Organisational Capital

There is much debate as to how companies carry out their activities in the context of new information and communication technologies influencing organisations to decentralise and develop new managerial practices, including outsourcing and networking. Recent theories have emphasised the importance of organising as a key component for building corporate competitive advantage and scholars have looked at this from a range of perspectives including in relation to intangible assets, human capital, work training and the process dimension. Yet the concept of organisational capital as such – in spite of its indubitable relevance and attractiveness – is still to be clarified until now.

In this book the subject is approached in four ways. First, from an analytical perspective: what is the status of organisational capital as a concept, and how is it defined? Second, from a ontological perspective: what type of (implicit) orders can be designed and implemented around organisations? Third, from the measurement perspective: what kind of frameworks and what type of metrics can be prototyped? And finally, the implementation perspective: how should organisations integrate the organisational capital perspective in the definition and implementation of their strategies for resources' allocation. The book provides the first multifaceted and international effort from a broad perspective, aiming at clarifying the concept of organisational capital and determining its analytical and operational implications.

Covering a large area of theoretical and empirical evidence, this book will be of great interest to students and researchers engaged with organisational design, innovation modelling and change management, as well as consultants in IT and organisational design.

Ahmed Bounfour is a professor at The University Paris-Sud, and the founder and titular of the European Chair On Intellectual Capital Management.

Routledge Studies in Innovation, Organisation and Technology

1 **Innovation in the US Service Sector**
Michael P. Gallaher, Albert N. Link and Jeffrey E. Petrusa

2 **Information and Communications Technologies in Society**
E-Living in a digital Europe
Edited by Ben Anderson, Malcolm Brynin and Yoel Raban

3 **The Innovative Bureaucracy**
Bureaucracy in an age of fluidity
Alexander Styhre

4 **Innovations and Institutions**
An institutional perspective on the innovative efforts of banks and insurance companies
Patrick Vermeulen and Jorg Raab

5 **Knowledge and Innovation in Business and Industry**
The importance of using others
Edited by Håkan Håkansson and Alexandra Waluszewski

6 **Knowledge and Innovation**
A comparative study of the USA, the UK and Japan
Helen Brown

7 **Industrial Innovation in Japan**
Edited by Takuji Hara, Norio Kambayashi and Noboru Matsushima

8 **Managing and Marketing Radical Innovations**
Marketing new technology
Birgitta Sandberg

9 **Mobility and Technology in the Workplace**
Edited by Donald Hislop

10 **Energizing Management Through Innovation and Entrepreneurship**
European research and practice
Edited by Milé Terziovski

11 **Innovating for Sustainability**
Green entrepreneurship in personal mobility
Luca Berchicci

12 **Organisational Capital**
Modelling, measuring and contextualising
Edited by Ahmed Bounfour

Organisational Capital

Modelling, measuring and contextualising

Edited by Ahmed Bounfour

Routledge
Taylor & Francis Group
LONDON AND NEW YORK

First published 2009
by Routledge
2 Park Square, Milton Park, Abingdon, Oxon, OX14 4RN

Simultaneously published in the USA and Canada
by Routledge
270 Madison Avenue, New York, NY 10016

Routledge is an imprint of the Taylor & Francis Group, an informa business

Typeset in Times New Roman by Pindar NZ, Auckland, New Zealand
Printed and bound in Great Britain by TJI Digital, Padstow, Cornwall

British Library Cataloguing in Publication Data
A catalogue record for this book is available from the British Library

Library of Congress Cataloging-in-Publication Data
Organisational capital : modelling, measuring and contextualising / edited by Ahmed Bounfour.
p. cm.
Includes bibliographical references and index.
1. Organizational learning. 2. Corporate culture. 3. Human capital. 4. Intellectual capital. I. Bounfour, Ahmed.
HD58.82.O74295 2008
658.4'038—dc22 2008025830

ISBN 13: 978-0-415-43771-4 (hbk)
ISBN 13: 978-0-203-88521-5 (ebk)

ISBN 10: 0-415-43771-4 (hbk)
ISBN 10: 0-203-88521-X (ebk)

Contents

Illustrations

Figures

Tables

Boxes

Contributors

Anjali Bakhru is a Senior Lecturer in Strategic Management at Middlesex University Business School in the UK. Her research focuses on resource-based and evolutionary approaches to competitive advantage, and her specific interest is in the processes through which organisations are able to create and develop capabilities over time.

Ahmed Bounfour is a professor at University Paris-Sud, where he is the founder and titular of the European Chair on Intellectual Capital Management. Ahmed Bounfour conducts research on intellectual capital, as a part of a large reflection on industrial competitiveness and future socioeconomic systems development. He has published numerous papers on strategic management, organisation design and competitiveness, in academic as well as professional journals. Ahmed Bounfour works as reviewer and/or Member of the Scientific Board for several journals in innovation, intellectual capital and management science. Among his recent books on intangibles and intellectual capital are *Intellectual Capital for Communities, Nations, Regions and Cities*, Elsevier Butterworth-Heinemann, Burlington, MA (with Leif Edvinsson), 2005; *Capital immatériel, Connaissance, et performance*, (Editor), L'Harmattan, Paris, (2006). *The Management of Intangibles, The Organization's Most Valuable assets*, Routledge, London & New York, 2003. Ahmed Bounfour speaks regularly on innovation and the knowledge economy in business and policy forums. He also works as an expert for national and international institutions, as well as for large corporations.

Yves Caseau is Executive Vice-President in charge of Services and Innovation for Bouygues Telecom (the third largest mobile phone operator in France). He was Chief Information Officer (CIO) for Bouygues Telecom from 2001 until 2006, in charge of the overall strategy and development of the IT divisions. His new assignment includes the development of new telecommunication services, research and development, and total quality management, which includes sustainable development, security and business process management.

Gwenaëlle Grefe is currently working at a major metallurgic company, researching knowledge exchange incentives related to maintaining the organisational technical memory. A graduate from the French Audencia Business School, Gwenaelle has a master's degree in International Management of Human Resources. She worked for a major computer manufacturer for five years in the role of business analyst during the worldwide implementation of a new ERP system. Gwenaëlle is a doctoral candidate at University Paris-Sud.

Sarah Hom is a Research Associate at the Naval Postgraduate school and a market research consultant specializing in custom research projects. With extensive experience in market research, industry analysis, marketing and business planning, she has completed a broad range of projects for technology and healthcare companies. She has also launched market research departments in several organizations, including Oracle Corporation, that provided market research, industry analysis and customer insights for enterprise applications in 14 vertical markets.

Dr Tom Housel specializes in valuing intellectual capital, telecommunications, information technology, value-based business process reengineering, and knowledge value measurement in profit and non-profit organizations. He is currently a tenured Full Professor for the Information Sciences (Systems) Department and Executive Director of the California Homeland Security Consortium. As Executive Director he is responsible for a growing organization with a budget in excess of $3 million annually. His current research focuses on the use of "Real Options" models in identifying, valuing, maintaining, and exercising options in military decision making. Prior to joining NPS, he also was a Research Fellow for the Center for Telecommunications Management and Associate Professor at the Marshall School of Business at the University of Southern California. Tom has been the Chief Business Process Engineer for Pacific Bell, where he completed numerous reengineering projects and developed a new objective method for objectively measuring the value-added by reengineering. His last assignment in the corporate world was as the Chief of Consumer Market Research for Telecom Italia in Venice, Italy where he developed new methods for predicting the adoption rates for new interactive multimedia broadband applications. He won the prestigious Society for Information Management award for best paper in the field in 1986. His work on measuring the value of intellectual capital has been featured in a *Fortune* cover story (October 3, 1994) and *Investor's Business Daily*, numerous books, professional periodicals, and academic journals.

Christine Komoroski is a lieutenant in the United States Navy on assignment abroad.

Florian Kohlbacher is a Research Fellow at the German Institute for Japanese Studies in Tokyo. From April 2005 to March 2007 he was a visiting researcher at Hitotsubashi University, Tokyo, where he conducted research in knowledge management, international business and marketing. He is the author of *International Marketing in the Network Economy: A Knowledge-based Approach*, (Palgrave Macmillan 2007) and holds a master's degree and a doctorate from the Vienna University of Economics and Business Administration.

Bernard Marr is Director of Research at the Advanced Performance Institute. Prior to that, he held research positions at the University of Cambridge and Cranfield School of Management. Bernard Marr is widely recognised as a leading expert and researcher on strategic performance management and intellectual capital. He has edited the academic book *Perspectives on Intellectual Capital*, which explores the topic of intellectual capital from different academic disciplines and perspectives. In addition, he has written over 200 academic articles, reports, and books including the best-selling book *Strategic Performance Management*. Bernard Marr is a member of the editorial board for many leading academic journals in the field and holds different visiting professorships.

Jan Mouritsen's research is oriented towards understanding the role of management technologies and management control in various organisational and social contexts. He focuses on empirical research and attempts to develop new ways of understanding the role and effects of controls and financial information in organisations and society. He is interested in translations and interpretations made of (numerical) representations (e.g., as in budgets, financial reports, non-financial indicators and profitability analysis) throughout the contexts they help to illuminate. His interests include intellectual capital and knowledge management, technology management, operations management, new accounting and management control. Jan Mouritsen is currently editorial board member of a series of academic journals in the various areas of management and business research including accounting, operations management, IT and knowledge management, and he has published in journals including *Accounting, Organizations and Society*; *Management Accounting Research*; *Scandinavian Journal of Management*; *Accounting, Auditing and Accountability Journal*; *Journal of Intellectual Capital* and *Critical Perspectives on Accounting*.

Dr Johnathan C. Mun is a research professor at the US Naval Postgraduate School (Monterey, California) and teaches executive seminars in quantitative risk analysis, decisions sciences, real options, simulation, portfolio optimization, and other related concepts. He has also researched and consulted on many Department of Defense and Department of Navy projects and is considered a leading world expert on risk analysis and real options anlaysis. He has authored nine books on real options and integrated risk management. He is also the founder and CEO of Real Options Valuation, Inc., a consulting, training and software development firm specializing in strategic real options, financial valuation, Monte Carlo simulation, stochastic forecasting, optimization and risk analysis, located in Northern California. He is also currently a finance and economics professor and has taught courses in financial management, investments, real options, economics, and statistics at the undergraduate and the graduate MBA levels.

Thierry Nabeth is a Research Fellow at INSEAD CALT (Centre for Advanced Learning Technologies). His research is in particular focused on the investigation of the next generation of agent enhanced collaborative platforms supporting the knowledge exchange in communities, both from a technical perspective (the mechanisms supporting and stimulating collaboration), usage perspective (how to translate this in terms of the user's experience) and sociological perspective (what motivates the user's participation). Recent fields of research include the application of Web 2.0 for enterprise collaboration, the support of attention in a social context, the concept of identity in the social web (social networking services) and the profiling of digital traces.

Steve Pike gained both his Doctor of Philosophy in Science and a Bachelors of Science with Honours from the University of Sussex in the UK. With his long experience in the defence sector and in business consulting, Dr Pike has worked, lectured and taught widely in the US, Europe and the Far East and has served on European Industry Management Associations and EU panels in a variety of capacities. He has published numerous book chapters and is a regular author of academic and cased-based articles for peer-reviewed journals and is a regular contributor at international conferences. He won the 2005 Literati Club Awards for Excellence outstanding paper award for a paper on measuring intangibles in the Journal of Intellectual Capital. Dr Pike is Research Director at Intellectual Capital Services where he splits his time between researching innovation, intellectual capital measurement and assessment methodologies, value measurement methodologies and direct client interaction. Most recently he has focused on intellectual capital, value measurement methodologies especially in the areas of the assessment of university research and the assessment of the value delivered by governmental agencies and initiatives.

Claudia Roda is a Professor of Computer Science, and co-chairs the Computer Science, Math, and Science department of the American University of Paris (France). Her current research interests focus on theoretical and applied models for attention computing, and she has extensive experience in the design, implementation, and validation of multi-agent systems supporting cognitive and social processes related to learning and collaboration.

Göran Roos is Honorary Professor at Warwick Business School in the UK, Visiting Professor of Innovation Management and Business Model Innovation at VTT Technical Research Centre of Finland, as well as Visiting Professor of Intangible Asset Management and Performance Measurement at the Centre for Business Performance at Cranfield University. He is also the founder of Intellectual Capital Services Ltd and the co-founder of B+I STRATEGY S.L. He is one of the founders of modern intellectual capital science, a recognised world expert in this field and a major contributor to thinking and practice in the areas of strategy and innovation management. He is the author and co-author of numerous books and articles on intellectual capital, innovation management and strategy, many of which have been recognised with awards

J.C. Spender was commissioned in experimental submarines in the Royal Navy, then studied engineering at Oxford (Balliol). He has worked as a nuclear submarine reactor engineer with Rolls-Royce & Associates, a sales manager with

IBM (UK), a consultant with Decision Technology International (Boston), and a merchant banker with Slater-Walker Securities. His Ph.D. thesis (Manchester Business School) won the Academy of Management's 1980 A. T. Kearney Ph.D. Research Prize, later published as Industry Recipes (Blackwell 1989). He served on the faculty at City University (London), York University (Toronto), UCLA and Rutgers, and as Dean of the School of Business and Technology at SUNY/FIT, before retiring in 2003. He now researches, writes and lectures on strategy and knowledge management in US, Canada, and Europe, with Visiting Professor appointments at ESADE and the Lund School of Economics and Management. He currently occupies the 2007–2008 Fulbright Research Chair at Queen's School of Business, Kingston, Canada.

Pirjo Ståhle's main area of specialization is the capability of organisations and societies for renewal and innovation. She has been involved in several business renewal and innovation projects for more than 20 years in Finland, and served on many national and international expert panels in the areas of innovation, education and foresight. Over the years she has often occupied a bridge-building position between business, academia and government. Professor Ståhle has published several books and more than 100 articles in popular and scientific publications, and given numerous lectures and presentations on themes related to organisational renewal, innovative management, and knowledge-intensive economy. She is currently a Professor at the Finland Futures Research Centre, Turku School of Economics.

Introduction

Ahmed Bounfour

This book is about organisational capital and organisational design. Why should we consider such a topic now? Because of the deep transformation of our socio-economic systems, where the traditional vertical paradigm – e.g. the enterprise – is less and less relevant. Indeed, in the context of the knowledge economy, the way organisations carry out their activities is being challenged on all levels. Whereas new information and communication technologies have induced more pressures towards a decentralised organisation, companies themselves have developed new managerial practices (outsourcing, networking and joint intangible assets building), which have challenged their most embedded routines. This, of course, has a deep impact on how we can view business modelling in the knowledge economy.

This problem has been largely debated in applied economics literature over the last five years. Via the internet, several views have been put forward, some of which have been naïve, especially when they emphasised the role of transparency and resources mobility. In many respects, the knowledge economy is considered to be endowed with characteristics similar to those proposed by classical economists for characterising market structures, especially those related to atomicity and free entry and exit of firms in the market.

The main issue to be considered here concerns the extent to which the knowledge economy admits specific characteristics that need (or include) a deep change in business modelling, from the industrial point of view (the value-added chain). Are there alternative (complementary) ways of doing business in the knowledge economy? Is co-production of value now an alternative form to production?

From the industrial point of view, value creation is sequential, unidirectional and transitive, realised in transactions and measured in monetary terms. Economic actors are analysed in one sequence. It is best described in value-added chains. From the co-production view, 'value creation is synchronic, interactive, best described in "value constellations"' (Ramirez, 1999:61). Consumers are considered as a factor of production and contribution to the value creation process. From an inter-organisational perspective, value creation might be related here to the relationship dimension of activities and their intangible dimension (Baxter, Matear, 2004). Does this mean that Porter's value-added chain (Porter, 1985) is no longer relevant? According to Stabell and Fjedstad (1998), three types of value creation models should be retained: chains, shops and networks. From this distinction, we can derive different forms and mechanisms for coordination of activities in the knowledge economy. We can also derive problematic issues for further consideration. The equilibrium between transaction and information (knowledge flow) is certainly one of those issues considered relevant. Indeed, in the industrial view, transaction is the hub of value creation. Transaction is expressed in monetary terms. Economic agents create value, whereas their customers destroy it (by consuming it). In the new (knowledge) economy, value is created by co-production. Transaction is only one dimension of the value process. Constellation (interstices) is a complementary way of value creation to sequences (Normann and Ramirez, 1998).

In this context, what should be the most suitable way of organising? Over the last five years, several theories and works have emphasised the importance of the organisational dimension as a key component for building corporate and more generally organisation's competitive advantage. Resource-based views, as well as dynamic capabilities approaches, are among those who strongly contributed to such an emphasis. Several scholars tried to circumscribe the concept of organisational capital by considering it from the general perspective of intangible assets. Some of them consider that organisational capital can be defined in close relationship to human capital – and work training and design – whereas others put more emphasis on the process dimension. Yet the concept of organisational capital, as such – in spite of its indubitable relevance and attractiveness – is still to be clarified, from at least four perspectives: the *analytical (epistemic) perspective* (What is the status of organisational capital as a concept? How to define it?); the *ontological perspective* (What type of (implicit) orders can be designed and implemented around organisations, especially in a context dominated by a strong weakness in social links?); the *measurement perspective* (What kind of frameworks and what type of metrics can be prototyped?); and finally, the *implementation perspective* (How should organisations integrate the organisational capital perspective in the definition and implementation of their strategies for resource allocation?).

This book aims at addressing some of these issues. It is structured into fourteen chapters.

Chapter 1, by Spender, puts forward the issue of organisational capital, taking a broad theoretical perspective. It discusses the semantic issue of organisational capital by relating it to other categories of capital – human capital and social capital, among others. Spender also discusses the status of the concept, both from a positivist and a constructivist perspective.

In Chapter 2, Mouritsen discusses the power and frailty of organisational capital. Indeed, in many contexts, organisational capital constitutes a powerful resource that needs to be mobilised. But under what circumstances might such leverage intervene? By considering two case studies, Mouritsen argues that organisational capital is a power only when it is mobilised into action. Therefore, we as scholars should move from – or beyond – establishing analytical categories, towards understanding developing organisational capital narratives.

Chapter 3, by Roos and Pike, addresses the issues of business modelling, taking an intellectual capital perspective. An *ad hoc* approach is proposed, in order to show concretely how different blocs of the suggested framework – the intellectual capital navigator, including organisational capital – interact, and how a business innovation model can be defined and implemented.

In Chapter 4, taking a prospective approach, I consider the issue of community development and its impact on how to create value in the new capitalism – what I have named elsewhere 'communautalism' (Bounfour, 2006). Here, I am building mainly on the theory of recognition, as it has been developed mainly by two philosophers (Honneth, 2000; Ricoeur, 2004), in order to propose a taxonomy of intellectual assets, the most suitable to the new forms of organising: communities. Here, I will suggest two types of communities: natural communities (nations, regions, cities) and emerging communities (constrained communities, quasi-organic communities, and organic communities). From this perspective, the most intelligent vertical enterprises are certainly those who will mostly be able to take advantage of these new forms of organising.

In Chapter 5, with Gwenaëlle Grefe, I consider the issue of designing sequences for knowledge creation and dissemination. This is an emerging and important issue in the knowledge economy. We should not only stress the importance of knowledge, but also design how to create and leverage it. By mobilising an *ad hoc* theory, the Hau-Ba theory (Bounfour, 2000, 2003), we show in a concrete context – a large industrial company – how the issue of sequences is essential to the creation and leveraging of knowledge.

Chapter 6 considers further this issue, especially from natural communities' perspective. Here, I am taking the dynamic capabilities approach and indicating how it fits well to the issue of natural communities, such as nations. The case of Finland is indicated here for illustration.

In Chapter 7, Ståhle considers the issue of systems-thinking in dynamic environments. This is of course related to the issue of self-organising, which is of particular criticality nowadays. Ståhle discusses in detail different systems theories for self-organising, including their operational implications.

With Chapters 8 and 9 we return to one major analytical and practical issue: how to modelise and manage the conditions for value creation. In Chapter 8, Housel *et al.* apply the Knowledge Value Added (KVA) analysis, with risk simulation and strategic real options, to a shipyard case. The methodology aims at helping top Navy executives in making decisions with regards to PML technology acquisition.

In Chapter 9, Caseau reviews different approaches to value creation in the context of information systems. Taking advantage of his previous position as CIO, here he clearly indicates the importance of establishing value contracts with the executives in charge of the lines of business.

In Chapter 10, Marr considers the issue of organisational capital from a strategic perspective. He indicates how mapping value – using a tree approach – helps to leverage corporate competences, via internal processes, e.g. organisational capital.

In Chapter 11, Roda and Nabeth put forward the importance of a very singular resource: attention. In an increasingly digitalised and networked world, attention is a primary resource. A model is proposed showing different levels of attention support: perception, deliberative, operational and meta-cognition.

In Chapter 12, Kohlbacher considers the issues of organisational capital from a marketing view. Building on the knowledge creation approach (Nonaka, 1994; Nonaka and Takeuchi, 1995), the author defines a set of marketing processes most suitable to the co-creation relationship, especially with customers.

In Chapter 13, Bakhru discusses the issue of competence building, taking both an intellectual capital and a capability perspective. The author stresses the importance of a more integrative approach, as well as further empirical research on the subject.

Finally, in Chapter 14, I consider the issue of organisational capital, value creation and reporting, taking as a starting point the issue of Information Technology (IT) and Information Systems (IS) investments. Different angles have been put forward in the literature. But whatever the efforts provided by scholars, we still lack data on how much resources do companies really invest in organisational processes. The second part of Chapter 13 addresses this issue from a B2B perspective.

References

Baxter, R. and Matear, S. (2004), 'Measuring intangible value in business-to-business buyer-seller relationships: an intellectual capital perspective', *Industrial Marketing Management*, 33: 491–500.

Bounfour, A. (2000), 'Gestion de la connaissance et systèmes d'incitation: entre théorie du "Hau" et théorie du "Ba"', *Systèmes d'Information et Management*, 2(5): 12–40.

Bounfour, A. (2003), *The Management of Intangibles: the organisation's most valuable assets,* London and New York: Routledge.

Bounfour, A. (2006), 'Connaissance, reconnaissance et "communautalisme"', in A. Bounfour, (ed.) *Capital Immatériel, Connaissance et Performance*, Paris: L'Harmattan.

Honneth, A. (2002), *La Lutte pour la Reconnaissance*, Paris: Le Cerf.

Nonaka, I (1994), 'A dynamic theory of organizational knowledge creation', *Organization Science*, 5(1): 14–34.

Nonaka, I. and Takeuchi, H. (1995), *The Knowledge-Creating Company: how Japanese companies create the dynamics of innovation*, New York: Oxford University Press.

Normann, R. and Ramirez, R. (1998), *Designing Interactive Strategies: from value chain to value constellation*, New York: John Wiley & Sons.

Porter, M.E. (1985), *Competitive Advantage: creating and sustaining superior performance*, New York: Free Press.

Ramirez, R. (1999), 'Value co-production: intellectual origins and implications for practice and research', *Strategic Management Journal*, 20: 49–65.

Ricoeur, P. (2004), *Parcours de la Reconnaissance: trois études*, Paris: Stock.

Stabell, C.B. and Fjeldstad, Ø.D. (1998), 'Configuring value for competitive advantage: on chains, shops, and networks', *Strategic Management Journal*, 19(5): 413–37.

1 Organizational capital

Concept, measure, or heuristic?

J. C. Spender

Human and social capital

Management and organization theorists' interest in "organizational capital," as something distinct from the organization's financial and physical capital, goes back at least to the time of Adam Smith and his political-economy colleagues. In spite of their obvious academic interests they were practical men and closely observed the workings of the world around them. Unlike many of our economist colleagues, they had no problem seeing the economic impact of people's knowledge and skills. They also recognized the very real costs of acquiring them and so were interested in an economics of human knowledge.

In this line of reasoning Smith concluded there were four types of capital: machines, buildings, land, and people's "acquired and useful abilities." He believed an effective division of labor would significantly facilitate the development of such value-adding skills, and experienced people should be recognized as economic assets. Indeed, human assets were to be understood as the post-mercantilist basis of the nation's wealth (Ekelund and Tollison, 1980). But post-Smith and post-slavery there was considerable sensitivity to defining people as transferable goods and a corresponding reluctance to use terms like "human capital" – until Marshall's and Pigou's reminders that what working people know must surely be made central to any workable theory of economics (Marshall, 1964; Pigou, 1928). Their comments tempted a new generation of macro-economic and management theorists to probe the rising importance of intangible or "soft" assets (Kendrick, 1956; Schultz, 1961; Tobin, 1969). Thus today's view, that an organization's total capital comprises both tangible and intangible elements, has been around for a while (e.g. Gort *et al.*, 1985; Prescott and Visscher, 1980); especially since "human capital theory" was opened up by macro-economists such as Johnson, Schultz, Kendrick, Solow, Becker, and others (Becker, 1964; Johnson, 1960; Solow, 1956).

Human capital theorizing was mostly at the macro level, estimating the national returns to using new technology (Solow, 1957) or to expenditures on education, estimating those investments and returns at an aggregated level. This revealed, for example, that "the income of the US has been increasing at a much higher rate than the combined amount of land, man-hours worked and the stock of reproducible capital used to produce the income" (Schultz, 1961: 6). Schultz pointed to the "discrepancy" between what can be observed, in terms of GDP growth, and what could be "explained" by conventional economic theory. That this discrepancy was labeled "human capital," in spite of Becker's misgivings, does not help us much unless we can get further into and theorize its workings. But it is clearly important economically and, for that reason, theoretically, politically, and managerially. Many economists tried to estimate the nation's stock of intangibles and its economic contribution. In 1969, for example, Kendrick argued around 50% of the entire US capital stock was of this "immaterial" nature (Mankiw *et al.*, 1992: 415). We can surmise the proportion is even greater now we are in the Information Age (Castells, 1996; Drucker, 1988) and have a service-dominated economy. For the US corporations, the Brookings Institute estimated that the soft assets of the *Fortune 500* companies represented 38% of their market value in 1982, but had risen to 62% by 1992 (Dzinkowski, 2000: 32). Again, we can presume this proportion has continued to rise along with the financial services and "knowledge-intensive" high-tech industries. But estimating the scale of these assets does little to reveal the mechanisms that connect investments in education and so forth to the human capital generated or the national economic outcomes. In fact there is surprisingly little empirical evidence about whether such common-sense links actually exist (Hotchkiss, 1993).

As an alternative to working at the macro level, trying to size the economy's aggregated human capital and compare it against other more tangible types of capital, is to try and identify human capital's components, coming up with subtypes, and thence move towards a more comprehensive theory. For instance, it is clearly helpful to distinguish background educational investments, not related to any specific value-generating activities, from firm-specific activities – such as training in making and marketing products like Oracle Data-base 11g or the Xerox Nuerva 288 Digital Perfecting System; or in learning how specific organizations, say TIAA-CREF, might make profitable use of these afore-mentioned products (Becker, 1964). Background or infrastructural investments may well make for a more civil society, but economists recognize business managers operate with specifics rather than academic generalities, and are reluctant to expend time and money training employees into forms of human capital when the resulting skills, such as C++ programming, can "walk across the street" and be readily applied by their competition (Kessler and Lülfesmann, 2002).

Work itself is often educational, as individual employees undertake new initiatives to make their practice easier or in some other way more effective. Indeed, this job-related learning so intrigued Adam Smith that he made it the core of *The Wealth of Nations*, famously illustrated in his pin-making example. A modern instance would be "quality circles" or any of the other institutionalized "learning-by-doing" practices (Arrow, 1962; Bahk and Gort, 1993; Yelle, 1979). In addition to this discovery of new knowledge wealth by "drilling down" into a specific practice, beneficial results in one area also spill over to colleagues. Employees are constantly educating each other and increasing each other's human capital in ways that make it difficult to distinguish the consumption and generation of knowledge, or indeed to know whether the processes are individual or collaborative. There is the SECI (socialization, externalization, combination, internalization) model, in which individual or small group discoveries of novel methods are shared with the rest of the organization (Nonaka and Takeuchi, 1995), though this may be little more than a restatement of Coleman's macro-micro model of the social process (Coleman, 1990). Aside from raising difficult questions about soft capital's source, location and who might actually own it, this approach also implies three levels of analysis – socio-economy wide, the "meso-level" of the firm or institution (Field, 2003: 139), and the individual employees – so adopting hierarchical categories familiar from the work of Parsons and Gurvitch (Gurvitch, 1972; Parsons, 1960). Both tangible and intangible capital may be present at all levels and, if so, we sense important questions about the relationships between the levels.

Other researchers move in different directions, contrasting different types of "soft" capital at each level. At the meso-level of firms and institutions, in addition to employees, equipment and financial capital, organizations have structure, rules and accounting arrangements to help everyone understand what they are being asked to do, and to measure and help integrate their work with others. These can be considered non-human components of the organization's "structural capital" – part of the bundle of resources developed to help the firm integrate its factors of production and division of labor, and ensure the employees' skilled activities are well aligned to its objectives (Grant, 2003). While much of this structural capital could be taken to be tangible – written rules, performance metrics, and so forth – we realize much is informal and cultural. Such relational assets seem to be "of the organization"; persisting beyond any particular employee's tenure, and standing apart from them and their skills, and so differentiable from the individualistic or personal dimensions of "human capital." From this point of view, organizational capital might be defined as a sum of the organization's human and structural capital. Some have labeled this the organization's "intellectual capital" to distinguish it more clearly from the organization's tangible financial and physical capital (Edvinsson, 1997; Edvinsson and Malone, 1997). The organization is also embedded in a network of relations with suppliers, customers, regulators, competitors and so forth (e.g. Porter, 1980). Its place there is earned as the firm becomes a legitimate and functioning part of the industry's structure, so this place too is a dimension of its structural capital; engaging customers and suppliers, and reducing its external transaction costs.

Complementing the economists' interest in human capital formation, the intangible outcome of education, training or learning-by-doing, is the sociologists' interest in "social capital." This is a way of measuring the strength or richness of a society's distributed intangible relational resources. Social capital is broadly defined as the system or network of relations between people, organizations and other social entities that facilitates their activity, both individual and coordinated. Social networks are evidence of social capital, infrastructural and institutional investments made intentionally or unintentionally (perhaps arising as spillovers from the intentional activity of individuals). Individuals and socioeconomic entities such as organizations and institutions are embedded in the social networks that result from previous interactions. Often costly to make happen, these generally leave memory traces that ease and facilitate further interaction. Thus, to see an industry's structure is to see an aspect of the constituent firms' social capital.

Social capital theorizing has exploded over recent decades, adding new twists and questions to traditional sociological concerns (Baron *et al.*, 2000; Field, 2003; Halpern, 2005; Lin, 2001). To date, the theorizing has been largely shaped by the work of Putnam, Coleman and Bourdieu, who nevertheless had rather different ideas about what social capital was and how it worked to open up new possibilities and facilitate others. Putnam, following De Toqueville's interest in "association," argued at the macro level that the US's social capital is in decline – that is, we Americans are now "bowling alone" and making less investment in our social relationships, even though we know these are useful when we want to get things done or deal with the unexpected (Putnam, 2000). In socioeconomic terms, Putnam argued, the transactions costs of social life are increasing. In sociological terms, we have less access to and are less supported by our society, and are obliged to depend more on our own endeavors or on deliberately engineered social policies and government institutions, such as welfare.

Coleman focused at the meso-level, mostly on the effects of community culture on educational achievement. His model is more about where particular social capital is located, who can access it and how, and thus about the interaction between the social capital of particular communities and the life-chances of those within them. Bourdieu, from a Marxist perspective, focused even more narrowly on how particular forms of social capital were generated and harnessed to protect the privilege and interests of those who possess it – particularly on how elites help each other sustain their advantages; old boy networks and so forth (Field, 2003; Whitley *et al.*, 1981). Instead of probing for where we might find and maybe measure such soft capital, most of the debate among human capital theorists has been about whether there are empirically verifiable links between educational expenditure and economic growth at the macro level (Bils and Klenow, 2000; Hartog and van den Brink, 2007; Mankiw *et al.*, 1992). Social capital theorists, in contrast, have been more concerned with the family as social capital's principal mode of action and debating – for instance, whether supporting families can have results that are more beneficial to individuals than government funded programs (Becker *et al.*, 1990). In short, there has been more focus on the causes and effects of these two types of soft capital than on identifying or measuring their occurrence.

Theorizing along these lines has led to a proliferation of adjectives for "soft capital"; intellectual, immaterial, relational, cultural, symbolic, innovation, environmental, customer, consumer, reputational, or social (Dean and Kretschmer, 2007). Some argue this has gone way too far, reducing the entire "soft" capital discussion to a mish-mash of conflicting definitions (Robison *et al.*, 2002). Paxton, for example, questions Putnam's conclusions and empirical findings (Paxton, 1999), while Fine thinks the explosion of talk about social capital has seriously damaged both sociological theorizing and social policy (Fine, 2000).

There are both theoretical and empirical difficulties. On the empirical side, the attempts to measure either human or social capital have probably added to the confusion. From the theory side, one difficulty is the idea that either human or social capital can be conceived, measured or theorized independently of the other. Social capital is about individuals and their interactions, just as human capital presupposes those interactions, too. Consequently, it may be more productive to think about how the concepts are related in spite of major differences in method, assumption and orientation in the two literatures. The micro-economic foundations of human capital theory lead to its prioritizing the individual and her/his processes over those of the collective, especially evident in "rational choice theory" arguments that human capital would only be properly generated by individuals for their own benefit (Lucas, 1988). Social capital theory partially complements this view, arguing that social capital facilitates the development of and so shapes the individual's human capital, especially influencing those who are disadvantaged and not in a good position to make the rational choices assumed by the human capital theorists – that is, social capital theory sees society as made up of individuals with heterogeneous resources and challenges. Thus human capital theory is inherently individualistic and politically conservative, while social capital theory is inherently collectivist and liberal, and the distinction between them may be more political than fundamental. Social capital theorists see the community's social capital as a crucial form of collectively constructed infrastructure that helps raise the constituents' quality of life, just as efficient utilities or legal institutions do. They also feel this infrastructure should not be left to chance or market forces, and that national or regional policies are implied, i.e. social capital is something to be managed. Relying on spillovers from individually directed activities is clearly not adequate. In contrast, human capital theorists adopt a more "methodologically individualistic" approach, and presume the world works better when investments are made individually, intentionally and rationally, with personal benefit in mind. Thus human capital is an essentially private good, while social capital is more of a public good. Alternatively we might say that human capital is what individuals bring to their lives and market choices, while social capital supports them when market failures occur.

Theorizing organizational capital

When theorizing organizational capital we might be able to draw on both sides of this discussion. Social capital theory can be applied by imagining the organization as a society writ small, with mutual trust and interdependence between its members. Social capital theory does not require the capital in question to be wholly inter-subjective like language, distanced or held in some place other than by the organization's members. While it clearly can be held in documents, rules and so forth, and be an aspect of the relations between the community's members, it can also be held as the common knowledge they share (Grant, 2003; Middleton and Edwards, 1990; Sunder, 2002). These elements of the organization's knowledge and skills are semi-public goods as far as that particular community is concerned, i.e. they operate as public goods within the meso-level context of a particular organization (Coleman, 1974). When such collective capital exists, much of the organization's knowledge and experience will be available to other employees without their engaging in any explicit or implicit contractual activity, i.e. members are able to access each other's knowledge without incurring the corresponding liabilities that would arise from market relationships (Bechky, 2003). Social capital implies some suspension of market forces, just as friendship is defined as "not keeping score" of the exchanges. In contrast with those who believe the market is the key to efficiency, many social capital writers assume collaboration provides for improved economic efficiency as transactions costs are lowered under circumstances of partial market failure. Thus one employee, facing a particular problem, is able to appeal to expert others within the organization (community), as custodians of the firm's accumulated expertise (Gray and Meister, 2004). We can also argue that when social capital is present, newcomers have to go through a period of training and socialization before they can access it, so becoming educated or institutionalized into the organization's social capital assets and processes (Karseras, 2006; Wanous, 1992).

But social and human capitals become increasingly entangled the more closely we look at them. Instead of assuming, as much of the literature does, they are different merely because they are defined by different languages and theories, we might more usefully wonder how they interact as they contribute to a middle-ground concept like "organizational capital." One of the risks with seeing the organization's capital through the prism of distributed social capital notions like "trust," "shared knowledge" or "networks" or, contrasted with this view, thinking of it as the sum of human capital components like the employees' "skills," is that organizations may differ significantly from both societies and individuals. If this is the case, then mapping intuitions from either social or human capital theory into the organizational realm might well prove problematic. While these theories can obviously furnish some insights, their relevance is contingent on the theorist's assumptions about the nature of the firm or organization. What counts as organizational capital, whether distributed and holistic or reductionist and atomic, must somehow fit into or with an appropriate theory of the organization.

We know organizations are often considered mini-societies and that much use can be made of sociologically based theorizing. But an organization may be much more than that (e.g. Morgan, 1997). *Inter alia* it may be a contrived quasi-mechanical device for achieving specific objectives, and this is not an entirely satisfactory metaphor for a society which, we presume, has organic qualities. Alternatively an organization may be considered a special market for human capital such as managerial capabilities (Williamson, 1970). Or it may be a political system (March and Olsen, 1989). Of particular relevance to theorizing organizational capital is the view of the firm as a device for converting some kinds of capital (such as the factors of production, including human and social capital) into other kinds of capital (finished goods, services, reputation, profit, etc.). Both human and social capital theorists are sensitive to questions about the transformation of one kind of capital into another; indeed their interplay was central to Coleman's analysis as he probed how social capital contributed to the emergence of human capital (Field *et al.*, 2000; Pennings *et al.*, 1998). Thus social capital theorists might argue that investing tax revenues in education raises educational attainment and the individual's human capital – and that improves the culture and the economy and, in turn, raises tax revenues. Human capital theorists might argue that decreasing taxes gives individuals more disposable income that they might choose to invest in their own education and so increase their life chances, and as a spillover, expand the tax base, allowing government to create more social capital – and so it goes. But if the application of social capital results in human capital, and the application of human capital results in social capital, the distinction between them becomes less a matter of definition and more to do with the analyst's points of view and departure.

Economists treat individuals as the principal objects of their analytic attention, and their interaction is what economics theorizes. By "black boxing" firms, economists reconceive them as individuals that can be brought into the framework of rational actors economists regard as their subject-matter (Khalil, 1997). Sociologists presume society exists and is the object of their attention. They then explore, perhaps, how the social structure constrains and shapes those human choices that are not mere self-maximization, which in turn leads to restructuration and new forms of social capital (Giddens, 1984). In short, the distinction between the human and social kinds of intangible capital may be no more than a methodological contrivance that reflects the theorist's initial assumptions. Social capital is inter-subjective, relational, and distributed between individuals, while human capital is intra-subjective, a measure of what individuals bring to the world; but as we consider their interactions within the organization, things get even fuzzier. The basic distinction between tangible and intangible assets seems to stand up, but that between the social and human types of organizational capital seems increasingly frail.

But where might organization capital fit into this? If we take it that the organization's capital comprises some human capital – an aggregation of the knowledge assets of the organization's individual members and their participating affiliates, those working for the firm's outsourcers, sub-contractors, etc. – plus some social capital – that of the productive relationships within the firm and those with the industry's other participants – the boundaries between the interacting categories become blurred, as the SECI model suggests. Just as the differences between human capital theory and social capital theory depend on assumptions about what individuals and societies are, and become increasingly problematic as the focus moves onto their interaction, inter-penetration and mutual constitution, so the sub-categories of organizational capital blur as we consider how they interact and transform each other. When workers are trained into the firm's way of working are they developing their individual capital, or taking on board the firm's collective (social) knowledge? This fading of categories gets even more serious when we think of the firm's social capital as partially tied up in the network of its relations with customers, suppliers and so forth. Does the social capital of this network belong to the firm or to its related entities? Along these lines we see that much of the organizational capital literature's seeming clarity is actually dependent on uncritically adopted assumptions about the firm as an isolated system of production, an abstraction with clear boundaries and without theoretically significant strategic ties to the agents of supply, demand, competition and regulation among which it is embedded. This is not to say the analysis of organizational capital collapses, rather that it shifts its purpose. Instead of being an academic step towards a tenable theory of the organization as a distinct entity, it becomes, instead, more about managers' everyday practice and drawing their attention to the firm's intangible capital, part of the heuristics they might use to guide their allocation choices.

The root question, as ever, is about the underlying concept of organization into which these notions of capital are supposed to fit. The organization capital theorist is obliged to clarify what s/he means by "the organization," given the number of alternative views, in the same way human and social capital theorists put forward notions of individuals and societies. While their choices are often implicit, they reflect the greater coherence of the economic and sociological disciplines within which they work. In contrast, as the popularity of Morgan's *Images of Organization* shows us, organizational science lacks this coherence, and we traffic in many images. Some are contradictory; others are mutually exclusive. In general, we organization theorists are reluctant to admit that there is no really satisfactorily coherent theory of organizations. Consequently, the organizational capital theorist must stake out the ground quite carefully. The resulting concept of organizational capital may be more contingent on the particular historical period, industry, regulatory regime and so forth, and so less universal and useful to the discipline as a whole. But perhaps we cannot have a general concept, as indeed we may not be able to find a general concept of the organization either. There is an implicit criticism of organizational theorizing here, especially of its multiple terms and general conceptual instability, along the lines of Pfeffer's call to establish some empirically reliable theory rather than continuing to proliferate unestablished and contradictory alternative theories (Pfeffer, 1993). Economists, on the other hand, seem to be more honest about their failings, more or less agreeing there is, as yet, no satisfactory theory of the firm (Demsetz, 1991). But we should bear in mind Coleman's project to employ human and social capital concepts to unite economics and organization theory (Field, 2003).

Capital itself?

An alternative to defining what we mean by the organization, and using that definition to then define what we mean by its capital, is to turn the analysis around and consider how the notion of organizational capital might be useful to practicing managers. Why are we chasing this concept anyway? If the meaning of organizational capital – and its usefulness to practicing managers – is being examined, then it may be enlightening to switch the focus from "the organization," as in the preceding paragraphs, and onto "capital" itself. One of management's roles may be to make resource allocation decisions, such as choices about how to allocate the firm's capital to different activities, in the manner suggested by March's distinction between exploitation versus exploration (March, 1991). Capital, as the organization's most fundamental resource, may be what is being allocated in the strategic decision process and that may be why it seems so important to identify and theorize it. A slightly odd definition of management, perhaps, especially to those who think it is about organizational design and "command and control." But this definition has the merit of being consistent with an economic approach. Indeed we can argue that when managers make decisions about where to locate activities – in transactions costs terms, inside or outside the organization, or in deciding to consume one kind of capital rather than another in the production of a third type – it is really the capital resources that facilitate activity that are being re-allocated, so rephrasing Fisher's definition of capital as the durable result of past activity capable of transforming future production.

If we look at capital itself, rather than the organization in which it is located, theorizing organizational capital seems to hinge on the distinction between the organization's tangible and intangible resources. Given the difficulty of dealing with intangible resources, this literature gains most of its traction from the seeming solidity of the notion of tangible resources; land, buildings, equipment, inventories of raw materials and finished goods, and so forth. Intangible capital is what they are not, yet what still seems of value. Tangible resources are what we might find both in the factory and valued on the firm's balance sheet, although these values are far from being the same thing as the objects and resources themselves, as the long history of accounting reminds us. The accounts are simply a model of things that exist, contingent on some agreed method of valuation, and this value is determined before the capital is applied and revenues generated. A firm's accounts only make sense because they include terms like "capital" and "revenues," yet they are so familiar we scarcely stop to think how they came into use or why they are useful, and this is where Dean and Kretschmer offer us a fine review (Dean and Kretschmer, 2007). As they show, the term capital has several important functions. One is to distinguish between the value of the firm's assets and the cash flow that is generated from the previous application of capital. Capital and revenue differ and it is important to realize that money in the till may not mean the assets shown on the firm's balance sheet are useful for earning future revenue. Likewise, even when the firm's intangible assets – such as goodwill or employee skills – can be identified, they need not be of value. The relationship between the firm's assets and their revenue potential is becoming increasingly problematic, and it is widely appreciated that standard accounting practice is less and less able to identify the firm's real economic value (Brainard and Tobin, 1968).

This is not the place to rehearse the entire history of the concept of capital (Harcourt, 1972). Dean and Kretschmer's review helps us see the term has served many different purposes as, over the millennia, the notion of economic activity itself has changed. Two things seem evident. First, following Fisher, the concept of capital points to those durable assets, either acquired directly or accumulated from past activities, that are applicable in future periods. Capital is that which is still held separate from the on-going processes of resource transformation, in this sense un-applied and available for application in the future. It can therefore carry across time periods into the future, to be applied by melding it with labor, equipment, and land to generate revenue. In its standing apart from labor it is distinguishable from the other factors of production, for they embody labor and are prisoners of time, both through depreciation and erosion. Capital seems free of time's constraints.

Equipment and technology may be purchased out of capital, but are themselves products of a melding of capital and labor elsewhere or in a different time period. We also need to remember the way the term is used may reveal its true meaning. As the history of the theorizing reveals, capital remains a puzzle that may do no more than refer to a socioeconomic system, as a religious symbol refers to a system of belief and practice. Or it may exist as a thing in itself that seeks its own accretion, much as we might argue individuals and society are the apparatus our genes have chosen to move towards a higher evolutionary possibility. Or should we treat it as a model of something else, such as the tangible and intangible resources necessary to move the organization along the non-zero cost evolutionary path implicit in, say, Nelson and Winter's model? (Nelson and Winter, 1982.) Is the use of the term less scientific and theoretical in the sense of its being a fundamental category of resource, like human intelligence, or is speaking of capital merely rhetorical, something to do with the rhetoric of the managerial process that actualizes their power? (McCloskey, 1998.)

Measuring organizational capital

Even assuming we are looking at capital as an independent variable in an organizational model, the notion is meaningless if it cannot be valued. Even when the term is used metaphorically, it is assumed that it is at least potentially possible to value the intangible resources being referred to. Thus a next step might be to explore measuring an organization's capital directly – or at least its change from one time to another. There is already a substantial literature on this (Bontis, 2001; Dzinkowski, 2000; Kannan and Aulbur, 2004) and there are three bases on which to construct such measures. Two correspond to ordinary accounting measures, inputs and outputs, resource costs versus anticipated revenues. Thus skills training can be measured in terms of inputs, years schooling and so forth, or in terms of future revenues, wage increases perhaps. Market valuations are more likely to be based in future earnings, while many book values reflect cost and allowable depreciation. Thus Tobin's q and the idea of "intellectual capital" itself grew out of the increasing divergence between market and book valuations. The third method of valuation is based more on comparison. Revenue per employee, for instance, can be compared for two firms, and the difference – assuming the firms are in the same business and the results are corrected for any difference in tangible capital allocation – can be considered a surrogate measure of each firm's intellectual capital as it is applied in their respective business models.

As interest in intangible assets grew at Skandia and other firms, many capital measurement schemes were constructed, often mixing all three modes of valuation in spite of their heterogeneous theoretical bases. Thus the Balanced Scorecard offers four dimensionally or theoretically distinct metrics: financial, customer, internal, and innovation (Cooper and Kaplan, 1988; Kaplan and Norton, 1996). These might be seen as four distinct views of the organization: financial as the shareholders' view, then the customers' view, the employees' view, and an overall view of the organization's future. The point being that by melding four different theories of the organization, this multi-dimensionality captures more of the organization, and the dynamics of its strategic situation and potential, than any single-dimensioned view can. The Skandia and IC-Index approaches offer many sub-measures, raising serious questions about the scheme's implementability (Bontis, 2001). On the one hand there is the methodological temptation to search for a single underpinning rationality; on the other, the challenge of helping practicing managers get a sense of, for instance, how to bring the Balanced Scorecard's different dimensions into a coherent basis for resource allocation decisions. This is the same kind of challenge that is presented by trying to take both human and social capital considerations into account in any particular strategic situation. The issue, as noted earlier, is the implicit theory of the organization that is the basis for meeting these theoretical challenges. Mapping human and social capital notions into the organization's capital – suggesting this can ultimately be defined as the sum total of both kinds – is all very well on paper, but of no great consequence to managers who need to know how to trade off, say, seven units of human capital against five units of social capital. The challenge is no more easily met if the categories are changed to those of the Balanced Scorecard. One might observe, charitably, that the literature is remarkably silent on these questions. Thus while we seem on sound ground suggesting that the organization's capital is some sum of subsidiary types of capital, the flaw in the proposal is that we do not know how this sum can be calculated given that we have no coherent theory of socioeconomic capital that can include, say, the different human, social and organizational types (Barney, 1991). In the background here is Barnard's notion of the organization's "system" as an executive-generated synthesis of its three subsidiary types of system: physical, social, and psychological (Barnard, 1968).

Before we reconsider Barnard's approach towards a notion of organizational capital, we might examine the doubts that Dean and Kretschmer raise about the wisdom of using the term capital for intangibles, in particular to probe the managerial need to describe and maybe measure those aspects of the organization's resources that can be carried from one time or place to another. The separation of capital from the firm's other resources, such as land and labor, creates an epistemic space for managerial or entrepreneurial decisions about bringing them together again, Humpty Dumpty style. Without this separation we have no description of management's decisions and thus no clear notion of what it is that managers are contributing to the organization. The separation implies a theory of management and, as a corollary, a theory of the organization to be managed. Thus behind the economic notion of capital stands a Smithian notion of the firm that it is not too far from what we might call the CMU (Carnegie Mellon) view of the firm as a mechanical apparatus within which management is the cognizing and decision-making component and therefore a specific type of resource in and of itself (March and Simon, 1958). The Smithian, or rather Marshallian, entrepreneur compounds land, labor, and capital so as to maximize profit, just as the CMU decision-maker is allocating the firm's tangible and intangible resources to best effect. The underlying insight is that land, labor, capital, and entrepreneurship are economic resources with different dimensions; land's essential nature is that it is fixed and cannot be moved elsewhere, while labor is only valuable when applied, and that must be in a particular time. Capital, on the other hand, is both durable and movable, across both space and time, and in these respects a more perfect resource, the most fungible and risk-free. It is an economist's dream, as Fisher's definition suggests. Paradoxically, it is only in its application and exposure to risk through managerial decision that capital has the possibility to increase itself, leading, perhaps, to Marx's analysis of the money-commodity capital cycle. Dean and Kretschmer note that applying the term capital to intangibles generally, and ideas and knowledge in particular, is highly problematic given that only in the most anecdotal way can one argue intangibles are the durable result of past activities. The analysis seems to stress causality and deny invention, insight and the very flexibility of the creative mind. In the same way that value can spring from next to nothing, escaping a causal analysis, so ideas and knowledge can become obsolete in the way that vacuum tubes, like the dinosaurs, were quickly extinguished by semiconductors. Nor can ideas and knowledge ever be really comprehended as separable from the particular individuals who know how they can be applied.

On the other hand, Dean and Kretschmer miss the way the term "capital" is now being used to help managers discuss allocating the variety of resource types that they see comprising the organization. More and more these include ideas, learning – as in the SECI model – and specific items of knowledge like patents and intellectual property (IPRs). That these are intangible and thus unlike the organization's other resources – land, equipment, financial capital, and labor – does not remove the manager's need to talk about their application (Teece, 2000a). Dean and Kretschmer probably make a categorical error in assuming that managers should talk and think like academics, respecting the purity of their concepts, rather than as practitioners with approximate measures and tangible problems to solve. Perhaps their objective should have been to research how the term capital is being used strategically, especially in the context of Tobin's q and the rising attention to intangibles, which – as we have seen already – triggered an interest in human and social capital as well as the development of the presently hugely popular Balanced Scorecard. Given that intangible organizational capital now figures largely in most managers' resource allocation discourse and process, the absence of ideas or theories of how the various types of capital are reconciled in their decisions becomes ever more pressing. This process of combination or coordination is the real problematic for a theory of organizational capital, not the tangibility or otherwise of the resources being considered.

The positivist researcher is likely to be searching for a universal theory of intangible capital valuation and measurement, along the lines, perhaps, of rational choice theory. Or even an empirically embedded one like transactions cost theory; empirical in the sense that the relative costs within and without the firm are likely to be contingent on its particular circumstances and these need to be discovered before the allocation decisions can be made. These theories presuppose a conjunction of rational decision-making and the determining facts of a particular context. Organizational capital is, then, the knowledge the firm has available about its context and the options open to it. Some of this will be objective knowledge of the situation, or scientifically correct theories of the situation, while some may be known tacitly as successful practice in that situation. Steel-making, for example, involves dealing with chemical processes, some of which are scientific, some embedded in the work practices, some articulated into rules, procedures and routines, some representing the firm's knowledge of its customers, suppliers and competitors (Khanna *et al.*, 2005). Here we are focusing on what is known about the organization's situation and the action options available rather than on the form that knowledge might take, scientific data which can be communicated with precision, or tacit knowledge that can only be communicated with difficulty in the manner suggested by the SECI model. Many of the comprehensive definitions of organizational capital as including the identifiable tangible assets, together with the employees' skills and the network of relationships they have available, point towards this imagined "total understanding of the situation," positivist in the sense of being a complete model of that situation's "reality," described in the language of, perhaps, land, labor, equipment, and so forth. A contemporary description of the business's environment might also be framed in the language of Porter's 5-forces model (Porter, 1980). Here the environmental description is actually of those with the power to disturb the firm's quasi-monopolistic rent stream. The hope of many who use the Balanced Scorecard is of such a four-dimensional understanding of the organization's external and internal situation and strategic possibilities.

Along these lines, we can define the organization's "capital" in terms of its managers' secure grasp of the business opportunities available through their decision-making, a practice-based complex of what they know about its situation, and the resources at their disposal to change it. It comprises the firm's past choices of land, labor, equipment, customers, and so forth, and the consequences of these choices, such as accrued profit and organizational learning, together with what the organization's managers know of the situation and the options available through all possible alternative allocations of those resources. Along similar lines, we might define social capital in terms of what a particular community knows of its situation and its options to change that, such knowledge being manifest as that society's institutional arrangements (North, 1990). A similarly framed definition of human capital spins around each individual's knowledge of her/his situation and options to change or be accepting of that. The impulse behind education, say, is that it increases one's life chances by both informing individuals of their options and by giving them some of the resources they need to change their reality. We can likewise work up a definition of organizational capital. In practice, of course, we know the positivist dream of complete knowledge and power over the situation leads to an impractically academic and unpragmatic notion of what an organization's managers really do. While Simon's celebrated attack on Rational Man and total understanding is widely appreciated (Simon, 1997), we have, as yet, few well-articulated responses in terms of theories of managerial decision-making under uncertainty together with a corresponding theory of the organization (e.g. Mintzberg, 1973). The proposition, therefore, is that a definition of organizational capital must turn on the theory of the organization that underpins it, just as theories of human or social capital turn on the models of the individual or the society that underpin them. The theory of the organization also includes a statement or theory of the organization's environment – be that a system of perfect markets, political power, or whatever. Ultimately, to meld human and social capital theories into a comprehensive theory of the socioeconomy requires bringing the underpinning definitions of the individual and their social arrangements together, a search for a socioeconomic "theory of everything" that matches the physicists' search for a natural science "theory of everything." This theory would position organization as Man's primary instrument for creating value, for achieving both individual and social objectives, and so for shaping society; and its capital would be a measure of its power to effect this.

Organization theorists face a less ambitious task, which takes us back to Barnard's model. That called on the executives to synthesize what was known in the dimensions of three subsystems into the "organizational system." The outcome fits with the above definition of organizational capital, suggesting it is what the managers create through their explorations of the bounded physical, social and psychological aspects of the organization, and the process of integrating what they find into a coherent, actionable model. It is also a statement of the organization's options available futures, given both the executives' bounded rationality and the organization's finite resources. A rather similar approach underpins Penrose's theory of the growth of the firm, encapsulated in her oft-quoted sentence that the firm's nature and options are less to do with its resources than with the services they provide (Penrose, 1995). In her analysis, the "management team" is responsible for developing that body of situated knowledge that separates the services gained from the resources provided – this difference being a Penrosian definition of the organization's capital.

Organizational capital as a workable heuristic

From this vantage point we can look back at the Balanced Scorecard as an intermediary step in a methodological shift from the search for positivistic or scientific definition of organizational capital towards one grounded in the subjectivity and imagination of the executive team. The difference between these approaches grows out of Simon's critique and his suggestion that if the organization's situation and options are ultimately unknowable because of the managers' bounded rationality, then a more useful definition of the organization's capital can only arise from what has been learned from an exploration of its options. Since we know that the term capital demands we focus on what can be transferred from one time/space context to another, we end up with a notion that is contingent on what has been learned remaining relevant in the next time-period or in the next place. Since, under circumstances of bounded rationality, the managers have no comprehensive knowledge of the world, they can never be certain that the organization's capital will remain valuable. The organizational capital is shaped by their expectations of its future value, a matter that neo-classical economists ignore because they presume total knowledge and, with this assumption, reject the contingencies of both time and space. Thus the notion that the organization's capital is the sum of its assets, plus its employees' skills, and so forth, masks all doubt about its future value under different circumstances – another way of saying that a post-Penrosian definition must recognize the time/space-past in which the management team's knowledge has been acquired, together with their expectations of the time/space-future in which it is to be applied.

As we adopt a theory of the organization as something unique and impossible to know completely, the ephemeral and transient creation of a specific group of managers immersed in a specific situation, we move towards an inherently constructivist notion of organizational capital. This shifts our attention away from looking for a positivist definition of the organization's resources, both tangible and intangible, that can be completely known and abstracted from the situation in the manner considered by Dean and Kretschmer. We move instead towards the situated and embedded expression of Bowman and Swart (Bowman and Swart, 2007). While these authors offer no definitive theory of either the organization or its capital, they argue the possibility of organizational capital depends instead on resolving the issues of knowledge ownership – what we might call "intellectual property rights" issues in the broadest sense. If the employees' skills are available only at their discretion, rather than being at the beck and call of the organization's management, they cannot really be considered as part of the organization's capital, and must remain the employees' own human capital. Bowman and Swart show that, even if we resolve the substantive issues of discovering and measuring the resources applicable to a particular situation, we cannot properly speak of organizational capital without also establishing the organization's ownership of those resources, an issue that stands behind Teece's analysis of appropriating their full value (Teece, 2000b).

A Penrose-style analysis suggests that if we define capital – either "hard" or "soft" – as something built up in the past, but now made available for application in the future, we are in danger of missing its essentially subjective nature. To measure it presumes it can usefully be considered objectively, beyond the particular time and space circumstances in which it is either created or to be applied. In fact this point is applicable to human and social capital as much as it is to organizational capital. Two different people will clearly extract different value from the same educational inputs. Similarly, two different societies will make different use of the same tax revenues. Organizational capital, however defined, must still be comprehended and integrated into the organization's processes if it is to contribute to value, and this process must be managed. Management's knowledge mediates any measurable value but escapes the possibility of being valued itself because, as Penrose's analysis shows, it is the point at which the management team's entrepreneurial capability enters the economic system (Romer, 1994). Even at this point in the analysis, the capital's ownership remains problematic.

In conclusion, we cannot make sufficient sense of organizational capital if we merely map the notions of human and social capital into the organizational context as if the organization was both an individual writ large and a society writ small. It only makes sense if we see the organization as a mechanism that both separates the organization's capital from what is present individually and socially, and establishes the organization's ownership of what has been separated. Organizational learning, that being managed within the context of the organization's power and practice, is so central here because it seems easier for managers to establish the results as organizational property; an argument that elides the complexities which Bowman and Swart explore. But we can see that whatever we might mean by organizational capital is contingent on several supporting analyses: (a) a theory of the organization in which it is created and applied, and (b) a theory of entrepreneurship as mediating the current stock of capital, which thereby shapes the management team's expectations of the future value of what can be carried from the past. We have much work to do in these areas. The widespread use of the terms human, social, and organizational capital is a strong indication that we face an eager audience of practitioners, be they individuals, managers, or public policy-makers.

Bibliography

Arrow, K. J. (1962). The Economic Implications of Learning by Doing. *Review of Economic Studies*, 29(3): 155–73.

Bahk, B. H. and Gort, M. (1993). Decomposing Learning by Doing in New Plants. *Journal of Political Economy*, 101(4): 561–83.

Barnard, C. I. (1968). *The Functions of the Executive* (30th Anniversary Edition). Cambridge MA: Harvard University Press.

Barney, J. B. (1991). Firm Resources and Sustained Competitive Advantage. *Journal of Management*, 17(1): 99–120.

Baron, S., Field, J., and Schuller, T. (eds.) (2000). *Social Capital: Critical Perspectives*. Oxford: Oxford University Press.

Bechky, B. A. (2003). Sharing Meaning Across Occupational Communities: The Transformation of Understanding on a Production Floor. *Organization Science*, 14(3): 312.

Becker, G. S. (1964). *Human Capital: A Theoretical and Empirical Analysis, with Special Reference to Education*. New York: NBER.

Becker, G. S., Murphy, K. M., and Tamura, R. (1990). Human Capital, Fertility, and Economic Growth. *Journal of Political Economy*, 98(5): S12–S37.

Bils, M. and Klenow, P. J. (2000). Does Schooling Cause Growth? *American Economic Review*, 90(5): 1160–83.

Bontis, N. (2001). Assessing Knowledge Assets: A Review of the Models Used to Measure Intellectual Capital. *International Journal of Management Reviews*, 3(1): 41–60.

Bowman, C. and Swart, J. (2007). Whose Human Capital? The Challenge of Value Capture When Capital is Embedded. *Journal of Management Studies*, 44(4): 488–505.

Brainard, W. and Tobin, J. (1968). Pitfalls in Financial Model-Building. *American Economic Review*, 58(2): 99–122.

Castells, M. (1996). *The Information Age: Economy, Society and Culture*. Malden MA: Blackwell.

Coleman, J. S. (1974). *Power and the Structure of Society*. New York: W. W. Norton.

Coleman, J. S. (1990). *Foundations of Social Theory*. Cambridge MA: Harvard University Press.

Cooper, R. and Kaplan, R. S. (1988). Measure Costs Right: Make the Right Decision. *Harvard Business Review*, 66(5): 96.

Dean, A. and Kretschmer, M. (2007). Can Ideas be Capital? Factors of Production in the Postindustrial Economy: A Review and Critique. *Academy of Management Review*, 32(2): 573–94.

Demsetz, H. (1991). The Theory of the Firm Revisited. In O. E. Williamson and S. G. Winter (eds.) *The Nature of the Firm: Origins, Evolution, and Development*. Oxford: Oxford University Press, pp. 159–78.

Drucker, P. F. (1988). The Coming of the New Organization. *Harvard Business Review*, 66(1): 45–53.

Dzinkowski, R. (2000). The Measurement and Management of Intellectual Capital: An Introduction. *Management Accounting*, 78(2): 32.

Edvinsson, L. (1997). Developing Intellectual Capital at Skandia. *Long Range Planning*, 30(3): 366–73.

Edvinsson, L. and Malone, M. P. (1997). *Intellectual Capital: Realizing Your Company's True Value by Finding Its Hidden Roots*. New York: Harper Business.

Ekelund, R. B. and Tollison, R. D. (1980). The Mercantilist Origins of the Corporation. *Bell Journal of Economics*, 11:715–20.

Field, J. (2003). *Social Capital*. Abingdon: Routledge.

Field, J., Schuller, T., and Baron, S. (2000). Social Capital and Human Capital Revisited. In S. Baron, J. Field, and T. Schuller (eds.) *Social Capital: Critical Perspectives*. Oxford: Oxford University Press, pp. 243–63.

Fine, B. (2000). *Social Capital Versus Social Theory: Political Economy and Social Science at the Turn of the Millenium*. London: Routledge.

Giddens, A. (1984). *The Constitution of Society: Outline of the Theory of Structuration*. Berkeley CA: University of California Press.

Gort, M., Grabowski, H., and McGuckin, R. (1985). Organizational Capital and the Choice Between Specialization and Diversification. *Managerial & Decision Economics*, 6(1): 2–10.

Grant, R. M. (2003). The Knowledge-Based View of the Firm. In D. O. Faulkner and A. Campbell (eds.) *The Oxford Handbook of Strategy* (Vol. 1). Oxford: Oxford University Press, pp. 197–221.

Gray, P. H. and Meister, D. B. (2004). Knowledge Sourcing Effectiveness. *Management Science*, 50(6): 821–34.

Gurvitch, G. (1972). *The Social Frameworks of Knowledge* (trans. M. A. Thompson and K. A. Thompson). New York: Harper & Row.

Halpern, D. (2005). *Social Capital*. Cambridge: Polity Press.

Harcourt, G. C. (1972). *Some Cambridge Controversies in the Theory of Capital*. Cambridge: Cambridge University Press.

Hartog, J. and van den Brink, H. M. (eds.) (2007). *Human Capital: Advances in Theory and Evidence*. Cambridge: Cambridge University Press.

Hotchkiss, L. (1993). Effects of Training, Occupation, and Training-Occupation Match on Wage. *Journal of Human Resources*, 28(3): 482–96.

Johnson, H. G. (1960). The Public Economy of Opulence. *Canadian Journal of Economics and Political Science*, 26(4): 552–64.

Kannan, G. and Aulbur, W. G. (2004). Intellectual Capital: Measurement Effectiveness. *Journal of Intellectual Capital*, 5(3): 339–413.

Kaplan, R. S. and Norton, D. P. (1996). Using the Balanced Scorecard as a Strategic Management System. *Harvard Business Review*, 74(1): 75.

Karseras, H. (2006). *From New Recruit to High Flyer: No-Nonsense Advice on How to Fast Track Your Career*. London: Kogan Page.

Kendrick, J. W. (1956). Productivity Trends: Capital and Labor. *Review of Economics and Statistics*, 38(3): 248–57.

Kessler, A. S. and Lülfesmann, C. (2002). The Theory of Human Capital Revisited: On the Interaction of General and Specific Investments. CESifo Working Paper No. 776.

Khalil, E. L. (1997). Is the Firm an Individual? *Cambridge Journal of Economics*, 21:519–44.

Khanna, A., Mitra, D., and Gupta, A. (2005). How Shop-Floor Employees Drive Innovation at Tata Steel. *KM Review*, 8(3): 20–3.

Lin, N. (2001). *Social Capital: A Theory of Social Structure and Action*. New York: Cambridge University Press.

Lucas, R. E. (1988). On the Mechanics of Economic Development. *Journal of Monetary Economics*, 22:3–42.

Mankiw, N. G., Romer, D., and Weil, D. N. (1992). A Contribution to the Empirics of Economic Growth. *Quarterly Journal of Economics*, 107(2): 407.
March, J. G. (1991). Exploration and Exploitation in Organizational Learning. *Organization Science*, 2:71–87.
March, J. G. and Olsen, J. P. (1989). *Rediscovering Institutions: The Organizational Basis of Politics*. New York: Free Press.
March, J. G. and Simon, H. A. (1958). *Organizations*. New York: John Wiley.
Marshall, A. (1964). *Elements of the Economics of Industry*. London: Macmillan.
McCloskey, D. N. (1998). *The Rhetoric of Economics* (2nd edition). Madison WI: University of Wisconsin Press.
Middleton, D. and Edwards, D. (eds.) (1990). *Collective Remembering*. Newbury Park CA: Sage Publications.
Mintzberg, H. (1973). *The Nature of Managerial Work*. New York: Harper & Row.
Morgan, G. (1997). *Images of Organization* (new edition). Thousand Oaks CA: Sage Publications.
Nelson, R. R. and Winter, S. G. (1982). *An Evolutionary Theory of Economic Change*. Cambridge MA: Belknap Press.
Nonaka, I. and Takeuchi, H. (1995). *The Knowledge-Creating Company: How Japanese Companies Create the Dynamics of Innovation*. New York: Oxford University Press.
North, D. C. (1990). *Institutions, Institutional Change and Economic Performance*. Cambridge: Cambridge University Press.
Parsons, T. (1960). *Structure and Process in Modern Societies*. Glencoe IL: Free Press.
Paxton, P. (1999). Is Social Capital Declining in the United States? A Multiple Indicator Assessment. *American Journal of Sociology*, 105(1): 88–127.
Pennings, J. M., Lee, K., and van Witteloostuijn, A. (1998). Human Capital, Social Capital, and Firm Dissolution. *Academy of Management Journal*, 41(4): 425–40.
Penrose, E. T. (1995). *The Theory of the Growth of the Firm* (3rd edition). New York: Oxford University Press.
Pfeffer, J. (1993). Barriers to the Advancement of Organization Science: Paradigm Development as a Dependent Variable. *Academy of Management Review*, 18:599–620.
Pigou, A. (1928). *A Study in Public Finance*. London: Macmillan.
Porter, M. E. (1980). *Competitive Strategy: Techniques for Analyzing Industries and Competitors*. New York: Free Press.
Prescott, E. C. and Visscher, M. (1980). Organization Capital. *Journal of Political Economy*, 88(3): 446–61.
Putnam, R. D. (2000). *Bowling Alone: The Collapse and Revival of American Community*. New York: Simon & Schuster.
Robison, L. J., Schmid, A. A., and Siles, M. E. (2002). Is Social Capital Really Capital? *Review of Social Economy*, 60(1): 1–21.
Romer, P. M. (1994). The Origins of Endogenous Growth. *The Journal of Economic Perspectives*, 8(1): 3–22.
Schultz, T. W. (1961). Investment in Human Capital. *American Economic Review*, 51(1): 1.
Simon, H. A. (1997). *Administrative Behavior: A Study of Decision-Making Processes in Administrative Organization* (4th edition). New York: Free Press.
Solow, R. M. (1956). A Contribution to the Theory of Economic Growth. *Quarterly Journal of Economics*, 70: 65–94.
Solow, R. M. (1957). Technical Change and the Aggregate Production Function. *Review of Economics and Statistics*, 39:312–20.
Sunder, S. (2002). Knowing What Others Know: Common Knowledge, Accounting, and Capital Markets, *Accounting Horizons*, 16(4): 305–18.
Teece, D. J. (2000a). *Managing Intellectual Capital: Organizational, Strategic, and Policy Dimensions*. Oxford: Oxford University Press.
Teece, D. J. (2000b). Managing Knowledge Assets in Diverse Industrial Contexts. In

C. Despres and D. Chauvel (eds.), *Knowledge Horizons*. Woburn MA: Butterworth-Heinemann, pp. 131–47.

Tobin, J. (1969). A General Equilibrium Approach to Monetary Theory. *Journal of Money, Credit, and Banking*, 1:15–29.

Wanous, J. P. (1992). *Organizational Entry: Recruitment, Selection, Orientation, and Socialization of Newcomers* (2nd edition). Reading MA: Addison-Wesley.

Whitley, R. D., Thomas, A., and Marceau, J. (1981). *Masters of Business? Business Schools and Business Graduates in Britain and France*. London: Tavistock Publications.

Williamson, O. E. (1970). *Corporate Control and Business Behavior: An Inquiry into the Effects of Organization Form on Enterprise Behavior*. Englewood Cliffs NJ: Prentice-Hall.

Yelle, L. E. (1979). The Learning Curve: Historical Review and Comprehensive Survey. *Decision Sciences*, 10:302–28.

2 The power and frailty of organisational capital

Jan Mouritsen

Organisational capital is typically presented as dead. It is what has been left behind after human capital has left the building. Its 'internal structure includes patents, concepts, models, and computer and administrative systems' (Sveiby, 1997), it 'doesn't go home at night' (Stewart, 1997), and it is 'everything left at the office when the employees go home' (Edvinsson and Malone, 1997). Organisational capital is a leftover which is abandoned every afternoon by human capital leaving to live other lives; it is doomed to stay behind. Organisational capital is not heroic in this picture of things; and it appears to be a production of humans, just as it is a tool for humans. It is systematically 'after human capital'.

However, organisational capital may be more. It has also been described as 'an agglomeration of technologies: business processes, practices and designs, including incentive and compensation systems that enable firms to consistently extract out of a given level of resources a higher level of output and at a lower cost than other firms' (Lev and Radhakrishnan, 2003). Here, it is presented as 'the only factor of production that is unique to the firm and is thus capable of yielding above the cost of capital returns' (ibid.). Thus, organisational capital may not only be a residue, a leftover from human capital, but a resource and prior to human capital. Therefore, organisational capital may not be dead, not passive, not waiting, but alive, participating – and even dominating – the productivity of humans. It may create superior constellations of knowledge resources referred to as 'intangible capabilities' (Itami *et al.*, 1987), 'core competencies' (Prahalad and Hamel, 1990) or 'dynamic capabilities' (Teece *et al.*, 1997). These are the result of the gradual accumulation of competence over time, specific to the individual firm, which makes it adept at a particular set of processes and procedures. Organisational capital concerns this reservoir of organisational capabilities. Therefore, analysing organisational capital, it is possible to identify processes of organisational capabilities. Thus, organisational capital may be powerful; but how is this power actualised?

There is a schism here. One the one hand, organisational capital may be powerful, but how does it mobilise its power? It is typically described in broad functional terms so that overall it has effects on value creation, but rarely is organisational capital described when it acts and thus creates value. In this essay I venture to discuss how organisational capital makes a difference. In this discussion I pay particular attention to the formative role of organisational capital, but I also extend this proposition and develop a reflection, not only on the conditioning effects of organisational capital, but also on its contingent existence; and end in a non-intuitive proposition about the curious boundaries of organisational capital. It appears from this analysis that organisational capital can neither keep an identity as a set of organisational residues after human capital, nor as a singular driver of value. On close inspection, organisational capital may not even be a unique entity.

Below, I present two examples of organisational capital and analyse their involvement with organisational processes and procedures. Both examples have been reported in full length elsewhere, where they focus on a different set of research questions. I, however, want to use these examples in a different and new way to exemplify how organisational capital is involved in the constitution of organisational action and the development of organisational competencies.

The power of organisational capital

Many studies have shown that there are relations between the three components of intellectual capital indicated by captions such as human, organisational and relational capital. They show that human capital rarely drives effects singularly (Marr *et al.*, 2004; Roos *et al.*, 2005). Bontis (e.g. 1998, 1999, 2004; Bontis and Fitz-enz, 2002) has shown many times that for many entities such as private firms, public institutions and nation-states, human and relational capital rarely influences value creation if not through organisational capital; the primary effect of intellectual capital goes through organisational capital (see also Wang and Chang, 2005). Organisational capital thus has a role to play, but which one?

One possible role is to assure predictability and efficiency through codification and re-use of knowledge, compared with human capital, which is accorded the powers of creativity and imagination. Another possible role is to occupy the space of tradable assets, while human capital is unpredictable as it can refuse to return to the workplace. In both capacities, organisational capital is a black box. While it is possible to identify the actions of human capital, the actions of organisational capital are hidden because its powers are explained as purposes or as functions. It is not clear how it is an actor.

Some examples of how it is an actor are therefore needed (see also Mouritsen and Koleva, 2004). One example of organisational capital is the patent (Mouritsen and Koleva, 2005), and another example is a management model – the BS 7750/ ISO14001 standard on environmental management (Mouritsen *et al.*, 2000). I will use these examples and develop them to discuss how organisational capital acts.

Example 1: Patents at Palm Computing

Mouritsen and Koleva (2005) develop the case of Palm Computing based on their analysis of a Harvard Business School teaching case (1996). They illustrate how patents circulate between individual innovation decisions, companies and markets.

The inventor Hawkins created a patent on a pattern recognition algorithm (PalmPrint). He licensed it to *GRiD Systems*, which then turned out to be a 'leader in pen-based computing'. Upon licensing, the company acquired rights over all product developments made hereafter. Thus, the extracted individual knowledge ('he was able to claim sole ownership rights to the patent') is packaged and exercised as an option shaping the relationships between individual and company, negotiating positions and profit distribution.

Even with his exceptional talent and multiple intellectual interests, Hawkins could not do it alone. He needed the infrastructure in which to experiment and test his ideas: he was in the software industry for more than 10 years before he started Palm Computing. He also needed the institution of patenting, because his 'experience in Silicon Valley had taught him that patents have real value – even more so than copy rights'. Thus 'Hawkins chose to patent rather than copyright even though it was more difficult'. Once codified, the information could circulate: 'I couldn't go out and prevent someone else from using it [the patented algorithm]'. He recognised the use of patents as a signalling instrument to the market: 'It is the currency of intellectual property that you can sell to investors or license to other companies'. Hawkins the asset owner was concerned about protecting his knowledge, while Hawkins the entrepreneur was interested in the tangibility of this knowledge, which can be used to overcome the resistance of other companies and investors. He mobilised his patent both as a mechanism for protection of key knowledge and as a signal ensuring its value.

The circulation of the patent enforced the circulation of the individual: he 'frequently spoke at business and industry meetings and he was often called on to meet with new and potential GRiD clients'. Not only did the inventor enact his codified knowledge through the institution of patenting, but the patent also acted upon him, forcing him to take decisions and to redefine relationships. The patent allowed the inventor to tell a story; it invested him with eloquence and with the power of ownership.

When Hawkins rearranged the market for PDA, he discovered that there were resistances to overcome. To start a company on its own for consumer palmtop (PDA), he had to convince GRiD to participate in his project and accept the role he had assigned to it. Setting up a new company started with knowledge extraction, protection and circulation. The original disentanglement of knowledge became entangled in being made an element of the firm. Even if the patent was instrumental in developing an idea of a new firm, the new firm was the condition that could make the patent valuable. Thus the legal protection of knowledge created a 'new world'; a new company mobilised as a symbol for the future of both industry and inventor: Palm is an 'independent software and services developer'. It is an actor around which 'cooperative efforts of several business partners' are mobilised in order to achieve success.

Hawkins was thus not the lonely knower any more. Through his patent he became a node in a network (*'The firm had opted not to invest in that future venture, but the partners had seen potential in Hawkins and had added his name to their list of candidates for future investment'*), he increased his size (*'He could design the software himself, but he needed a staff of highly qualified software engineers to do the development and writing'*), he negotiated relationships, assigned roles (*'Tandy might be able to satisfy this goal ...'*) and communicated via representations of his endeavours (*'he would have to report his progress ... '*) in the world.

The patent became an entangled matter. It altered competitive constellations (*'GRiD entered into negotiations to buy the patent, but it was competing with Microsoft and GO for the rights'*) and enacted the competitors (*'the license to use the device patent did not include rights to make software ... '*). Competition was suddenly something to be enacted in the patent game and which accepted definitions (*'NEC, NCR, Samsung, Sanyo, and IBM were among the first to announce their intent to develop pen-based products'*), the environment created through the patent developed more and more, and was no single actor's work. The inventor and the patent were no longer in control of the entangled knowledge; they had become part of a context, the relations of which they helped to shape, but they could not keep in place.

The patent rearranged the investment decisions. It was both a signalling instrument and a hedging operation, because it was a stored value, which could be exchanged and capitalised on the market (*'the venture capitalists with whom Hawkins was in contact were actively involved in industry intelligence – always looking for the most talented people already working in the area's high technology firms'*). Financial calculations occupied the back stage in this case through the 'dance of patent rights'. Royalties and financial results were incentives for all actors; but hardly the only incentive (*'I could make a lot of money and naturally, I'd like that. It's not unimportant, but it's clearly not the motivating factor'*). The financial results of entrepreneurship were important and created an overlay of management control, but they were not the only stimulus for visionaries. They are part of the mechanism to make patents develop into networks because they help with grasping – or, more exactly, pointing out – the tangibility of knowledge, the results of value creation. They are currency, which can be shown to the stockholders.

Example 2: The environmental management standard BS 7750/ISO 14001

Mouritsen *et al.* (2000) illustrate how a management model in the form of a green standard (the BS7750, which later became part of ISO 14001) could not only report a firm's environmental performance, but indeed also develop a firm's strategies in various ways. The standard was quickly recognised as more than a reporting tool that could be used to develop a firm's environmental performance. It could also be a driver in extending a firm's business strategies more generally, in at least four ways, illustrated in Figure 1.

Appease the Public (political domination)

Mouritsen *et al.* (ibid.) illustrate one strategy reproducing the following dialogue between interviewer (Q) and manager (R):

Q: Why did you get certified?

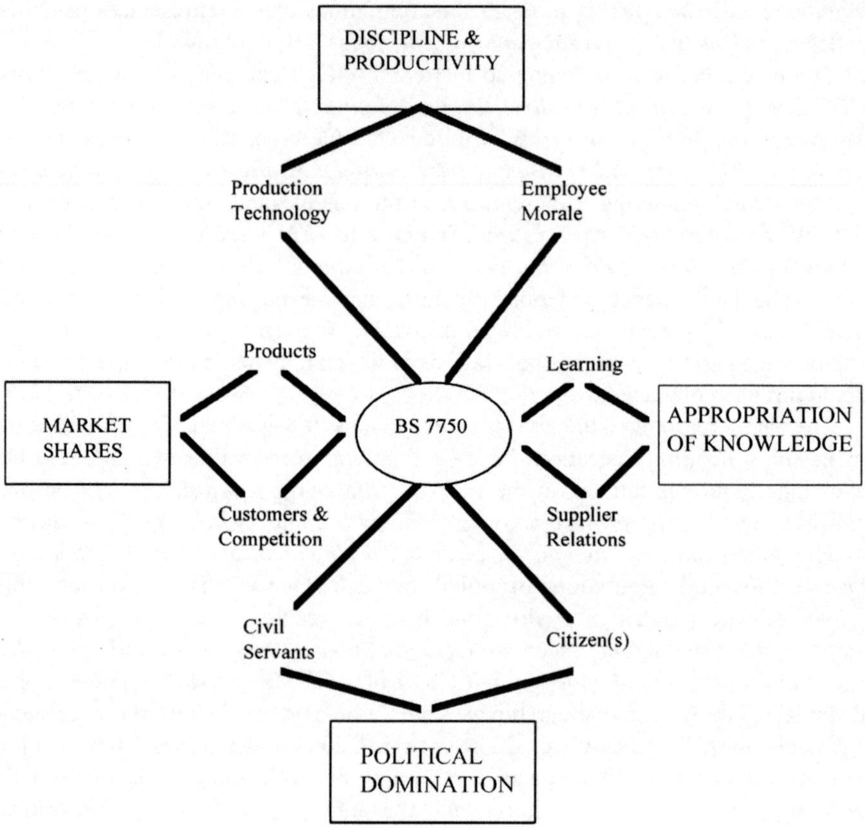

Figure 2.1 Narratives of BS 7750.

R: Because it is a 'must'. In future industry, all have to account for their actions to look after the environment. In addition, there is great uncertainty among citizens about what type of firm this firm really is. We have been exposed to a set of strange attacks where a certain Mrs Petersen, under a false address, complained about us to the Community Chief Engineer's Department, who then came to us and asked what was going on. This Mrs Petersen complained about smoke, noise and dirt, but this was simply a provocation because we have less than 35 dB noise, we don't have smoke and no dirt. But because of the lack of knowledge about what we do here we have to explain ourselves …

We have to mind the public opinion, which is often very aggressive and 'lefty' and if they start asking questions it will take a lot of time to respond. We don't have anything to hide, and we want to show that we are not only a serious firm that has a first class product at a fair price, and that we are profitable. We also want to show that we take the environment into regard, and as there is uncertainty as to what we do, we have decided to tell about it. This is why we wanted to get certification.

Q: So, it was because of an anonymous letter that you decided to get certified.

R: We had already heard some rumours, as people were saying that this is really a terrible place as they use cyanide in their production. Everybody knows from books that this has been used to kill people for centuries. These people are, however, not knowledgeable about how we do it. And we could take the heat off the debate by saying that there are no problems with us because we are in control. The certification shows this.

Q: Have there been any effects of working with BS 7750?

R: We have described how we for a long time have been doing things. We have written down how we handle toxic production flows.

This interchange shows that BS 7750 developed relations to external constituents, appeasing neighbours and the community. BS 7750 persuaded the public that the firm's production processes, albeit perhaps potentially dangerous, were well controlled and looked after. It used the certification to fend off critique and to establish to the wider public that the firm's activities were not dangerous. BS 7750 brought the environment into the equation.

Develop Production Methods

Mouritsen *et al.* (ibid) also identify how BS 7750 may increase workforce productivity. They produce the following evidence from a firm:

> In 1991 we decided to get ISO 9000 certified and when we had finished this project we decided to go ahead with BS 7750 certification. We have to change things in order to proceed continuously. We have to blow a bomb to alert attention.
>
> Paradoxically, we are in principle opposed to systems but we proceeded anyway for several reasons. Firstly, we had to shake the organisation a bit. Secondly, we wanted to be pioneers in the industry, and we are ahead concerning environmental issues, and I believe we were the first on quality, as well. In addition, when in Denmark we had the pension reform where lots of people went on early retirement; firms were suddenly paralysed because they lost their expertise. We avoided this since we had our processes written down on paper. Actually, we could fire all employees tomorrow and still relatively quickly start again. Now, we are not any more afraid to lose employees. When a new employee comes in, he or she can just read instructions and follow another more experienced employee for a week or so, and then he or she will know the whole system.
>
> If a new instruction is produced, it is immediately sent to the employees who are concerned with that specific process and then it is corrected and sent back again. All employees have to sign a paper saying that they have read it. Then the instruction will be published.

BS 7750 was an extension to ISO 9000 as an opportunity to control a set of environmental cost objects. It helped to direct attention and produce motivation in the workforce, to improve production processes. BS 7750 was more than a set of aspirations to improve 'the environment'. It was also an information system that mobilised workers towards more efficiency and productivity in the name of 'the environment'. This was a process of making production processes *visible and controllable.*

Create a Marketing Platform

Mouritsen *et al.* (ibid) also illustrate that BS 7750 could help to manage the market, as exemplified in the following statement by a third firm:

> We use our '5 R philosophy' to improve: Reject, replace, reuse, reduce and recycle. These are published on internal posters in the whole firm so our employees understand that we mean it seriously when we say that we have to think and act environmentally. We have put so much knowledge into 'environment' that our competitors have to take it seriously. It has to be customers' only choice. We have, though, to consider the borders to trustworthiness, which is difficult because we are actually communicating a lot of knowledge.
>
> It is no problem to find suppliers because they want to use us as a frame of reference. We are approached from interested possible suppliers every day, but we just give them our questionnaire on environmental protection. The important thing about a supplier is not technology, but their attitude to our environment concept. They have to change their strategy to fit ours. Our method is a questionnaire with multiple choice questions, and I can thus compare 'best practices' and on that basis make the cut-off point.
>
> If one wants to use the environment factor seriously in the marketing activities then one has to be serious about the environment. If you don't, you will be challenged and you will be questioned and these are attacks on the 'nerve' of the concept to the environment.

BS 7750 was part of competitive advantage, just like price, design, quality, etc. A 'green' tag could take market shares. The green certification made it possible for the customer to discriminate between products that may look similar on the outside but were different on the inside. When products do not discriminate themselves by their appearance on shelves in shops, they could by pushing BS 7750 in front of them. Without the standard, the products' qualities would be fabricated aimlessly because they would be 'non-communicable'.

Develop Competencies

The last strategy identified by Mouritsen *et al.* (ibid.) is to develop and create a competence based strategy for its development:

> It appeared 'natural' to start working with the environment as the firm was to consider toxic liquids anyway. We already worked with ISO, and when BS

> 7750 came by, it just seemed right to take it on. One of the reasons to take on the environment was that we could as well do today what otherwise we would have been forced to tomorrow. In addition, it does not matter that when people say 'environment' they think about this firm.
>
> The environment has been important both for the internal environment and for the external environment, where we have focused on the latter in order to ensure that we didn't send toxic products on the market. From management's side there has not been an explicit requirement to come up with cost savings. It has more been a question of documenting our capabilities, although if there was a potentiality for savings we should take them.
>
> The firm has very close links with its suppliers and we pay for the adapted components that we get. We try to substitute environmentally defective materials in co-operation with suppliers. BS 7750 has provided a stronger internal knowledge and we can interact more precisely with suppliers. Likewise, the customers will in due course be required to buy 'green' products, and they express great concern for the firm's activities *vis-à-vis* environmental issues.
>
> One example of the implications of the role of the environmental issue is investments in new production technology, where we have become a test firm for a particular piece of machinery to cut up timber so that thinner variants of a wooden product would be as durable. This machinery minimises waste but it also makes the firm more flexible and efficient, as the development of products will have more degrees of freedom. Likewise, the new painting method will ensure that workers will not have to work in rooms with toxic fumes, and the painting is of a better quality, just as we use less paint.

This firm developed and produced outdoor play-tools for children, and part of the quality process was to actually design play-tools that fit children rather than grown-ups. BS 7750 helped to develop new relations between the firm on the one side, and both employees and suppliers on the other; and also relations to internal production spaces.

Organisational capital and organisational activities

Organisational capital in action

The two examples of organisational capital presented above are different but each illustrates how organisational capital may work, and they offer new insights.

The case of the patent in Palm Computing teaches us that first the patent has to be disentangled from a multitude of different relations to become a patent, and then it has to be re-entangled into multiple relations to be of value. The patent is constantly in circulation, where it persuades others to engage and help identify and realise its potentiality. It extends its relations and engages with actors and companies, the existence of which the inventor may never have imagined. There are no linear relationships between the patent and its effects as it constantly spirals away from a situation to a new space. A patent is thus rarely storage of knowledge, but is a mechanism to relate and organise actors of various kinds.

Likewise, the case of the management technology BS 7750 shows that its power resides it its ability to distribute and organise actors of various kinds. BS 7750 is never a small item in the management closet of the company. It is constantly searching for issues to incorporate, and is able to do many different things. Being able to develop political mediation, develop markets, mobilise and possibly appropriate employees' and suppliers' knowledge and motivation, B 7750 circulates many types of ambitions and performance criteria all the time. Again, the item of organisational capital does not primarily store knowledge – it distributes relations and extends them in time and space, within and beyond the firm.

Both examples show that organisational capital is not dead and not a leftover from human and relational capital. The things left in the office when employees go home are not on hold, but they engage activity. The principle here is that the length of relations that can be extended by organisational capital develops its power and value. When organisational capital mobilises many actors of different kinds, it gets more power; but also, when organisational capital extends these relations and includes more and more actors, it changes identity and character. In its meeting with these others, organisational capital will get new properties – this is how it can develop concrete possibilities, rather than presenting abstract potentialities.

Travelling between internal and external users, as the case of Palm Computing shows, the patent gains relevance and strength, even if its purposes had to co-develop with the development of the relations. It can generate products, it can develop industry standards and it can even make competitors go out of their way to accommodate it. It is in this network of highly concrete activities that the patent changes from being an asset *on hold* (where in some sense it just is there; but unmovable and 'dead') to an asset *in action* (where in some sense it is only something in relation to other things and thus difficult to separate from the other things happening in the network; it is movable and 'alive', but difficult to assess individually).

Likewise, when BS 7750 engages in developing relations, it can radically colour its own identity. The four translations into concrete possibilities illustrate that even if the core item of organisational capital remains, the identity and character of BS 7750 are radically different between the four situations. BS 7750 can reach into the production space, it can extend into the supply chain, it can co-produce the market, and it can alleviate political risk. These four translations illustrate that the linkages forged by BS 7750 develop potentiality, but also that its power is tied to the length and durability of the relations it extends in time and space.

The two examples show that organisational capital is more than codified knowledge that is available when employees have gone home. This is a very poor metaphor for understanding the character of organisational capital. In order to make sense of organisational capital, it is necessary to inquire into its abilities when in action, rather than when on hold. This requires us to understand organisational capital in situations where it makes a difference; when it mobilises actors and relations including connections to people, processes, procedures, technologies, politics and strategy. Understanding organisational capital more as a network of entities in constant interactions (in action), rather as an object lying in an inventory (on hold), is useful because this directs attention to its openness and the degrees of freedom by which it can be put to use. Following closely what organisational capital can do expands the space of possibility where the item of organisational capital gains colour and identity by its relations (see also Mouritsen, 2006).

Generally, these relations are found in human and relational capital. In both examples, it is impossible to talk much about the item of organisational capital without referring to human and relational capital. In both examples, organisational capital reaches out to employees, political actors, suppliers, financers and competitors, and it gains its identity by these relations. To determine whether organisational capital is an input or an output is not easy because in both examples the item of organisational capital does exist at a certain point in time, but it does not exist with stable traits and identity over time. Neither is it easy to say exactly whether human imagination or organisational process-knowledge is the creative part because both BS 7750 and the patent develop relations consisting of ideas, propositions and possibilities. And, in addition, it is not easy to distinguish between the conditions for good effects and bad effects of organisational capital, because it extends and builds network-relations that colour its power, and thus it has no fixed properties from which predictable outcomes arise smoothly. This is why, for example, BS 7750 can be four distinct things, and not just an agglomeration of them all.

The strategic ambiguity arising out of this discussion is that, since an item of organisational capital can take on many identities and characteristics, the management concern is often reduction rather than expansion of the identities it can have. The more identities and possible characteristics, the more uncertain is the power with which it operates. The implication is not that management would be uninterested in exploring the potentialities of organisational capital, but that there is a tension to exploration. This is not only because exploration extends the period of time in pre-production mode, which at least creates opportunity costs of some sort, but also because exploration extends the time where people are confused and unaware of where the totality of the business is going. Increasing confusion hinders creativity. So, the dilemma is that exploration of organisational capital could be of value, but it is also of value to stop exploration and get to exploitation.

The boundaries of organisational capital

As suggested above, organisational capital does many things, and not only things that are predictable. Also, organisational capital rarely travels alone. It only has power when intermingled with other types of intellectual capital and, therefore, it is easy to question the strong separation in the rhetoric of human, organisational and relational capital. These kinds of capital may not exist, as such, apart from in some descriptive accounts of the size and/or value of intellectual capital, or of its amount in disclosure practices, or in statistical models of its various powers.

As practice, organisational capital may not have any strong boundary and it may not have any unique existence. It shares this problem with human and relational capital. Take, for example, an event such as ‘Training’ – one would expect this to be a clear case of human capital. Assume then that we learn this training is to develop computing competencies to make people use the firm's newly acquired sophisticated technology. Is it still human capital, or is it now suddenly organisational capital? Training is used to develop the productivity of information technology, so it can be both human and organisational capital. Further assume that we learn this information technology is a customer relationship module (CRM) in an ERP package, and then the training is suddenly an investment in stabilising the firm's relations to its customers. Is it not then relational capital?

Thus, a 'Training' event can be human, organisational or relational capital, depending on how it is explained. The three concepts, which make intuitive sense, have a problematical organising capability because their ability to make sense of events is weak. They are good metaphors; but they are not good classifications.

This dilemma expresses itself in a series of different ways. Firstly, human capital is typically seen to be about creativity and heightened attention to the individual's pursuits. Novelty and new ideas are functions of this entity/variable. However, many propositions about human capital are not about individuals at all. They are about collectives, such as breakdown of the workforce according to age, gender, education, satisfaction, sickness, tenure, etc. These are statistics about a collective, and are much more a description of institutionalised competencies than of risk taking, creativity and novelty. Human capital is rarely about oddballs making new ideas and inventions; it is rarely about the value of the unexpected. It is much more about attempts to master the workforce and make it amenable to intervention, not in terms of person per person but by structuring of patterns of competencies needed to stabilise the firm (O'Donnell *et al.*, 2006; Roslender and Fincham, 2001; Thorbjørnsson and Mouritsen, 2003). Does this not make human capital an organisational resource?

Second, when we look at organisational capital, for example, through the lens of information technology, it can turn out to have many different possible properties. It can be used to document or codify information (e.g. Hansen *et al.*, 1999) where items of knowledge and documents are made available via an intranet. This is where knowledge is made common between all people, and all people get access to the same information and knowledge. Another possibility is where information technology is used to create corporate 'yellow pages' or directories in which people can access each other. In this situation, people are acknowledged as experts, and technology merely creates connections. But this is a very different notion of knowledge sharing than the first example. In the first example, attention is to corporate resources such as documents and common knowledge, while in the second case, knowledge is still an individual possession and therefore the ambiguity is in whether this intranet is really organisational capital and not human capital.

Third, as Orlikowsky (1992) illustrates, information systems are tools, but tools are strange. As means for humans we should expect them primarily to assist human pursuits, but Orlikowsky shows how the tool prescribes tasks, procedures and principles that even the expert human cannot dispense with. They are one thing. Also, Orlikowsky suggests, the combination tool-human together prescribes the services and products that can be directed to a client or customer, and together structure-human defines the fate of relational capital by manoeuvring and defining which customers can have a place in the firm. It may not be easy to untangle either human or relational capital from structural capital. Their effects are collective and not separable into structural, human and relational effects.

All these examples illustrate that it may not be easy to separate out the activities that pertain to organisational capital and those that are relevant for other types of intellectual capital. If this is difficult, it is also difficult to accept both Sveiby's (1997), Stewart's (1997) and Edvinsson's (1997) claim that organisational capital is a leftover after human capital has gone home; and it is difficult to accept Lev and Radhakrishnan's (2003) claim that investment in organisational capital is, on average, profitable. The concern is that organisational capital does not devise a strong criterion for its boundary and, when in place, it cannot survive alone.

Managing organisational capital

As suggested above, organisational capital is an unruly resource. Analytically, it is possible to define a box of items that remain in the office during the night and separate them from other knowledge resources. Analytically, it is also possible to identify items whose purpose is to generalise and codify knowledge resources. The empirical problem is, however, that such analytical distinctions say little about the role of items of organisational capital in action.

The organisational capital box may contain patents, concepts, models, and computer and administrative systems, but these only share properties when they are on hold – when they sleep during the night. When they are in action – when they are awake and participate in organisational activities – they are different from each other; and the stronger they are, the more types of resources they engage with that are also outside the organisational capital box. This is the management challenge: when organisational capital is valuable, it cannot be contained in the box – it has to be mobilised vis-à-vis many other types of resources, such as is illustrated, for example, by Marr *et al.*'s (2004) visualisation of the dynamics of value creation through mapping techniques.

These techniques introduce a set of dynamic aspects to the role of elements of intellectual capital, illustrating that the purposes, roles and effects of various elements of intellectual capital are overlapping, complex and perhaps also to a degree impossible to define a priori. The relations depend on the (strategic) situation at hand.

One way to understand this is to liberate the various elements of intellectual capital from their effects at the outset. In this case the effects are a network of entities (Andon *et al.*, 2003; Habersam and Piber, 2003; Mouritsen, 2006, Mouritsen and Larsen, 2005; Vaivio, 2004). The separation between items of various types of intellectual capital and the functioning of the firm suggests that they are contingently related to action (Huges *et al.*, 2002). Therefore, the elements of intellectual capital have to be related together, e.g. in a narrative of achievement where the elements of intellectual capital are related in a sequence of activities. This is the strategy that makes knowledge a relevant resource.

This *narrative of achievement* has Time (events constitute a sequence of things and phenomena that are related over time), a Plot (events are developed around some kind of dilemma that can have several possible resolutions), a Voice (somebody or something has to put the plot into words, which develops a strategy for setting up what the narrative is about), and a Point of View (the voice suppresses other voices, which can be inserted into the Plot by other voices if they are allowed to speak) (see, for example, Czarniawska-Joerges, 1997; Gabriel, 2000). The elements of intellectual capital are materials used to develop the narrative. So, the narrative weaves together the proposed items of intellectual capital. This is obviously a hypothesis, but this is exactly the task of management: to point out the relations between the various types of elements of intellectual capital and items in each of its categories. Management makes a flow of the items of intellectual capital; the flow is action that mobilises the items of organisational/intellectual capital and makes them propositions of how they can make a difference, how they can create value of some kind. Management fills out the space between the items of intellectual capital that, when described, are often on hold in an inventory, and the narrative of achievement, which adds organisational events in action, in a coherent proposition about the role of knowledge resources in value creation (Mouritsen and Larsen, 2005).

The narrative is indispensable and yet unstable because, in principle, all can participate in defining and interpreting organisational events. This is, as Bruner (1986) says, exactly the logic of a narrative – it identifies and organises events – but others can also speak about and reorganise them. They can also reorganise the boundary between the events that are included and those that remain outside the narrative. It is therefore very clear that the problem facing firms and managers is to develop a credible narrative or storyline about the relations between items of intellectual capital, and to suggest how items of organisational capital can be woven together with other types of knowledge resources (see e.g. Mouritsen and Larsen, 2005).

Researching organisational capital

The research agenda concerns the role of research in developing knowledge about the roles and effects of organisational capital, specifically, and intellectual capital, generally. Most research on organisational and intellectual capital is 'pro-organisational/intellectual capital'. The claim and hope is that organisational/intellectual capital is a resource that works towards some idea of value. Cloaked in the analytics of positive arguments, the normative aspiration is very clear. This is problematic because intellectual capital then can become a rhetorical device by which attention to the 'objections' made by intellectual capital to be mobilised in a particular way is omitted.

As suggested by the above analysis, given the problems of understanding how organisational capital works in the specifics of the local, it is useful to go beyond the statistical generalisations (which also have to be made) and then inquire into how many elements have to be in place and how they should be connected for organisational/intellectual capital to be able to take up a role (see also Mouritsen, 2006). It is useful to try to decompose the three conventional analytical elements – human, organisational and relational capital – and recompose them in new ways. If the previous arguments are useful, we should expect various combinations of the human, organisational and relational capital to an extent that it is impossible to see them separately in practice.

This is the challenge; until now research has pretended that these capitals are separable, but this is only possible when they are inscribed in an intellectual capital statement where they are listed as resources and described as separate from each other. Only in the description of organisational/intellectual capital are its items separated and on hold. When they are in action, they have to be translated into narratives of achievement – i.e. propositions of how the various items of intellectual capital are related and produce something valuable (however differently value may be defined).

Therefore, the challenge to research is to get beyond the 'pro-organisational/ intellectual capital' attitude and develop a set of nuanced accounts of the actual working hereof. This will probably require us to develop hypotheses that integrate various kinds of resources in our understanding of intellectual capital as a collective that mediates between knowledge and performance.

Conclusion

This essay problematises not only organisational capital, but also central parts of the discussion of intellectual capital. Starting with organisational capital, however, the essay proposes that the received wisdom about organisational capital – i.e. that it is a leftover from human capital – is based on a very coarse observation. On the contrary, organisational capital is an intriguingly active actor because its spins a net of relations to many other entities, including some which are not within the confines of conventional definitions of its boundaries.

Drawing on two examples of organisational capital – patents and a standard on environmental management – the essay shows how organisational capital extends its relations. It rarely stands still and in practice it hardly abides by the confines of the conventional boundaries around it. It simply operates by extending its services to more and more elements and actors. It is so integrated with human and relational capital that distinctions between them appear to be superfluous – at least, the distinctions do not have a lot of power in explaining practices of intellectual capital mobilisation. The distinctions are useful to describe organisational/intellectual capital on hold (in an inventory), but hardly when it is described in action (when it performs). The management concern is to make use of information about organisational/intellectual capital when it is on hold, to develop narratives of achievement of it in action.

Therefore, there is a curious conclusion; namely, that items of organisational capital are important and may have transformative powers, but the class of organisational capital is not homogeneous and does not have transformative powers as an entity. There may not be such a thing as a 'box of organisational capital' whose elements can be ranked and integrated according to one principle that has causal effects. In contrast, each item of organisational capital carries out its own trajectory, but always by interesting and mobilising human and relational capital. In this movement, items of organisational capital change colour since, by developing links, organisational capital also changes its traits and gains new properties. Therefore, the power of organisational capital resides in its ability to adapt to relations so that it intermingles and changes identity.

Bibliography

Andon, P., Baxter, J. and Chua, W.F. (2003) Management accounting inscriptions and the post-industrial experience of organisational control, in Bhimani, A. (ed.) *Management Accounting in the Digital Economy,* Oxford University Press, Oxford.

Bontis, N. (1998) Intellectual capital: an exploratory study that develops measures and models, *Management Decision*, 36(2): 63–76.

Bontis, N. (1999) Managing organizational knowledge by diagnosing intellectual capital: framing and advancing the state of the field, *International Journal of Technology Management*, 18(5/6/7/8): 433–62.

Bontis, N. (2004) National intellectual capital index: a United Nations initiative for the Arab region, *Journal of Intellectual Capital*, 5(1): 13–39.

Bontis, N. and Fitz-enz, J. (2002) Intellectual capital ROI: a causal map of human capital antecedents and consequents, *Journal of Intellectual Capital*, 3(3): 223–47.

Bruner, J. (1986) *Actual Minds, Possible Worlds*, Harvard University Press, Cambridge MA.

Czarniawska-Joerges, B. (1997) *Narrating the Organization: dramas of institutional identity*, University of Chicago Press, Chicago.

Edvinsson, L. and Malone, K. (1997) *Intellectual Capital: realizing your company's true value by finding its hidden brainpower*, Piatkus, London.

Gabriel, Y. (2000) *Storytelling in Organizations*, Oxford University Press, Oxford.

Habersam, M. and Piber, M. (2003) Exploring intellectual capital in hospitals: two qualitative case studies in Italy and Austria, *European Accounting Review*, 12(4): 753–79.

Hart, Myra M. (1996) Palm Computing Inc. (A), Harvard Business School Cases 396-245 (Harvard Business School course materials).

Hughes, J.A., Rouncefield, M. and Tolmie, P. (2002) Representing knowledge: instances of management information, *British Journal of Sociology*, 53(2): 221–38.

Itami, H. and Roehl, T.W. (1987) *Mobilizing Invisible Assets*, Harvard University Press, Cambridge MA.

Lev, B. and Radhakrishnan, S. (2003) The measurement of firm-specific organisation capital. Working paper 9581 at National Bureau of Economic Research, Massachusetts.

Marr, B., Schiuma, G. and Neely, A. (2004) The dynamics of value creation: mapping your intellectual performance drivers, *Journal of Intellectual Capital*, 5(2): 312–25.

Mouritsen, J. (2006) Problematising intellectual capital research: ostensive versus performative IC, *Accounting, Auditing and Accountability Journal*, 19(6): 820–41.

Mouritsen, J. and Koleva, G. (2004) The actorhood of organisational capital, *Organisational Learning and Intellectual Capital*, 1(2): 177–89.

Mouritsen, J. and Koleva, G. (2005) Packing and unpacking knowledge: patents and intellectual capital, *Journal of Intellectual Capital* 6(3): 308–21.

Mouritsen, J. and Larsen, H.T. (2005) The second wave of knowledge management: the management control of knowledge resources through intellectual capital formation. *Management Accounting Research*, 16(3): 371–94.

Mouritsen, J., Ernst, J. and Møller Jørgensen, A. (2000) 'Green' certification as a managerial technology, *Scandinavian Journal of Management*, 16(2): 167–87.

O'Donnell, D., Tracey, M., Henriksen, L.B., Bontis, N., Cleary, P., Kennedy, T. and

O'Regan, P. (2006) On the 'essential condition' of intellectual capital: labour!, *Journal of Intellectual Capital*, 7(1): 111–28.

Orlikowsky, W. (1992) The duality of technology: rethinking the concept of technology in organisations, *Organisation Science*, 3(3): 398–427.

Prahalad, C. K. and Hamel, G. (1990) The core competence of the corporation. *Harvard Business Review*, 68 (May–June): 79–91.

Roos, G., Pike, S. and Fernström, L. (2005) *Managing Intellectual Capital in Practice*, Elsevier, London.

Roslender, R. and Fincham, R. (2001) Thinking critically about intellectual capital accounting, *Accounting, Auditing and Accountability Journal*, 14(4): 383–98.

Stewart, T.S. (1997) *Intellectual Capital: the new wealth of organisations*, Nicholas Brealey Publishing, London.

Sveiby, K.E. (1997) *The New Organizational Wealth: managing and measuring knowledge-based assets,* Berrett-Koehler, San Francisco.

Teece, D., Pisano, G. and Shuen, A. (1997) Dynamic capabilities and strategic management, *Strategic Management Journal*, 8 (August): 509–33.

Thorbjørnsen, S. and Mouritsen, J. (2003) Accounting for the employee in the intellectual capital statement, *Journal of Intellectual Capital*, 4(4): 559–75.

Vaivio, J. (2004) Mobilizing local knowledge with 'provocative' non-financial measures, *European Accounting Review*, 13(1): 39–71.

Wang, W-Y. and Chang, C. (2005) Intellectual capital and performance in causal models: evidence from the information technology industry in Taiwan, *Journal of Intellectual Capital*, 6(2): 222–36.

3 An intellectual capital view of business model innovation

Göran Roos and Steve Pike

This chapter addresses the key features of innovation and, in particular, business model innovation. The first part of the paper addresses the general characteristics of innovation and concludes with an appreciation of the many factors or resources in innovation that affect a firm and its efforts to innovate. Particular attention will be given to business model innovation. While business model innovation lacks the near infinite possibilities of research-based innovation, it can be as important to the success of a company. Although the possibilities are relatively limited, there are a number of resources, actors and exogenous effects which must be understood and managed effectively to achieve viable business models. Therefore, a methodology that exposes what is actually happening in firms is required; intellectual capital is a perspective based upon resources and their employment and so has the potential to facilitate this understanding. The second part of the chapter presents a simple review of the main features of intellectual capital and how it may be used as a practical diagnostic. The third and final part of the paper brings the first two parts together and shows how intellectual capital methodologies and their underlying discipline, the resource-based view of the firm, can examine innovation in firms.

The need for innovation

Innovativeness is most generally considered to be the ability to create novel products and/or processes and it is usually the critical component of business competitiveness. The need to build and maintain innovation-enabling capabilities is necessary not only to flourish, but often in fact to survive. Bender and Laestadius (2005) argue that, in principle, these general statements apply to all firms, and that there is no special means of knowledge generation or innovation that separates research intensive, high-tech companies from non-research intensive firms.

In 2006 IBM (2006a) carried out a global study based on interviews conducted with 765 CEOs from corporate and public sector leaders worldwide. They found that 65 per cent of leaders anticipated a fundamental change in their industries during the following two years. As a result, many CEOs claimed to be undertaking innovations in operations and/or products and services. The most significant result of the study was that the financial outperformers put twice as much emphasis on business model innovation as did the underperformers.

Innovation is the key driver for economic growth on the company level, industry level, national level and even the global level, and the OECD estimates that at least 50 per cent of sustainable growth is due to innovation. Only innovation drives above-average sustainable financial returns on both the industry and company level. In company terms, this means that at least half of the future value component of the share price of any company should come from innovation.

The chairman's summary of the OECD Council at Ministerial Level in Paris, 15–16 May 2007, included a section entitled 'Innovation: Advancing the OECD Agenda for Growth and Equity' (OECD, 2007a). The section recognised ministers' agreement that innovation performance is a crucial determinant of competitiveness, productivity and national progress. Ministers agreed that there is a need to improve the framework conditions for innovation through further opening and integrating the product and labour markets. They underlined the pervasive nature of innovation, noting in particular the importance of education systems to ensure the supply of skills and researchers, and the need to foster greater private investment in innovation. At a more practical level for companies, ministers welcomed the publication of two reports: 'Moving up the Value Chain – Staying Competitive in the Global Economy' (OECD, 2007b) and 'Globalisation and Innovation in the Business Services Sector' (OECD, 2007c).

At the European level, the EU extols similar views. The Directorate-General for regional policy has published a working document, 'Innovation in the National Strategic Reference Frameworks' (EU, 2006). The document concludes that the role of innovation in the National Strategic Reference Frameworks is positive. It recognises that innovation will play an increased role in regional policy for the period 2007–2013 but cautions that it is important for national and regional governments to ensure that the intentions set out in the National Strategic Reference Frameworks are implemented in reality.

Innovation

It is convenient to consider three basic types of innovation (process, product/service and strategy/business model). There is, however, significant debate on the acceptability of grouping products and services, and strategy and business models. As the issue of business model innovation is central to this paper, it is important to develop the arguments on this issue further. Osterwalder (2004) believes that, when considering the differences between strategy and business models, the picture is unclear – with some people using the terms 'strategy' and 'business model' interchangeably, as noted by Magretta (2002). According to Stähler (2002), 'business model' is frequently used as a term to refer to everything which gives a firm a competitive advantage. However, the literature shows that the view that business models and strategy are linked, but distinct, is more common (Magretta 2002; Mansfield and Fourie 2004). Osterwalder seeks a practical distinction and uses Magretta's description of a business model as 'a system that shows how the pieces of a business fit together, while strategy also includes competition'. In contrast, others understand the business model as subordinate to a firm's strategy and having the potential to apply to many firms (Seddon *et al.* 2004). In general however, business model literature seems to fit the former definition better, because most of it focuses on describing the elements and interactions that define how a company creates and markets value.

Gordijn (2002) shows that in the literature, the concept of the business model is interpreted in two ways:

1 As a *taxonomy* (such as e-shops, malls, auctions).
2 As a *conceptual model* of the way we do business.

Taxonomy in this instance means the *finite* number of business model *types* (e.g. Bambury 1998; Timmers 1998; Rappa 2001; Weill and Vitale 2001), since it deals with a finite set of resources. The conceptualisation of 'business model' means the *meta-model* or *reference model* for a specific industry. This is a more open definition since it opens the way to an *infinite* number of business models suggested by many authors (e.g. Chesbrough and Rosenbloom 2000; Hamel 2000; Linder and Cantrell 2000; Mahadevan 2000; Amit and Zott 2001; Applegate 2001; Petrovic *et al.* 2001; Weill and Vitale 2001; Gordijn 2002; Stähler 2002; Afuah and Tucci 2003; Osterwalder 2004).

It is generally agreed that there are three basic types of innovation – process, product/service, and strategy/business model – each varying in its level of innovation, from sustaining to discontinuous or from incremental to radical. There are also important relationships between these types of innovation. For example, a strategy innovation may necessitate product or process innovations.

Levels of innovation

As explained above, innovation ranges from *incremental* to *radical*, these terms being generally a measure of novelty. Innovation can be new within a particular limited context or new in terms of the overall marketplace of ideas. Similarly, it can be a new twist on an old theme or a radically different idea. In terms of the impact of innovation, the effect can range from a fairly small contribution to the improvement of a product or a process; or it can cause a fundamental transformation in the resulting products or services and/or the process technology of an entire industry; or it can transform the marketplace and/or the economy as a whole. Due to possible confusion caused by the two factors of novelty and impact, Christensen (1997) suggested a means for separating the ideas. Since radically new innovations do not always have a significant impact, the distinction of *sustaining* innovation and *discontinuous* innovation were introduced. Sustaining innovation improves the performance of established products or services, while discontinuous innovation involves marketing very different products or services that have the potential to replace established products and services in the particular market sector. Christensen cites steel mini-mills as an example of a discontinuous innovation. While the product was not significantly changed, a change in the production process led to a drastic change in prices, firms and markets. Discontinuous innovation does not always have greater utility; it can result in a product that under-performs established products since the momentum of ongoing sustaining innovations can push product and service functionality beyond what customers want. Christensen explains that the development of innovations to establish products and services can eventually overshoot a large segment of the market. He therefore advises companies in all industries to be continually attuned to a potentially discontinuous innovation that could cause their demise if they do not quickly adapt and adjust to the fundamentally changing situation.

Types of innovation

The three main types of innovation (process, product/service and strategy/business model) will be considered in more detail. However, the latter – business model innovation – will be afforded a more extensive review in a separate section.

Process innovation

Process innovation, as explained by Baker, became an important topic with the rise of the quality and continuous improvement movements which emerged from Japan in the 1980s and was reprised with the recent emphasis on change management, organisational learning and knowledge management. Firms, at least in the developed world, are reaching the limits of incremental process improvement, and Hammer and Champy (1994) note the growing desire for radical process innovation. They introduced the concept of *radical reengineering* based on their belief that if firms are to achieve maximum efficiency and effectiveness, then this requires a radical process reengineering of the firm and their processes. Since processes tend to lag behind what is possible given technological advancement, they argue that it is not possible to achieve the necessary transformation through incremental reengineering.

Carter (1999) states that the argument for radical reengineering seemed plausible, and many organizations undertook large scale reengineering efforts, but the results have disappointed with many firms having expended a lot of effort for little return. One possible reason for this is that management itself needed to be radically reengineered, since it has often been a barrier to change. Others suggest that firms are often not capable of changing as much and as quickly as radical reengineering requires and, hence, transition management has emerged as an area that has not been sufficiently addressed. There appear to have been two problems with reengineering. The first concerns planning change wherein an ambitious plan to reengineer a firm has been initiated without a sufficiently detailed and realistic plan of how to manage current operations during the transition to the new model. The second is a lack of the sustained effort needed to ensure success. In addition, as Carter (1999) notes, downsizing is often called reengineering; this 'confusion' in terms is perhaps a means of disguising a painful process under the banner of another process whose aim is wholly positive. In addition, downsizing tends to have short-term and limited benefits, since its aims are concerned with scale and not scope. The origins of discontinuities in process innovation are often found to have been imported from outside the industry, either as a result of a deliberate search or by luck. Thus, in addition to intentional process improvement and reengineering, firms must monitor other industries and have the ability to adapt potential innovations that could affect how they currently operate.

Product/service innovation

Product/service innovation also can be radical or incremental. In its incremental form it is designed to improve the features and functionality of existing products and services, whereas radical product/service innovation involves the creation of wholly new products and services. Jonash and Sommerlatte (1999) observe that general reductions in product life-cycles have meant that a firm's survival depends on new product development and, increasingly, on the speed of innovation in order to develop and bring new products to market faster than their competition. Companies must direct greater attention to new product development, while maintaining and improving their existing products. The likelihood of discontinuous products and services is increased with ever-faster new product/service development, and firms must be vigilant in their search for emergent products and services. Although product/service innovation and process innovation are not identical, they are often interconnected. For example, process innovation may well be required to support product or service innovations, since the new product or service may require delivery processes that have not hitherto been needed. Also, it has been argued that organisational processes and structures oriented towards incremental product innovation are not the same as those needed to foster and facilitate new product development. It is usual to separate these activities and to introduce wholly new process innovations that will help promote and speed up radical product innovation.

Business model innovation

Strategy or business model innovation involves major changes to the way a company makes money, or, for a new company to the industry, may involve a rejection of the business model prevalent in the industry. The IBM (2006b) study shows that business model innovation can have a far more profound effect on profitability than either process or product/service innovation. While it is possible to improve a firm's business strategy incrementally, Hamel (1996, 2000) contends that radical business concept innovation is now paramount. He claims that the current business environment is hostile to those who have been static in their industry and have become established and hospitable to industry revolutionaries. In order to ensure a firm's success it is necessary to review continually the firm's strategy and business model. Hamel states that this requires three things:

1 A radical reinvention of products and services, not just the development of new products and services.

2 Redefining market space.
3 Redrawing industry boundaries.

If radical business concept innovation is successful in accomplishing these objectives, it is by definition discontinuous.

Osterwalder *et al.* observe that research in business models is maturing, although 'researchers do not yet rely on each others' work and findings extensively'. Based on an extensive literature review they propose five phases in the evolution of business model literature. During the first phase, when the term business model started to become prominent, a number of authors suggested business model definitions and classifications (Timmers 1998). In the second phase, authors started to complete the definitions by proposing what elements belong in a business model. At first, these propositions were simple 'shopping lists', just mentioning the components of a business model (Chesbrough and Rosenbloom 2000; Linder and Cantrell 2000; Petrovic *et al.* 2001; Magretta 2002). It is interesting to note that the discipline of intellectual capital is of similar age but seems to be struggling to get past Osterwalder's second phase. In the third phase, detailed descriptions of these components become available (Hamel 2000; Weill and Vitale 2001; Afuah and Tucci 2003). In the fourth phase, researchers started modelling the components conceptually, and this naturally led to the proposition of business model meta-models in the form of reference models and ontologies (Gordijn 2002; Osterwalder 2004). In this phase, models also started to be evaluated or tested more rigorously. The most modern of intellectual capital methodologies has just reached this phase. In the fifth phase, which is current, the reference models are being applied in management applications.

Again, in common with the views of Pike and Roos (2007) concerning intellectual capital research, there remains considerable discussion about 'what it is'. Some of the business model innovation issues discussed concern the possible distinction between business models and business process models (Gordijn, Akkermans *et al.* 2000), the difference between strategy and business models (Linder and Cantrell 2000; Porter 2001; Stähler 2002; Seddon *et al.* 2004), or the distinction between enterprise models and business models. Gordijn *et al.* (2000) emphasise that the distinction between business models and business process models must clearly be understood. They reviewed the business model literature and concluded that the business model concept is generally understood as a view of the firm's logic for creating and commercialising value, while the business process model is more about how a business case is implemented in processes. Aguilar-Savén (2004) believes that part of the confusion comes from the expression 'business modelling' being used mainly for the activity of business process modelling while business models refers to more structural concepts. Furthermore, there are many tools available for business process modelling, and their scope and dependence on an underlying business model blurs the distinction between the underlying architecture (the model) and the actual implementation (the process model).

Practical interpretations

Bender and Leastadius (2005) found the not unsurprising result that the only feature shared by all the firms in the low-tech sector of industry they studied was that none of them based their competitiveness on recent scientific findings. For them, their firm's innovation was to a large extent the outcome of transforming and configuring generally well known knowledge, components and technologies developed elsewhere. They also explain that in principle, the knowledge formation processes in their firms are similar to those in other firms, including those thought of as high-tech or medium high-tech. Their concept of 'innovation enabling capabilities' was designed to be generic, since it is concerned with the general organisational and cognitive preconditions for innovation. The discrimination between transformative and configurational capabilities is strictly analytical, and helps to reduce complexity, but is not an empirical description. The mix of transformative and configurational capabilities varies between firms but both are necessary; in order to configure distributed knowledge in novel ways, transformative capabilities are required. Transformative capabilities concern cognition and learning and, according to Cohen & Levinthal (1990), are based to a large extent on absorptive capacity. The nature of the knowledge being formed is not a matter of principle but an empirical question. It is about the ability to learn.

Thus far, the discussion of innovation has taken a perspective that is predominantly inward-looking in nature. The aim of innovation is to make money through the sale of products and services in new ways and in new business forms to the customer. If the role of the customer in both these aims is accepted, then it is important that the customer is involved in the innovation process to the greatest possible extent. It should be noted that 'the customer' often means the end consumer, but this is not always the case if there are well established and diverse routes from a primary supplier to the end user that involve intermediaries.

Piller *et al.* (2004) developed a three-step framework for an 'open innovation process' that involves the customer wherever appropriate. According to Von Hippel (2001) and Reichwald *et al.* (2003), customers are becoming co-designers in the innovation processes.

In the first step, innovation, Grumer and Homburg (1999) found that the degree of consumer interaction in the different phases of new product development varied. A high degree of customer involvement in the early and late stages increased success. Building on this, a four-stage model of the innovation process following Wheelwright and Clark (1992) was used: Idea, Concept, Prototype and Market.

Studies concerning obtaining a contribution from the customer in the second (concept) step revealed that there were three types of interaction observed:

1 Within *decision activities* – customers decide or evaluate given facts. Besides simple yes/no decisions, customers are able to assess the potential of a product idea, concept or prototype on the basis of, for example, nominal scaling. Additionally given products can be ranked according to the customers' preferences.
2 *Information* refers to the possibility that customers are able to articulate

preferences or solutions regarding a specific challenge of the product development process. Customers express their personalities, needs, preferences, or solutions to a specific problem.

3 *Creation* requires that customers are able to be creative on their own – instead of giving information or deciding how to solve a specific innovation challenge, customers come up with their own creations as a solution.

In the third step, customer referred to specific characteristics that mark them as successful contributors in terms of integration in the innovation process. Following the approach of Lüthje (2000), application and object knowledge of customers are the two dominant customer characteristics. Application knowledge refers to practical experience with a product through intensive usage. Object knowledge focuses on knowledge concerning, for example, the technology, procedure or material of a product (physical conditions of the product and how single components work together). While Lüthje argues that only advanced customers with high application and object knowledge qualify for open innovation, it may be possible that other types of customer, with other mixes of application and object knowledge, may be able to contribute.

One common misconception is the tendency to think of innovation as a fixed process. Morris (2003), in his article on business model warfare, explores the problems with such thinking. Morris points out that while innovations in any area within an organization may be important, innovations that are broadly and directly relevant to the business model will be life-sustaining. He illustrates this with an analysis of the mortality rate amongst major quoted firms. Morris shows how innovation is affected by the transparency of the market and its tendency towards positive feedback.

> Because the market is so transparent and the performance of every public company is subject to detailed scrutiny by investors and analysts, subtle changes in an organization's performance can lead to broad swings in stock price. Improving performance and increasing stock price are both self-feeding cycles that create more favourable conditions for companies to develop and implement future innovations, both by improving stock currency for making acquisitions and by lowering the overall cost of capital. Conversely, declining performance and a falling stock price can lead to a downward spiral that makes it progressively more difficult for companies to compete for attractive acquisition fodder, and which can also increase the cost of capital that could be invested in innovation-related activities such as R&D and product development. Get ahead and push farther ahead; get behind and fall farther behind.
>
> (Morris 2003)

Morris believes that while managers may be thinking about change and its impact on their firms, they must be doing so in a way that is ineffective and suggests that thinking about and enacting business model innovation is important for established businesses. Despite this, the temptation to build a business according to a fixed structure that is expected to endure for the long term remains strong with managers focused on stability and continuity, instead of on disruption and change. Morris contends that to survive, all organisations must develop a comprehensive innovation framework, and the perspective offered by the Business Model Warfare framework can help leaders to be more effective.

In their 2006 survey of CEOs, IBM concluded that there were three types of business model innovation strategies These were an industry oriented model, a revenue model and an enterprise model (IBM 2006a).

The industry model involves innovating the industry value structure and can be accomplished through horizontal moves into new industries. It can also be accomplished by redefining existing industries by, for example, eliminating intermediaries and going directly to customers. They found that the most dramatic example of industry model innovation involved the development of entirely new industries or industry segments. This is an example of the occupation of white spaces in the competitive environment.

The revenue model focuses on innovations in how companies generate revenues by reconfiguring products and service and/or by introducing new pricing models. This is a dimension that leverages customer experience, choices and preferences and that can also leverage new technologies.

The enterprise model approach involves innovations in the structure of the enterprise and the role it plays in new or existing value chains, and focuses on redefining organisational boundaries. Enterprise model innovation can also be accomplished via specialisation, in which organisations focus on core competencies or high-margin activities and outsource the rest. Enterprise model innovation can be accomplished via network structures, in which companies rely on external collaboration.

The IC perspective

The previous section has examined innovation and, in particular, business model innovation. The resource-based view of the firm (RBV) would describe the components involved in innovation, be they tangible or intangible as resources. In the mid-1990s, RBV was used as the basis for the discipline of intellectual capital (IC). This section describes IC in more detail and the final section of the paper shows innovation from the IC/RBV perspective.

Pike *et al.* (2005) have shown that the work of Chamberlin (1933) and Robinson (1933) on the identification of the key capabilities of firms laid the foundations of what was to become intellectual capital in the inter-war years. Their views were taken up by Penrose (1959), amongst others, whose much cited work on the theory of the growth of the firm dismissed the view that a firm was just an administrative unit and saw it instead as productive resources at the disposal of managers. She suggested that a firm is best gauged by some measure of the productive resources it employs. This led directly to the development of ideas concerning competitive advantage in the last third of the twentieth century.

Barney (1991) showed that sustainable competitive advantage demands the possession of certain key resources, and that they have characteristics such as quality or value, high barriers to duplication, and so on. Penrose's work provided further guidance for the development of intellectual capital as an approach to business management. For example, the clear definition of what a resource can be and how it differs from activities and services is crucial. This led to the notion that services yielded by resources depend on the resources that are used. A given resource can be used in different combinations with other resources to give different services or generate a variety of other resources. Furthermore, the development of a firm is constrained to an extent by the nature and qualities of the resource it currently possesses. This thinking led others to consider the development and deployment of resources (Amit and Schoemaker 1993; Barney 1986, Barney and Zajac 1994, Lei *et al.* 1996; Schoemaker 1992) and the relationship between resources and the scope of the firm (Chatterjee and Wernerfelt 1991; Markides and Williamson 1996; Prahalad and Hamel 1990; Robins and Wiersema 1995). As the rise of the new economy gathered pace, traditional Porterian structures were found to be inadequate to describe firms, and the performances of firms, even in the same industry (Cubbin 1988; Hansen and Wernerfelt 1989). This immediately brought in researchers concerned with strategy and strategic decision making (Amit and Schoemaker 1993; Barney 1986; 1991; Dierickx and Cool 1989; Lippman and Rumelt 1982; Peteraf 1993; Reed and DeFillippi 1990).

The treatment of value extraction from innovation expounded by Teece (1986), and human resources by Itami's (1987) treatment of the 'mobilization' of resources, added to these foundations and led to the publication of a complete IC approach by Roos *et al.* (1997).

Pike and Roos (2007) compare the common methods of categorising and discussing intellectual capital. These methods usually involve a hierarchical menu of resources starting with 'Level 1' which comprises monetary, physical, human, organisational and relational resources. These are defined by sets of underlying resources at finer levels of granularity.

As stated by Penrose and noted above, it is the combination and use of resources that generates value through the creation of other saleable resources or services. For example, products to money, creativity to new processes, relationships to reduced search costs, brands to increased revenues and so on. The analysis requirement is to identify and evaluate the firm's unique transformations structure. There are two problems which are encountered:

- Few of the firm's resources are additive in the way they are 'used'. For example, doubling the number of people does not double the human resource value. This means that the relationship between the amounts of resources involved in a transformation and the amount of the resource(s) produced is complex.
- Outwardly similar transformations may actually be rather different in detail. For example, parallel and similar production lines may be dependent on resource quality to very different degrees. This makes backward interpretations

of aggregated results problematical, and small volume transformations may be missed altogether, even though they are important.

The Intellectual Capital Navigator (ICN) is a numerical and visual representation of how management views the deployment of resources to create value in the organisation. The ICN displays transformations from one resource into another and can be presented at any level of granularity and with any level of filtering. Filtering of the results is undertaken to remove clutter from the picture by excluding transformations relatively unimportant to company managers. Several features can be seen in navigators but perhaps the most obvious and interesting is the adherence or otherwise to the recognised forms of firm value creating architecture (Stabell and Fjeldstad 1998). Stabell and Fjeldstad postulate three basic firm architectures: the (Porterian) value shop typical of production orientated companies, the value shop typical of professional service companies and the value network typical of market facilitating companies. Production orientated companies are typified by important physical to physical transformations supported by human and organisational to physical influences. Professional service companies exhibit a triangular structure involving human, organisational and relational resources, that is, a learning process. Market facilitating companies can either be physically based (such as the physical resources of a telecom firm) or organisationally based (such as the software and processes of an online market place). While the underlying structure is variable, all market facilitating companies have a strong relational to relational transformation representing client transactions. There are also relational to monetary and relational to human links representing earning and feedback respectively. The degree, balance and completeness of these basic structural forms measure how effectively the company is following its chosen operating form.

Further analyses based on the navigator matrix can be carried out. One of the most revealing is to inspect the balance between how influential a resource is in a firm, and the extent to which it is influenced by other resources. Resources with a ratio greater than unity are sources of value since they influence more than they are influenced. Resources with a ratio less than unity are termed 'sinks of value'. The ratios for all resources (usually expressed as the logarithm of the ratio) can be plotted against the absolute importances of the resources in what is known as an 'effector plot'. Important resources that are significant sources of value should be inspected for robustness according to the criteria of Barney. Those that are significant sinks should be inspected to see whether there are reasonable prospects that they will deliver more value in future. In an extension to this depiction of the influence of resources, the methodology of Pike (2007) permits the connection of the resources, deployed in the numerous activities of the company, to be assessed for their contribution to income, costs and net profitability. The plot shows the instrumental importance of the resources on the x-axis and the financial measure on the y-axis. Resources which generate little or negative net income can be examined for the role they play in the company. Clearly, if important resources are net negative profit makers, then either some changes need to be made to their costing or some more radical and innovative changes to the business model should be investigated, in which the role of these resources in the company's activities is changed.

Characteristic innovation forms shown by IC

The IC Navigator process developed by Roos *et al.* (1997) and Pike (2007), and as described in the previous section, offers a powerful diagnostic into how firms actually operate, the importances of the resources and the numerous value-creating pathways that connect them. Some groups of pathways will represent innovation processes, while wholesale changes to the structures will represent changes to the business model.

It is possible that the resource-based view of the firm can indicate how different functional (technological and marketing) and integrative (internal and external) capabilities affect product development efficiency (lead time and productivity) and product effectiveness (fit with market needs and quality). However, only the most modern and sophisticated IC methodologies, such as that presented by Pike (2007), have the capability to explain the detailed interactions and explain real outcomes.

Pike's methodology is developed from RBV and does not build upon existing IC models, thus it does not confuse the intrinsic nature of the resources with their instrumental attributes. Thus, putative intangible assets such as cross-functional team working are not resources in themselves (the team is the resource and its ability to function when composed of cross-functional members is its instrumental capability). Early IC models omit the critical combination of these three elements, but the approach of Roos *et al.* (1997), derivatives of this method and the method of Pike (2007) specifically include resource interactions. The resource-based research on innovation is based on the fundamental premise that organisational resources and capabilities are those that underlie and determine a firm's capacity for innovation. Within this perspective, organisational, human and relational resources (including the customers) are taken to provide the input that in turn is combined and transformed by capabilities to produce innovative forms of competitive advantage.

The resource-based view has been used to identify those resources critical for innovation. Adequate financial resources can expand a firm's capacity to support its innovative activities (Lee *et al.* 2001; Delcanto and Gonzalez 1999; Harris and Trainor 1995), whereas the lack of financial funds may limit firm level innovation (Baysinger and Hoskisson, 1989; Teece and Pisano, 1994; Helfat, 1997). According to transaction-costs economics and agency theory, internally generated funds are more conducive to R&D activities and investments than external funds, primarily because there exist information asymmetries between the firm and the external capital market, and the potential to lose control or degrade the impact of innovation. Physical resources have also been found to positively affect innovation (Song and Parry 1997; Gatignon and Xuereb 1997; Mitchell and Zmud 1999; Liyanege *et al.* 1999). Carrying out innovation activities in many cases requires a minimum prior investment in appropriate technical equipment, which raises the possibility of producing innovative output of increased value for the firm.

Intangible resources have non-linear effects and are often more important from a strategic point of view since they tend to be valuable, rare and difficult to imitate or replace by competitors (Barney, 1991; Hitt *et al.* 2001b). The increasing role of intangible resources has led to the emerging knowledge-based view (KBV) of the firm as an extension of the RBV. Viewing a firm from a knowledge-based perspective places particular emphasis on the firm's stock of knowledge (tacit or explicit) as a strategic resource and as an important determinant of its competitive success (Kogut and Zander 1992; Nonaka 1994; Decarolis and Deeds 1999). Therefore, according to RBV, not only must firms be able to create knowledge within their boundaries, but they must also expose themselves to a bombardment of new ideas from their external environment in order to prevent rigidity, to encourage innovative behaviour, and to check their technological developments against those of competitors (Leonard-Barton 1995).

Entrepreneurship refers to the articulation of a long-term vision for the firm that aims at higher growth through innovation at the expense of short-run profit maximisation, and Drucker (1985) has suggested that innovation is the primary activity of entrepreneurship. This has been expanded by Lumpkin and Dess (1996), who argue that a key dimension of an entrepreneurial orientation is an emphasis on innovation. Other studies by Lal (1999), Iansiti and West (1999), Pillai and Meindl (1998) and Markham (1998) reached similar conclusions, examining US and Japanese industrial settings. Teece *et al.* (1997) proposed a 'dynamic capabilities' framework. Dynamic capabilities refer to the firm's ability to integrate, build, and reconfigure internal and external competences (groups of resources in use) to address rapidly changing environments. In their view, coordination/integration, learning and transformation are the fundamental dynamic capabilities that serve as the mechanisms through which available stocks of resources (e.g. marketing, financial and technological assets) can be combined and transformed to produce new and innovative forms of competitive advantage.

The IC Navigator and the associated "Effector" plots described by Roos (1997) go a long way towards showing the fitness of a company for effective innovation and its capacity to operate different business models. Stabel and Fjeldstad (1998) presented three generic value creation forms found in business. The first was the Porterian value chain, while the others were the value shop and the value network. The value chain appears as a branched but effectively linear structure in which physical resources are converted to other physical resources and thence into monetary resources. The other, more intangible resources appear as branches, for example, the injection of process (organisational capital) and human capital into a dumb manufacturing process. The value shop is typified by the consultancy in which the offering to the market is improved with each application, and is hence cyclical in nature. In IC terms there is always a triangular interplay between relational, human and organisational capitals, which shows delivery of solutions in one direction and the learning process in the other. The true value network has a less structured appearance but is typified by relational capital to relational capital interactions supported by either physical resources (such as a telephone network) or organisational capital (such as the software in an online market).

The simplest depiction of these forms is known as 'Level 1' in which only the five top level resource groups appear (human, organisational, relational, physical and monetary). As far as the analysis of innovation is concerned, this level is too coarse to be of use. At the next level of granularity, each of the top level resource groups is typically split into four to 10 'Level 2' groups and at this level it is usually possible to judge the efficiency, effectiveness and economy of a business model. At 'Level 3' the resources are so well divided that a complete, if crowded, view of the firm is always available. However, at this level, detail may obscure the key messages.

Examples

The methodology of Pike (2007) is optimised to permit analysis at Level 2; but in addition to intrinsic resource importance, it is also concerned with the qualities of those resources in accordance with classical resource-based theory, and especially the resource characteristics of Barney (1991). Of crucial importance are the quantity and quality of the resources. It appears rare that any firm achieves pre-eminence in all the categories suggested by Barney, but at the same time, companies innovate. At this depth of analysis undertaken, the basic business model is readily exposed and, due to the inclusion of quality and quantity, it is possible to see whether a business model that works in theory would actually work in practice.

The example shown in Figures 3.1 to 3.4 is the outcome of a set of simulations of an innovative consultancy company that conforms to the value shop structure of Stabel and Fjeldstad. Figure 3.1 shows the Level 1 navigator. In the navigator, the size of the bubble representing a resource is a measure of its intrinsic importance, and the thickness of the arrow from one resource to another is a measure of the instrumental importance of that transformation. The Level 1 navigator clearly shows the two-way, triangular configuration between human, relational and organisational capitals, which confirms that the predominant business model is a value shop; but beyond that, it gives little extra detail. Figure 3.2 shows the navigator at Level 2, one level of disaggregation lower, and here it is possible to see the components of human capital (innovation team), of organisational capital (codified and proprietary knowledge) and of relational capital that are important for the innovation process. In the case of this consultancy, innovation appears to be a largely internal activity with no or little involvement from the customers.

'Effector' plots usually show the relationship between intrinsic importance and instrumental importance. They show which resources are net sources of value and which are net sinks of value (they affect other resources more than they are affected by other resources). In the modified 'effector' plot of Figure 3.3, the y-axis, normally the instrumental balance, has been replaced by the financial measure of the net contribution to profit. In other words, the notion of value has been replaced by the simpler notion of financial contribution. Here again, the importance of the key Level 2 resources involved in innovation can be seen both to be important to the company (shown by their high x-value) and also to be significant contributors to the financial well-being of the company (shown by their high y-value). A deeper

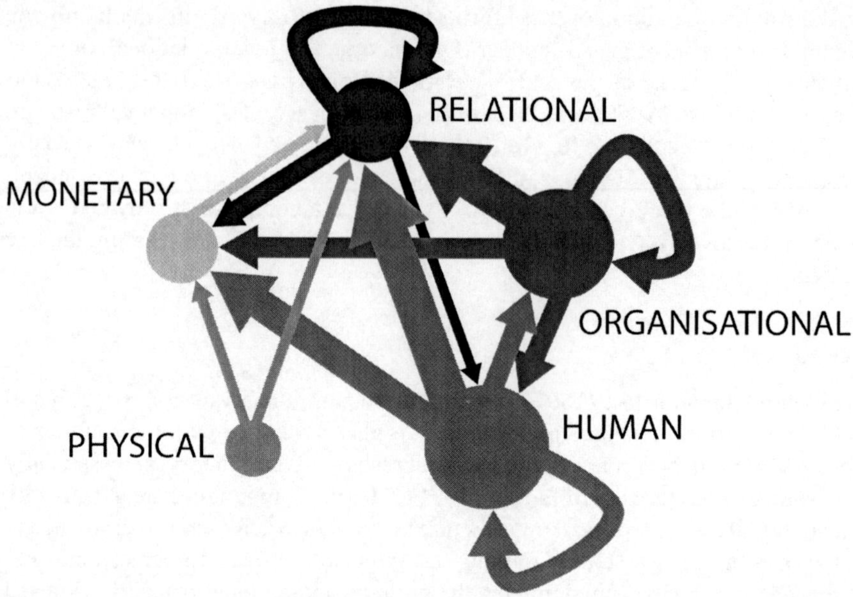

Figure 3.1 Level 1 Navigator.

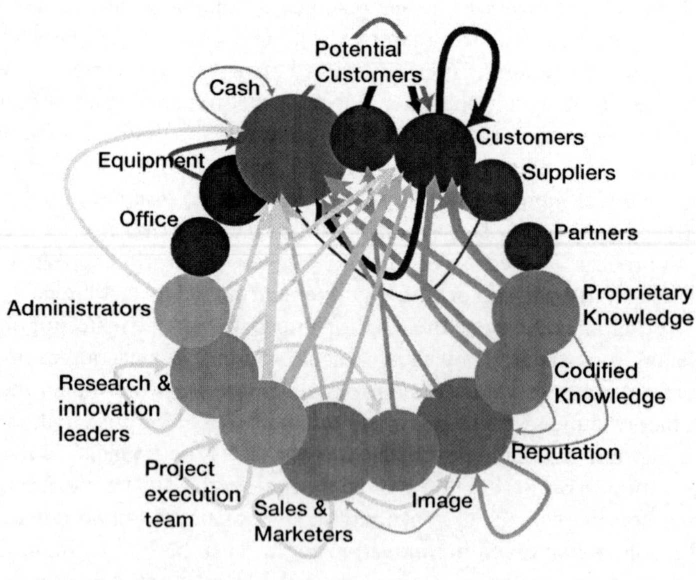

Figure 3.2 Level 2 Navigator.

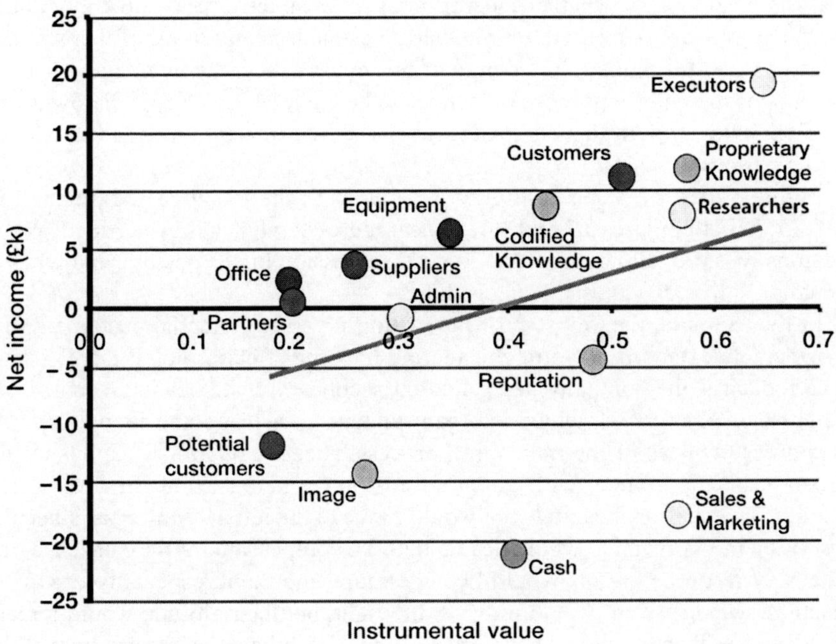

Figure 3.3 Effector plot.

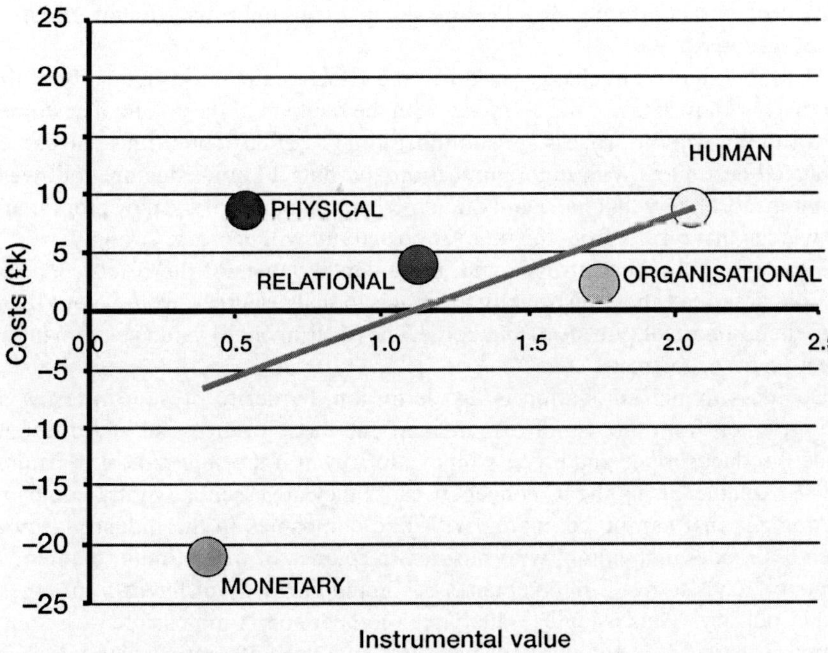

Figure 3.4 Effector plot at Level 1.

analysis would reveal whether the attributes of those resources – notably quality and quantity – are optimised, or whether investment in any or all of them would be good value for money. In the case of this consultancy, the innovation process was judged to be fit for purpose but tended to be vulnerable to financial downturns in sales. Innovation in this company was one of the first activities to be reduced during periods of stress.

Figure 3.4 is the same as Figure 3.3, but with the resources aggregated to Level 1. In both Figures 3.3 and 3.4, a linear regression line has been added. When a company is profitable, the gradient of the regression line is positive and when it is making a loss, the gradient is negative.

In the example, the key step of innovation involved potential customers to a considerable extent. It is worth considering how the effector plot at Level 1 may have looked if the company had relied on secondary customer input (e.g. from commissioned surveys), which is organisational knowledge and its own people as sources of ideas in the innovation process. Clearly, relational capital would decrease in importance, with potential customers being excluded from a key activity. The relational capital spot would move to the left and upwards, since the cost of their involvement would be avoided. To compensate for their absence, the other key resource groups would become more important, especially organisational knowledge. Both would move to the right, but their altitude would remain unchanged as there would be no volume change. It is likely that the gradient of the regression line would decrease.

A comparison of the company's plots with others in the same industry with equivalent market offerings would allow comparisons to be made on the effective use of resources.

The most significant change would be the effect on the intrinsic quality of the proprietary knowledge of the company with the removal of the potential customer from the innovation process. Assuming Lüthje's (2000) conditions for use of advanced customers with high application and object knowledge are followed, then it is most likely that the quality (and perhaps quantity) of the new proprietary knowledge that results from the innovation activity will decrease strongly.

Figure 3.5 plots the intrinsic and instrumental values of the resources. The changes described above, especially to organisational resources, would move them from their important (intrinsic) and borderline (instrumental) value position in the direction of 'problematic stars'.

Business model innovation is, by definition, harder to present in terms of a progression from the use of resources in one mode to their use in a different mode. Product/service and process innovation, even if they are radical in nature, can be explained using the IC concept because they are essentially intra-company phenomena that can be compared with like companies in the industry sector. Business model innovation, with business resources of more limited numerical diversity, tends to result in companies becoming distinctly different from others in the industry. Thus a logical, analytical comparison is impossible – the only comparison tends to be in outcome measures and, most often, financial ones.

An illustrative example of this is the change in the travel industry over the last

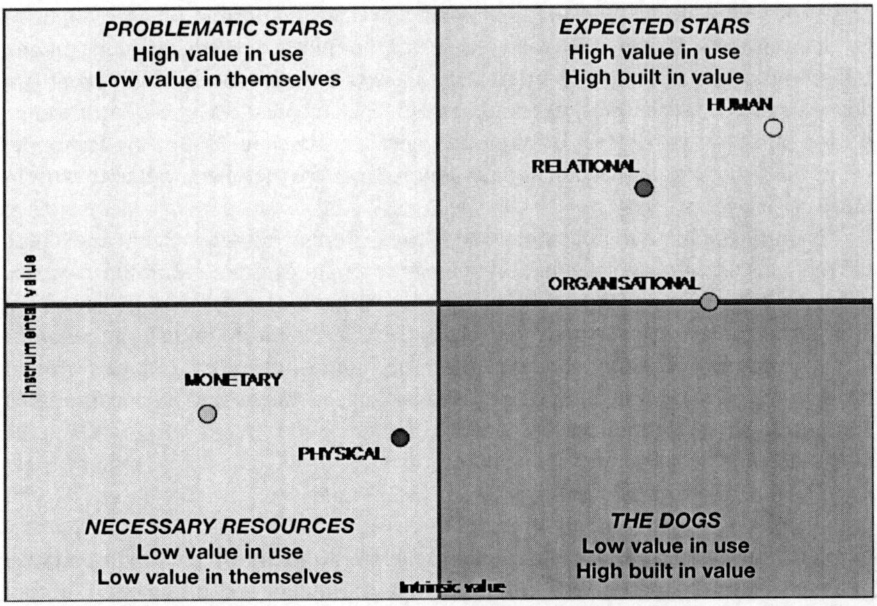

Figure 3.5 Instrumental and intrinsic values of the resources.

decade. A simple outcome statistic which illustrates this is the rise of the online travel company. For example, from its foundation in 1995, Expedia has become one of the world's largest travel agents. An audit of their intellectual capital resources and their mode of use, and a comparison of this with traditional travel companies, is instructive.

Traditional travel companies generally operate a commission-based model, on shops as a physical resource. Traditional travel companies enjoy commissions from a relatively limited pool of airlines, hotels and other service providers with physical resources to maintain. With competition amongst end providers, commissions are reduced or even eliminated, which means that commission fees have to be replaced by higher charges to the customer. Some traditional travel companies have changed their business model by, for example, horizontal integration, in that they now own or control their own airline or 'resort'. The intellectual capital resources used are dominated by monetary, physical and relational resources, although the latter are not diverse. Organisational capital is confined to booking systems, and human capital comprises 'representatives' and office staff.

Online travel companies operate in the same industry but use the 'merchant model'. Most of these companies were new starts and did not evolve from traditional travel companies. Nevertheless, they represent innovative thinking. Typically, an online travel company receives inventory of blocks of aeroplane seats, hotel rooms or rental cars at wholesale rates from end providers. Then, acting as the merchant of record, they sell the inventory at variable prices, deriving profit from the difference. The business carries no inventory risk because unsold rooms or seats are returned to the supplier within a certain time frame. The problems of falling commissions are avoided or at least minimised. Expedia's management, for example, has expended great effort to shift its business model in the merchant direction as far as possible. For the six-month period ended 30 June 2001, revenue from commissions was nearly twice the merchant revenue. But in the following year, the company collected 35 per cent more from the merchant model than from the commission model.

The intellectual capital resources are quite different. With a very diverse range of possible end providers and networked partner organisations, relational capital is clearly much more important. Organisational capital is also more important since, in addition to booking software, its Expert Searching and Pricing (ESP) platform offers more priced itineraries to travellers, and allows them to combine different elements to build diverse but personalised packages. Human and physical capitals are reduced to the minimum.

Conclusions

This chapter had several purposes. The first was to demonstrate the importance given to innovation in companies and in governments and other international organisations. This was developed into a description of the key elements of the innovation process – the key issue revealed is that innovation is not a simple process, and it is not the same as research and development. The paper has shown that to be a successful innovator, a company needs to bring together, coordinate and manage a broad range of resources. This range includes a variety of different human resources and organisational resources, depending on the business it may include physical resources and money. It also includes relational resources that, again, may be of more than one type. It may include partners and suppliers but, more importantly, it should involve the customer in some way. The chapter has also reviewed the issue of business model innovation where it can be seen that fixed formulae for the delivery of innovative products or services is a recipe for eventual failure. The literature explains that not only must products and services be innovative, but so too must be the way they are delivered, and that requires an agile business model.

The chapter reviews the key points of the intellectual capital approach to business management and the resource-based view of the firm. Since it is comprehensive and holistic in nature, the intellectual capital approach has shown itself to be capable of describing any facet or activity of a firm. Together, these approaches are shown to have the power, in theory, to explain and illustrate both business model innovation and product and service innovation, although only the most advanced of the available approaches has the capability to do it in practice. A case study using the most advanced intellectual capital methodology was used briefly to illustrate the capability of intellectual capital analysis when applied to a consulting firm. Finally, the case of online travel agencies compared to traditional travel agencies was used to illustrate business model innovation and to show that the importance of the intellectual capital resources used in the two models is quite different.

In conclusion, innovation is one of the most pressing business issues today. The intellectual capital approach has the ability to explain and guide innovation processes, innovation management and business model innovation to achieve the best outcome for the firm.

References

Afuah, A. and Tucci, C. (2003). *Internet Business Models and Strategies*. Boston: McGraw Hill.

Aguilar-Savén, R. (2004). Business process modelling: review and framework, *International Journal of Production Economics* Vol. 90, pp. 129–49.

Amit, R. and Schoemaker, P. (1993). Strategic assets and organisational rent, *Strategic Management Journal* Vol. 14, pp. 33–46.

Amit, R. and Zott, C. (2001). Value creation in e-business, *Strategic Management Journal* Vol. 22, Nos. 6–7, pp. 493–520.

Applegate, L. (2001). E-business Models: making sense of the internet business landscape. In G. W. Dickson and G. De Sanctis (eds) *Information Technology and the Future Enterprise: new models for management*. NJ: Prentice Hall.

Baker, K. (2002). *Innovation in Communication*. Management Benchmark Study, Office of Science, US Department of Energy, Chapter 14.

Bambury, P. (1998). A taxonomy of internet commerce, *First Monday* Vol. 3, No. 10. Available at www.firstmonday.org/issue3_10/bambury/index.html (accessed October 2007).

Barney, J. (1986). Strategic factor markets: expectations, luck and business strategy, *Management Science* Vol. 32, pp. 1231–41.

Barney, J. (1991). Firm resources and sustained competitive advantage, *Journal of Management* Vol. 17, pp. 99–120.

Barney, J. and Zajac, E. (1994). Competitive organisational behaviour: toward an organisationally-based theory of competitive advantage, *Strategic Management Journal* Vol. 15, pp. 5–9.

Baysinger, B. and Hoskisson, R. (1989). Diversification strategy and R&D intensity in large multi-product firms, *Academy of Management Journal* Vol. 32, pp. 310–32.

Bender, G. and Laestadius, S. (2005). Non-science based innovativeness: on capabilities relevant to generate profitable novelty. Paper presented at the conference Low-Tech as Misnomer: the role of non-research-intensive industries in the knowledge economy, Brussels, 29–30 June 2005.

Carter, A. (1999). *The Aftermath of Reengineering: downsizing and corporate performance*, Philadelphia: Haworth Marketing Resources.

Chamberlin, E. (1933). *The Theory of Monopolistic Competition*. Cambridge, MA: Harvard University Press.

Chatterjee, S. and Wernerfelt, B. (1991). The link between resources and type of diversification: theory and evidence, *Strategic Management Journal* Vol. 12, pp. 33–48.

Chesbrough, H. and Rosenbloom, R. (2000). *The Role of the Business Model in Capturing Value from Innovation: evidence from Xerox Corporation's technology spinoff companies*. Boston: Harvard Business School.

Christensen, C. (1997). *The Innovator's Dilemma: when new technologies cause great firms to fail*. Boston: Harvard Business School Press.

Cohen, W. M. and Levinthal, D. A. (1990). Absorptive capacity: a new perspective on learning and innovation, *Administrative Science Quarterly* Vol. 35, pp. 128–52.

Cubbin, J. (1988). Is it better to be a weak firm in a strong industry or a strong firm in a weak industry?, London Business School, Centre for Business Strategy, Working Paper No. 49.

Decarolis, D. and Deeds, D. (1999). The impact of stocks and flows of organizational knowledge on firm performance: an empirical investigation of the biotechnology industry, *Strategic Management Journal* Vol. 20, pp. 953–68.

Del Canto, J. and Gonzalez, I. (1999). A resource-based analysis of the factors determining a firm's R&D activities, *Research Policy* Vol. 28, pp. 891–905.

Dierickx, I. and Cool, K. (1989). Asset stock accumulation and sustainability of competitive advantage, *Management Science* Vol. 35, pp. 1504–11.

Drucker, P. (1985). *Entrepreneurship and Innovation: practice and principles*. New York: Harper Business.

European Commission (2006). Innovation in the National Strategic Reference Frameworks: working document of the Directorate General for Regional Policy. Available at http://ec.europa.eu/regional_policy/innovation/2007/innovation_nsrf.pdf (accessed October 2007).

Gatignon, H. and Xuereb, J. (1997). Strategic orientation of the firm and new product performance, *Journal of Marketing Research* Vol. 34, pp. 77–90.

Gordijn, J. (2002) Value-based Requirements Engineering : exploring innovative e-commerce ideas. PhD thesis. Amsterdam: Vrije Universiteit.

Gordijn, J., Akkermans, J. M. and van Vliet, H. (2000). Business Modelling is not Process Modelling. In *Conceptual Modeling for E-Business and the Web: ER 2000 workshops on conceptual modeling approaches for e-business and the World Wide Web and conceptual modeling, Salt Lake City, Utah, USA, October 9–12, 2000*. Lecture Notes in Computer Science 1921, pp. 40–51. Springer-Verlag.

Gruner, K. and Homburg, C. (1999). Does customer interaction enhance new product performance?, *Journal of Business Research* Vol. 49, pp. 1–14.

Hamel, G. (1996). Strategy as revolution, *Harvard Business Review* (July–August), pp. 69–82.

Hamel, G. (2000). *Leading the Revolution*. Boston: Harvard Business School Press.

Hammer, M. and Champy, J. (1994). *Reengineering the Corporation: a manifesto for business revolution*. New York: HarperBusiness.

Hansen, G. and Wernerfelt, B. (1989). Determinants of firm performance: the relative importance of economic and organisational factors, *Strategic Management Journal* Vol. 10, pp. 399–411.

Harris, R. and Trainor, M. (1995). Innovations and R&D in Northern Ireland manufacturing: a Schumpeterian approach, *Regional Studies* Vol. 29, No. 7, pp. 593–604.

Helfat, C. (1997). Know-how and asset complementarity and dynamic capability accumulation: the case of R&D, *Strategic Management Journal* Vol. 18, pp. 339–60.

Hitt, M., Bierman, L., Shimizu, K. and Kochlar, R. (2001). Direct and moderating effects of human capital on strategy and performance in professional service firms: a resource-based perspective, *Academy of Management Journal* Vol. 44, pp. 13–28.

Iansiti, M. and West, J. (1999). From physics to function: an empirical study of research and development performance in the semiconductor industry, *Journal of Product Innovation Management* Vol. 16, pp. 385–99.

IBM (2006a). *Paths to Success: three ways to innovate your business model*, IBM Institute for Business Value, Somers, NY. Available at www-935.ibm.com/services/us/gbs/bus/pdf/g510-6630-01-paths2success.pdf.

IBM (2006b). *Business Model Innovation – the new route to competitive advantage*, IBM Institute for Business Value, Somers, NY. Available at www-935.ibm.com/services/us/cio/flexible/enflex_wp-business-model-innovation.pdf.

Itami, H. (1987). *Mobilizing Invisible Assets*. Cambridge, MA: Harvard University Press.

Jonach, R. and Sommerlatte, T. (1999). *The Innovation Premium: how the next-generation companies are achieving peak performance and profitability*. Reading, MA: Perseus Books.

Kogut, B. and Zander, U. (1996). What firms do? Coordination, identify, and learning, *Organization Science* Vol. 7, pp. 502–18.

Lal, K. (1999). Determinants of the adoption of information technology: a case study of electrical and electronic goods manufacturing firms in India, *Research Policy* Vol. 28, pp. 667–80.

Lee, C., Lee, K. and Pennings, J. (2001). Internal capabilities, external networks, and performance: a study on technology-based ventures, *Strategic Management Journal*, Vol. 22, pp. 615–40.

Lei, D., Hitt, M. and Bettis, R. (1996). Dynamic core competences through meta-learning and strategic context, *Journal of Management* Vol. 22, pp. 549–69.

Linder, J. and Cantrell, S. (2000). *Changing Business Models: surveying the landscape*, Accenture Institute for Strategic Change. Available at www.woodwardequity.com/pdf/Strategy-ChangingBusinessModels.pdf (accessed October 2007).

Lippman, S. and Rumelt, R. (1982). Uncertain imitability: an analysis of interfirm differences in efficiency under competition, *Bell Journal of Economics* Vol. 13, pp. 418–38.

Liyanage, S., Greenfield, P. and Don, R. (1999). Towards a fourth generation of R&D management model-research networks in knowledge management, *International Journal of Technology Management* Vol. 18, pp. 372–93.

Lumpkin, G. and Dess, G. (1996). Clarifying the entrepreneurial orientation construct and linking it to performance, *Academy of Management Review* Vol. 21, pp. 135–72.

Lüthje, C. (2000). *Kundenorientierung im Innovationsprozess*. Wiesbaden: Deutscher Universitäts-Verlag.

Magretta, J. (2002). Why business models matter, *Harvard Business Review* Vol. 80, No. 5, pp. 86–91.

Mahadevan, B. (2000). Business models for internet-based e-commerce: an anatomy, *California Management Review* Vol. 42, No. 4, pp. 55–69.

Mansfield, G. and Fourie, L. (2004). Strategy and business models: strange bedfellows? A case for convergence and its evolution into strategic architecture, *South African Journal of Business Management* Vol. 35, pp.35–44.

Markham, S. K. (1998). A longitudinal examination of how champions influence others to support their projects, *Journal of Product Innovation Management* Vol. 16, pp. 490–504.

Markides, C. and Williamson, P. (1996) Corporate diversification and organisational structure: a resource-based view, *Academy of Management Journal* Vol. 39, pp. 340–67.

Mitchell, V. L. and Zmud, R.W. (1999). The effects of coupling IT and work process strategies in redesign projects, *Organization Science* Vol. 10, pp. 424–38.

Morris, L. (2003). *Business Model Warfare: the strategy of business breakthroughs*. InnovationLabs and Ackoff Center for Advancement of Systems Approaches (A-CASA). Available at http://innovationlabs.com/BusModelWarfare.pdf (accessed October 2007).

Nonaka, I. (1994). A dynamic theory of organizational knowledge creation, *Organization Science* Vol. 5, pp. 14–37.

Organisation for Economic Co-operation and Development (2007a). *Chair's summary of the OECD Council at Ministerial Level, Paris, 15–16 May 2007 – Innovation: advancing the OECD agenda for growth and equity*. Available at www.oecd.org/document/22/0,3343,en_2649_201185_38604566_1_1_1_1,00.html (accessed October 2007).

Organisation for Economic Co-operation and Development (2007b). *Moving up the Value Chain: staying competitive in the global economy*. Available at www.oecd.org/document/54/0,3343,en_2649_33703_38726774_1_1_1_1,00.html (accessed October 2007).

Organisation for Economic Co-operation and Development (2007c). *Globalisation and Innovation in the Business Services Sector*. Available at www.oecd.org/dataoecd/18/55/38619867.pdf (accessed October 2007).

Osterwalder, A. (2004). The Business Model Ontology: a proposition in a design science approach. PhD thesis. Lausanne: University of Lausanne.

Osterwalder, A., Pigneur, Y. and Tucci, C. (2005). Clarifying business models: origins, present, and future of the concept, *Communications of AIS* Vol. 15, Article 13.

Penrose, E. (1959). *The Theory of Growth of the Firm*. Oxford: Blackwell.

Peteraf, M. (1993). The cornerstones of competitive advantage: a resource-based view, *Strategic Management Journal* Vol. 14, pp. 179–91.

Petrovic, O. and Kittl, C. (2001). Developing Business Models for eBusiness. Paper presented at the International Conference on Electronic Commerce, Hofburg Conference Centre, Vienna, 31st October – 4th November 2001.

Pike, S. (2007). Intellectual Capital and Financial Accounts: a methodology and case study. Paper presented at the IC Congress, Haarlem, 3–4 May 2007.

Pike, S., Fernström, L. and Roos, G. (2005). Intellectual capital: management approach, *ICS Ltd Journal of Intellectual Capital*, Vol. 6, No. 4, pp. 489–509.

Pike, S. and Roos, G. (2007). Intellectual Capital Research: a personal view. Paper presented at the IC Congress, Haarlem, 3–4 May 2007.

Pillai, R. and Meindl, J. R. (1998). Context and charisma: a 'meso' level examination of the relationship of organic structure, collectivism, and crisis to charismatic leadership, *Journal of Management* Vol. 24, pp. 643–71.

Piller, F., Schaller, C. and Walcher, D. (2004). Customers as Co-Designers: a framework for open innovation. München: TUM Business School, Department of General and Industrial Management, Technische Universitaet München, Paper 116.

Porter, M. (2001). Strategy and the Internet, *Harvard Business Review* Vol. 79 (March), No. 3.

Prahalad, C. and Hamel, G. (1990). The core competence of the corporation, *Harvard Business Review* Vol. 68, pp. 79–91.

Rappa, M. (2004). The utility business model and the future of computing services, *IBM Systems Journal* Vol. 43, No. 1, pp. 32–43.

Reed, R. and DeFillippi, R. (1990). Causal ambiguity, barriers to imitation and sustainable competitive advantage, *Academy of Management Review* Vol. 15, pp. 88–102.

Reichwald, R., Piller, F., Jäger, S. and Zanner, S. (2003). Economic evaluation of mini-plants for mass customisation. In M. Tseng and F. Piller (eds) *The Customer Centric Enterprise: advances in mass customization and personalization*, pp. 51–70. New York: Springer.

Robins. J. and Wiersema, M. (1995). A resource-based approach to the multi-business firm: empirical analysis of portfolio interrelationships and corporate financial performance, *Strategic Management Journal* Vol. 16, pp. 277–99.

Robinson, J. (1933). *The Economics of Imperfect Competition.* London: MacMillan Press.

Roos, G. and Roos, J. (1997). Measuring your company's intellectual capital performance, *Long Range Planning* Vol. 30, No. 3, pp. 413–26.

Schoemaker, P. (1992). How to link strategic vision to core capabilities, *Sloan Management Review* Vol. 34, pp. 67–81.

Seddon, P. and Lewis, G. (2004). The case for viewing business models as abstraction of strategy, *Communications of the Association for Information Systems* Vol. 13, pp. 427–42.

Song, X. and Parry, M. (1997). The determinants of Japanese new product success, *Journal of Marketing Research* Vol. 34, pp. 64–76.

Stabell, C. and Fjeldstad, O. (1998). Configuring value for competitive advantage: on chains, shops, and networks, *Strategic Management Journal* Vol. 19, pp. 413–37.

Stähler, P. (2002). Business Models as a Unit of Analysis for Strategizing. Paper presented at the International Workshop on Business Models, Lausanne, 4–5 October 2002.

Teece, D. (1986). Profiting from technical innovation: implications for integration, collaboration, licensing and public policy, *Research Policy* Vol. 15, pp. 285–305.

Teece, D. and Pisano, G. (1994). The dynamic capabilities of firms: an introduction, *Industrial and Corporate Change* Vol. 3, pp. 537–56.

Teece, D., Pisano, G. and Shuen, A. (1997). Dynamic capabilities and strategic management, *Strategic Management Journal* Vol. 18, No. 7, pp. 509–33.

Timmers, P. (1998). Business models for electronic markets, *Journal on Electronic Markets* Vol. 8, No. 2, pp. 3–8.

Von Hippel, E. (2001). *Open source shows the way: innovation by and for users – no manufacturer required*, MIT Sloan School of Management Working Paper No. 4163.

Weill, P. and Vitale, M. (2001). *Place to Space: migrating to ebusiness models.* Boston: Harvard Business School Press.

Wheelwright, S. and Clark, K. (1992). *Revolutionizing Product Development.* New York: The Free Press.

4 Knowledge, recognition and 'communautalism'

Ahmed Bounfour

This chapter is about communities, recognition and their related and subsequent intangibles. In some of my recent works (Bounfour, 2005, 2006), I advanced the argument that the community perspective is essential to understanding the new capitalism dynamics. More and more activities are organised around and within communities, and less and less within the vertical unique organisations.

The chapter is structured as follows: Section 1 presents the arguments towards the community as a perspective; Section 2 considers the issue of community and recognition; Section 3 proposes a typology of intangible assets most suitable to the community regime.

Why communities now?

The issue of community is posed because of the deep transformation in organisational implicit order. By implicit order, I mean the fact that in many contexts people observe certain rules of behaviour which do not need any effort of explicitation. But now, due to the deep transformation of socioeconomic system, most of the rules governing organisations are under pressure for transformation, and new rules have to be defined in the new context. We really need an adapted map to the emerging social forms; for example, the new capitalism.

If we look at the issue from a long-term perspective, at least three types of orders can be distinguished (Bounfour, 2005):

- *Pre-industrial orders*, e.g. the orders predominating before the advent of the industrial revolution. Generally, societies in that context were governed by specific rules, and at this level we can differentiate between a community (*Gemeinschaft*) and a society (*Gesellschaft*), as they have been defined by the German sociologist F. Tönnies (1887). *Gemeinschaft* refers to an absolute unit where there is an indistinctive and compact relationship between members. The conscience of members is so high that none can move without the others (Durkheim, 1889: 4). The perfect form of a community is the family. But it might also be a village or extensively a small town. *Gesellschaft*, on the contrary, refers to a group of individuals who, while leaving peacefully, are fundamentally separated. Under this regime, the individual is the centre whereas under the community regime, it is the community, which represents the hub.

- *Industrial-manufacturing orders* refer to the organisational forms which were born and developed after the industrial revolution. Typically, while large hierarchies – whether they are private (e.g. General Motors at the beginning of the twentieth century) or public (e.g. Department of Defence, Health Departments) – emerged and developed, other organisational forms had been tested and implemented: Communism in East Europe, China and other parts of the World, clans in Japan and market transactions almost worldwide. Each of these regimes corresponds to specific characteristics but, globally speaking, bureaucracies are more important than market forms.
- *Service-intangibles orders.* These orders correspond to the present situation of (knowledge) capitalism. We have now one global socioeconomic system – the 'transaction regime' – putting pressure on every organisation for more and more performance improvement. Hence the increase in spot market transactions (the archetype being the financial market transactions) and the emergence of hollow corporations and networks. But because of that, communities emerge as a complementary – and even, under specific circumstances, as alternative ways of carrying out activities and growth. The Linux Community represents the archetype of such a regime, but other communities are now observable in different places, being physical (part of towns as small villages), and /or virtual (facebook communities).

The service-intangibles orders, allied to the high potential of internet as well as to the deployment of managerial practices, induced a large deconstruction of social links. More importantly, and for the first time in modern capitalism, what is leading in innovation is not what is happening *intra muros* within vertical companies, but *extra muros* within societies and communities. I develop this argument further, and distinguish between different types of communities. The emergence of the community as an organisational mode of governance leads us to the distinction between two regimes: the transaction regime and the community regime – what I have named elsewhere, 'communautalism' (Bounfour, 2006).

Two regimes

Indeed, from a systemic perspective, two parallel and potentially conflicting regimes can be put forward: the transaction regime and the community regime.

The transaction regime

This is still the dominant nature of capitalism. Companies and collective systems are mainly driven by efficiency requirements, and therefore any individual or collective action should be appraised from this perspective. To be schematic: return of invested resources is the alpha and omega for the assessment of any decision or behaviour. The shareholder value is the archetype of such reasoning.

The community regime

I suggested introducing this concept of community regime due to the deep crisis we all observe in our societies with regards to 'recognition mechanisms'. It is clear that, at least since the mid-1970s, there has been a steady and deep tendency towards 'fragilising' socioeconomic links within the traditional vertical corporations. Outsourcing and networking activities, as well as the emergence of the services economy, create a deep change in the way individuals see others and their organisation; and therefore, how they recognise themselves. This crisis – or at least transition – in recognition mechanisms is a stimulating perspective for understanding the whole dynamics of capitalism. From a microeconomic point of view, to a certain extent, the market – and its transactions – are now the dominant forms of exerting activities. But because of that, individuals are now orphans and seek new spaces of recognition; hence the relevance of the concept of community. By community, we should understand here '*a set of individuals for whom relationships are governed to different degree by "recognition mechanisms"*'. This naturally has nothing to do with 'communities of practice', as often promoted within and around companies and organisations, because most of the time these so-called communities are in fact artificial groups of individuals, nominated or co-opted by the management, without the necessary recognition mechanisms.

This concept of recognition, which has been developed by Hegel (in his earliest work at Iena), and recently elaborated further by French and German philosophers (Ricoeur, Honneth), is central to the elaboration of a critical theory of present and future societies, and therefore for building new social links within societies; in brief, for searching a new path for happiness in societies. Finns are Finns because they recognise others as Finns, as do the French, Germans, Austrians, Japanese and others. They do not need 'communities of practice' for that – they form a natural community. A natural community is therefore a set of people who spontaneously recognise the others as fellows. Villages, cities, regions and nations are natural communities, shaped by history. Beside these forms of communities, I will distinguish new forms of communities that emerge basically due to the transformation of large companies, as well as to the emergence of new forms of social-economising outside the traditional vertical form.

I will then distinguish three forms of emerging communities:

- *Constrained communities*, e.g. communities that individuals belong to basically because transactions costs are high under the transaction regime. Typically such a regime can be – and is already – perfectly applied to a network of experts or knowledge gurus. These individuals will exchange contacts, references, websites citations and reputation, in order to increase their market power. They do so because they do not have the choice, nor do they have the resources and time to afford concluding contracts.
- *Quasi-Organic communities*. These communities, while leaving under the transaction regime, develop norms and behaviours corresponding to those norms and rules defined by Tönnies. This is specifically the case for the Linux community in the IT area, but also for other communities of knowledge

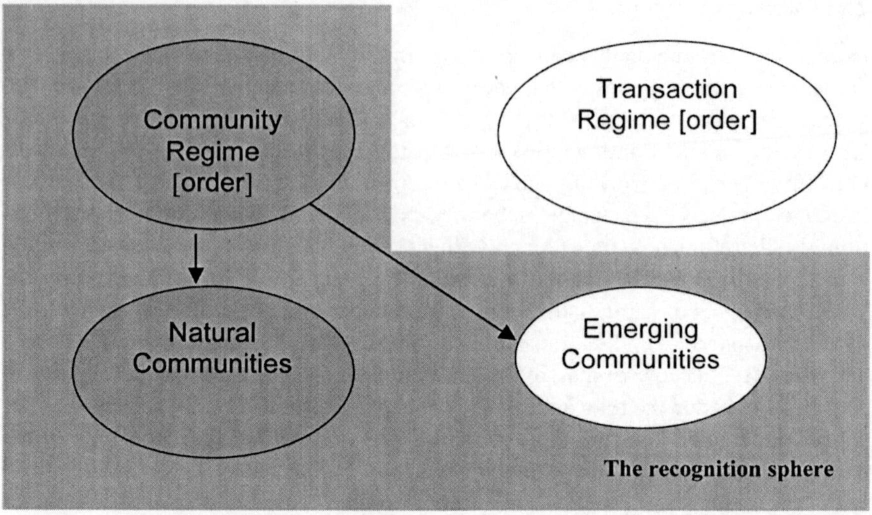

Figure 4.1 The new capitalism map: Transaction Regime versus Community Regime, Natural Communities versus Emerging Communities.

exchange. This also might apply to local communities such as districts, cities or villages.

- *Organic Communities*. These communities are still to be observed. Under the organic communities, there is a full congruence between individual expectations and behaviours and the community rules of governance.

Mapping organisational orders and dynamic of cognitive capitalism

These three categories are separated here for pedagogical reasons, since what is important is primarily the dynamic interrelation between the distinguished spaces:

- between the transactional order and the community order;
- between the three community orders themselves;
- between the private space, the transactional space and the organic space;
- finally, between natural communities and emerging communities.

Let us consider each of these points.

The articulation between the transactional order and the community order

From a global perspective, we must look at the question of how the transactional order, currently dominant within organisations, can maintain relations of overlap

– or integration in some form or another – with the community order. In other words, will companies – particularly the largest ones – deploy management tools sophisticated enough to integrate ongoing innovations, or that might intervene within the community order?

In short, what possible articulation can there be between the transactional order and the community order? The answer to this question is not obvious at this stage, but we can make some guesses at corporate behaviours, in particular on the development of sophisticated mechanisms of articulation between community order and transactional order. This especially concerns the so-called 'global companies', in which the reduction in the role of hierarchical forms of organisation activities and networking tends to suggest greater attention to community forms of work organising. One of the uncertainties at this level concerns managerial routines that will be dominant in the long term: what coexistence is there between the Anglo-Saxon mode – dominated by outsourcing and other destructuring managerial practices – and Chinese, Indian and Japanese managerial modes (the latter being currently the subject of a full transformation).

This overall conjecture has to be refined based on the three distinguished community orders: it is clear that constrained communities are closest in their governance mode to the transactional order and adopt, for the most part, the same rules. No obstacles to their articulation exist: in fact, they are already articulated. Independent consultants, former business executives, are already articulated to their firm(s) of origin and its (their) networks. The articulation between the transactional order and the quasi-organic communities (the Linux community or, on another level, scientific diasporas, for example) is certainly the most interesting to observe. We could assume that sophisticated articulation mechanisms will develop, allowing companies to benefit from the knowledge disseminated within these communities. Finally, an articulation between the transactional order and the organic community is not very clear at this stage, but it can be assumed that the observation of emerging practices will provide us with some arguments to the formulation of strong conjectures at this level.

The articulation between the three community orders

What type of back-and-forth movement can be observed between the three types of communities: constrained communities, quasi-organic communities and organic communities? Some hypotheses can be formulated here: the constrained communities are closer to the transactional order in their own mode of governance, and it is likely that their relationship to the other forms of communities will be weak. But it is possible to observe, here and there, changeovers and overlapping between members of constrained communities forced towards quasi-organic communities (gurus and freelancers at the end of their 'intellectual life cycle').

The articulation between quasi-organic communities and organic communities is interesting to consider; there might be a back-and-forth between the two in terms of members; and it is possible that some quasi-organic communities turn into organic communities (in the case of a crisis for them or disappearance of any form of professional reference for their members). It is also possible that some organic communities incorporate the transaction sphere in part, and thus become quasi-organic communities.

The articulation between transactional space, 'organic' space and private space

At the crossroads of the two previous overlaps, we can also raise the issue of the relationship between transactional space, organic space and private space for individuals. This is an important issue, particularly because of the elastic boundaries of working time and the intangible nature of the relationship between individuals and organisations. We are attesting more and more to a shift in the reality of the company from its material dimension – offices, meeting rooms, corridors, factories, cafeterias – to an intangible reality, the intranet, which radically changes the problem of the employment relationship and therefore the relationship to others.

Understanding the dynamics of these interactions is essential to the design of a management – public or private – adapted to the new form of capitalism: 'communautalism'. More generally, the weakening of the social contract – and work within companies, and dematerialisation of the psychological relationship to the organisation – and at the same time, increased anxiety of individuals, calls for a reflection on how reinvention of the business relationship happens. The individuals themselves are forced to innovate, and thus to reshape their way of navigating between the transactional space – their enterprise, their organisation, the organic space (the community) – and the private space (the family), more and more invaded and weakened by work constraints. Within the transaction space itself, companies tend to encourage the development of private spaces for innovation by individuals that these companies are trying to capture in the 'official' transaction space, as soon as these innovations have reached a certain level of maturity.

The articulation between natural communities and emerging communities: the new dynamic capabilities

The assessment of possible modes of articulation between natural communities (nations, regions, cities and districts) and emerging communities is very important for research and action, both for enterprises and for public management.

For a nation, innovation policies, training and labour law are closely linked to the dominant structure of the activities (and of course also to history). If constrained communities became the dominant mode of production in a country, it is clear that training policies will be affected; the same is true of the work laws, as well as for intellectual property rights. Similarly, at the international level, countries with strong scientific and business diaspora will benefit the most from these communities. By contrast, those countries that do not (such as Japan and Finland) should seek alternatives to enable them to better absorb knowledge flows within organised scientific and technological communities.

The same issues arise more or less for a region, a city or a district: how to encourage the formation of more or less organic communities, in order to ensure a smooth flow of intangible capital for the benefit of these natural communities. This is typically what people are doing, or seeking to do, in cities such as Barcelona, Grenoble and Rhône-Alpes, or city-states such as Dubai, for example. Conversely, for emerging communities themselves, they may be looking for physical, virtual or mental spaces, enabling them to better organise and develop their exchanges.

We see therefore, in a dematerialised economy, the analysis of the dynamics of the relationship between natural communities and emerging communities is a major field for research, as well as for the design of new instruments for public management.

Community and recognition

By considering the community as a valuable analytical perspective for the analysis of the dynamics of the new capitalism, I would like to emphasise the importance of organic links in the relationship between human beings. We propose to do this by introducing the concept of recognition as a philosophical and analytical concept allowing us to better analyse the modalities of formation, re-articulation and redeployment inter-and intra-organisational links, and thus redesigning accordingly, instruments and exchange of artefacts of different types, in alignment with the different organisational order distinguished earlier (especially what I proposed to name: 'recognition assets').

We should emphasise at the outset that, semantically, the French language distinguishes between *connaissance* (knowledge), which is a link from subject to object, and *reconnaissance* – recognition, which is a link between subjects (not the case in English, which uses two different terms: knowledge and recognition). On a more theoretical level, we will refer here to the French school of the gift, around the Revue du MAUSS led by Alain Caillé, but also to recent developments within the philosophical school of recognition (those led by Axel Honneth and Paul Ricoeur, in particular). Our intention here is not to describe in detail the trajectory of the philosophical and anthropological concept of recognition, but to consider its possible translations in the field of economic-based communities, and especially from the point of view of the formation of new economic assets: recognition assets.

Axel Honneth and the fight for recognition

In his Habilitation Thesis, Axel Honneth (1992, 2004), successor to Habermas at the University of Frankfurt, attempted to draw a model of normative content, from the lines of the model of the 'fight for recognition' by the young Hegel (in his Iena period). According to Honneth, Hegel has given a new meaning to Hobbes's concept of 'fight', on the basis of the Fitchian theory of recognition:

> A subject as long as he knows himself as recognised in some of his capabilities

> and qualities, by another, as long as he is reconciled with the latter, still finds aspects of its own identity, where he distinguished himself undoubtedly from other possible subjects and opposes again them as a particular subject. (p. 26).

In this context, the crime in a society appears as – and is the result of – a lack of recognition. The criminal is a person for whom 'I' is not sufficiently recognised by society. The person whose rights are affected by the criminal reacts then follows a divergent cycle of 'fight' for recognition. Extended to social conflicts, this perspective suggests that interindividual relationships should be considered in a holistic way. This is a fundamentally dissonant view compared to that of Hobbes. In the conception of Hegel, unlike that of Hobbes, 'if the individual socially ignored affects the property of others, it is not to satisfy the physical needs, but in order to exist again in the eyes of others' (p. 58). The individual who was attacked understands that through this violence, the attacker is looking for a signal of recognition. This perspective allows a different interpretation of the state of nature by Hobbes, indicating that people are at the outset ontologically enrolled in a relationship of dependency and fight for recognition. The same reasoning is extended to intra-societal legal relationships, for which respect is ensured by an institutional part: the State.

From the Hegelian model of the fight for recognition, Honneth conditions the achievement of a normative theory of recognition to the performance of three core tasks (p. 83–84):

1 The Hegelian model is based on a speculative thesis: the interaction of "I's". But, says Honneth, we cannot be satisfied with a speculative basis of this type, hence the importance of rebuilding the original thesis of Hegel from an empirical social psychology. (This will be done on the basis of the social psychology of George Herbert Mead.)
2 From his intersubjective thesis, Hegel suggests different successive times of recognition: 'love', 'right' and 'ethnicity'. This succession of phases of recognition relationships also requires empirical demonstration.
3 As their identities are formed, individuals are forced to engage in intersubjective conflicts of recognition.

These are the three points that Honneth sought to address later in his book. A structuring relation of recognition is proposed. It should especially be noticed with Honneth that the relations of solidarity in modern societies are dependent on relationships of symmetricity and esteem between autonomous individuals. By symmetricity, it is understood here the possibility for an individual to see that his/her abilities and qualities are recognised as valuable. According to Honneth, these developments 'are opening for the first time an horizon within which individual competition for the social esteem can take place without suffering, i.e. without putting the subject through the experience of contempt' (p. 158).

Paul Ricoeur and the *Parcours de la reconnaissance*

In *Parcours de la reconnaissance*, Ricoeur stresses in his foreword that 'it is a fact that there is no theory of recognition worthy of the name in the way there is one or more theories of knowledge'(p.9). The purpose of the book, which is the result of three lectures at Institut für die Wissenschaften Menschens of Vienna, is to help to fill this gap through the confrontation of two major dictionaries of the French language: the *Dictionnaire de la langue française* composed and published by Emile Littré from 1859 to 1872, and *Le Grand Robert de la langue française* (1985), directed by Alain Rey. Stemming from the analysis of the long-term parcours of the concept of recognition, there are three possible philosophical meanings:

- Recognise means identify and differentiate: 'recognise something like the same as identical to oneself and not as something other than oneself, means to distinguish it from any other' (Ricoeur, p. 34).
- Self-recognition; and mutual recognition.

For our purposes here, let us consider the last form of recognition. Here Ricoeur rereads Hobbes, and Hegel and his fight for recognition. In Section V – 'la lutte pour la reconnaissance et les états de la paix' (pp. 319–355) – he develops an alternative thesis to the struggle for recognition: 'The alternative to the idea of fight in the process of mutual recognition lies in peaceful experiences of mutual recognition, based on symbolic mediations removed both from the legal system as well as from trading exchanges.' (p. 319) We should focus particularly here on Ricoeur's developments around the paradoxes of the gift and counter-gift and the logic of reciprocity, and more specifically his reading of the three requirements outlined by Mauss, in his essay on gift. As stressed by Mauss in his essay (p.147), the riddle of the gift is not so much in giving, or even in receiving, but in giving back.

That is the 'Hau spirit', says Mauss, which makes those three obligations structurally related, i.e. a magical spirit is present in exchanged objects. It is known that this argument was clearly rejected by Claude Lévi-Strauss (in his preface to the book by Mauss), who wondered whether Mauss was not mystified by the natives. But then, how to clarify the riddle of the gift? Ricoeur responds by mobilising the developments by Marcel Henaff in his book *Le prix de la vérité* (2002), especially the double break provided by this author: on the one hand with the moralistic vision associated with its sumptuous and festive peak; and on the other hand, vis-à-vis the economist analysis, which sees the phenomenon as an archaic gift compared to modern exchanges in markets, without solving the riddle of the gift, and in particular the obligation give-back. For Ricoeur, a detour through the gift does not lead to a state of perpetual peace, it only suspends the dispute:

'The experience of the gift, in addition to its symbolic indirect, unusual or even exceptional nature, is inseparable from its load of potential conflicts related to the creative tension between duty and generosity; it is these aporias raised by the analysis of the ideal type of gift, that the experience of gift brings in its coupling with the fight for recognition.'(p. 355)

In short, says Ricoeur, if the fight for recognition is endless, the effective experiences of gift suggest an alternative to the fight for power and violence.

We should then state with the philosophy of recognition that social organisation is a constant fight for recognition. Also, fighting is an inherent part of human existence. Finally, we should notice that the Maussian theory of gift is of an extreme modernity and that it offers opportunities for designing times of truce in this fight for recognition. Now, let us then translate these concepts in the field that concerns us: the creation and dissemination of recognition resources under the community regime, e.g. 'communautalism'.

Community and Recognition assets: a typology

From the viewpoint of economic analysis – and the formation of value in the knowledge economy – the perspective proposed here allows us to distinguish different types of resources/assets, collective and individuals, that we propose to name recognition assets. They are to be considered dynamically, as part of a global constellation of intangible resources, for which it is necessary to specify the content as well as the contours. By reconsidering the mapping of regimes (organisational orders) distinguished earlier, we can proceed to the typology of these resources.

Typology of intangible resources /assets

In each of the two major regimes distinguished, there were associated *ad hoc* intangibles.

Transactional regime

Here, two types of resources can be distinguished:

- *Intangible resources for idiosyncratic hierarchies.* By hierarchy we mean a defined company and any other form of organisation (a public administration) endowed with instruments for recording (balance sheet, income statement or similar instruments), *ad hoc* reporting, and with clearly delineated borders, specified by strong ownership rights. Among these intangible resources, some are idiosyncratic, as they are specifically related to business lines of the company and its business model: technological knowledge, procedures, specific and standard methodologies, patents, etc. Some of these resources may be protected by *ad hoc* intellectual property rights.
- *Intangible resources for Taylorised hierarchies* (the unified enterprise). Some discourse on the knowledge economy, suggests a *tous azimuts* deployment of intelligence in society. This is obviously a strong argument, which should be considered in a serious way, but it does not need to be interpreted in a naïve way: in other words, a large number of tasks and activities continue to be organised in a Taylorised way, mainly through the development of tools, based on explicit knowledge (not to mention that whole parts of the society

are excluded from the benefits of the knowledge economy). In other words, in the knowledge economy, the deployment of idiosyncratic intelligence is not necessarily the general rule. Two types of Taylorist activities can be distinguished: those performed by people and those filled by artefacts. For the former, we refer here particularly to call centres, in which resources are deployed in the form of an explicit knowledge. For this type of activity – this is particularly true of call centres of Level 1 – the operator has no room for manoeuvre. He/she merely (or rather he/she is forced) to deploy a knowledge formalised and written by others. This type of resource tends to develop within the transactional system, for reasons of productivity and because of the opportunities afforded by offshoring. Besides Taylorised resources associated with the tasks performed by people, other tasks are increasingly being performed by artefacts: intelligent agents. These, both in transactional order as well as elsewhere, will perform tasks of interface of a commercial or productive nature (aid for ordering on the internet). Again, the formalisation of a prior tacit knowledge is the dominant rule.

Interpenetration between idiosyncratic resources and Taylorised resources

What interpenetration is there between idiosyncratic and Taylorised resources within the transactional order? The answer to this question will depend on a number of factors: technological, organisational and legal. It should be noticed, at this stage, the high potential offered by the development of research in information systems around intelligent agents, the possible return to insourcing practices including those actually offshored, and the potential offered by new intellectual property rights, for example, if the Taylorisation of an idiosyncratic knowledge is likely to generate a rent on secondary markets (including at the international level).

Community regime

Our mapping of new organisational forms suggests two types of intangible resources for communities: individual idiosyncratic resources, for constrained

Table 4.1 Transactional regime, community regimes, types of resources and IPRs

	Transactional Regime	*Constrained Communities*	*Quasi-Organic Communities*	*Organic Communities*
Ad hoc Resources (Assets)	Idiosyncratic intangible resources for hierarchies Taylorised intangible resources	Individual idiosyncratic resources	Recognition resources (Assets)	Recognition resources (Assets)
IPRs regime	Exclusive intellectual property rights	Joint resources (Assets)	Open or quasi-open rights	Open Rights

Source: Bounfour (2006: 186)

communities; and recognition resources, for organic communities and quasi-organic communities.

- *Individual idiosyncratic resources*: this type of resource covers knowledge, skills, assets, and sometimes expertise that individuals as members of constrained communities have developed, or are seeking to develop. Individual victims of transformations induced by the transactional regime (restructuring, outsourcing, offshoring) are forced to develop these kinds of resources. That is, not only resources inherently deployable or observable (e.g. skills, know-how, expertise), but also resources that can help navigate through the jungle ahead of constrained communities (reputation resources, for example). The idiosyncratic individual resources will be particularly critical in cases where the scenario 'all freelance' becomes the dominant mode of organising activities.
- *Recognition resources*: the same resources as before, but deployed within communities in which relationships between members are governed by organic or quasi-organic links. Within this type of community, the effectiveness of the recognition requires the deployment of recognition resources. This is already observable in scientific communities, where the recognition dimension (as defined by Ricoeur) is present for a long time. But we can reasonably estimate that as the transaction deploys itself and sees its underlying mechanisms being visible for individuals, recognition emerges as a complement, if not a substitute. One can also reasonably think that with the spreading of virtual proximity, the effectiveness of recognition becomes possible. The deployment of recognition within more or less stable communities can be done through mechanisms of gift and counter-gift assets and resources of tacit knowledge, formalised intangible resources (assets) or related to reputation. (The old practices of patronage and recommendation may find here a large scope for renewal.)

IPRs regimes

The types of regimes of intellectual property rights to be distinguished, flow naturally from the typology of intangible resources just made. For the transactional system, we have already noticed the deployment of intellectual property rights for exclusive hierarchies (companies and organisations). This is the continuation of the current dominant mode of exercise of intellectual property, patents, trademarks, copyright, and in some countries for business methods and software.

For the community regime, two types of modes of exercise of intellectual property rights can be distinguished:

Joint intellectual property rights for constrained communities

As we have already pointed out, constrained communities are formed because of the inability of individuals to bear exorbitant transaction costs for their daily professional activities. They are therefore forced to enter into the process of wise confidence, implying the sharing of joint intangible assets, in particular those related to intellectual property rights: trademarks, software, and business methods, among others. The methods for the sharing of such resources could be the subject of legal proceedings ahead. They will certainly be the subject of innovation by the players themselves, for the sharing of the joint rent.

The regime of open-source (copyleft) for quasi-organic or organic communities

In such communities, the organic links of exchange and gift constitute the ontological reason of the community: they are the basis of its existence and philosophy. This is the overall regulatory regime. Of course, especially for the quasi-organic communities, some articulation to the transaction sphere cannot be excluded; it is even effective in the case of software, or on another level, in the case of diasporas.

References

Bounfour, A. (2005). 'Modeling Intangibles: transaction regime versus community regimes', in A. Bounfour and L. Edvinsson (eds) (2005). *Intellectual Capital for Communities, Nations, Regions and Cities*. Burlington, MA: Elsevier Butterworth-Heinemann.

Caillé, A. (2000). *Anthropologie du don*. Paris: Desclée de Brouwer.

Caillé, A. (2004) *De la reconnaissance: don, identité et estime de soi*. Revue du Mauss, No. 23, 1er semestre. Paris: La découverte.

Durkheim, E. (1889). 'Communauté et Société selon Tönnies', *La Revue Philosophique* 27. Reprinted in: Emile Durkheim (1975). *Textes/1. Eléments d'une théorie social*, pp. 383–90. Collection Le Sens Commun. Paris: Editions de Minuit.

Hénaf, M. (2002). *Le Prix de la vérité, Le don, l'argent, la philosophie*. Paris: Editions du Seuil.

Honneth, A. (2002 [1992]) *La lutte pour la reconnaissance*. Trans. Pierre Rush. Paris: Les Editions du Cerf. Collection Passages. Original title: *Kampf um Anerkennung*. Frankfurt am Main: Suhrkamp Verlag.

Mauss, M. (1950 [1924]). 'Essai sur l'économie du don', in: *Sociologie et Anthropologie*. Paris: Presses Universitaires de France.

Nonaka, I. (1994). 'A dynamic theory of organizational knowledge creation', *Organization Science* Vol. 5 (February), No. 1, pp. 14–37.

Nonaka, I. and Konno, N. (1998). 'The concept of "BA", building a foundation for knowledge creation', *California Management Review*, Vol. 40, No. 3, pp. 40–54.

Nonaka, I. and Takeuchi, H. (1995). *The Knowledge-Creating Company: how Japanese companies create the dynamics of innovation*. New York: Oxford University Press.

Ricoeur, P. (2004). *Parcours de la reconnaissance, trois études*. Paris: Editions Stock.

Tönnies, F. (1977). *Communauté et société: catégories fondamentales de la sociologie pure*. Paris: RETZ-CEPL.

5 Designing sequences for knowledge exchange

The Hau-Ba model

Ahmed Bounfour and Gwenaëlle Grefe

The question of knowledge is becoming more and more closely related to the issue of organisational design. So far, the issue of knowledge creation and dissemination has been considered mainly by taking into account the intrinsic nature of knowledge. But we argue here that, beyond this important perspective, we should further consider the issue of organisational design sequences, in the context dominated by the instability in social links. To tackle this latest perspective, a model has been developed: the Hau-Ba model.

The chapter is organised in five sections: the first section addresses the issue of the intrinsic nature of knowledge and its implications for organisations; the second section addresses the issue of organisational design in relation to the intrinsic nature of the knowledge economy; the third section presents the key components of the Hau-Ba model; and the fourth section presents in detail how the Hau-Ba model can be applied in a concrete setting, i.e. the community of founders within a large aluminium company. Finally, the last section puts the Hau-Ba model into perspective.

The intrinsic nature of knowledge[1]

Within complex economies, innovation is a major requirement for competitiveness. Innovation must be understood, not in the traditional sense, i.e. as product or process innovation, but in the generic sense – namely, the introduction of any break with pre-existing situations. It is an extensive approach to innovation, one which does not reduce it solely to its mere output component: a new product/service. Innovation, from this point of view, can be understood here as any new supply resulting from combining organisational resources, mainly of an intangible nature.

Innovation is an essential component of intangibles management. It is the way by which an organisation can take the initiative to change the rules of the game. But it is not naturally about a new problematic: the economic theory since Schumpeter and the various publications on the management of technology, to which academic or professional reviews are entirely devoted, have long been interested in this question.

Innovation has a multidimensional and trans-functional character. What is at stake for companies is not only putting new products or new processes in the marketplace, but, more importantly, a means of self-renewal. Therefore, the organisational dimension appears today as an important field for research and action. By organisational dimension, we understand here the organisational modes or collective effort for innovation, i.e. for orchestrating radical or incremental breaks with pre-existent situations.

All these dimensions must be considered from the organisational perspective, i.e. how organisations develop new ontological perspectives, including their positioning in spatial and temporal terms, and new routines, which lead them to develop new competitive approaches. Naturally, such an attempt is path-dependent. Indeed, past routines influence organisational capabilities in innovation. Innovation processes are to be considered here as complex exercises, which lead to a deep definition of the role of project managers and executives in charge of innovation within organisations.

Knowledge taxonomies

If the question of knowledge creation is at the heart of this continuous process of re-invention, we should start by considering its taxonomy. Understanding the complexity of knowledge creation within organisations can be appreciated by starting from a definition of the concept of knowledge itself, especially as it can be differentiated from information. Many scholars in various disciplines (information economics, IT, statistics) have dealt with this problem. According to Dosi *et al.*, information

> entails well stated and codified propositions about (i) states-of-the-world (e.g. "it is raining"), (ii) properties of nature (e.g. "A causes B."), (iii) identities of other agents ("I know Mr.X and he is a crook.") and (iv) explicit algorithms on how to do things. Conversely, knowledge … includes a) cognitive categories; b) codes of interpretation of the information itself; c) tacit skills, and d) search and problem-solving heuristics irreducible to well defined algorithms'.
>
> (Dosi *et al.*, 1996: 23–24)

Such a definition can be combined with that suggested by Machlup: knowledge is a stock that might be influenced by a flux (information).

Among the characteristics of knowledge, the distinction between tacit knowledge and explicit knowledge, due to Polanyi, can be regarded as a very stimulating starting point to a new approach to knowledge production within organisations. This differentiation was enlarged by Winter (1987), who integrated several criteria, thus leading to the definition of a detailed taxonomy of knowledge within organisations. Nonaka (1994), on the other hand, in a founding paper, proposes an integrated approach to knowledge creation within organisations, and thus to innovation. The principal thesis of the author is that the process of innovation intervenes by a continuous dialogue between tacit knowledge and explicit knowledge.

By stressing the importance of knowledge in complex economies, Nonaka calls for a change of the design of innovation in large organisations, and in particular for a break with the perception of the latter as a set of simple tools for data-processing or the resolution of problems.

The author believes that innovation, which is a key form of organisational knowledge creation, cannot be sufficiently explained in terms of information processing or problem solving. Innovation can best be understood as a process in which the organisation creates and defines problems and then actively develops new knowledge to solve them (Nonaka, 1994: p. 14). Therefore, 'the organisation *should be studied from the viewpoint of how it creates information and knowledge, rather than with regard to how it processes these entities*' (ibid. p. 15, italics in original). This point of view constitutes a break compared to the approach suggested by Itami, and discussed earlier. Here, the focus is on the organisational dimension of innovation, starting from a strong criticism of the traditional perception of organisation as a system that processes information and solves problems, i.e. the 'input-process-output dimension'.

The Nonaka model is defined from the universal point of view. It is intended to explain the mechanisms of innovation in organisations, whether they be public or private, with an economic vocation or not, and in whatever cultural or competitive context is being considered. The theory developed aims at showing how knowledge is held by individuals and organisations and how its development can be ensured by an amplified spiral between tacit knowledge and explicit knowledge.

From the previous definitions and analysis, we can see that the specific characteristics of knowledge that go into making its creation, and more generally its management, are very complex. At least five characteristics are considered to be particularly critical from the managerial point of view:

- The *tacit dimension of knowledge* (Polanyi, 1964), a concept that has been further developed by Winter (1987): this characteristic of knowledge is a critical factor for most managerial dimensions of intangibles, especially with regards to their building and valorisation. Here, the human dimension must be stressed, especially with regards to the type of common beliefs shared by most of the people within an organisation about innovation as a value. Their belief in the equity feeling principle is another dimension that is often underestimated by analysts and executives in charge of the definition and implementation of innovation policies.
- The *nonprogrammable, unpredictable nature of tacit knowledge*: this is certainly an important characteristic of tacit knowledge. To illustrate this idea, take the case of a meeting on a given project with few participants, even in the case of a very precise agenda and clearly anticipated outputs: nobody can predict with great precision the type of exchange that will take place among participants. This clearly attests to the predominance of tacit knowledge among people within organisations. Tacit knowledge is difficult to insert into programmes; it is also difficult to predict. Tacit knowledge is like a volcanic eruption: it may be brutal and it is difficult to predict with precision, whatever the importance of the organisational effort.
- The *dialectical nature of knowledge creation*: this characteristic is important,

especially for innovation. As Nonaka (1994) showed, innovation intervenes via the various modes of a dialogue between tacit knowledge and explicit knowledge. Indeed, the relationship between these types of knowledge is dialectical; i.e. we need tacit knowledge for building explicit knowledge, and vice versa. Put differently, and using other works of intellectual capital management, an organisation cannot develop its structural capital (brands, methods, patents) without using (reinforcing) its human capital, which is mainly of a tacit nature. An organisation needs to manage these two types of intangible resources in a very distinctive, specific and dialectical way.

- *The importance of complementary assets*: the observation of innovation practices shows that the implementation of an innovation requires that developed technical know-how be used in conjunction with other company services or assets, such as marketing, production, distribution or after-sales service. There is a need for complementary assets, mainly of an intangible nature, for the development of a process of innovation in the organisation. This idea is now widespread among the innovation community. Indeed, the trans-functional character of innovation, in particular between research and development and marketing, has by now been pointed out for more than 15 years, both in Europe and elsewhere.

Teece (1989), emphasising the importance of the concept of complementary assets, especially for the success of innovating strategies, suggested that three types of assets be retained: generic assets, specialised assets and co-specialised assets.

These characteristics have important implications for action.

Strong implications for action

What type of implications should be derived from these characteristics for action? Figure 1 summarises possible recommendations for managers.

The *tacit knowledge dimension* is important for the management of innovation as a break within and around organisations. Its success is fully dependent upon people (especially champions, but not solely), trust in organisational rules and principles held in common. As we will see later, sharing tacit knowledge especially in the now largely service economies – is to a great extent dependent upon people's confidence in the level of implementation of the so-called principle of 'equity feeling', i.e. in the level of the 'justice' in individuals ⇔ groups ⇔ organisational transactions.

This distinction also has fundamental implications in other emerging areas of practice. It makes it possible to highlight extremely operational stakes which can arise, for example, from the fortuitous destruction of mechanisms patiently implemented, or the outsourcing of processes or key resources, of a more or less tacit nature.

In outsourcing decisions, for example, differentiation between tacit knowledge and explicit knowledge is important, since it underlines their dynamic complementarities. In the case of the transfer of an activity in which the tacit dimension is prevalent, it is obvious that the transferring organisation loses a key share of its intangible heritage, necessary to its competitiveness. This is all the more important to note as in many outsourcing contracts, the customer is not at all in a position to master the allowance of externalised human resources. It is also advisable to add that the fragmentation of resources necessarily resulting from outsourcing carries in itself some risks of the destruction of processes of knowledge creation, which until now have been under the control of the organisation.

In addition, this differentiation makes it possible to highlight the level of strategic importance of the knowledge considered, with that considered as non-strategic knowledge being potentially assimilated to the level of 'commodities'.

There are also implications at a more general level for strategic choices, especially with regards to the type of knowledge to be developed and the type of value to be derived from such knowledge. With regards to the second question in particular, Winter (1987) stressed that, insofar as the company must maximise the value drawn from its competences and knowledge, these must be kept – as far as possible – non-transferable, i.e. as dominantly tacit. But by doing so, the company becomes strongly dependent upon key individuals and therefore more vulnerable to any increase in personnel turnover. If, on the other hand, the company finds it beneficial to develop a policy of licence or of co-operation (due to the fact, for example, of a difficulty in protection) then the company must accentuate the transferable character of the knowledge, i.e. its formalised character.

On the whole, the tacit dimension has important implications for the management of knowledge in organisations. Indeed, a component of knowledge is all the more strategic, as it comprises ipso facto an inimitable aspect, i.e. it is strongly specific to the organisation and hence non-transferable to the firm's competitors.

The *non-programmable, unpredictable nature of tacit knowledge* also has its proper managerial implications. Two of them must be stressed particularly here: the importance for organisations to develop empathy as a principle of management, especially with regards to a 'not generally believed' or 'not native here' idea on innovation; second, as far as the management of innovation projects is concerned, the importance of devoting a substantial effort to overlap tasks and efforts, especially in the earlier stages.

The *dialectical nature of the dialogue between tacit knowledge and explicit knowledge* is certainly one of those dimensions that are very difficult to tackle. A lot of projects in knowledge management fail because of the weak integration of this dimension by those in charge of their implementation. At the instrumental level, *ad hoc* processes, mechanisms of cross-fertilisation and incentive systems must be implemented. At the monitoring level, specific metrics and scorecards have to be designed and widely diffused within organisations. New rules for reducing people's anxiety about the transfer (explicitation) of their tacit knowledge are still to be defined and made known. In short, this dimension is certainly among those for which companies, and more generally organisations, do not allocate sufficient effort.

At a more general level, the utilisation of IPR policies constitutes a field for action: this is especially due to the reinforcement of legal rules at the international

Key Characteristics of Knowledge	Implications for Knowledge creation and Innovation
The tacit dimension of knowledge	Successful innovation is fully dependent upon people's trust in organisational rules and common beliefs.
The nonprogrammable, nonpredictable nature of tacit knowledge	An important effort should be allocated to empathy, acceptation of ideas generally not held, and selection of research areas overlapping among projects, especially in the earlier phases.
The dialectical nature of knowledge creation	The general management has to make a special effort, via ad hoc processes, towards the organisation of a dialogue – and cross-fertilisation – between tacit knowledge (human capital) and explicit knowledge (structural capital). Specific indexes for performance measurement and monitoring should be implemented. Development of a strong IPR policy (patents, brands, methods protection).
The importance of complementary assets	Knowledge creation should be implemented by integrating several functional competences from the start. Risks of failure will be then reduced. Complementary assets should be looked for within as well as outside the organisation.
Creating knowledge is path-dependent	"What is good for the goose is not necessarily good for the gander". The general management has to evaluate carefully the organisation's absorptive capacity with regards to the planned innovations (products, processes, norms, etc.)

Figure 5.1 Key characteristics of knowledge and implications for action.

Source: Bounfour (2003: 106)

level, including in the European arena. Protection methods for innovation are among the areas of scholarly research, due in particular to the generalisation of RTD networks, including at the European level. This question was raised by Winter (1987) in a piece of research undertaken within the framework of the *Yale Survey of R&D Executives*. This survey consists of a broad investigation relating to various facets of innovation, in particular with regards to the protection dimension of knowledge. One of the questions raised relates to the evaluation of the effectiveness of protection methods for innovation. The results show that, except for petroleum refining, patents are considered better suited to protecting the innovations of products than those relating to the processes themselves. A second element of Winter's conclusion is that it is not necessary to engage in a process of protection by the patents to innovate. This is the case in particular for the semiconductor industries, where the recorded rates are scarcely higher than the average of the sectors considered. The importance of the patent in sectors such as pharmaceuticals is strongly argued by the articulable, observable and independent nature of innovation in this industry.

This differentiation is also important for innovation strategies: the concept of being first to enter the market was analysed by Teece (1989). Strategic behaviour and related results are naturally dependent upon several factors: the mode of appropriability of results, the paradigm of prevailing design and the importance of complementary assets (see above). The mode of appropriability refers to the environment of the innovation. The points considered here are those relating to the nature of the technology developed (a product or a process, on a given level of 'tacitness'). However, one can see the extent to which the distinction between tacit knowledge and explicit knowledge is stimulative, insofar as the more tacit knowledge is, the less easy it is to transfer out of the organisation, with the resultant low imitability factor.

By recalling the importance of *complementary assets* for innovation, my aim is to stress that innovation no longer takes place as a linear process. In modern organisations, innovation takes place by mobilising different disciplines and different competences, from research to after-sales service. This is, in fact, an idea that is widely held within innovation communities and among practitioners.

Finally, by stressing the fact that *creating knowledge is path-dependent*, I would like to emphasise the importance of organisational contingency in innovation efforts. We must stand that old saying on its head; what is sauce for the goose is definitely not sauce for the gander. This is one of the main messages of the evolutionary approach that we fully support for intangibles management. Therefore, top management should be very careful in managing innovation projects. In fact, the absorptive capacity of the organisation should be carefully evaluated – an equilibrium has to be found between past routines and new routines.

Enabling conditions for knowledge creation

Considering innovation as mainly an organisational issue necessitates not only the analysis of its managerial implications, but also the definition of its conditions for enablement. The main concepts for this have been defined by Nonaka and Takeuchi (1995) in their joint book *The Knowledge Creating Company*. Five conditions are considered necessary here; the role of the organisation being to provide the necessary context for knowledge accumulation at the individual level, as well as at the level of activities and groups of activities.

But whatever the complexity of knowledge and its management, most of the literature developments, at least those dealing with knowledge creation, are built on one major hypothesis: the existence of a single organisation, with relatively stable frontiers. So far, we do really have a general theory of knowledge creation and dissemination within unstable organisations, e.g. with unstable frontiers. In short, we still lack research that really addresses the issue of joint intangible assets.

The next section will address the issue of organisational design as an important issue for understanding the dynamics of organisations, networks and communities, and therefore for knowledge creation and dissemination. We make the hypothesis that organisations are evolving: concrete and modelisable sequences need to be conceived, and tested in new organisational settings, so as to understand the real knowledge economy dynamics.

Knowledge and the issue of organisational design

In the knowledge economy, several questions are posed to organisations and their management:

- How should organisations articulate their knowledge innovative capabilities?
- What type of organisational design should be privileged to meet the knowledge economy's key requirements?
- What kind of sequences are, or should be, observed?
- What type of knowledge assets are mobilised according to the different observed, or to be observed, sequences?
- Under what conditions do organisations better leverage their knowledge creation and dissemination capabilities?

The Hau-Ba model addresses this issue in a very concrete and, from our perspective, very innovative way. The model considers that space design is a particularly relevant perspective for managing innovative capabilities within and around organisations in the twenty-first century. Hence the high potential of building on the Japanese Ba approach, as it has been developed by Professors Nonaka and Konno (1998). However, this perspective, instead of its powerful potential, does not address clearly the issue of sequences of knowledge exchange, their articulation in time, or the conditions of their embeddedness in organisational processes. Hence the Hau-Ba theory (Bounfour, 2000, 2003), which completes the Ba theory with an important component, specifically addressing these conditions of embedness and, as we move forward, helps to solve the critical issue of sequences.

In concrete terms, for any organisation, the model aims at:

- Identifying the most critical spaces for innovation: physical spaces, virtual spaces and mental spaces. This of course necessitates a deep analysis of the content and characterisation of each of these spaces, as well as of their relative importance.
- Defining the critical sequences for leveraging innovation capabilities. From the managerial point of view, the critical issue lies not only in characterising and identifying the relative importance of spaces but, more importantly, in defining and articulating sequences. This issue of sequences is certainly one of the most critical ones. It aims at addressing this concrete managerial question: how do you start building innovative spaces? And in what type of order?
- Defining the contingent factors for leveraging innovation capabilities (conditions of embedness). This question of embedness is, of course, not really

new in the literature. The debate of organisational routines to a certain extent already covers this issue. But the problem is posed here from a slightly different angle. This issue is as follows: how can organisations make the knowledge flow really embedded into its routines? Under what conditions might such an embeddedness be achieved? The Hau-Ba model addresses this issue by considering it from two complementary angles: the anthropological view, which focuses on mechanisms of social exchange, and the philosophical view, which puts forward the issue of recognition in societies as a key mechanism for socialising.

The Hau-Ba model

The Hau-Ba model has been developed on the basis of the consideration of the deep transformation of socioeconomic systems, and especially the emergence of the community as an importance perspective for organising activities, which leads to the emergence of what has been conceptualised elsewhere as 'communalism' (Bounfour, 2006). Indeed, the question of communities governance, beyond the designing and articulating of mental, physical and virtual spaces, is clearly posed: how is it possible to embed some rules within groups and communities, without necessarily making them explicit – as a basis of a new 'organisational implicit order' (Bounfour, 2005).

In previous works (Bounfour 2005, 2006), a taxonomy of socioeconomic systems has been proposed, based on the issue of emerging communities to which are associated specific types of intangibles, as well as specific types of IPRs regimes. These points will be developed further in this chapter. But besides these categories, a managerial issue is still posed: how can we articulate the transactional regime to the community regime, and what type of conceptual approach should be privileged? Answering this question, we suggest reconsidering certain principles of the theory of gift; more precisely those developed by the French anthropologist Marcel Mauss (1924), especially the Hau principle; and confront them with the Japanese Ba theory, developed by Nishima and applied by Nonaka and Konno (1998) in the management science area. The confrontation of these two theories led to a hybrid theory, named by Bounfour elsewhere the Hau-Ba Theory (Bounfour, 2000, 2003).

The Ba theory insists on the importance of articulating three spaces (Ba) in conducting any process of innovation: the physical Ba, the virtual Ba and the mental Ba. But beyond innovation practices per se, this approach is very stimulating for designing and implementing any form of collective organising: innovation, production, marketing, human resources and networking (Figure 5.2).

The Hau theory refers to the triple obligations of behaviour in primitive societies, brought to the fore by Mauss: the obligation to use, to circulate and give back exchanged objects. Applied to our present societies, these obligations appear extraordinarily modern. Indeed, modern organisations are seeking to implement these principles of knowledge exchange within – as well as around – their boundaries, and this is the basic reason for the existence of knowledge

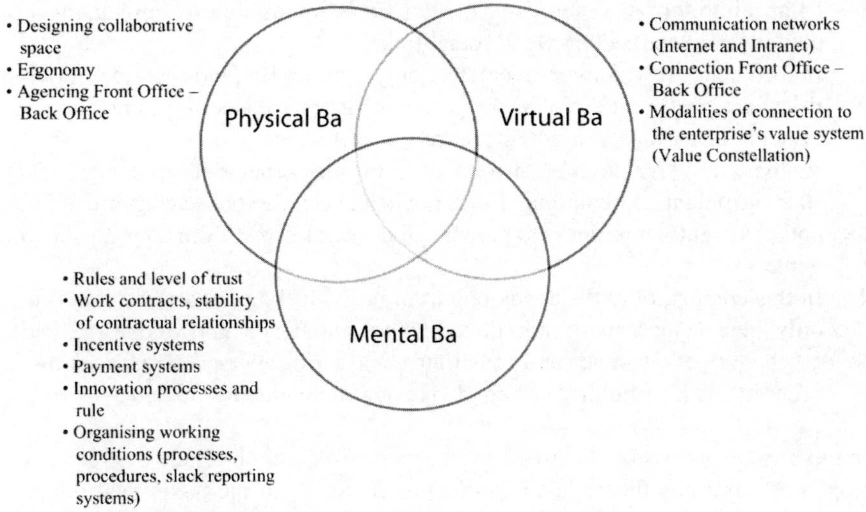

Figure 5.2 Modalities of organising: the triple Ba approach.

Source: Bounfour (2006: 188)

management. Organisations are seeking to make these rules as embedded as possible in innovation processes, and more generally for any process of information and knowledge exchange (Bounfour, 2000). This, of course, raises the issue of the feeling of equity between individual and organisation relationships (Adams, 1963; Wilkins and Ouchi, 1983).

At this stage, three questions are posed:

1. How can we articulate the 'Hau'with the 'Ba', and what should be the building blocks of a Hau-Ba model?
2. What types of sequences should be considered in implementing such a model in practice?
3. And finally, what are the contingency elements to be considered, taking into account the two distinguished orders (transactional order versus community order)?

With regards to the first question, we can already stress that among the barriers relative to the implementation of any process of innovation and, more generally, to the management of intangibles, those related to the mental Ba are the most difficult to tackle, because they are the most problematic. They are substantial mainly because of the deep transformation of social links within organisations and their increasingly short-termist behaviour. Development of stress and the increasing resort to managerial 'palliatives' such as coaching, perfectly illustrate such a crisis. What should be the component of a mental Ba, the best adapted to such a context?

Four possible responses or arguments can be put forward:

1 In absolute terms, a stabilised mental Ba is impossible to implement in a context characterised by weak social links;
2 In a context of dynamic movements, only moving Ba (and therefore moving rules) are possible to implement (which calls for considering intra-organisational relationships as a whole and real spot market);
3 As the sociologist strategic theory recommends (Crozier et Friedberg, 1977), 'faire semblant' ('pretending') does not help, because social actors are rational and sufficiently intelligent to perceive the weak interest from them to play the game;
4 In this context, only the development of individual games are relevant (here, only the development of individual human capital – i.e. knowledge and social assets – are of relevance and constitute a real serious perspective for action, in order to ensure a fluidity of knowledge at a more global – societal – level).

In this case, is it possible to envisage an articulation with the Hau? There are two responses here: one theoretical and one empirical. From the theoretical point of view, it is clear that the Hau can be fastened to the Ba, and vice versa. The Ba theory tells us simply that it is important to allocate a singular place to the mental space in organisations in order to get things going. We have just learned the extremely critical character of this dimension, as well as its difficulties, but it shows us how to implement the Ba (we mean here a conceptualised 'how', beyond the case quoted here and there. The Hau theory tells us the extreme modernity of the observation of the embedded rules of usage, circulation and restitution of intangible resources in the knowledge economy. From this point of view, the Hau refines the Mental Ba, of which it constitutes an advanced stage.

From the conceptual point of view, to talk about the Hau-Ba consists of suggesting a particular deployment of the mental space, and to certain extent, an advanced stage of it. We can then name 'Hau-Ba' a singular mode of articulation within a community, allying the 'Hau spirit' with the Mental Ba while surpassing it.

By suggesting, we re-loop with the recognition rules considered earlier: the Hau-Ba corresponds to a mode of collective action in which recognition – via knowledge – becomes or tends to become a 'total organisational fact' (Mauss spoke about a total social fact – *'un fait social total'*) recognisable in quasi-organic or organic communities, according to our initial typology.

From an empirical point of view, if the conditions of the implementation of a mental Ba become more and more difficult to assemble, the same situation applies, but in a more accentuated way to the Hau-Ba. The Hau-Ba model can be fully deployed only in organic or quasi-organic communities, localised for the most part outside the transactional space (even if we observe the survival of industrial workers' communities in specific sectors – metal workers for instance – but for how long?)

In brief, a Hau-Ba model is conceivable, but its conditions of implementation are hard to assemble; only the community order is likely to respond. From this point of view, investments in knowledge management programmes by companies, in the context of a transactional order, might be considered as a waste of resources. Naturally, the reality of organisations is more nuanced; and contingency factors, in particular those related to the existence of a strong industrial culture, should be considered with great attention.

With regards to the second question – the question of sequences – what types of sequences should be considered in implementing such a model in practice? We would consider here three spaces, in a syncretic way, and articulate them to the gift and recognition dimensions.

Six sequences can then be briefly considered both from theoretical and empirical perspectives.

Sequence 1: Physical Ba ⇒ Mental Ba ⇒ Virtual Ba

This is the most observable and common way for organisations to create a dynamic space for innovation and socialising. Traditional human activities have been created based on interaction in physical spaces. The physical space allows interacting and recognising others as similar peers. Workshops as Physical Ba provide the opportunity to test, exchange and build respect and confidence. The Physical Ba is a way of preparing the Mental Ba. Initial gifts often intervene in the Physical Ba. Depending upon the type of activities, different Physical Ba might be mobilised: shops, offices, cafeterias, meeting rooms, conference rooms and transportation. In most activities, the Physical Ba is a proven way of creating a Mental Ba; people

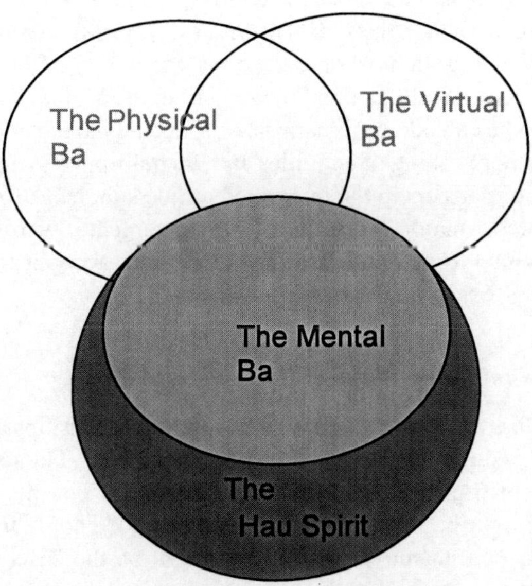

Figure 5.3 The building blocks of the Hau-Ba model.

Source: Bounfour (2006: 191)

can gauge others and recognise them as similar fellows. They can see their eyes, and even develop physical 'contactivity', depending of course upon the considered future. The undertaking of a Physical Ba is a good condition for the Mental Ba, and a prerequisite to it. The introduction of the Virtual Ba does not pose a problem, in a further step, but the question of a full substitution to the two previous Ba might legitimately be posed.

Sequence 2: Physical Ba ⇒ Virtual Ba ⇒ Mental Ba

This sequence can be understood in different ways; first, in the case of organisations seeking to create a community based on the physical experience of the Physical Ba as a starting point. In many manufacturing industries, this is still the dominant – and even the only – way of hiring new workers (see "The Hau-Ba model put into practice" below). The Physical Ba is the way to start, but the movement to the Virtual Ba does not work in this context.

Hence, the second category of organisations seeks to move from the Physical Ba to the Virtual Ba. This is observed more and more often in value-added services activities such as IT, consulting and all activities where freelancing and nomadism is becoming the dominant way of carrying out activities. After migration from the Physical Ba to the Virtual Ba, people become orphans; hence the importance of creating a Mental Ba arises. In most cases, this is initiated by a reintroduction – at least in part – of the Physical Ba. This was the case for Gemini Consulting, as described by Von Krogh *et al.* (2000). Gemini Consulting was forced to invite its consultants to meet in their offices on Fridays, as a way of recreating the Mental Ba and therefore socialising. In most organisations, the *passage* from the Physical Ba to the Virtual Ba does not allow a real movement to the Mental Ba. But, of course, the question has to be considered dynamically, especially in the inter-organisational context. Here, the networking of activities and the multiplicity of partnerships (see the large number of partners in the integrated projects in the European framework programme) creates a major constraint of the movement towards the Virtual Ba. The problem has also to be considered by taking into account the habit-forming effect of the virtual world on the new generation.

Sequence 3: Virtual Ba ⇒ Physical Ba ⇒ Mental Ba

This sequence refers to a context in which business relationships are firstly built in virtual spaces. This might be the case for spot transactions, but also for permanent or semi-permanent transactions and/or relationships. The movement towards the Physical Ba might be induced by the necessity for people to socialise under permanent or non-permanent contexts. This might be the case, for instance, for residential seminars organised with the main purpose of reinforcing social links among an *ad hoc* community (for instance, marketing teams or researchers). In this case, the Physical Ba will be used as a way of building and preparing for the advent of the Mental Ba. This might also be the case with temporary relationships outside the vertical organisation (e.g. freelance business).

Sequence 4: Virtual Ba ⇒ Mental Ba ⇒ Physical Ba

This will certainly be the case for the new generation, for whom the Virtual Ba is the reality of the world. In this case, the Virtual Ba might be the preparatory phase for the Mental Ba, which will then be followed by the Physical Ba.

Sequence 5: Mental Ba ⇒ Physical Ba ⇒ Virtual Ba

This might be considered as quite a theoretical process. Can an organisation, a network or a community start by building a Mental Ba without any Physical Ba or Virtual Ba? Or to ask the question differently: can a Mental Ba pre-exist the Physical or Virtual Ba? This is not observable, so far, in commercial organisations. However, this is not true for specific communities where the exchange is embedded in the profile of people. Research communities, for instance, do exchange ideas, concepts and publications without necessarily meeting in physical spaces. For these communities, the Mental Ba is embedded in the nature of activities and the profile of people. This might also be the case for the people in charge of security questions within organisations.

Sequence 6: Mental Ba ⇒ Virtual Ba ⇒ Physical Ba

The same question is posed here. Stating that a Mental Ba pre-exists the virtual Ba implies a spontaneous mental order, without any social interaction (be it in virtual or in physical spaces). Also, so far, we should consider this sequence as more observable in specific concrete settings.

With regards to the third question, what are the contingency elements to be considered when taking into account the two distinguished orders (i.e. transactional order versus community order)? (See Table 5.1)

The Hau-Ba model put into practice[2]

This case study was explored to build the Hau-Ba model, which is a combination of two theories initially associated by Bounfour (2000, 2006): the theory of the Hau, which describes a system of exchange; and the theory of the Ba, which presents the different physical, virtual or mental spaces enabling knowledge creation and transfer. Thus, at the intersection of anthropology, sociology and management, the Hau-Ba model establishes a knowledge exchange global incentive approach, in which 'community' members give, receive then give back knowledge or symbols, based on a fight for recognition within their organisation.

An immersion in a French foundry during 18 months provided the background for this case, which is the first of a series of three. This enabled us to follow knowledge exchanges between senior and junior employees during the critical period of a demographic and social transition.

On one hand, from the theoretical perspective, we open the scope of the social exchange theory (Mauss 1950, Blau 1964, current works of the *Ecole française du don*). On the other hand, we call the concept of Ba developed by Nonaka and Konno

Table 5.1 The Hau-Ba Model, type of organisational regime, barriers and practices

	Transactional Regime	*Constrained Communities*	*Quasi-Organic Communities*	*Organic Communities*
Physical Ba	An important barrier that is more and more observable, due to pressures on costs for resource allocation to physical Ba (offices) – hence the difficulties in organising collaborative work, as well as distributing recognition among individuals.	An important barrier, due to the fact that most constrained communities do not have access to enough proper resources to invest in Physical Ba.	Weak to strong barrier, depending upon the type of community considered (software communities are a priori the most prepared for surpassing this barrier).	Barrier to be considered depending upon the community to emerge, as well as the available resources.
Virtual Ba	Investment efforts for the virtual Ba. No particular barriers, except those related to the level of investment.	An articulation effort of the individual Ba of the community members.	Articulation of the virtual space to the mental space, to which it serves as a support.	Barrier to be considered according to the available resources.
Mental Ba	A crucial barrier, due to the weakening of the work contracts. Barriers to be considered according to the considered activities.	A reasoned Mental Ba, generally governed by relationships near to the spot market.	A Mental Ba fully deployed.	A Mental Ba fully deployed.
The Hau-Ba Model	A quasi-impossible deployment under a pure transactional regime.	Unsuited model.	An adapted model. (This is the case for the communities governed by the copyleft principle.)	A fully adapted model.

Source: Bounfour (2006: 191)

(1998). If the Ba theory explains knowledge creation through knowledge transfer, it also provides the conditions for knowledge exchanges. Finally, we refer to the German philosophy of the fight for recognition, which can be read as the backdrop of the Hau-Ba model (Honneth 2000; Caillé, 2007). As a synthesis, we propose the design of the Hau-Ba system, confirming the intuition that these two concepts are associated, and highlighting *how* they are correlated within a unique model.

Problematic and questions of research

The organisation that hosted the case agreed to the intervention of a researcher, in order to help it face the critical situation of losing its technical memory. Affected by the demographic transition and the desertion of blue-collar jobs by the younger generation, plants had to deal with another threat related to the dislocation of their memory during a merger, and the associated structural changes imposing a market-oriented design instead of a trade-oriented one.

In this turbulent period, the primary and pragmatic focus was to provide research on how to save the organisational memory. We decided to choose as a theoretical backcloth, the analysis of the ongoing knowledge exchange system that led to the Hau-Ba concept.

Thus, we could word the problematic as follows:

> *Primary question*: What are the exchange modalities that characterise the saving of the intra-organisational technical memory?

… and its four secondary questions:

1. What is the *composition* of the exchange initialised by the knowledge transfer? What structure, form and content characterise the circulation of the assets included in the exchange?
2. What is the *spatial circulation* of the exchange assets? What are the places that we can identify to describe where the knowledge exchanges happen?
3. What is the *consensus* adopted by the actors of the exchange? What are the exchange principles and the underlying motivations that sustain the observable rules and rites inside the groups?
4. What is the impact of the organisational *context* on the exchange system? What are the contingencies of the model?

We conducted the explorations within several 'trade communities' and then we synthesised our results, in order to produce a global model.

Presuppositions before defining our proposals

- The 'gift' model applied to knowledge exchanges is possible within organisations.
- Actors involved in the exchanges are shop workers, technicians, engineers and researchers, all belonging to a specific 'trade community'.
- The nature of the exchanged knowledge is constitutive of the technical memory, which is made of:
  - knowledge called 'trade knowledge'
  - declarative, procedural and judgmental knowledge (Girod-Séville, 1995)
  - individual and/or collective, official and/or underground knowledge
  - explicit and tacit knowledge (words, documentation, gestures, gazes and inter-subjectivity).

At this stage, the problematic can be clarified by four proposals, which all stemmed from the questions of the research (see Table 5.2).The theoretical backup of the research can be summarised as follows in Table 5.3.

Table 5.2 What are the exchanges modalities that characterise the saving of the intra-organisational technical memory?

Q1. What is the composition of the exchange initialised by the knowledge transfer?	*Q2. What is the spatial circulation of the exchange assets?*	*Q3. What is the consensus adopted by the actors of the exchange?*	*Q4: What is the impact of the organisational context on the exchange system?*
P1: Four types of assets are noticeable in the exchange: the transferred knowledge, the used and appropriated knowledge, the created knowledge, and the symbols, all related to the 3 moments of the gift.	P2: Some physical, mental and virtual Ba entice Hau assets circulation. The observation of the Hau depends on the coexistence and the development of specific Ba.	P3: The mutual recognition sustains the Hau-Ba, working as an intrinsic motivation for the gift, issued from people who can be considered as members of quasi-organic communities.	P4: The survival context influences the model positively. In some respect, the limit is to consider that such a context is the lone justifying factor. The sharing of this emotional climate erases 'the strategic games' logic in favour of the adoption of the Hau.
Temporary conclusion: Confirmed proposal. Sometimes, the gift back is symbolic when the capacities are not enough to create knowledge. Function of the gift-back: the recognition. This exchange is a cycle.	*Temporary conclusion:* The presence of a mental Ba is essential to the full development of the Hau. The physical Ba is the origin of the process; it houses the initial gift. The virtual Ba is minor in the model.	*Temporary conclusion:* The recognition principle, once satisfied, reinforces the psychological contract. This feeling is all the more obvious because the community is organic.	*Temporary conclusion:* The survival background puts us into the perspective of the 'transmission', where not giving means losing. This feeling causes a kind of 'union sacrée'. This dimension constitutes one of the limits of our research, which remains to be tested in a context free from the survival anxiety.

Schema of the design

The transfer base of the memory saving process is included in an exchange cycle, which is the core of our research object. We are going to try to characterise the modalities of this exchange in order to be able to draw roadmaps for action on every lever involved in the cycle. (See Figure 5.4.)

As a summary, the model we want to end up with articulates itself with the system as set out in Figure 5.5. This diagram shows the outputs of the Hau-Ba application – the links and the occurrences between the different dimensions remain to be discovered.

The methodology and the design of the research

Adopting a 'moderate' constructive paradigm was the best way to reconcile the early theory of the Hau-Ba with new elements directly drawn from the field. With regards to the 'Grounded Theory' (Glaser and Strauss, 1964), we were able to mix our initial 'intuition' from the coverage of the Hau and Ba literature with the results of an in-depth exploration, fed by a qualitative longitudinal study, and based on participant observation, within a major metallurgic company. Three cases out of fourteen were retained to conduct the analysis.

Table 5.3 What are the exchanges modalities that characterise the saving of the intra-organisational technical memory?

Q1. What is the composition of the exchange initialised by the knowledge transfer?	*Q2. What is the spatial circulation of the exchange assets?*	*Q3. What is the consensus adopted by the actors of the exchange?*	*Q4: What is the impact of the organisational context on the exchanges system?*
Hau theory: Mauss 1950; Blau 1964; current works of the 'Ecole française du don'. (Karsenti, Godbout, Caillé); Godbout, 2007.	Ba theory: developed by Nonaka et Konno, 1998. Knowledge transfer: Nonaka, 1994; Nonaka et Takeuchi 1995.	Recognition theory: Honneth 2000 ; Caillé, 2007. Psychological contract: Delobbe, 2005.	Professional identity, survival: Sainsaulieu, 1985; Sardas, 2004; Dubar, 2003, 2004; Osty, 1998 ; Blin, 2005. Poltier, Guenette, Henchoz, 2004; Boisseroles de Saint Jullien, 2005; Molinié, 2004; Flamant, 2005.

Sources: Organisational memory: Walsh and Ungson, 1991; Aschcraft, 1994; Girod-Séville 1995, 1997; Moorman and Miner, 1998. Socialisation: Dubar, 1991; Lacaze, 2005. Quasi-organic community, community of practice: Bounfour, 2006; Lave and Wenger, 1991; Esposito, 2000.

Note: question Q4 will not be pursued independently, but will be embedded in Q2 and Q3, as Q4 is an integral part of them.

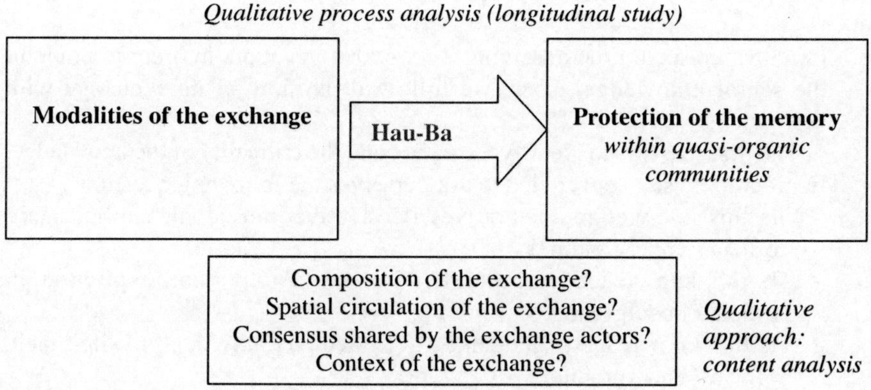

Figure 5.4 The specific Ba active in the foundry workers' community.

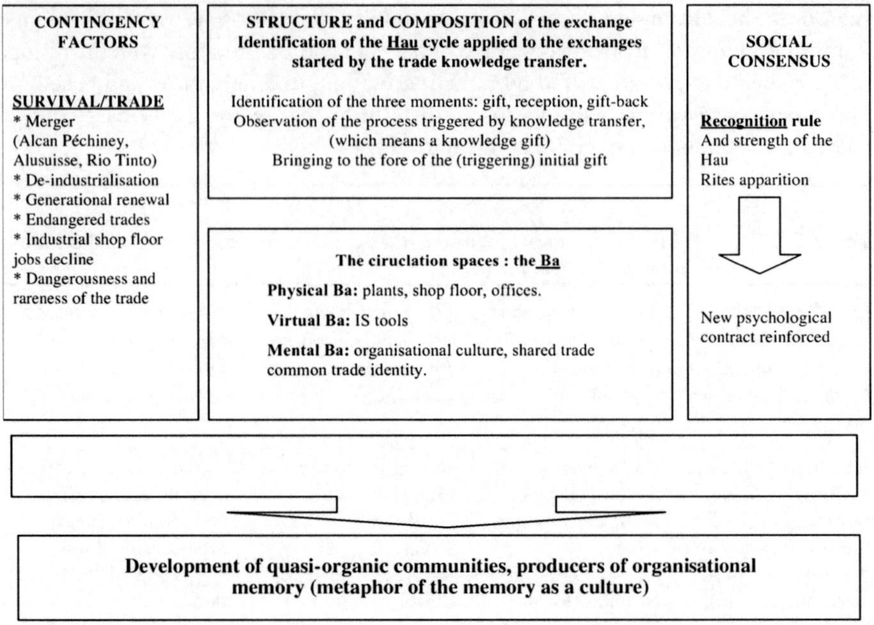

Figure 5.5 Hau-Ba model.

The one we are presenting in this paper is related to the exploration within a community of French foundry workers.

Much like ethnographers embedded totally in the field, we collected all data without discrimination: major events in the foundry (e.g. strikes, turnover, training, management activity, etc.) were entered, in chronological order, into a matrix.

We also identified the category of knowledge that was concerned in each exchange, and in the memory saving process.

- Initially, we spent time observing the workers in action, in order to pinpoint the senior knowledge. Then, we followed the flow of its exchange with newcomers.

  The first step was to identify the nature and the criticality of the knowledge. In order to do so, we were led to ask ourselves the following questions:
  - Is this knowledge declarative? (Collective/individual, explicit/tacit, official/ underground?)
  - Is this knowledge procedural? (Collective/individual, explicit/tacit, official/ underground?)
  - Is this knowledge of judgement? (Collective/individual, explicit/tacit, official/ underground?)

At this time, we were able to list and characterise the know-how and the knowledge (tacit or explicit) which were at stake in the transfer, as the core of the memory. This helped to track the four stages of the SECI matrix involved in every knowledge transfer occuring in the Ba (Nonaka & Takeuchi, 1995).

The next part of the process reveals the Hau cycle and its social rites:

- Is this knowledge given (transferred by seniors to newcomers)?
- Is this knowledge received (used by newcomers)?
- Is this knowledge returned (new knowledge creation)?
- Is anything else returned (gifts of symbols, etc.)?

At this stage, we were able to confirm *the gift model* within the context of an organisational knowledge exchange.

- Second, we observed what kinds of 'Ba' were in place at the time:
  - Was any physical, mental or virtual Ba identifiable?
  - Are they developed in synchronisation or not? (What is their order of apparition?)
  - What kind of knowledge transfer do they characterise? (in reference to the SECI matrix, Nonaka & Takeuchi, 1995)
  - What moment of the gift do they sustain?

This part was conducted as a longitudinal study combined with a process analysis.

- As a second section of our exploration, we analysed the logic of actions that were supporting the exchange:
  - What values are justifying the knowledge exchange: interest or recognition?
  - What are the recognition assets?
  - What are the effects on the organisation (on the psychological contract)?

This was done by analysing from the content of a collection of unsolicited speeches and interviews.

Data treatment

The primary data from day-to-day observations and interviews were assigned codes, as a way to categorise the data and determine the nature of the assets in the gift, as well as the different steps in the exchange process. The data was collated to tie the Ba and the Hau concepts together and bring forward their connections, in addition to the sequences of the Ba inside the Hau process.

In short, as an output of the research, and at the crossroads of the two previous overlapping theories, we proposed a specific version of the Hau-Ba model. This model was inspired by the early works of Bounfour (2000, 2006) and fed by the empiric approach of our field research, which, in this particular case, deals with a very specific category of people: heavy industry workers in the 'old' western society.

The case study outputs

A. Description of the field of research: an old foundry community of workers

As mentioned before, the studied organisation was facing a critical issue related to the loss of its memory. The departure of many workers over the years, in conjunction with different restructuring plans and the baby-boomer phenomenon, meant that the company was losing a large set of skills, expertise and experience from its shop-floor. Senior employees were no longer used to orient and train new workers; the climate was typical of an organisation in crisis (Sainsaulieu, 1985). Employees were feeling like 'survivors' (Boisserolles Saint-Julien, 2005) and were no longer dynamically involved; most of the seniors were passively waiting to leave the company, considering their plant without a future.

At the same time, recruiting and retaining staff had become more and more of a challenge for managers, who had very few answers as to how to reverse such a fatalistic social trend. Nevertheless, the context changed when the decision was made, by the business unit's upper management, to move a production activity from another foundry. This new project brought the perspective of development and it also presented the organisation with a new challenge: not only to recruit people, but also to transfer knowledge from the seniors (the 'few who knew') to twenty newcomers, in a very short time (18 months).

The social background was also hindering the situation. The junior generation was poorly perceived by the seniors, and vice versa: after an attempt in 2001 to integrate four employees, who all left within the year, senior employees considered that the value they placed on the job was not shared anymore. They felt underestimated or disrespected by newcomers. It is a fact that young people nowadays do not desire the job nor the conditions (working in shifts, facing risks) associated with blue-collar positions. In many cases, when they enter the foundry, it is not the result of a choice. They walk a difficult path and face a breaking point in their career, so the necessity of working is then stronger than reluctance; nevertheless, we know that it is not enough to sustain long-run motivation. Furthermore, much like with mining and miners, a foundry is characterised by the pride of the people who work in the industry. Thus, we point out here one of the strong values shared by the members of what can be called a community. If pride is not felt right at the beginning of the integration process, or even worse, if the trade is not respected, the acceptance of the newcomer is difficult, if not impossible.

B. A specific model from the Hau-Ba theory

On-the-field preliminary actions: the implementation of a tutorial system

Before exploring and comparing the results with the Hau-Ba theory, we initially had to be sure that the conditions were right for the model to be potentially activated.

From survey results gathered by interviewing new employees, we noted that newcomers believed that on-the-job employees were not involved in their training. This triggered another wave of interviews, this time targeting the experienced workers. The conclusion indicated that the experts did not feel any recognition for training from the organisation. If knowledge transfer is considered a duty, they would want to be officially recognised for this role. The middle management took this request under consideration; as a result, they built a tutorial system and nominated specific tutors. This role, which had been historically very important, was considered to be proof of their respect and value. If employees were not nominated, they did not want to 'act' like a tutor in the foundry. This opinion was held by a high percentage of the seniors.

Also, one of the tacit rules in the foundry is that nobody questions the knowledge of someone else. An informal hierarchy does exist and employees must pay attention to avoid offending the pride of the 'experts'. Taking responsibility for the training of a newcomer could be considered within the community as having a defiant attitude, at least to the 'natural leaders'. As for them, they were waiting to be asked before getting involved. This is why management had to formalise the integration process: old experts would not have involved themselves in a training process without the official recognition of their 'value', and other on-the-job workers would not have replaced them in the training mission as it would have broken one of the tacit rules of the community, i.e. to respect the 'chiefs' (furnace pilots). In conclusion, it is important to notice that no monetary compensation was requested by the experts; a pure question of recognition was at stake, and strongly tacitly expressed.

The foundry workers team: the definition of a community

The return to a practice from the 'glory years' was a way to reconcile 'survivors' with their past. It also refreshed their memories about the fact that they all belonged to a historic, prestigious and glorious company. Therefore, the sense of pride was revived, and the seniors remembered the value of their company and their jobs in the French industrial frame. The complexity of the trade, the high level of risk, the contact with molten metal, and the gigantic size of the machinery used to produce the material, all made workers feel empowered, like they coexisted with 'tamed monsters'. All these aspects built a very strong job identity, shared by what can be called a 'community' – a community that can be defined in several ways. First, the foundry workers can be called a community of blood, since most of them have come from the same village, for many generations. Second, it can also be seen as a community of space: they all share the same shop-floor and face the dangers together on the furnaces. They use a common space to work in tight coordination.

Finally, we can evoke a community of spirit as well, when they have developed the same social identity. Belonging to the same historic organisation/industry, being involved in the union activities and sharing similar jobs with very specific trade characteristics (danger, nobility) developed a feeling of belonging and a strong trade identity. Then, in conjunction with Tonnïes (1977), we can declare the foundry workers a collective community.

It is a matter of fact that every community applies its own social rituals and initiation rites; thus it is interesting to find a possible connection between the concept of community and the knowledge exchange system, especially for the rites that they can share. These rites are analysed at the same time as the Hau principles are brought to the fore. This is what will be covered in the next section.

The trigger of the Hau-Ba system: the original gift

Once the tutor's role was formalised and agreed on, the knowledge exchanges started. Thus, it became possible for us to track them.

As a consequence, the first result of the tutorial system was to restore the psychological contract tacitly established within the organisation, making it favourable again. In short, the psychological contract defines the sense of equity felt by an employee towards his/her company, and influences the level of commitment (Delobbe, 2005).

Indeed, once nominated as 'tutors', the senior employees involved in the training process felt that equity was respected. Then, they considered it a duty to help the new generation take over the trade. For them, it was an opportunity to leave a legacy. After 25 to 30 years spent in the same plant, passing on their experience was considered a way to legitimise their whole career. It was not considered a task or a 'chore', but a necessary *gift* (this word 'gift' was formulated in interviews). Nevertheless, they would not have given the gift if it had not been recognised. The organisation had to show explicit signs of recognition of this potential gift. This recognition, from the management, can be seen as the *'original gift'*, the symbolic one that triggers the start of the Hau process.

It is worth noting that this original gift is double. It concerns both tutors and newcomers. For them, the initial gift to make newcomers act as 'receivers' is to give the promise of a long-term job, after the training period. Without this outlook, the involvement in the training and the ability of receiving would be non-existent.

The start of the Hau-Ba system: the first gifts of phase 1

Based on the reassurance of the psychological contract, first gifts from the tutors were noticeable but as a gift that was not 'risky'. Acting like a test, the first gift dealt with declarative and procedural knowledge (Girod-Seville, 1995), a kind of 'easy to hold' memory. No tacit or personal knowledge was at stake in this stage. This knowledge transfer happened in what can be called the 'cold area' of the foundry, which is physically separated from the real life of the foundry workers' community. This later happens in the 'hot area', close to the molten metal and the furnaces, during casting phases. In the cold area, a tutor with vast experience spends three months with the newcomers, delivering key messages on safety and molten metal knowledge. The initial three months are absolutely critical in the integration process, and most of the employee departures happened during these initial phases.

The reasons for the break are twofold:

- The new employees can initiate the departure:
  - They realise the danger and understand that they cannot control their fear. They know that in this context, they cannot receive, nor give back.
  - They have learnt the conditions associated with being part of the community: facing the danger and dominating the fear. These conditions are intimately linked with the success of the gift process.
  - The ones who can not adjust to these conditions are those who leave.
- The tutor can also initiate the departure:
  - Testing the ability of the newcomer to receive the gift, if the tutor considers he is failing in the early stage of the gift process, he will not sponsor his integration.
  - On this basis, the tutor decides if the newcomers will become trustworthy in the 'hot area'. Before receiving the trade secrets in the heart of the foundry, they must have passed the confidence test.

With regards to this integration process from the cold to the hot area, there is no risk of knowledge waste because the training is started in the most basic area. They may sacrifice some 'trivial knowledge' to test the ability of the recipient to be a receiver; if they pass the test, then the risk of the gift is fully accepted. At this stage, we cannot speak about a total gift-gift back model.

This introduction to the application of the system of exchange (done in a physical and original Ba, 'the cold side') does not expect more than finding the hope for a new member. The newcomer is not asked to give back, but most show the proper attitude (the respect for the trade, which means the recognition for the knowledge gift) so that they will be endowed with the trust of the community. We understand that this also implicitly means the respect of the Hau. Indeed, if they know how to receive the first gift, then we can *trust* that they will give back somehow. Humility, respect and the desire to do well are all part of the right mind-set for future members of the community. These are also the behaviours which mean the 'reception'. At this stage, integrating the hot side of the foundry is acceptable; it is a step towards the acceptance in the group of experienced casting workers. Within the primary physical Ba (the hot section), the furnace pilots are going to transfer the ultimate knowledge, which is richer in terms of tacit and personal dimensions (Polanyi, 1983) – this knowledge cannot be transferred without social interactions.

The total Hau-Ba system: the gift-back boucle of phase 2

The training on the hot side of the foundry lasts 18 months. However, three years is the comprehensive time it takes to become a full fledged 'foundry worker'. At the very beginning, the newcomers only observe the process. They learn how to alleviate their fears and to integrate the codes expressed between workers.

These codes are used to work in synchronisation; often in conditions where no word is spoken, as the protective gear worn can cover up their voices. This close interaction takes place in the space composed by the furnaces, and that can be assimilated to a physical Ba. We can advance that the sharing of this Ba supports the socialisation (phase 1 in the SECI matrix of Nonaka and Takeuchi, 1995: 71–2, 89). Nevertheless, it should also be brought forward that this physical Ba would only work temporarily if a second, invisible one did not exist.

As a matter of fact, another Ba must be developed, this time a mental Ba. The characterisation of this mental Ba, discovered after coding, is the sharing of a common *emotional climate*. Indeed, in the hot section, danger is omnipresent. Lethal injuries or burns from explosions are always possible. Workers must stay vigilant, secure and the ability to control their own fear is absolutely necessary. The only way to face the risk and make the situation liveable is to deny the danger. Then, between acceptance and denial, the casting workers dominate their fear and never even allude to it: showing fear is tacitly forbidden or the whole balance would be disturbed.

The newcomers who are receiving knowledge of the trade on the hot side slowly integrate this demonstrated mental Ba. They give obvious proof of membership by accepting, one day, to assist the furnace pilots during the casting operation. If they are not ready to express a form of self-confidence at this stage, those who are not able to share this mental Ba cannot be part of the knowledge exchange anymore, and will leave the foundry.

The mental Ba enables the Hau fulfilment: the gift-back step

In the case of the foundry workers' community, the Hau-Ba system requires not only the investment of a physical Ba, but quickly a subsequent mental Ba. If it does not happen, the Hau mechanisms are jammed and the physical Ba is not strong enough to sustain the knowledge transfer alone. On the contrary, if the mental Ba is shared, then the Hau mechanism is fully realised and the physical Ba continues its role in the knowledge transfer.

From the viewpoint of the completion of the Hau, we allude to this stage of the cycle when it is time to give back. Even if nobody can identify the exact moment, all the actors involved in the Hau-Ba have faith that it will happen, anyhow. In this case, the gift-back takes multiple forms (intermediary gifts), but one seems stronger and is a greater determining factor because it is systematic and highly personal. Indeed, the gift-back is perceived tacitly by a kind of self-sacrifice: the symbolic 'gift' of the body, the acceptance to risk injury. Accepting the danger and hiding fear both belong to the same dimension of gift-back. After a transfer (of knowledge) from father to son, the reciprocity happens at a symbolic level: "I give you my body to go on with your life." The meta-meaning of the Hau is nothing other than a story of generational transmission.

However, although this gift-back is the major one compared to the others, it cannot happen right away. It needs time for the newcomer to build the start of a *trade identity*, the time of interaction where the *mental Ba* is embedded. This delay

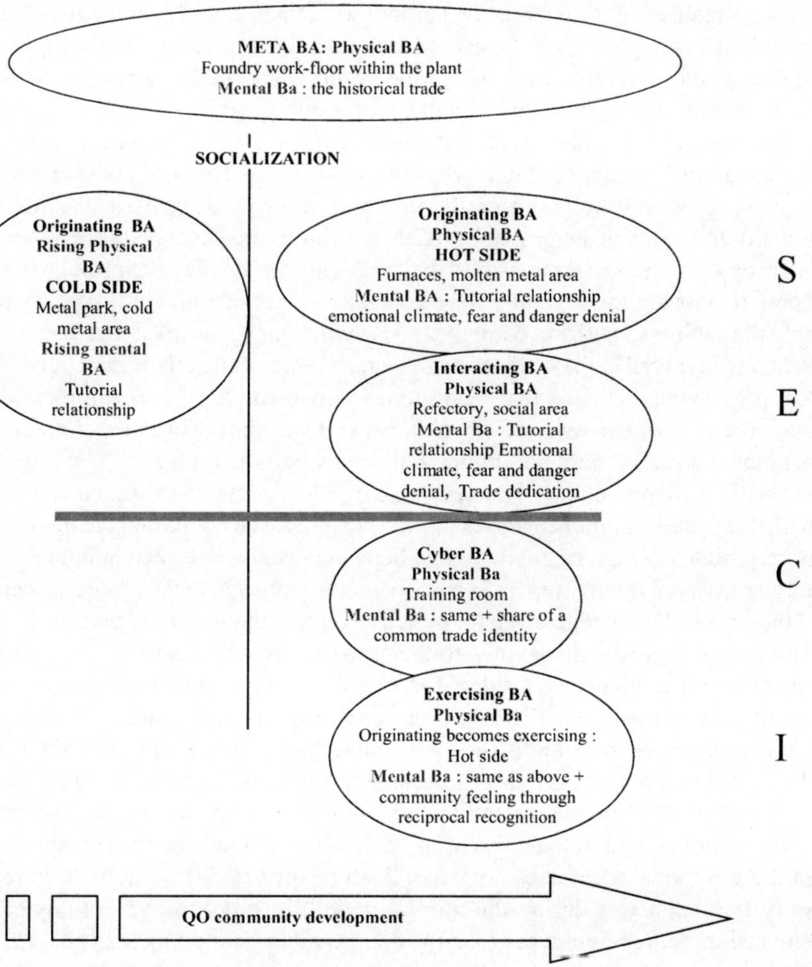

Figure 5.6 Active Ba in the foundry workers' community.

is also what gives the value of the gift (the gift is rare) and what defines the gift model (it requires patience from the initial givers).

In the meantime, as this main gift-back takes time to be returned, it is then important to show smaller signs of recognition, signs which confirm the status of giver to the receiver and proof that they are real members of the Hau. The role of intermediary gifts is to confirm the trust and the faith put into the receiver, trust that transforms him/her into a future giver. Nevertheless, the newcomers cannot give back knowledge of their trade experience when it is too short to be relevant. As a matter of fact, returning this new knowledge too early could also be seen as questioning the expertise of the ones who 'know', and may appear to be a lack of respect. This does not mean that the knowledge received, once incorporated, will not be transformed into a higher degree of know-how. The 'trade' knowledge creation realises itself, but it is not part of the exchange, as a counter gift. The new knowledge is personal, but valuable for the whole community; the competencies of one member influence the life of the group when the foundry men work as a single team – a danger for one is a danger for everybody.

Therefore, we understand that the gift-back cannot intervene during the socialisation, but happens later, when the workers have arrived at the end of their learning process (the one socially admitted, after three years in the foundry). Loyalty to the job is the primary gift-back. Prior to this, knowledge receivers find other opportunities to demonstrate their recognition and play their role in the Hau. Some may bring food (if they were cooks or bakers in a previous career), others help the seniors to perform computer tasks with which they are not at ease, most of them are involved in the summer maintenance tasks, while others may build a team to represent the casthouse in a local sports tournament. All these examples fall into the same category of intermediary gifts-back. If we take the instance of the summer maintenance tasks, they traditionally happen when the foundry is shut down and the seniors are on holiday. The newcomers stay and help the maintenance service with their yearly equipment check-up and cleaning. We notice that the involvement is very high as a sign of goodwill and benevolence towards the community.

Yet, it is not totally impossible to give back *knowledge*; it becomes acceptable if the area of knowledge does not directly concern the *technical* part of the trade. The pure technical side belongs to the 'experts' as stated earlier, and during the socialisation, it might be considered as an offence to question it. Receivers are then going to investigate other areas, such as security or ergonomics. We notice that both are the concerns of altruism (work conditions improvement). In the Hau-Ba theory applied to our case, this dimension provides opportunities of gifts-back as a sign of recognition and gratitude, although we must point out that this form of return is not related to the concept of debt, which defines the transactional mode. In the gift model, debt does not exist. With regards to this point, we can relate a story that happened during the tutorial period. In order to express this no-debt dimension, senior employees took the opportunity of a training session, organised by the management to explain theoretical concepts to the newcomers. Surprisingly, the tutors who were usually reluctant regarding formal in-class training asked to participate in the session, arguing that, thanks to it, they could learn or relearn what they might have forgotten. They pointed out that they could also learn from the newcomers and admitted that, like the junior workers, they did not know everything – especially when it came to declarative knowledge regarding casting theory.

Using a topic of knowledge that is not emotionality invested (theoretical knowledge is the 'engineer's property'), they preserve their core of competence and the know-how which defines them. But in another way, by adopting this attitude they reduce the gap between themselves and the new generation, symbolically erasing the *power* influence and the weight of the debt, and showing signs of similarity. They call for *solidarity* inside the community now fully opened to the newcomers, actors in the Hau-Ba. One worker says: "*The young generation is more at ease than us with calculating, they spend a longer time at school, they know more than us in some respects, both can learn from the others.*"

Trust, which was the first condition for opening the Ba to the newcomers and for risking the Hau principles, slowly evolved into a higher concept: reciprocity and mutual recognition. It can be seen as a consequence of the Hau-Ba application, which strengthens the intrinsic attributes that characterise a community.

Interim conclusions

On the whole, this case illustrates that the gift-back is free and unconditional. Applying the value of the Hau is a question of faith, not the result of a request or a contract. It also brings proof of evidence that if the gift-back does not happen, a recognition offence will break the social consensus and the ability to integrate the

Table 5.4 The fulfilment of the Hau cycle inside the Ba

Hau cycle		*Activated Ba*
Initial Gift	From the organisation to the old experts: Recognition of the tutor mission. Tutor assignment. From the organisation to the newcomers: promise of a long-term position if the training period is successful. **Result:** the psychological contract respects equity. The Hau can start and the Ba can work.	New project (transfer of activity) + tutorial mission reactivate the Meta Ba and the original Ba for the first givers (tutors). Application (physical) Ba: cold area for both tutors and newcomers. Interaction (mental) arousing Ba: tutorship interaction.
First Gifts/ Gifts-back	From the tutor of the cold area to the newcomers: non-critical knowledge. From the newcomers to the tutors: Modesty, respect, humility. **Result:** Trust appears. The newcomers are perceived as either potential receivers or not. The ones who fail the test leave the foundry.	Applicative and physical Ba of the cold area.
Hau Gifts and Gifts-back	From the tutors of the hot area to the 'receivers': critical tacit and personal knowledge gift (trade secrets). From the receivers to the first givers: • Intermediary gifts: ideas in ergonomics or safety, help, food. • Primary gift: job acceptance.	Applicative and physical Ba of the hot area. Interacting and mental Ba: emotional climate and job/social identity.
	Result: the psychological contract is stronger; the trade is desirable again. Newcomers are socialised and join the 'community' as full members. The sense-making process of socialisation (Pratt *et al.*, 2001) is a kind of personal and judgement **knowledge creation**.	The application Ba is stronger. But the Meta Ba is not active for the new generation. The interpersonal links are strong, but not the links with the organisation; they know how precarious their position can be.

newcomers into the foundry community. This fragile balance is then cautiously taken care of by the exchanges of intermediary minor gifts that announce the future and primary gift-back.

On another hand, the effects of the Hau are made possible by the investment in the elementary Ba (original, physical and upcoming mental Ba), closely followed by primary ones (nearly simultaneous strong physical and mental Ba). Furthermore, we can note that in this specific context, original, interacting and application Ba are joined as a single Ba, the Meta Ba which is the foundry itself.

In this space, slowly but surely, the beginner ends the transfer process by integrating the knowledge. At the same time, this instigates the symbolic gift-back, which is the involvement in the trade. When someone accepts a new trade that is no longer socially desired, then adopting a dying culture, sharing the pride of community and controlling one's own fears are the major components of this gift-back. In this case, *receiving and giving are merged.* By properly receiving (by adopting and integrating the knowledge in order to use it and to perpetuate it, despite the lack of attractiveness) the receiver gives back to the community. They become the ones who justify the past and ensure a future. The receiving of the trade memory and of the role is the gift itself, because receiving is not desired prior to the socialisation.

In conclusion, the gift-back has a secondary effect, this time, on the organisation: by building loyalty within the firm, the new employee tacitly accepts the psychological contract and reinforces it. This acceptance is a strong sign for others; it makes the trade desirable again. We saw that the psychological contract was the starting point of the model; it also finishes off the Hau-Ba system in this particular case. The theory starts when the contract is clear between the organisation and the tutor, which means when equity is fairly perceived. Once this has happened, the system can deploy itself, submitting to the newcomer's capacity to become a 'receiver' in the Hau cycle. Once the cycle completes, one of the last outputs is the reinforcement of the psychological contract. In this circumstance, the gift-back, which is also the receiving of the trade knowledge, becomes the acceptance of a foundry worker's position. (See Box 5.1 and Figure 5.7.)

In this specific variant of the Hau-Ba theory, receiving and giving-back join together under the framework of the main Ba, which is the mental one. The gift-back is highly symbolic and is not a pure return of knowledge. If knowledge creation happens through the sense-making creation process of the socialisation, it is not as an element of the Hau cycle, but as a positive 'side-effect' of the Hau-Ba. It is not an asset of the exchange. Lastly, the mental Ba cannot arise without the primal existence of several physical Ba, which enable the cooperation, the experiment of the other source of trust. Trust is somehow indispensable, to believe in the future gift and to have the associated patience to wait for it, without requesting a debt.

This model is built around the 6 'A's:

Artifice: defines the introductory gift (test). Senior casting workers cultivate the myth of the imaginary notebook holding the trade secrets. They use this trick to express that the knowledge is not a right, but a gift to be honoured with. The recipient of the transfer of memory must be worth the gift; this means he must act as a receiver. Since this capacity is not proven, the knowledge transfer remains partial and superficial. At this stage, only the procedural and official memory is staked in the transfer, as a test.

Allegiance: defines the way a recipient receives the gift. He recognises the transfer as a gift, and reacts accordingly, expressing his gratitude. This behaviour announces the possibility of a gift-back. As a submission, this form of receiving shows respect and recognition to the giver. At this stage, the circle of the gift can really get under way. The underground memory can be delivered, its procedural and judgement, individual and collective side.

Allegory: the gift-back is symbolic. The loyalty to the trade and the merging with the workers' community, the acceptance of the legacy, all this within a danger denial, compose the return. The gift-back, made of knowledge, is expressed through the know-how and the ability, which are necessary during risky operations. The gift-back implies the gift of the body to the guild, and the acceptance of possible injury.

Asymmetry: The return is not the equivalent of the initial gift, and this is admitted. The stake is elsewhere, on the side of recognition, esteem and gratitude.

Abnegation: in order to create some similarity and some proximity, senior tutors erase the asymmetry of the exchange to make the debt invisible. To do so, they express their own limits, admitting they also need training in the theoretical side of the trade. In the very small emotional field of the official and declarative knowledge which composes the official memory (not the underground one, elaborated by the occupational community), the symbols of the 'Father' step aside and announce the end of the unilateral transfer (a symbolic father-to-son transmission and inheritance). The initial givers can also become the 'receivers'. The socialisation ends and the community is one again, a community where each member can start the gift cycle.

Adoption: the meta gift-back appears as the adoption of a "non-desired" trade by a new generation. In this design, the meta gift is the trade memory, while the "receipt" is seen in the acceptance of its heritage. Alliance becomes stronger than fear or danger. The underlying motivation that fits the HAU BA incentive in mutual recognition is developed by individuals who search for a meaning to their past or to their future.

Box 5.1 The Hau-Ba in case 1: the '6 A model'

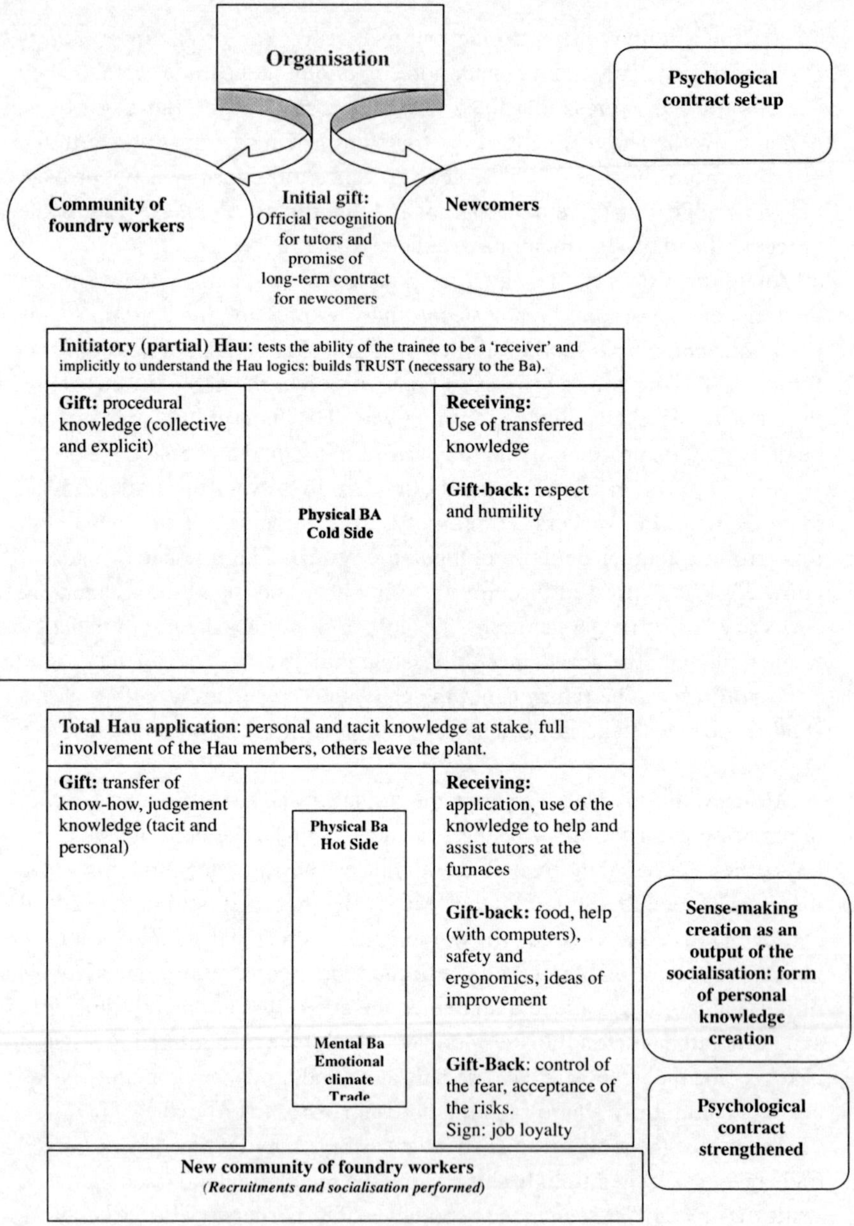

Figure 5.7 Synthesis schema of the Hau-Ba model applied to the case of a community of foundry workers.

The Hau-Ba model and the future of organising

In this chapter we have tried to address one of the major issues for organisations: how to design sequences for knowledge exchange and innovation. Building on two theories, the Hau-Ba model proposed here addresses this issue in terms of concrete settings. A case study has been used to illustrate the feasibility of the model, as well as its limits. Our ongoing research on the subject tends to suggest that the question of sequences and knowledge exchange's embedness is a stimulating perspective for research and action. The model should be refined, by taking into account the socioeconomic system dynamics, and especially the issue of 'communalism', as it has been underlined in Chapter 4 of the present volume.

Notes

1 This section reprints some of the previous developments in Bounfour (2003), Chapter 4: Knowledge Creation.
2 This section refers to the ongoing research conducted by G. Grefe, in the framework of her PhD study at the University Paris-Sud, which aims at testing and refining the Hau-Ba model in the context of a major manufacturing company.

References

Adams, J. S. (1963), 'Towards an understanding of equity', *Journal of Abnormal and Social Psychology*, Vol. 67, pp. 422–36.

Aschcraft, M. (1994). *Human Memory and Cognition.* New York: Harper Collins.

Blau, P. M. (1964). *Exchange and Power in Social Life.* New York: Wiley.

Blin, J. F. (1997). *Représentations, pratiques et identités professionnelles.* Paris: L'Harmattan.

Boisserolles de Saint Julien, D. (2005). *Les survivants, vers une gestion différenciée des ressources humaines.* Paris: L'Harmattan.

Bounfour, A. (2000). 'Gestion de la connaissance et systèmes d'incitation: entre théorie du "Hau" et théorie du "Ba", *Systèmes d'information et management*, Vol. 5, No. 2, pp. 12–40.

Bounfour, A. (2003). *The Management of Intangibles: the organisation's most valuable assets.* London and New York: Routledge.

Bounfour, A. (2005). 'Modeling intangibles: transaction regime versus community regimes', in A. Bounfour and L. Edvinsson (eds). *Intellectual Capital for Communities, Nations, Regions and Cities.* Burlington, MA: Elsevier Butterworth-Heinemann.

Bounfour, A. (2006). 'Reconnaisance, reconnaissance et "communautalisme"', in A. Bounfour (ed.) *Capital immatériel, Connaissance et performance.* Paris: L'Harmattan.

Caillé, A. (2007). *La quête de reconnaissance, nouveau phénomène social total.* Paris: Editions La Découverte.

Crozier, M. and Friedberg, E. (1977). *L'acteur et le système.* Paris: Le Seuil.

Delobbe, N. (2005). 'Le contrat psychologique', in N. Delobbe, O. Herrbach, D. Lacaze and K. Mignonac, *Comportement Organisationnel: contrat psychologique, émotions au travail, socialisiation organisationelle*, Volume 1. Brussels: de Boeck, pp. 21–68.

Dosi, G., Marengo, L. and Fagiolo, G. (1996). 'Learning in evolutionary environments', WP 1996–05, Department of Economics, University of Trento.

Dubar, C. (1991). *La socialisation: construction des identités sociales et professionnelles*, Paris: Armand Colin.

Dubar, C. (2003). *La crise des identités, l'interprétation d'une mutation*, Paris: Presses Universitaires de France.

Dubar, C. (2004). 'Mutation de l'emploi et crise identitaire', in H. Poltier, A. Guénette and A. Henchoz (eds) *Travail et fragilisation*. Paris: Payot, pp. 129–33.
Esposito, R. (2000). *Communitas: origine et destins de la communauté*. Paris: Presses Universitaires de France.
Flamant, N. (2005). 'Les jeunes, les séniors et l'entreprise', Study No. 250. Paris: Entreprise et Personnel.
Girod, M. (1995). Mémoire et organisation. PhD Thesis, Université Paris-Dauphine.
Glaser, B. G. and Strauss, A. L. (1967). *The Discovery of Grounded Theory: strategies for qualitative research*. London: Weiderfield & Nicholson.
Honneth, Axel (2002). *La lutte pour la reconnaissance*. Paris: Le Cerf.
Lacaze, D. (2005). 'La socialisation organisationnelle', in N. Delobbe, O. Herrbach, D. Lacaze and K. Mignonac, *Comportement Organisationnel: contrat psychologique, émotions au travail, socialisiation organisationelle*, Volume 1. Brussels: de Boeck, pp. 273–341.
Lave, J. and Wenger, E. (1991). *Situated Learning: legitimate peripheral participation*, Cambridge: Cambridge University Press.
Mauss, M. (1950) 'Essai sur le don, forme et raison de l'échange dans les sociétés archaïques', chapter 2 in *Sociologie et Anthropologie*. Paris: Presses Universitaires de France.
Molinie, V. (2004). 'Peur, méfiances et défi face à la machine', *Terrain* No. 43, pp. 47–62.
Moorman, C. and Miner, A. S. (1998). 'Organization improvisation and organizational memory', *Academy of Management Review*, Vol. 23, No. 4, pp. 698–723.
Nonaka, I. (1994), 'A dynamic theory of organizational knowledge creation', *Organization Science*, Vol. 1 (February), No. 1, pp. 14–37.
Nonaka, I. and Konno, N. (1998). 'The concept of "Ba": building foundation for knowledge creation, *California Management Review*, Vol. 40 (Spring), No.3.
Nonaka, I. and Takeuchi, H. (1995). *The Knowledge-Creating Company: how Japanese companies create the dynamics of innovation*. New York: Oxford University Press.
Polanyi, M. (1983 [1966]). *The Tacit Dimension*. Gloucester, MA: Peter Smith.
Poltier, H., Guenette, A. M. and Henchoz, A. M. (2004). *Travail et fragilisation*. Paris: Payot.
Sainsaulieu, R. (1985). *L'identité au travail, Les effets culturels de l'organisation* 2nd ed. Paris: Presses de la FNSP.
Sainsaulieu, R., Franckfort, I., Osty, F. and Uhalde, M. (1995). *Les mondes sociaux de l'entreprise, sociologie économique*. Paris: Edition Desclée de Brouwer.
Sardas, J. F. (2004). 'Dynamiques identitaires et transformations au travail', in *Travail et fragilisation*. Paris: Payot, pp. 137–56.
Teece, D. (1987). 'Profiting from technology innovation: implications for integration, collaboration, licensing and public policy', in D. J. Teece (ed.) *The Competitive Challenge: strategies for industrial innovation and renewal*. New York: Harper & Row.
Tönnies, F. (1977 [1922]). *Communauté et Société, Catégories fondamentales de la sociologie pure*. Introduction and trans. J. Leif. Paris: Presses Universitaires de France, in collection Les classiques des sciences humaines. Original German title: *Gemeinschaft und Gesellschaft*.
Von Krogh, G., Ichijo, K., Nonaka, I. (2000). *Enabling Knowledge Creation*. Oxford: Oxford University Press.
Walsh, J. P. and Ungson, G. R. (1991). 'Organizational memory', *Academy of Management Review*, Vol. 16, No. 1, pp. 57–91.
Weick, K. E. (1995). *Sensemaking in Organizations*. London: Sage Publications.
Wilkins, A. L. and Ouchi, W. G. (1983). 'Efficient cultures: exploring the relationship between culture and performance', *Administrative Science Quarterly*, Vol. 28, pp. 468–81.
Winter, S. (1987). 'Knowledge and competence as strategic assets', in D. J. Teece (ed.) *The Competitive Challenge: strategies for industrial innovation and renewal*, New York: Harper & Row.

6 Dynamic capabilities of communities

Ahmed Bounfour

Dynamic capabilities emerged as a central perspective for making more explicit how companies create value in the knowledge economy. This concept does indeed help in solving the causal ambiguity weakness of the resource-based view. In this chapter, I consider this concept further by articulating it to the concept of community, as it has been defined and implemented in the two previous chapters. Section 1 will consider the issue from the strategic literature perspective. Section 2 will go further by considering the dynamic capability issue from the national perspective (using the case of Finland). Section 3 will briefly address the issue of dynamic capabilities and communities from the intelligent enterprise perspective. Finally, Section 4 will conclude by putting forward how dynamic capabilities might be related to the issue of organisational design.

Dynamic capabilities in the strategic literature: a résumé[1]

The concept of dynamic capabilities has been central in the strategic literature over the last ten years. Several scholars have put forward the argument that beyond the importance of intangible resources, as they have been emphasised by the resource-based view, dynamic capabilities are the adapted lever for articulating and combining intangibles in a very idiosyncratic way. The dynamic capabilities approach aimed at addressing some of the RBV weaknesses, especially by providing a more operational analytical framework. Teece *et al.* (1997) defined dynamic capability as 'the firm's ability to integrate, build and reconfigure internal and external competencies to address rapidly changing environments' – a concept similar to the 'combinative capabilities', defined by Kogut and Zander earlier (1992). This definition has been criticised by Zollo and Winter, as they consider it 'as troublesome near-tautology in defining a capability as ability' (Zollo and Winter, 1999: 4), and from their perspective the conditions of formation of capabilities are not explicitly defined by Teece *et al.* They connect *capability* with *routine*, especially in the context of what they called 'knowledge evolution cycle'. Therefore, the authors defined a dynamic capability as 'a learned pattern of collective activity through which the organization systematically generates and modifies its operational routines in pursuit of improved effectiveness' (Zollo and Winter, 1999: 10). In a later paper Winter (2002) addressed in more detail the issue of dynamic capabilities. He made a distinction between ordinary 'zero level' capabilities (i.e. those capabilities that *'permit the firm to make a living in the short term'*) and dynamic capabilities that contribute to the extension, modification or creation of ordinary capabilities. These have been named elsewhere 'high-order capabilities' (Collis, 1994).

Eisenhardt and Martin (2000) defined dynamic capabilities as a set of identifiable and specific processes (development processes or alliance processes, etc.) dedicated to articulating resources and competencies within companies, for example, Toyota's system for product development, Cisco's approach to competences building and web-based articulation or Nokia's development processes. These processes are endowed with commonalities in key features and idiosyncrasy in details. Recently Leoncini *et al.* (2003) proposed an interesting literature review on dynamic capabilities from two perspectives: the organisational lens (strategic and evolutionary) and environmental lens (*milieu innovateur*, industrial district, regional system, new industrial space approaches). They also suggest a system approach for analysing dynamic capabilities. A system-based dynamic IC view has also been developed in Finland by Ståhle (Ståhle and Grönroos, 2000; Ståhle and Ståhle, 2006) and its practical applications have been widely implemented in the country. Kianto (formerly Pöyhönen) has further developed this Finnish approach on dynamic IC (Pöyhönen, 2004) and she notably put forward the lack of a shared understanding with regards to this dimension. Kianto concludes with the importance of developing a roadmap for intellectual capital dynamics in the research area and praxis (Kianto, forthcoming).

As Eisenhardt and Martin (2000) made clear, dynamic capabilities are basically a set of processes dedicated to articulating resources and competencies within companies. In brief, dynamic capabilities might be defined as specified earlier, as: *'The ability to integrate, build, and reconfigure internal and external competencies to address rapidly-changing environments.'* (Teece *et al.*, 1997). From this definition we can derive a hypothesis: in economies nowadays, the way companies and organisations articulate their resources and competences should evolve continuously, otherwise these organisations will lose their competitive advantage. In other terms, the present (static) capabilities should be continuously challenged and changed in order to build *ad hoc* dynamic capabilities.

Dynamic capabilities of natural communities: nations, regions and cities

But from a community perspective, this definition should be extended, by taking into account the *recognition dimension* as well as the *emotive dimension* (especially with regards to collective positioning in space and time). Therefore, from a community perspective, a dynamic capability can be defined as: 'the *ability of a community to build its architectural and mental resources*, consisting in the *way these communities continuously renew and articulate their transaction and recognition spheres, according to their members' (and leaders') beliefs and positioning in space and time*'. It is this ability that will allow nations, as natural communities, to find a new path for development, beyond their existing intangible resources. This refers naturally to the emotive dimension of performance, which creates a sense of collective action and also allows building congruence with world demands and expectations, in terms of products, services, images and societal modelling. Via dynamic capabilities, hence defined, we understand the way the form of a community (a nation, such as Finland for instance, as we will see later) can articulate its present intellectual capital with pieces of intellectual capital not built so far. By doing so, a nation defines its 'innovative offer' to the rest of the world, and therefore its specific development path. Naturally, such capabilities are already defined by taking into account the dynamics of the whole global company, and its global issues.

If we agree on this definition, then the question of public policy can be considered from a different angle. In particular, one of the most important issues will concern the way public policy – and more generally, national strategies – will articulate natural communities (nations, regions, cities) strategies with emerging communities governance (Figure 1). It is the role of dynamic capabilities to make it possible to proceed as such. For instance, if we consider the clustering process now adopted by most nations (the 66 already labelled 'competitiveness clusters' in France, for instance), it is clear that such a clustering will only succeed if its conditions of functioning are clearly in congruence with the rules of governance of emerging communities. On another note, new entrepreneurship and new IPRs rules might be needed, if the constrained community's regime becomes a dominant one.

The new dynamic capabilities: the architectural collaborative capabilities

Two important factors characterise the intangible economy: the importance of 'the combinatory function' and the instability of competitive advantages (Bounfour, 1998). This needs from organisations a continuous renewal of their resources and their combinatory function. This can be done via the development

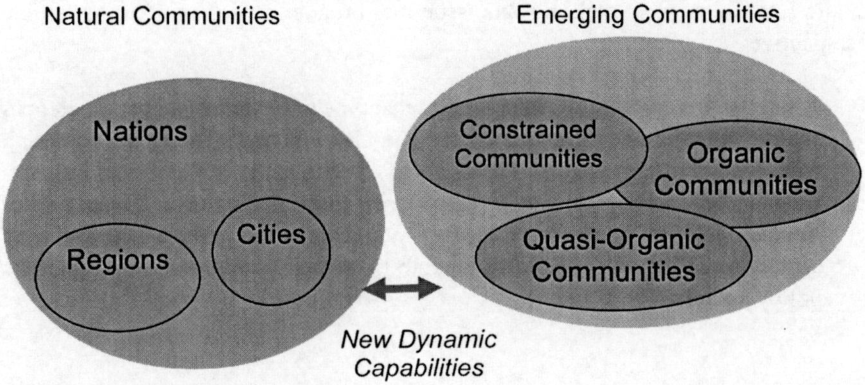

Figure 6.1 The articulation between Natural Communities and Emerging Communities.

of specific capabilities: dynamic capabilities. Within the framework proposed in Chapter 4 – the relationship between transactional order and the community order – these capabilities concern particularly the development of a 'collaborative' architecture that enables natural communities to integrate the dynamics of emerging communities (Bounfour, 2005, 2006). This is already observable in the case of scientific and technical diasporas for leading nations – via their governments – as they try to develop specific modes of articulation to the national space, through the creation of physical, virtual and mental spaces of recognition.

This is typically what India is trying to achieve with its scientific community. That could be the case tomorrow with Maghreb countries and their communities in Europe. The space for innovation here is vast, and building capacities for collaborative 'architecture' calls for a radical overhaul of how the instruments of public policy have been designed and adopted so far. The relationship between the tangible sphere and intangible (reputation) sphere is a factor to be considered in this context. For example, what scientific and technical capacities are the oil-producing countries likely to build today, given the resources accumulated through oil? How, on another level, can Japan compensate for the weak global articulation of its scientific and technical capacities? How will Finland enhance its 'resilience' capacity beyond Nokia? How is the city of Paris going to renew its image in a context of strong competition between cities? How likely is an old city like Liege, in Belgium, to recover in the context of an intangibles' economy? These are questions to which the concept of 'collaborative architecture' could provide some analytical answers, necessarily idiosyncratic. On a more functional level, these responses need to address modalities for developing collective intelligence, intellectual property rights, ways of knowledge fluidity inside as well as outside of the community space and, more generally, positioning in space and time.

Dynamic capabilities of nations: the case of Finland[2]

In concrete terms, and taking a broader perspective, how can we define a bundle of dynamics capabilities as the most relevant for Finland's new path of development? I would suggest tackling this issue in a broader sense, by taking a double perspective:

1 A supply-driven side, by considering what type of resources and competences are key ingredients of Finland's present intellectual capital and by considering what type of congruence can be established with some of the global issues;
2 a demand-driven perspective, by considering the global issues and what type of 'innovative offer' can be provided by Finland to the rest of the world, and what type of bundling of capabilities need to be primarily addressed by Finland's policy agenda.

Finland's dynamic capabilities from a supply side perspective

If we consider the issue of dynamic capabilities from the supply side, based on existing information about Finland's performance, we can already deliver some statements. Naturally, these are preliminary, and should be re-assessed in more detail. But, considering things from the outside, we can make some preliminary remarks.

First of all, as Finland is endowed with highly educated human resources, there is a clear fitness with global issues for *ad hoc* innovation. Needs for innovative capabilities might be sector specific, but also cross-sectoral. Therefore the existence of highly educated resources, and the fact that science and technology are of high value within Finnish society, is an important intellectual asset for the country. In a global innovative market, Finland's supply of innovation will certainly need global demands for its innovative offers. Naturally, this will not be a spontaneous process, and dynamic capabilities should be built for that.

As for clusters – as deposits of knowledge and outputs – we can, at this stage, state that at least three clusters are in accord with some global issues:

1 ICT and related applications appear to have high potential, taking into account some global issues. There should be a strong need for ICT solutions and artefacts, especially due to the emergence of strong social tendencies:

   a the dominance of individualism (and nombrilism) in societies;
   b the importance of ICT networks and infrastructure for communities (constrained communities and quasi-organic communities, mainly);
   c the aging population, which necessitates a full design of the whole ICT infrastructure (see the 'ubiquitous network' concept in Japan and South Korea);
   d urban design and management (for communication and security purposes, among others).

2 Water, paper and forest will probably have an open opportunity for providing innovative supply, taking into account global environmental issues, as well as the issue of water supply and management in many parts of the world. Is there any innovative supply coming from Finland on this very critical issue?
3 Biotech clusters are an important issue, especially when we consider the aging population. There is certainly a complementary between ICT and biotech, in this context.
4 Finally there are *ad hoc* intellectual assets which make the Finland model unique: equity principles, social cohesion, systematic innovative processes and the absence of corruption. These are specific assets that need to be leveraged in a bundle of intangible resources, to be offered to the rest of the world. They might contribute to building *ad hoc* responses under the community regime, and therefore to moderating some of the violent rules underway in most of the economies under the transaction regime.

Finland's dynamic capabilities from a demand-side perspective

Let's then consider the same problem, from a demand perspective, as a double-checking exercise. We can start by considering three blocks of issues: global societal functionalities, global societal issues and institutional governance (Figure 2). Those indicated in blue are the most relevant for Finland's ICT cluster, which seems to me to be of particular relevance for consideration here. The question here is that of ensuring a full congruence between Finland's intellectual capital and these global tendencies and issues.

Global societal functionalities

By societal functionalities, I mean here the expectations of societies, especially western ones, regarding their daily functioning. If we consider carefully what is underway both at the demand and supply sides, we can derive at least four major functionalities, the last three being of particular relevance for ICT: innovativeness as a value and practice; shortermism behaviour of people (due to the pre-eminence of the space of flows, as has been already stressed by Castells); real-time connectiveness (we can already observe this with the emergent young generation); and real-time surveillance (this should be one of the major issues, especially under the pressure of the insurance industry, but also as an implicit or even explicit demand of societies).

Global societal issues

These global issues are already known. We can at least remind them, in order to consider what type of dynamic capabilities should be considered for building by Finland. Among those issues of particular relevance are: the aging population; the rise of insurance expectations (see previous section), environmental issues, the crisis in recognition mechanisms within companies and societies (and emergence of orphan individuals); people migration; knowledge migration (via diasporas and other forms of quasi-organic communities); water management and disease.

In face of all of these issues, the Finland model has to be reassessed, in order to determine its level of relevance and congruence with these global issues.

Institutional governance

As for the institutional governance, taken from a broader perspective, we can already make some preliminary statements:

- The State, in its traditional centric form, is in crisis (and its slack is decreasing) due to the spreading of the transaction regime, including in the public sector (even in some of the 'Hobbesian' spheres such as security and education). Naturally, this is a general statement that needs to be moderated, taking into account the context of nations (Europe, Asia, North and South America, among others);

- Large vertical corporations are decreasing. They are no longer recognised as major spheres of recognition and security ensuring;
- The individual is becoming centric as well as – correlatively – the community (because individuals do not support being orphans, as they are in search of what Giddens (1991) names the 'ontological security');
- Supranational mechanisms for global issues regulation will increase. Only these mechanisms will allow environmental, peace and even criminal issues to be tackled.

Here again, we can expect Finland to provide a unique 'innovative offer' to the rest of the world. There will certainly be strong expectations for such an offer.

Finland's new path: a bundle of dynamic capabilities

Considering these two perspectives – supply and demand – we can already establish some points of strengths and weaknesses for dynamic capabilities that need to be considered for the future.

Dynamic capabilities with specific strengths for Finland might be listed as follows:

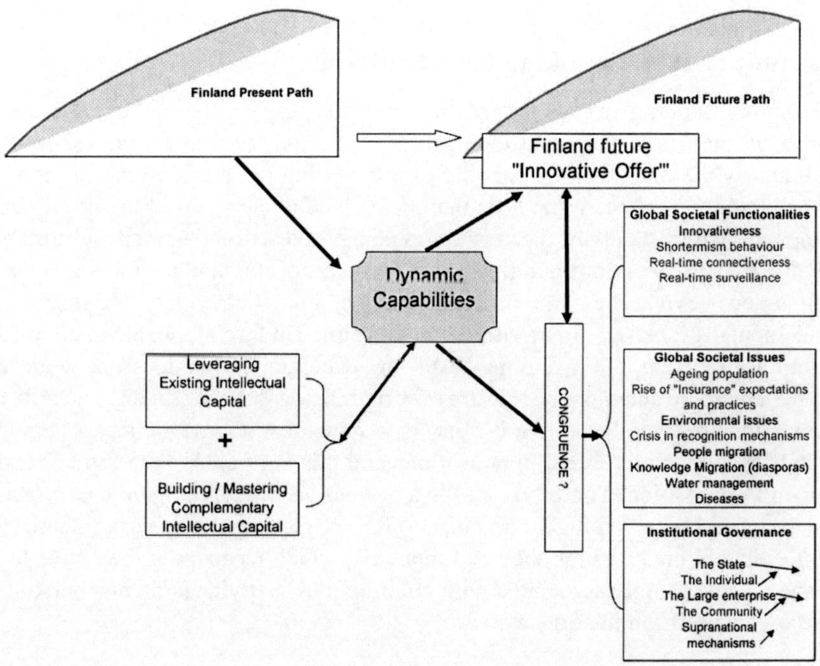

Figure 6.2 Finland's future path – the 'Innovative Offer': a tentative modelling.

Source: Bounfour (2007: 31)

- community building;
- renewability;
- social cohesion and systemic innovation.

These are certainly the central dynamic capabilities but, from a policy perspective, attention should also be paid to those capabilities with apparent weaknesses. Among these are:

- individual entrepreneurship and venture capitalism;
- communities bridging (especially from outside);
- diasporas building (this is also major issue for countries with similar strategies such as Japan);
- attractiveness of the best of class;
- policy instruments for individuals (since building individual intellectual capital might be a major requirement in the future);
- branding, image building and image projection (including for the whole country).

From these overall diagnostics, we can derive a bundle of dynamic capabilities with particular relevance for consideration for policy and decision making in Finland (Figure 6.3). Those in blue are particularly individual-centric.

Dynamic capabilities of intelligent enterprises

The same reasoning can be applied to companies, especially the largest ones. In my view, the most intelligent enterprises of the twenty-first century should be particularly the ones that are capable of articulating the transaction regime with the community regime. What does that mean in concrete terms? First of all, these companies will certainly be those who should have clearly understood and admitted that the dynamics of communities are at the heart of the new capitalism. This of course goes beyond the community of practice; a practice which is basically and fundamentally a biased organisational mode, aimed at forcing people to cooperate within a pure transaction regime. With few exceptions, this does not work any longer, and more and more people are now mobilising their intelligence outside the transaction sphere. We can see it every day: new ideas and new concepts emerge outside the walls of vertical organisations and this is of course the future central space for innovation. Therefore, and in a normative way, intelligent enterprises – and more generally, intelligent organisations – are requested to look for identifying *ad hoc* spaces under which they can innovate, which means that they have to be in one way or another associated with communities' activities: clients, personnel, freelancers of different sorts, etc.

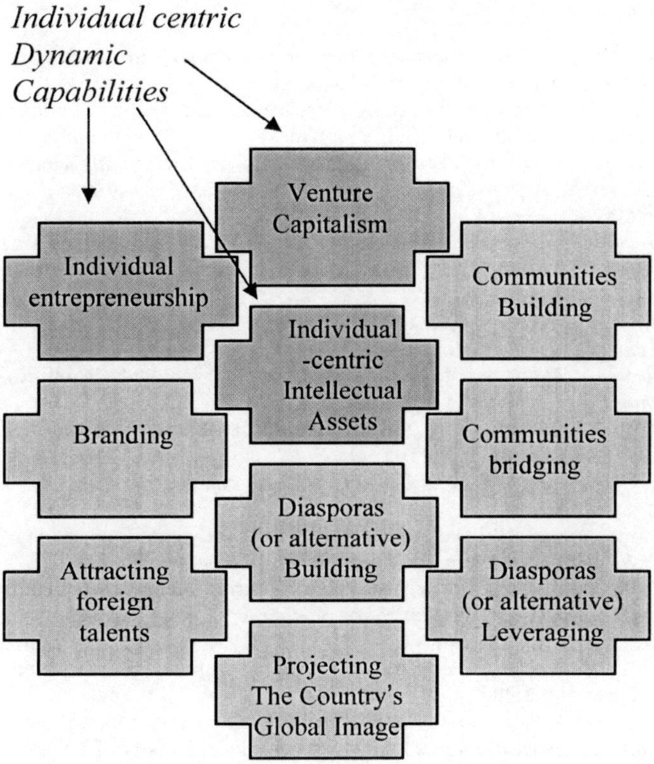

Figure 6.3 A bundle of dynamic capabilities for Finland's new path.

Source: Bounfour (2007: 33)

Dynamic capabilities and the organisation's design

The issue of dynamics of communities is naturally related to the issue of organisational design. This is a classical theme of organisational science that will be deeply influenced by the emergence of communities as the new hub of the new capitalism. Designing new organisational forms necessitates designing physical, mental and virtual spaces for knowledge flow, within the transaction sphere as well as within the recognition sphere. It also necessitates the consideration of how to articulate emerging communities within traditional vertical organisations, as well as with natural communities such as nations, regions, cities and districts. These are the topics of a new research agenda on dynamic capabilities.

Notes

1 This section refers to my joint paper with Pirjo Ståhle (Ståhle and Bounfour, 2008).

2 This section refers to my contribution to the New Club of Paris report to the Round Table with Matti Van Hanen, the Prime Minister of Finland. See Bounfour (2007) and for further reading: www.the-new-club-of-paris.org

References

Bounfour, A. (1998). *Le Management des Ressources Immatérielles: maîtriser les nouveaux leviers de l'avantage compétitif.* Paris: Dunod.

Bounfour, A. (2005). 'Modeling intangibles: transaction regimes versus community regimes', in A. Bounfour and L. Edvinsson (eds) *Intellectual Capital for Communities, Nations, Regions and Cities*. Burlington, MA: Elsevier Butterworth-Heinemann.

Bounfour, A. (ed.) (2006). *Capital Immatériel,Connaissance et Performance*. Paris: L'Harmattan.

Bounfour, A. (2007) 'Dynamic capabilities of communities and Finland's new path', in P. Ståhle (ed.) 'Five steps for Finland's future', *Tekes Technology Review* 202/2007, pp. 25–34.

Bounfour, A. and Edvinsson, L. (eds) (2005). *Intellectual Capital for Communities, Nations, Regions and Cities.* Burlington, MA: Elsevier Butterworth-Heinemann.

Collis, D.J. (1994). 'Research note: how valuable are organizational capabilities?', *Strategic Management Journal* Vol. 15, pp. 143–52.

Einsenhardt, K.M. and Martin, J.A. (2000). 'Dynamic capabilities: what are they?', *Strategic Management Journal* Vol. 21: 1105–21.

Giddens, A. (1991) *Modernity and Self-Identity: self and society in the late modern age.* Cambridge: Polity.

Kianto, A. (forthcoming). 'What do we really mean by the dynamic dimension of intellectual capital?', *International Journal of Learning and Intellectual Capital.*

Kogut, B. and Zander, U. (1992). 'Knowledge of the firm, combinative capabilities, and the replication of technology', *Organization Science* Vol. 3, pp. 383–97.

Leoncini, R., Montresor, S. and Vertova, G. (2003). 'Dynamic capabilities: evolving organisations in evolving (technological) systems'. University of Bergamo Economics Working Paper No. 4/2003.

Pöyhönen, A. (2004). 'Modeling and measuring organizational renewal capability'. *Acta Universitatis Lappeenrantaensis* 200, Lappeenranta University of Technology.

Pöyhönen, A. and Smedlund, A. (2004). 'Assessing intellectual capital creation in regional clusters', *Journal of Intellectual Capital*, Vol. 5, No. 3, pp. 351–65.

Ståhle, P. and Bounfour, A. (2008). 'Understanding dynamics of intellectual capital of nations', in Special Issue on Intellectual Capital for Communities, *Journal of Intellectual Capital*, Vol. 9, No. 2, pp. 164–77.

Ståhle, P. and Grönroos, M. (2000). *Dynamic Intellectual Capital: knowledge management in theory and practice.* Porvoo, Helsinki, Juva: WSOY.

Ståhle, P. and Ståhle, S. (2006). 'Intellectual capital and national competitiveness: conceptual and methodological challenges' in A. Bounfour (ed.) (2006). *Capital Immateriel, Connaisance et performance.* Paris: L'Harmattan.

Teece, D., Pisano, G. and Shuen, A. (1997). 'Dynamic capabilities and strategic management', *Strategic Management Journal*, Vol. 18, pp. 509–33.

Winter, S. (2002). 'Understanding dynamic capabilities', A Working Paper of the Regional H. Jones Center, The Wharton School, University of Pennsylvania, WP 2002–05.

Zollo, M. and Winter, S. (1999). 'From organizational routines to dynamic capabilities', A working paper of the Regional H. Jones Center, The Wharton School, University of Pennsylvania, WP 99–07.

7 The dynamics of self-renewal

A systems-thinking to understanding organizational challenges in dynamic environments

Pirjo Ståhle[1]

Introduction

Organizations today operate in a dynamic, highly unpredictable global competitive environment. The challenge is the same for both businesses and public organizations: how to constantly increase speed and efficiency, to improve quality and innovation? In order to succeed in the competition at both the company and national level, systems must show a capacity for continuous development and even radical change. Increasingly, competitiveness now boils down to a capacity for self-renewal in and by organizations, networks and nations. Continuous innovation and renewal capability in organizations has indeed attracted growing research interest in recent years (e.g. Nonaka and Takeuchi, 1995; Leonard-Barton, 1995; Weick and Sutcliffe, 2002; Brown and Eisenhardt, 1998; Ståhle *et al.*, 2003; Pöyhönen, 2004).

To achieve the capacity for self-renewal, it is necessary to amalgamate and integrate different kinds of expertise, interests, people and organizations. The management of these complexities presents a huge challenge for every organization, and cannot be adequately met without an internal capacity for self-organization. It is necessary therefore to understand the dynamics of self-renewal, which unfolds as a result of a process of change involving multiple agents and driven from within the system.

In this paper I examine the conditions for the process of self-renewal via two different systems theories. I begin with a general overview of the development of systems thinking, providing a backdrop to the discussion of the two theories in focus. I then proceed to a more in-depth treatment of Ilya Prigogine's theory of self-organizing systems. This opens the door to understand radical reform and renewal, particularly the *innovative development process and the function of collective intelligence.* Next, I move on to the autopoiesis theory of Humberto Maturana and Francisco Varela, and to its social science application by Niklas Luhmann. This theory is particularly useful for understanding *organizations as learning and evolving systems*.

The paradigms of systems thinking

Systems theories were developed in the twentieth century on both sides of the Atlantic, although they have received greater emphasis in Europe than in the US (Checkland, 1988, 13). In the late 1940s there were two main schools of systems thinking: *general systems theory* and *cybernetics*. These two approaches have provided the foundation for the development of systemic thinking and systems theory up to the present day. Cybernetics was originally very much dominated by the *Newtonian paradigm*, which means that systems were viewed mainly as ingenious machines. Systems were dominated by general laws and, as such, they were predictable and controllable (Dooley 1995, 1999). In perspective, this view is still an important part of the cybernetic systems thinking.

The Austrian biologist Ludwig von Bertalanffy founded general systems theory, and was the first scientist to develop systems research outside the field of physics. In the 1920s and 1930s, von Bertalanffy's theory focused on open systems. Initially grounded in organic biology, it was subsequently elaborated into a general systems theory (e.g. Bertalanffy, 1967, 1972, 1975). In this theory, systems are looked upon as open and living organisms that communicate with their environment. The processes taking place within the open system serve as continuous feedback cycles, which are described as chains of inputs, throughputs and outputs. The system never rests and the only force that maintains it is this perpetual motion. Feedback cycles generate a lot of information that allow the system to choose different paths of development. In spite of its perpetual motion, the system strives to achieve equilibrium and always remains in a steady state.

The other school of systems thinking was cybernetics, which was pioneered by American mathematician Norbert Wiener. Cybernetics, according to Wiener, referred to disciplines that were concerned with controlling machines and organisms by means of communication and feedback, i.e. with the dissemination, manipulation and use of information for purposes of controlling biological, physical and chemical systems (Wiener, 1948 and 1950; Porter, 1969, vii). Cybernetics is focused on machine-like systems, whose operation and outcome are predetermined, or at least predictable. A cybernetic system is a closed system in the sense that it has no exchange of energy or matter with its environment. An open system, on the other hand, has several options with respect to its aims and operation, and it is furthermore dependent on interaction with its environment.

From the 1960s onwards, systems thinking began to change. It was still mainly founded on the theory of open systems, but the main focus of attention began to shift to the complexity of systems and their innate capacity for change. This led to the emergence of new concepts and patterns of systems thinking, including Forrester's system dynamics, Checkland's soft systems methodology and Senge's learning organization. In 1956, Jay Forrester started the System Dynamics Group at MIT, leaning largely on cybernetic thinking. However, the group's main interest was in open systems that communicated with their environment (e.g. Forrester, 1961 and 1968). Although they focused on systemic change and problem-solving, Forrester (1991, 1) maintains that the approach has universal application because system dynamics provides both the foundation for understanding any processes of change and the tools to steer and influence them. Peter Checkland introduced his soft system methodology as a critique against what he regarded as oversimplification of reality (Checkland, 1981 and 1991, 1). His aim was to understand large social systems through feedback cycles. Checkland emphasized that people create their own reality and are always active and organic parts of the system. This is why systems formed by humans cannot be studied or manipulated from the outside. Checkland was chiefly interested in identifying systemic changes rather than regulating or manipulating them. From the early 1990s onward, Peter Senge's concept of learning organization gained wide currency. Organizational learning had previously been successfully addressed by Argyris and Schön (1978), so in this sense the notion of systemic learning of organizations was not entirely new. However, Senge (1990) was more clearly connected to the tradition of systems thinking, especially to the idea of continuous renewal. He was interested not only in the changes required by the environment or adaptive learning, but also in learning processes and organizational change that pave the way to generative learning (ibid., 14).

These three branches of systems thinking (systems dynamics, soft systems and learning organization) highlighted a new research interest: the attempt to *understand change* and its manifestations from a systemic point of view. Forrester, Checkland and Senge represented a new way of thinking, but initially they were still quite firmly anchored either to the discourse of open systems or cybernetics. However, at the same time (in fact starting from the 1960s), a whole new systems theory discourse began to evolve, and to gain ever-increasing recognition.

The evolving new systems paradigm was not based on open systems theory or cybernetics, but it marked a complete departure from old ways of systems outlining and thinking. The new paradigm focused on the chaotic and *unpredictable behavior* of systems (rather than on their stability) and on the *internal dynamics of systems* (rather than on feedback cycles). The new perspective grew out of three main sources:

1 Complexity and chaos research, as represented by Lorenz (1993 and 2005), Feigenbaum (1982 and 1993), Mandelbrot (1977 and 2004), the Santa Fe group (since 1984);
2 Prigogine's self-organizing systems (1980 and 1984);
3 Maturana and Varela's autopoietic systems (1981 and 1987).

Chaos and complexity research represent distinct traditions of their own, yet from a systems theory point of view they also cover a lot of common ground, i.e. intra-systemic dynamics and changes originating from within. Chaos theories emphasize the perspective of unpredictability and permanent, uncontrollable laws, whereas complexity research places more weight on emergent intra-systemic characteristics.

The most prominent instigator of this new line of thinking was American meteorologist Edward Lorenz, who brought along a whole new perspective on dynamic and chaotic systems in the area of meteorology. Whereas previously it was thought that chaos and discontinuity were instances of system malfunction, Lorenz

(1963) argued that they were in fact the normal state for many systems: some systems, such as climate conditions, were in a constant state of chaos, however in an orderly fashion. Chaotic systems are particularly sensitive to change because they are often composed of an infinite number of interactions and are therefore in perpetual motion. Even the slightest change in the original state of the system may have dramatic effects throughout the whole system. Another noteworthy chaos researcher is Benoit B. Mandelbrot, whose studies on fractals formed by chaotic systems have attracted much attention. Fractal theory means that the same structures and patterns can be found within the system at different levels, i.e. that the system repeats itself at both the micro and macro level (e.g. Mandelbrot, 1977). A major influence in this field is the Santa Fe Institute: founded in 1984, it is perhaps the world's leading research center on complex systems.

The chaos and complexity perspective implied three fundamental changes to the earlier systems views of open and closed systems. These changes concerned the conception of a system, possibilities to influencing the system and the focus of research interest.

The conception of the dynamics of the system. The focus shifted from equilibrium, stability and continuity to imbalance, change and discontinuity. In contrast to earlier beliefs, the continued existence of the system was not dependent on the maintenance of equilibrium. Chaos was not a disruption or aberration in the system but, on the contrary, often a prerequisite for existence and development.

Conceptions of how the system could be steered and influenced. The interest was no longer on manipulation or control of the system. Instead the system could be understood and it could be steered and influenced from within, through involvement and participation in the system, i.e. interaction. In order to glean information about the system, people had to be actively involved in the system. Objective, external observation was merely a delusion.

The focus of research interests. Whereas previously researchers were interested in searching for general laws, principles, symmetry and harmony, their interest now turned to understanding the nature of change, the unfolding of changes and processes of radical renewal.

We can distinguish between three different paradigms in the development of systems thinking. The first paradigm refers to systems that are controlled by universal laws, regularities and stability. Research under this paradigm aims to explain and define laws and principles and to predict events on a theoretical basis. According to the underlying theories, systems are machine-like and obey predetermined laws. Their foundation is provided by classical Newtonian physics, which is the paradigmatic basis of Western science.

The second paradigm is based on general systems theory as developed by von Bertalanffy. According to this theory, systems are not regarded as closed or mechanical machineries, but, on the contrary, as constantly evolving, open organisms that communicate and change with their environments. The paradigm emphasizes both the system's interaction with its environment and its alternative, open paths of development. Open systems are in a constant state of controlled change, yet they are striving all the time for a new equilibrium, and permanent disequilibrium would lead to system breakdown. The intra-system process is supported and maintained by input-throughput-output feedback cycles, which are regulated by the system from within.

The third paradigm focuses on the system's own internal, autonomous dynamics. Here, the system is looked upon as a highly complex entity that is in a state of inherent disequilibrium and chaos. The paradigm emphasizes a) the capacity of the system for self-organization and renewal; b) the system's discontinuity and non-determinism; and c) the non-locality of the system. *The main interests of the third paradigm lie in the system's self-renewal, self-organization and its capacity for radical change.*

The three paradigms can be seen as complementary perspectives on systems thinking. None of them is right or wrong as such, but can instead be seen as a (partly chronological) continuum of understanding systems. The paradigms also refer to the existence of different kinds of systems with different characteristics. Each paradigm still offers a valid point of departure, depending on the situation and the type of system under scrutiny. However, it is crucial to understand the paradigms and the different – even contradictory – prerequisites behind the respective systems. There is no such scientific point of departure as 'systems theory', since every analysis always involves certain tradition or perspective on systems, i.e. a system approach can refer to various theories on systems. To refer generally to 'systems thinking' or 'systems theory' (as is more often the case in the research literature) is meaningless unless one's point of departure is explicitly anchored to a certain systems paradigm or at least a systems tradition.

From a practical point of view, understanding the system paradigms sheds useful light on how organizations have been managed and continue to be managed today. These paradigms describe comprehensive beliefs and mental models that are employed in the design and implementation of change processes, as well as in the management and leadership of organizations. They also help us to understand the sometimes hard-to-resolve conflicts that arise between decision-makers and the people responsible for implementation. If a creative development project is

Table 7.1 The paradigms of systems thinking (adapted from Ståhle, 1998, 43)

Paradigm	*Origin*	*Characteristic*	*Research interest*	*Objective*
I Closed systems	Newton	Static, deterministic, mechanical	Principles, rules, laws	Prediction, control
II Open systems	von Bertalanffy	Balanced, near equilibrium equifinal, living	Feedback processes, changes, adaptation	Control, maintenance, development
III Dynamic systems	Lorenz Prigogine Maturana Varela	Imbalance, far-from-equilibrium, uncontrollable, complexity, chaos	Self-organization, self-renewal, intra-systemic dynamics	Understanding/ exploiting system dynamics, radical change, innovation

grounded in the first (mechanical) system paradigm, it is easy to predict how the approach and results will differ compared to the situation where the third (dynamic) paradigm of self-direction is adopted. An awareness of these differences may in itself allow for the effective treatment of emerging undesired conflicts or help in choosing an approach that is best suited to the situation.[2]

In this paper I focus on the third paradigm, which is the most informative with respect to the topic in hand: understanding organizational challenges to self-renewal in dynamic environments. The chapters below concentrate on the two major theories in this area: Prigogine's theory of self-organizing systems; and Maturana and Varela's theory of autopoiesis.

Self-organizing systems according to Prigogine

The results of chaos research only began to receive wider attention in the 1980s, even though many key studies were initially published much earlier. These studies had shown that some systems are capable of self-organization and self-development under the force of their own inherent (chaotic) dynamics. Ilya Prigogine published his study on dissipative or self-organizing systems in 1967: this provided the foundation for his analyses of *the process of becoming*, as well as the evolution of *order out of chaos* (Prigogine, 1967a, 1967b, 1967c). It was a revolutionary argument to suggest that systems were capable of self-organization, without any external control (e.g. Nicolis and Prigogine, 1977; Prigogine and Stengers, 1984); this marked a radical departure indeed from general systems theory. Prigogine showed that self-organization was not in fact an exception, but, on the contrary, quite a common systemic characteristic. Examples of self-organization include the operation of markets, human biology or the movement of flocks of birds. An economic system is created out of the countless decisions that are constantly made by people, consciously and unconsciously, to purchase and to sell. The system is neither designed nor controlled by anyone; the market simply creates and re-creates itself. In the same way, genes organize themselves in a certain way as they form a liver cell and in another way to form a muscle cell, and flocks of birds are organized without any external control. A modern example of self-organization is provided by the internet (see also the research on neuron networks by Kohonen *et al.*, 2004).

Prigogine describes the phenomenon of self-organization from various perspectives in various contexts. He points out that the phenomenon of self-organization is quite normal for different systems, yet not all systems are capable of self-organization. However, Prigogine does not offer a clear universal description of the preconditions for self-organization, but deals with the issue in several of his works. Based on the analyses of Prigogine's descriptions, we can identify five core concepts in self organization: 1) far from equilibrium, 2) entropy, 3) iteration, 4) bifurcation, and 5) time. These core concepts have been drawn primarily from four works in which Prigogine describes self-organization from different perspectives: *Order out of Chaos* (Prigogine and Stengers, 1984), *From Being to Becoming* (Prigogine, 1980), *Thermodynamic Theory of Structure, Stability and Fluctuations* (Glandsdorff and Prigogine, 1971) and *Exploring*

Complexity (Prigogine and Nicolis, 1989). The concepts have their origins in chemical and physical phenomena, but Prigogine frequently points out that they are also applicable more generally to social and human systems (e.g. Prigogine, 1976, 120–126; Prigogine and Nicolis, 1989, 238–242).

Far from equilibrium

According to Prigogine, most systems appearing in the world are capable of self-organization, but only in certain conditions. Self-organization can only occur in systems that are capable of remaining far from equilibrium, i.e. at *the edge of chaos*. Prigogine says that in all forms of life, chaos or disequilibrium is the source of new order. In the state of disequilibrium, external change and pressure constantly act on the structures and boundaries of the system: the system is being pushed, as it were, towards disorder and chaos and is therefore under constant threat of collapse. Instead of collapsing, however, the system is driven into a state of dynamic equilibrium, i.e. the system possesses a *dissipative structure*: continuously disintegrating and destroying old structures, the system subsequently re-organizes new structures again. The self-organizing system is in a constant state of chaos *and* order, i.e. it alternates between consecutive overlapping cycles of *chaos and order* and *order and chaos*: after organizing itself and being driven into chaos, it re-organizes and subsequently comes under threat and is driven into disorder, etc. It is noteworthy, however, that not all systems are capable of self-organization: when a stable or balanced mechanical system comes under pressure, it simply disintegrates and is unable to re-organize. (Prigogine and Stengers, 1984, 178, 278, 292; Prigogine, 1980, 100, 123.)

It is impossible to understand the process of self-organization without an understanding of disequilibrium, or what Prigogine refers to as 'far from equilibrium'. Disequilibrium refers to a state of intra-systemic conflict at the edge of chaos; for instance, in a thermodynamic system to the simultaneous presence of hot and cold, or in a social system to the co-existence of conflicting interests. These extremes create an inherent tension in the system and active interaction within the system. Disequilibrium also results from the system being exposed to pressures from the outside, or to stabilization being prevented by the system's internal *entropy*. (Glandsdorff and Prigogine, 1971, 278.)

Entropy

Entropy, Prigogine says, has a function of paramount importance in the process of self-organization. Entropy refers to energy or information that the system produces but that it cannot use. In this sense it may be described as a surplus residue. A high degree of entropy is also indicative of disorder, wasted resources, untapped information or insecurity within the system. Entropy is created when the system exchanges or produces information and energy beyond its needs, or when information is disorganized, unclassified or devalued. Established thinking and the second law of thermodynamics had it that entropy was superfluous and a threat to the system, and only increased the system's destructive instability. Prigogine, however, showed that in systems capable of self-organization, entropy was in fact necessary and indispensable. Entropy introduces uncertainty, imbalance and confusion into the system – and it is this very instability that gives the system its capacity for self-organization. In other words, in the process of self-organizing, excess entropy is both used and absorbed. (Glandsdorff and Prigogine, 1971.)

Iteration

The foundation of all self-organizing systems lies in abundant information exchange, abundant interaction. Intra-systemic interaction, when at its most sensitive and most abundant, refers to the second precondition for self-organization, i.e. iteration. Iteration means a continuous, highly sensitive feedback process or activity via which the information and models produced by the system are rapidly disseminated throughout the system. Iteration gives the system its capacity of self-renewal, its ability to copy internal models from the micro to the macro level, and vice versa. In a sense, it is the system's engine room. For iteration to work properly in the system, intra-systemic interaction must meet two criteria: first of all it must be non-linear, and second it must be based on feedback. The basis for feedback refers to the basic condition of iterative dynamics, i.e. sensitive dependence on the original circumstances. (Prigogine and Nicolis, 1989, 219; Prigogine, 1976, 95.)

Iteration as positive and negative feedback (and feed forward) functions makes the system spontaneous and utterly sensitive to change, i.e. the system dynamics are nonlinear. This often finds expression in what is known as the butterfly effect: initially the effect is seen in only a small part of the system, but it then advances and gradually gathers momentum so that 'the flap of a butterfly's wing in Brazil sets off a tornado in Texas' (Lorenz, 1993, 14). This would not be possible without a sensitive and continuous reciprocal feedback process between different components of the system. Iteration is the driving force of self-organization, because it constantly generates new information and new structures and carries the effect throughout the system. Iteration guarantees that whatever happens within the system, it spreads and multiplies. (Prigogine and Stengers, 1984, 154; Prigogine and Nicolis, 1989, 72.)

Bifurcation

Bifurcation is a zone in between determinism and free choice. It means that a) there are certain periods in the life of a system when it can make genuine choices, b) these choices cannot be predicted and c) the choices are irreversible. The system has a choice between two or more alternatives when it is driven ever further from its state of equilibrium. Bifurcation, therefore, is always 'a manifestation of a new solution' (Prigogine, 1980, 105), and it produces a solution that is not a logical or necessary extension of the previous structure. '*The event of bifurcation, therefore, is also always a source of innovation.*' (Prigogine and Nicolis, 1989, 74).

The change of a system to a new state of equilibrium happens suddenly, as if in a single (quantum) leap. At the point of bifurcation, the system rejects huge amounts of information, reducing the amount of entropy and paving the way to the creation of a new order, a new dynamic structure. Between the old and the new system structure there is a moment of *discontinuity* and non-*location*, i.e. neither old nor new system structure exist. The point of bifurcation is a key concept with respect to irreversible changes in self-organizing systems. When the system drifts ever further from its original state of equilibrium, it can only choose between existing new possibilities; there is no returning to the old. Bifurcation does not necessarily require chaos; a state of equilibrium will suffice, together with a genuinely open and non-deterministic situation. The choice made by the system cannot be predicted, i.e. the choice is never made by necessity, and in this sense it is a genuine *free* choice. (Prigogine and Stengers, 1984, 169; Prigogine 1980, 106; Prigogine and Nicolis, 1989, 72.)

The historical path that the system has followed in its development includes a series of stable stages dominated by deterministic laws, and a series of unstable stages or points of bifurcation where the system can make a *free* choice between several alternatives. This mixture of necessities and possibilities constitutes the *history* of the system. (Prigogine and Stengers, 1984, 169.)

Time

From the system's point of view, time is both subjective and objective. Subjective time means that the system creates its own history via its choices. Bifurcations not only create a new order, but also at the same time equip the system with new unique characteristics and structures. The constant production of entropy forces the system constantly to move forward, to continuously develop and find new forms. This kind of evolution requires time, and is built into the system: it is the system's way of being. Over time, all parts of the system and their subsystems contribute to driving forward the process of evolution. (Prigogine and Stengers, 1984, 106; Prigogine, 1980, 127.)

According to Prigogine, everything has its own forward-looking dynamics; all development is geared forward. In self-organization the main role is played by entropy, because entropy is also key from the point of view of time and evolution. In nature and in human life, entropy constantly produces development and forward movement, which has both an innovative and, on the other hand, a deterministic side. We live our lives on the interfaces of both necessity and creativity, of being and becoming. (Prigogine and Lefever, 1973, 132.)

In this sense, the perspective of timing is crucial to the process of creation, to the changeover from one point of bifurcation to another. Bifurcations appear unexpectedly, and the possibility of choice and change is only opened up with the occurrence of the point of bifurcation. All systems have their own history, an irreversible series of events that go together to form a path of a unique life. It can be argued that each process, with time, produces its own unique pattern out of the alternation between chaos and new order. For self-organizing systems, this means that it is essential to be able to master and cooperate with time. The accumulation of

Table 7.2 Self-organizing systems according to Prigogine (based on Ståhle, 1998, 72)

Main concepts of self-organization	*Far from equilibrium*	*Entropy*	*Iteration*	*Bifurcation*
Characteristic	continuous or periodic	excess residue, not directly applicable	non-linear, based on feedback	between necessity and freedom
Manifestation	fluctuations, intra-system conflicts, pressures from outside system	abundant information exchange, tolerance of insecurity and confusion	sensitive reaction and feedback, positive and negative feedback	proper timing
Significance to self-renewal	precondition for radical change	creation of new order	cumulative power	innovation and new solutions

entropy takes time, the exchange of information takes time, the iterative feedback process takes time – and points of bifurcation have their own timing that needs to be recognized. (Prigogine and Nicolis, 1989, 242; Prigogine, 1976, 124.)

Adaptations of self-organization in further research

Prigogine's work on the self-organizing process might have universal applicability, even though his findings were made in the context of chemistry and physics. He himself is convinced of the universal nature of the principles of self-organization (Prigogine and Stengers, 1984, 298). There are no detailed scientific analyses of the self-organizing process that would provide conclusive evidence in either direction. However, self-organization as such has raised increasing interest in various branches of research, and the angles and results of this work are closely connected to Prigogine's findings.

Prigogine's key concepts – 'order out of chaos,' 'self-organization through bifurcation' and 'dissipative structures' – have been applied in a variety of fields, ranging from quantum physics (e.g. Wheatley, 1999) to the mental process of knowledge creation and neurology (e.g. Piaget, 1975; Collier, 2005). Applications in the study of social systems in general (e.g. Mileton-Kelley, 2003), economics (e.g. Arthur 1994 and Chen, 2000), organizational systems (e.g. Marion, 1999; Griffin, 2002) and developmental and innovation processes (e.g. Fischer, 2001; Kuschu, 2001; Nonaka, 2006) are particularly interesting.

Self-organization has also attracted increasing research interest in social and organizational sciences, where it has been studied in the context of collective intelligence, among others, by Hakkarainen (2006) and Engeström and colleagues (Engström *et al.*, 1999). Collective intelligence refers to processes of intelligent activity that find expression at the collective rather than individual level. Many animals are capable of coordinating and self-organizing mutual activities at such a high level of sophistication that they can be considered to possess a kind of swarm intelligence. The swarm intelligence of ants, for instance, is a form of self-organizing activity. Humans engage in various processes of collective intelligence that resemble swarm intelligence, both metaphorically and literally. Many of the manifestations of human collective intelligence are outcomes of self-organizing activity rather than representing coordinated, organized or directed individual processes.

According to Hakkarainen, the highly complex problems that people have to resolve in knowledge work or in high technology require ever greater reliance on socially distributed intelligence and competence. Collective intelligence is based upon the self-organization of the social collectivity's intelligent systems into a collective intelligent system. The self-organization of intelligent activity within the social collectivity is crucial to overcoming and exceeding the individual's intellectual resources. (Hakkarainen, 2006.)

Engeström *et al.* (1999) have argued for the emergence of a historically new type of work, which they call knotworking. Knotworking is characterized by the absence of an organizing structure or centre; instead the participants collaborate to self-organize their work, its objectives and modi operandi. The approach, developed by Engeström and colleagues (1999, 1987) on the basis of the cultural-historical theory of activity, offers a conceptually advanced way of understanding collective intelligence. That approach is now emerging as an international metatheory of collective intelligence that provides a unified foundation for the analysis of human collective activity (Minnis and John-Steiner, 2001). Engeström's theoretical frame of reference does not draw directly upon Prigogine's work, but his research certainly stands as an excellent concretization of the phenomenon of self-organization as it is discussed in this article.

Social collectivities spontaneously produce an accurate understanding of the distribution of knowledge and know-how within an organization, which refers to *transactive memory* (Wegner, 1986; Moreland 1999). This is true particularly in situations where people are working with highly complex information and knowledge for extended periods of time. A team that works closely together for long periods, such as an elite anti-terrorist police group, a football team or an emergency room team may develop a *collective mind* (Weick and Roberts, 1993). Intensive interaction makes it possible to transcend the boundaries of the individual's skills and competencies and to form a socio-cultural system with *hybrid expertise* that cuts across those boundaries (Howells, 1997; Spinardi, 1998). It has also been suggested that the current era of information networks is changing our conceptions of how human intelligence works, indeed, that it calls for a new understanding of humans as networking cultural creatures whose *intelligence is socially and physically divided* (Salomon, 1993).

Theories of collective intelligence owe their origin to early pragmatists such as John Dewey and George Herbert Mead, but they have now been sidelined from mainstream psychology. Psychology, however, was dominated by a natural science ideal that did not provide solid enough premises for an investigation of social intelligence, and researchers in this field were unable to offer methodologically reliable tools. The situation has now changed, for three reasons. First of all, modern audio, video and network technology means that complex collective phenomena can be recorded. Second, the analysis of social networks provides the methodological tools that are needed to analyze relations between individual agents. And thirdly, the theory of self-organizing dynamic systems helps us to conceptualize complex phenomena of interaction. (Hakkarainen, 2006, 398.)

Autopoietic systems by Maturana and Varela

Prigogine described a process of renewal that does not necessarily lead to incremental development through small steps, but that is, on the contrary, geared to producing whole new solutions and structures. These may also be described as innovations, since the new solution always introduces genuinely *new information* to the system (Prigogine and Stengers, 1984, 307; Prigogine and Nicolis, 1989, 132, 140). Chilean biologists Humberto Maturana and Francisco Varela, on the other hand, approached the process of renewal from a different perspective. They focused in their research on living systems as self-copying, self-reproducing organizations, thus addressing the principles of a system's self-renewal from a completely new angle as compared to the perspectives adopted in earlier complexity studies. In the discussion below I first consider autopoietic systems by reference to Maturana and Varela, and then proceed to a social scientific application of their theory by German sociologist Niklas Luhmann.

Maturana and Varela published their study on autopoietic systems in the early 1970s. The concept of autopoiesis was originally coined in the field of biology to describe the capacity of cells for self-reproduction. The theory belongs to the category of new emerging paradigms dealing with spontaneous phenomena and the self-organization of physical, biological and social systems (Zelenyn, 1981a, xv).

Autopoiesis means self-production, self-maintenance, sameness and harmony (*autos* = self, *poiein* = to do, to produce, to maintain existence, to do again, to conceptualize). In autopoietic systems, *relations* and *interaction* constitute both the system itself and its boundaries, not just the system components, i.e. relations and interactions *are* the main components of a system. The constituent parts influence the whole, and the whole influences the constituent parts, i.e. the relations within the system are organized in such a way that they are constantly reproduced. Autopoiesis refers to 'the process of self-production and self-renewal in living systems' (Dobuzinskis, 1987, 214). The coherence of the autopoietic system is always the outcome of the close contacts and interaction between constituent factors (Maturana, 1981, 23).

According to Maturana (1981, 23) the autopoietic system is defined as follows: 'The unity of an autopoietic system is the result of the neighborhood relations and interactions (interplay and properties) of its components.' Thus autopoietic systems are entities a) where the components create the network and the network creates the components – i.e. interaction between the constituent parts of the system maintains and constantly reproduces the network, but on the other hand the network also produces and maintains the constituent parts; and b) whose boundaries are formed by the parts of the network that are involved in building the network (ibid., 21, 22).

All social systems are dependent on communication between their members. If there is not enough communication, the system cannot function properly. In the words of Varela: 'In defining a system, when conceiving something about it, one is already part of it.' (Varela and Johnson, 1976, 31). According to this theory, then, passive membership of an autopoietic system is impossible; membership has to be based on active involvement and interaction. Each individual in the network, for instance, influences the system and contributes to its reproduction, but at the same time the network also constantly changes the individual and the individual's relations of interaction.

The theory of autopoiesis emphasizes *being as something*. Being, however, is not seen as a static condition, but above all as a process in which the system continuously produces and reproduces itself. The aim of autopoietic organization, then, is the system itself and its existence – not 'doing' or 'representing.' *Autopoiesis is a property of a system, reproducing itself (internally) in a way so as to preserve its organization, which is to say its identity.* The way the system is organized is, in fact, the system's identity: it is on this basis that the system can be identified and distinguished from other systems (cf. Rapoport, 1986, 114).

The autopoietic system has a special relationship to its environment. Von Bertalanffy's open systems and Prigogine's self-organizing systems are both dependent on the environment – or at least the environment heavily influences them. The autopoietic system, by contrast, is essentially autonomous. Maturana and Varela say that the environment is a mirror – or point of reference – for the autopoietic system, i.e. the system lives in relation to the environment but is not dependent on it (Maturana and Varela, 1987, 75). Seen from the point of view of its organization and maintenance, then, the autopoietic system is closed. This means that the system only realizes its own autopoiesis, i.e. its own existence. However, autopoietic systems are closed only as far as their essence is concerned; this does not apply to any other of their functions. In order to ensure that their other functions remain effective, autopoietic systems must engage in exchange with their environment. *A cell, for example, communicates with its environment, unlike the genetic code that controls the cell.* Whereas structure and function in self-organizing systems can sometimes change quite radically, in autopoietic systems they usually remain constant (Jantsch, 1981, 65).

Varela described the autopoietic phenomenon in the context of a social system as early as 1976. He defined a system as a being that always has clear boundaries, although those boundaries vary depending on the observer. Varela argued that, in reality, persons who define the boundaries of the social system are themselves an integral part of the system, and personal needs and perspectives always influence their view on the system. This means that all *social systems are self-referential* in that they always define themselves (Varela and Johnson, 1976, 26–31). The logic of self-reference can be summarized as follows: *what we see is always a reflection of what we are.* According to Varela (Varela and Johnson, 1976, 29), every characteristic that we identify in an object is always dependent on ourselves as observers. In other words, objects never appear to us objectively, as assemblies of their own inherent characteristics, but every individual perceives an object through the lens of their own characteristics, and partly as a result of the interaction that they themselves have created. All system characteristics are thus filtered and expressed through the observer's own characteristics.

Renewal is not a fundamental characteristic of autopoietic systems; instead the key lies in the 'constitution of the unity to be reproduced' (Maturana, 1981, 23). Autopoietic renewal does not primarily mean regeneration, but rather *maintenance of the core of the autopoietic system.* As Kickert (1991, 198) has shown, renewal requires a constant and ongoing struggle. Even though autopoiesis refers primarily to maintenance, it also requires constant renewal of the system. As systems everywhere are in a constant process of natural degradation (according to the second law of thermodynamics), maintenance itself requires constant renewal. However, even maintenance does not simply mean the reproduction of the same models in similar conditions, but the system also works constantly to renew its elements and their mutual relationships.

To sum up, an autopoietic system has two distinctive characteristics:

1 *A core that finds expression through interaction.* The essence of a system cannot be understood without studying the interaction taking place within that system. The main purpose of an autopoietic system is its existence, which is characterized by the reproduction of its own core, i.e. the continuity of its own identity.
2 *An overall view of the system cannot be gained from the outside.* When an individual describes or defines a system, he or she is already part of that system (Varela and Johnson, 1976, 29). The process of defining is itself active involvement and participation, a process in which the individual's view of the system is formed only in interaction. The essence of the system cannot be defined from the outside; it can only be properly understood by someone actively involved in the system.

A human being, for instance, is an autopoietic system. In accordance with the first of these two characteristics, the sole purpose of the human individual is 'existence' and 'becoming a self.' The true nature of the individual is always expressed in his or her way of interacting with the environment and other people. In accordance with the second characteristic, it is impossible to define or characterize someone else without the person's own characteristics impacting that assessment. Whatever statements or arguments the person makes about another person, (s)he will always simultaneously reveal something about him- or herself. For example, from the comment that "he is an extremely dominating person," it will not be clear to the listener whether that person is bossier than usual, or whether the comment reflects more on the person making the statement, say that it is hard for that person to hold his own, or that he takes the view that people are supposed to be modest and humble.

Like Prigogine, Maturana and Varela also deal with the process of change and renewal. Their perspectives, however, are quite different. Prigogine emphasizes dramatic changes that affect structures and basic functions, i.e. vacillation between

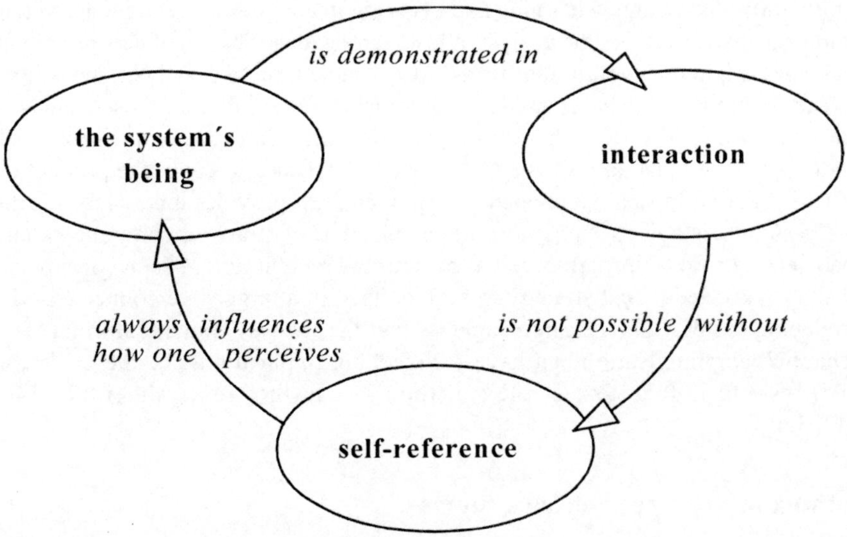

Figure 7.1 The autopoietic nature of systems (Ståhle, 1998, 81).

chaos and order. Maturana and Varela, by contrast, emphasize continuity and maintenance as core in a systemic function, which implies ongoing, incremental change for system maintenance. For instance, almost all cells in the human body are replaced over a period of two years, yet people can still be identified throughout their life. Thus both incremental change and stability are simultaneously present in autopoietic systems.

Applications of autopoiesis theory

The concept of autopoiesis has attracted widespread attention, and applications have been put forward in virtually all fields of systems research. The most significant applications have come in the fields of biology and medicine (e.g. Boden, 2000; Naohide, 2005) and in the fields of *human* networking (e.g. Plass *et al.*, 2002), knowledge management (e.g. Okada, 2004; Jackson, 2007) and knowledge creation (e.g. Ratcheva, 2007; Thompson, 2004), physics (e.g. Tsytovich *et al.*, 2007) and social sciences (Nomura, 2002). For the most part, however, the references are *recognitions of the phenomena* rather than rigorous theoretical analyses of autopoiesis. Consequently the applications suffer from some grave weaknesses. First, the interpretations offered tend to over-emphasize the concept by treating autopoiesis synonymously with autonomy. Second, no clear *conceptual* distinction is elaborated between autopoietic, complex, chaotic and self-organizing systems, i.e. it is assumed that complex systems are autopoietic and that self-organizing systems are autopoietic.

One noteworthy exception is Maula's (1999) more analytic treatment of autopoiesis. Her application of autopoiesis theory is embedded in the context of multinational companies' learning and evolving in complex environments. Maula points out that an autopoietic analysis allows for the identification of new principles that can explain the evolution of firms. At the same time this analysis sheds light on multinational companies' underlying structures and processes, especially on the knowledge flows and the consistency of their strategic composition. The findings indicate that autopoiesis theory can be extended to cover the production of various non-physical components. In particular, it provides a new tool for the analyses of strategic composition, i.e. a selection of strategic components and their relationships. Furthermore, it allows for the redefinition of such concepts as identity, knowledge and strategy to be redefined in a larger interconnected self-producing system. The research suggests that the less-structured "informal" and "chaotic" communication can have far-reaching implications for the evolution of firms and is therefore a relevant topic for further research. (ibid., 346, 347, 350.)

Luhmann's self-referential systems

Maturana and Varela were biologists and developed their theory of autopoiesis primarily in the context of natural sciences. German sociologist Niklas Luhmann has expanded this theory and applied it to social systems in a noteworthy manner. According to Fuchs (1988b: 21), "at present, Luhmann's theory of social systems is the only general theory that can claim to introduce a new paradigm … Luhmann's proposal will radically change the conventional ways of doing social theory." Luhmann is convinced that social systems are autopoietic, and it is a recurring theme in several of his works (1982b, 1984a, 1984b, 1986, 1990, 1995a, 1995b). He goes so far as to argue that the theory of autopoietic social systems requires a conceptual revolution in sociology.

According to Luhmann, the foundation of the system lies in communication. Social systems use communication as a means of autopoietic renewal: it is only by means of communication that the system is capable of maintaining and duplicating itself. By communication, Luhmann refers to activity or to an event rather than the subject of communication (Luhmann, 1986a, 174). In the theory of autopoietic systems, communication is the basic unit of self-referential processes (Luhmann, 1986a, 177). Communication is based on contacts that are constantly created and renewed by the network of interaction and that cannot exist outside of the network. In this sense autopoiesis means that continuity requires communication (Luhmann, 1990, 3, 14).

Maturana, too, repeatedly points out that the autopoietic (social) system is composed of communication, not components (e.g. people). An autopoietic system can be defined as an entity that consists of the *relationships* in which its components are reproduced (Maturana, 1981, 29). Luhmann agrees that the autopoietic system constantly creates itself, i.e. its essence. This is a process in which the system constantly reproduces its basic components in a network formed by those components. The outcome may be some form of biological life, consciousness or (in the case of a social system) communication. Whatever the outcome, the system that is created in the autopoietic process is always distinctive and clearly identifiable in relation to its environment. Autopoiesis is these systems' way of being and self-reproducing (Luhmann 1989, 143).

Communication as the basic unit of systemic processes refers to activity, an event and understanding. Understanding does not mean one has to approve of the content communicated, but that communication always leads in open situations either to approval or rejection of the content. In other words, the function of communication is not to achieve mutual understanding. By contrast communication may force situations to change because it leads to choices without which interaction would never happen. Only communication itself can create situations that open up new possibilities to achieve a point of bifurcation, which in turn pave the way to different future scenarios. (Luhmann, 1986c, 176.)

According to Luhmann (1995a, 37), the most important factor in the system's self-renewal is controlling its complexity. This is not, however, a matter of manipulation from outside the system, but rather of *controlling complexity from within*. This perspective is also reflected in the way that Luhmann defines the autopoietic system. In addition to open, closed and self-organizing systems, Luhmann introduces a new category of systems, namely, *self-referential* systems. Self-referential systems can regulate their own boundaries, i.e. they open and close autonomously and are thus at once both closed and open.

Below, I proceed to discuss Luhmann's concept of self-referential systems in somewhat more detail. I examine his main ideas via three of his main concepts: 1) self-referential closure, 2) double contingency and 3) processing meaning.

Self-referential closure: the foundation of autonomy

Luhmann (1995a) says that the autopoietic system is fundamentally autonomous and independent of its environment, and in that sense closed. Self-referential closure means that the system can choose either to open up or to remain closed and use the information gleaned from the environment in its own processes of renewal. In this way the system remains autonomous and independent, but at the same time communicates with the environment and is open to the environment on its own terms.

The self-referential autopoietic process is dependent on the ability to make a distinction between oneself and the environment. Luhmann says that if the autopoietic system did not have an environment, it would need to create one in which to reflect itself (Luhmann, 1986a, 175). However, Luhmann's notion of self-reference does not mean that the system would directly create an image of itself on the basis of what it sees in the mirror. Rather, it would be looking into what may be described as a 'negative mirror', which means that the system creates an image of itself on the basis of the image in the mirror, but it does not draw information about itself directly from the image; rather it uses the image to create a perception of itself as *distinct from its environment*. This process may be described as one of negative mirroring, in which the system learns to recognize what it is *not* like, i.e. how it differs from the other (systems).

According to Luhmann, *self-referential systems are characterized by the ability of self-referential closure* (Luhmann, 1990). Without this ability the system would be unable to set itself apart from the environment as an autonomous being and become interwoven as part of the environment. The system reflects its autonomy via self-defined and self-regulated boundaries. Because system renewal takes place via the system's internal dynamics, the role of the environment in transactions is seen in a different way when compared to the theory of open systems. Despite these differences the views are not fundamentally at odds with each other, because even self-referential systems exchange information with their environment – it is only that they regulate this interaction autonomously by opening and closing their boundaries depending on the situation. Luhmann (1995a, 29) emphasizes that the role of system boundaries is highly significant in new systems thinking. Boundaries represent the evolutionary peak of the system and reflect the operation of the most advanced systems.

Double contingency: trust and equality

According to Luhmann (1995a, 118), *the basic explanation for social action lies in the relationship between two persons*. Systemic change is not primarily reduced to individuals, but to their relationships. The core of a self-referential system is manifested in double contingency: all individuals in the system live in a network of reciprocal dependencies. Without these dependencies, the system lacks the necessary connectivity. It is precisely by virtue of its internal relationships that a system can form a coherent entity – without those relationships there would be no system.

From a social point of view the key issue with regard to autopoietic systems does not have to do with self-reproduction, but with systemic development: how the system moves from one point of departure to the next. According to Luhmann (1995a, 36) the answer lies in the system's relationships of double contingency: these contingencies determine *the possibilities of change and learning*.

Double contingency relations are always *symmetrical and voluntary*. Symmetry means that both parties are aware of their contingent relationship. Voluntariness, then, means that both parties accept this relationship of reciprocal dependence (Luhmann, 1995a, 108, 125). Communication in this type of relationship *always involves risks*. If the individual is unable to take risks, or to overcome the fear of the unknown, "the system is undetermined and thereby blocked" (ibid., 131). One of the key preconditions for double contingency is the development of *trust* or *distrust*. A person who shares a lot of trust also enhances his or her scope of action. However, trust inherently includes the possibility of distrust, and is therefore highly sensitive. Breaking trust will necessarily bring changes to the relationship (ibid., 128). Trust is always freely handed out according to the situation; it cannot be forced or manipulated. Trust makes it possible for the system to develop and on the other hand provides it with the power for ever riskier self-renewal. Trust is not based on reported factual information, but information serves as an indicator of trust. Trust is a universal precondition for action (ibid., 129). Luhmann emphasizes that every system first puts trust to the test and only then proceeds to process meanings – specifically, and only in this order (ibid., 112).

Processing meaning: information as an experience

The processing of meaning takes places in double-contingency relationships (Luhmann, 1995a, 113). When information is considered in a systemic context, it refers more to an 'event' than to a 'fact.' Information, in a systemic context, refers to the kind of facts, information or knowledge that have some impact on the system. In other words, information is defined not through its form or other characteristics, but only through its impact. Information that is repeated in a system no longer serves in that system as actual information, because it no longer changes the state of the system. When information is repeated in identical format, it does retain its meanings, but it can no longer impact the systems – therefore it does not function as information. *Information changes the state of the system. Information is more of an experience than a fact*. Information is the basic unit of an event in a system: this is not just data referring to facts, but information that affects people personally. Only if information causes reactions (i.e. changes the state of the system) will it become a process element (ibid., 67, 69).

According to Luhmann (1995a), meanings are core structural elements of the system. Psychic and social systems have developed in and through a process of evolution in which both complexity and self-reference are necessary. This achievement of evolution can be described as 'meaning' (ibid., 59). "Not all systems process complexity and self-reference in the form of meanings but for those that do, this is the *only* possibility ... Systems bound to meaning can therefore never experience or act in a manner that is free from meaning." (Ibid., 61–62). According to Luhmann, the core of interaction lies in meaning, because meaning is created and it materializes in the event of interaction. Meanings are created in an evolutionary process as a result of human interaction. In the search for meaning, the system realizes its potential: contradictory experiences and views engender activity, which in turn evolves into goal-oriented action. *The social structure in self-referential systems is always created through the processing of meanings* (ibid., 61–65, 113).

The speed of systemic renewal is proportional to the speed at which meanings develop. This refers to the ability of the system to make rapid choices to develop and create information. Systemic coherence is important, because without it there can be no double contingencies in the system; and without double contingencies, the system would not be able to produce or test meanings. The function and purpose of the system are based on meanings (Luhmann, 1995a, 119), and double contingency serves as a kind of internal accelerator in the system (ibid., 131).

The system's capacity for self-reference

Self-reference is the starting-point for all communication within the system. *Self-reference* is the core that is fundamentally autonomous, but it evolves in a reflective relationship with the environment. *Being and becoming thus lie at the heart of all renewal.*

Luhmann says that self-renewal can be seen as an event that is based on three decisive criteria. The first is double contingency. The quality of social relations is essential to the system's capacity for self-renewal, i.e. the participants must encounter one another at the same level. The mutual dependence must be recognized and admitted, the risk involved in developing relations of trust must be taken into account and the participants must act accordingly. Double contingency does not require mutually shared values, symbols or consensus (Luhmann, 1995a, 172–173, 126). Interaction does, on the other hand, necessarily require *mutual trust and recognition of a mutual relationship of dependence.*

The second criterion concerns the quality of information. Exchange of information, i.e. communication, is a necessary condition for the system to function, because no action is produced without communication. Whether or not the system is capable of autonomously renewing itself depends on the quality of information that is exchanged within the system. Luhmann emphasizes the importance of information that becomes a driving force and process element of the system. By this, Luhmann refers to information that is shared in the discourse of experience – i.e. information is related to the speaker's experience and at once engenders experiences in the listener. In practice this means that the information exchanged *influences* the people that constitute the system and in this way changes the state of the system. Information that does not change the state of the system is meaningless. A systemic message is never superficial but, on the contrary, it always has some impact or another. (Luhmann, 1986c, 174.)

The third criterion is related to meanings. Luhmann shows that meanings are created collectively within the system, as a consequence of collectively produced events. Meanings are never fully ready, nor can they be directly transferred to others. The creation of meaning always requires double-contingent relations, which in turn engender action. *Meanings are thus basic structural elements of a system* and all operations are based and steered by meanings.

From Luhmann's presentation we can extract the following criteria for self-renewal that serve as the basic operational preconditions for a self-referential system:

1 connection with other systems
   - use as a point of reference
2 double contingency
   - symmetric dependence (balance of power)
   - voluntary provision of trust
3 experiential information
   - information as an event
   - information produced in an experiential discourse that has the power to change the state of the system
4 creation of collectively produced meanings

Table 7.3 Description of self-referential systems

Main concepts	*Self-reference*	*Double contingency*	*Information*	*Meaning*
Characteristic	Identifiable core, self-reproduction	Mutual, recognized positive inter-dependency	Experience – not representation, Event – not fact	Basic element of system operation and structure
Manifestation	Definition of self, self-referential closure, contacts with other systems	Equality, trust, risk-taking	Information exchange, reactions and responses, dialogue	Collective processing (in double-contingent relations)
Contribution to self-renewal	Internal control of complexity	Internal system accelerator	Power of renewal	Actualizes system's potential

Source: adapted from Ståhle, 1998, 90.

These criteria are demonstrated in the way the system refers to itself. At the same time they demonstrate how self-reference is the way in which the system controls its own internal complexity.

Autopoiesis, as set forth by Luhmann as a *social systems theory*, has had an immense impact on social systems thinking and its recent development. The concept of autopoiesis has been developed in intrinsic detail in fields as diverse as gender research (Misheva, 2001) and history (Gregory, 2006). It has been deployed in a wide range of studies from organizational studies to small companies (Koivisto, 2005; Christensen, 2003) to research on global politics and law (Albert, 2002; Albert and Hilkemeier, 2004; D'Amato, 2003) and the competitiveness of multinational corporations (Hessling and Pahl, 2006). At the same time it has been the focus of conceptual criticism and development (Jalava, 2003; Gumbrecht, 2001).

The dynamics of self-renewal in organizations

The third paradigm of systemic thinking highlights the fact that each system has its own built-in spontaneous dynamics and potential that can be exploited in the right circumstances. In a mechanical way of thinking, the components of the system – say, the members of an organization – can be harnessed to pursue predetermined goals and objects with the support of management and control systems. But, for example, Prigogine's main idea is that in certain circumstances and under certain conditions, systems are capable of organizing themselves, i.e. producing completely new physical, social and mental structures that are not just an incremental step forward, but an innovation-like shift. How this happens in real organizations is a huge challenge that may generate significant competitive advantage for companies in knowledge economies where competitiveness is mainly based on brands (company 'self' and identity) and innovations.

The secret of innovative development and, by the same token, of organizational competitiveness, lies in whether or not people can learn to make good use of the capacity of self-organization, or whether that potential is constrained by excessive control. As Prigogine points out, in some circumstances, chaos produces nothing but confusion; in others it may produce radical innovations. The systemic pre-conditions for innovation are concentrated, for example, in the system's ability to cope constructively with conflicts and threats to its own power structures and ways of thinking. The questioning of the status quo and openness to new possibilities presents a huge challenge at both the individual and organizational level.[3]

The processing of information, i.e. an entropy-producing communication process, also runs counter to the order on the strength of which organizations have learned over time to operate. The process of self-organization requires a great deal of the participants involved. First of all, it is necessary to have a high tolerance of the uncertainty that grows out of the initial confusion. If a solution is forced before there is a sufficient amount of entropy, self-organization – and with it any new solutions or innovations – will not happen. On the other hand, self-organization also requires an ability to make good use of points of bifurcation, i.e. to reject even good templates or ideas and most of the work that has gone into them, to make the right decision and proceed accordingly. In this process, solutions do not come about by vote, but by communication: as a rule, the material will speak for itself and begin to self-organize so that the next steps are clearly evident. In the individual's creative work process, this stage often follows close on the heels of the moment of insight, with the solution effectively surfacing out of its own accord. It appears to come out of nowhere, but it has in fact been preceded by extensive, both conscious and unconscious, collection and processing of information.

For Luhmann, self-renewal is a rather different concept than it is for Prigogine. Whereas Luhmann emphasizes the established identity of the system, i.e. the capacity of the system to constantly reproduce itself as an identifiable self, Prigogine is interested to study the system's visible self-organization, its spontaneous transformation that eventually produces a new structure. Luhmann emphasizes continuity, process-like development without crises, whereas Prigogine emphasizes more sudden and dramatic change.

Assessments of organizational renewal and competitiveness tend usually to focus exclusively on action, on what the organization has done to achieve certain goals. In today's high-paced and insecure competitive environment, business organizations must constantly work to identify and define their own competitive assets. Much attention has been paid to products and services, but there is also a growing recognition that the creation of attraction, an image or brand is, in fact, often more important that the development of a specific product. People are intrigued by the aura and identity of a business, and their decisions are largely driven by their desire of identification. Persona or identity, the system's fundamental essence, Luhmann says, is reflected in interaction. In other words, the true essence of a business company is reflected not in what the company says it is, but in how it is reflected in all its activity. It is not enough that the company declares its mission and its values verbally or in writing, but the core of the system lies in its genuine action. The more strongly that core is transmitted to others, the greater its appeal and attraction – both from internal and external perspectives.

The quality of the information or knowledge processed in organizations is of paramount importance to the achievement of results. This means that the micro-level communication processes are quintessential from the point of view of the capacity for organizational self-renewal. Luhmann does not subscribe to the importance of the distinction between explicit and tacit information (elaborated by Polanyi, 1958, and made famous by Nonaka, 1995). Instead he underlines the impact of knowledge as communication: whatever the form of knowledge, it should act as a force that can change the system, i.e. knowledge is more an event than a fact. If product development people exchange information, either verbally or by technical means, but are not really interested in each other's arguments, the information exchanged will remain meaningless and will not contribute to development. Indeed there is good reason to ask whether development projects or change management today pay enough attention to making sure the information exchanged becomes a shared experience, or whether it merely remains a dead letter. Very often it is much easier to intervene in structures, processes and forms than it is to genuinely analyze what is really *happening* in an organization.

Both Prigogine and Luhmann encourage us to focus on communication processes at the micro level. They argue that the possibility of self-renewal is reduced precisely to communication. *The system's capability of interaction will at once determine its changes of renewal*, radical change, innovation and influence. Both Prigogine and Luhmann also draw attention to power structures and the manifestations of power that steer the processes of communication. In Prigogine's view, the production of entropy requires equal exchange of information without power concentrations, which is a key precondition for self-organization. Luhmann, on the other hand, emphasizes double contingency and the equality and mutual trust it requires, without which meanings cannot develop in a system. These are interesting preconditions for development in organizations and other social systems. When the aim is to put the system's development potential to full use, it is necessary, above all, to focus on the power structures demonstrated in communication. Recently studies of social capital in particular have paid much attention to the role of trust in economic productivity and in the success of partnerships (Blomqvist, 2002). In this sense, too, the pioneering work by Prigogine and Luhmann opens up important insights that can pave the way to building up competitive advantage in dynamic business environments.

Notes

1 The author is Professor at Finland Futures Research Centre, Turku School of Economics, pirjo.stahle@tse.fi

2 For more details on organizational applications of the mechanical, organic and dynamic paradigm see Ståhle and Grönroos, 2000.

3 For a detailed synthesis of the preconditions for a self-renewing system, see Ståhle, 1998, 227.

References

Albert, M. (2002). Governance and democracy in European systems: on systems theory and European integration. *Review of International Studies* 28:293–309.

Albert, M. and Hilkermeier, L. (2004). *Observing international relations: Niklas Luhmann and world politics.* New York: Routledge.

Argyris, C. and Schön, D. A. (1978). *Organizational learning: a theory of action perspective.* Reading, MA: Addison-Wesley.

Arthur, W. B. (1994). *Increasing returns and path dependence in the economy.* University of Michigan Press.

Blomqvist, K. (2002). Partnering in the dynamic environment: the role of trust in asymmetrical partnership formation. *Acta Universitatis Lappeenrantaensis* 122. Lappeenranta: Lappeeenranta University of Technology.

Boden, M. A. (2000). Autopoiesis and life. *Cognitive Science Quarterly* 1:117–145.

Brown, S. and Eisenhardt, K. (1998). *Competing on the edge: strategy as structured chaos.* Boston: Harvard Business School Press.

Checkland, P. B. (1981). *Systems thinking, systems practice.* Chichester: Wiley.

Checkland, P. B. (1988). Images of systems and the systems image. In W. J. Reckmayer (ed.) *General systems* (Vol. 31, pp. 13–20). New York: ISSS.

Chen, P. (1996). A random walk or color chaos on the stock market? Time-Frequency Analysis of S&P Indexes. *Studies in Nonlinear Dynamics and Econometrics Quarterly Journal* 1 (2) July 1996. Available online at: http://www.e-m-h.org/Chen96.pdf

Chen, P. (2000). The Frisch model of business cycles – a spurious doctrine, but a mysterious success. *CCER Working Paper* 1999007. Available online at: http://old.ccer.edu.cn/workingpaper/paper/e1999007.pdf

Christensen, K. (2003). Knowledge management in a project-oriented organization: three perspectives. *Journal of Knowledge Management* 7 (3) 2003:116–28.

Collier, J. (2005). Anticipatory systems: dealing with the unexpected. Available online at: http://www.kli.ac.at/theorylab/jdc/papers/CASYS2000final.pdf

D'Amato, A. (2003). *International law as an autopoietic system.* Max Planck Institute for Comparative Public Law and International Law. Available online at: http://anthonydamato.law.northwestern.edu/auto/PLANCK-1.pdf

Dobutsinskis, L. (1987). *The self-organizing policy: an epistemological analysis of political life.* Boulder, CO: Westview.

Dooley, K. (1999). Evolution and revolution in the history of the discipline. In D. Fedor and S. Ghosh (eds) *Advances in the management of organizational quality* (Vol. 5, pp. 1–28). Greenwich, CT: JAI Press.

Dooley, K. and Bush, D. (1995). TQM, chaos, and complexity. *Human Systems Management,* 14(4) (1995): 1–16.

Engeström, Y., Engeström, R. and Vähäaho, T. (1999). When the center does not hold: the importance of knotworking. In S. Chaiklin, M. Hedegaard and U. Jensen (eds) *Activity theory and social practice: cultural-historical approaches* (pp. 345–74). Aarhus: Aarhus University Press.

Faulkner, W. and Fleck, J. (eds) (1998). *Exploring expertise: issues and perspectives* (pp. 265–85). London: McMillan.

Feigenbaum, M. (1982). Universal behavior in nonlinear systems. *Physica D: Nonlinear Phenomena* 7 (1–3): 16–39.

Feigenbaum, M. (1993). The transition to chaos. In *Chaos: the new science*. Nobel Conference XXVI. University Press of America.

Fischer, M. M. (2001). *Knowledge, complexity and innovation systems.* New York: Springer.

Forrester, J. W. (1961). *Industrial dynamics.* Cambridge, MA: MIT Press.

Forrester, J. W. (1968). *Principles of systems.* Cambridge, MA: Wright-Allen.

Forrester, J. W. (1991). System dynamics and the lessons of 35 years. In De Greene, Kenyon

B. (ed) *The System Basis of Policy Analysis in the 1990s*. Available online at http://sysdyn.clexchange.org/sdep/papers/D-4224-4.pdf (accessed 3 November 2008).

Fuchs, S. (1988a). The constitution of emergent interaction orders: a comment on Rawls. *Sociological Theory* 6: 122–24.

Fuchs, S. (1988b). Introduction. In N. Luhmann, Tautology and paradox in the self-descriptions of modern society, trans. S. Fuchs. *Sociological Theory* 6: 21–37.

Glandsdorff, P., and Prigogine, I. (1971). *Thermodynamic study of structure, stability and fluctuations*. New York: Wiley.

Gregory, A. (2006). Systemic reflections on our past, present and future. *Systems Research and Behavioral Science* 23 (5): 685–94.

Griffin, D. (2002). *The emergence of leadership: linking self-organization and ethics*. New York: Routledge.

Gumbrecht, H. (2001). How is our future contingent? Reading Luhmann against Luhmann. *Theory, Culture and Society*, 18 (1): 49–58.

Hakkarainen, K. (2006). Kollektiivinen älykkyys. *Psykologia* 6 (3): 384–401.

Hakkarainen, K., Palonen, T., Paavola, S. and Lehtinen, E. (2006). *Communities of networked expertise: professional and educational perspectives*. London: Elsevier/Pergamon.

Hessling, A. and Pahl, H. (2006). The global system of finance: scanning Talcott Parsons and Niklas Luhmann for theoretical keystones. *American Journal of Economics and Sociology* 65 (1): 189–218.

Howells, J. (1997). Management and the hybridization of expertise: EFTPOS in retrospect. *Journal of Information Technology* 12 (1): 83–95.

Jackson, T. W. (2007). Applying autopoiesis to knowledge management in organisations. *Journal of Knowledge Management* 11 (3): 78–91.

Jalava, J. (2003). From norms to trust: the Luhmannian connections between trust and system. *European Journal of Social Theory* 6 (2): 173–90.

Jantsch, E. and Waddington, H. C. (eds) (1976). *Evolution and consciousness: human systems in transition*. Reading, MA: Addison-Wesley.

Kickert, W. J. M. (1991). Applicability of autopoiesis to administration science. In R. J. in 't Veld, L. Schaap, C. J. A. M. Teermeer and M. J.W. van Twist (eds) *Autopoiesis and configuration theory: new approaches to societal steering* (pp. 193–205). Dordrecht: Kluwer Academic Publishers.

Kohonen, T., Kaski, S. and Lagus, K. (2004). Mining massive document collections by the WEBSOM method. *Information Sciences* 163 (1–3): 135–56.

Koivisto, T. (2005). Developing strategic innovation capability of enterprises. VTT Publications 586. Espoo: VTT. Available online at: http://www.vtt.fi/inf/pdf/publications/2005/P586.pdf

Kuscu, I. K. (2001). An adaptive approach to organizational knowledge management. *Knowledge and Innovation: Journal of the KMCI* 1 (2) (15 January 2001): 109–26.

Leonard-Barton, D. (1995). *Wellsprings of knowledge: building and sustaining the sources of innovation*. Boston, MA: Harvard Business School Press.

Lorenz, E. (1963). Deterministic non periodic flow. *Journal of Atmospheric Science* 20: 130–41.

Lorenz, E. (1993). *The essence of chaos*. London: UCL Press.

Lorenz, E. (2005). Designing chaotic models. *Journal of the Atmospheric Sciences* 62 (5): 1574–87.

Luhmann, N. (1982). *The differentiation of society*. New York: Columbia University Press.

Luhmann, N. (1984a). *Soziale systeme: Grundrib einer allgemeinen theorie*. Frankfurt: Suhrkamp Verlag.

Luhmann, N. (1984b). *Religious dogmas and the evolution of societies*. New York: Edwin Mellan.

Luhmann, N. (1986c). The autopoiesis of social systems. In F. Geyer and J. van der Zouwen

(eds) *Sociocybernetic paradoxes: observation, control and evolution of self-steering systems* (pp. 172–92). London: Sage Publications.
Luhmann, N. (1989). *Ecological communication.* Cambridge: Polity Press.
Luhmann, N. (1990). *Essays on self-reference.* New York: Columbia University Press.
Luhmann, N. (1995a). *Social systems.* Stanford, CA: Stanford University Press.
Luhmann, N. (1995b). Why 'systems theory'? *Cybernetics and Human Knowing* 3:3–10.
Mandelbrot, B. B. (1977). *Fractals: form, change, and dimension.* San Francisco: Freeman.
Mandelbrot, B. B. (2004) *Fractals and chaos: the Mandelbrot set and beyond.* New York: Springer.
Marion, R. (1999). *The edge of organization: chaos and complexity theories of formal social systems.* CA: Sage Publications.
Maturana, H. R. (1981). Autopoiesis. In M. Zeleny (ed.) *Autopoiesis: a theory of living organization* (pp. 18–33). New York: Elsevier-North Holland.
Maturana, H. R. and Varela, F. J. (1987). *The tree of knowledge: the biological roots of human understanding.* Boston: New Science Library.
Maula, M. (1999). *Multinational companies as learning and evolving systems. A multiple-case study of knowledge-intensive service companies. An application of autopoiesis theory.* Helsinki School of Economics and Business Administration. Acta Universitatis Oeconomicae Helsingiensis A-154. Helsinki: HeSE print.
Minnis, M. and John-Steiner, V. P. (2001). Are we ready for a single, integrated theory? *Human Development* 44:296–310.
Misheva, V. (2001). Systems theory from a gender perspective. Paper presented at the annual meeting of The Swedish Sociological Association, Working Group on Gender Research, Uppsala, 25–26 January 2001. Available online at: www.soc.uu.se/plugins/pdfdownload.php?id=1203 (accessed 3 August 2005).
Mitleton-Kelly, E. (2003). *Complex systems and evolutionary perspectives on organisations: the application of complexity theory.* Netherlands: Elsevier.
Moreland, R. L. (1999). Transactive memory: learning who knows what in work groups and organizations. In L. L.Thompson, J. M. Levine and D. M. Messick (eds) *Shared cognition in organizations: the management of knowledge* (s. 3–31). Mahwah, NJ: Erlbaum.
Naohide, T. (2005). Basis of bioengineering: paradigm shift of bio function interpretation. *New Diamond Journal* 21 (3): 38–41.
Nicolis, G. and Prigogine, I. (1977). *Self-organization in nonequilibrium systems: from dissipative structures to order through fluctuations.* New York: Wiley.
Nomura, T. (2002). Formal description of autopoiesis for analytic models of life and social systems. In R. K. Standish, H. A. Abbass and M. A. Bedau (eds) *Artificial Life VIII* (pp. 15–18). Cambridge, MA: MIT Press. Available online at: http://alife.org/alife8/proceedings/sub358.pdf
Nonaka, I. (2006). *Organizational knowledge creation theory: evolutionary paths and future advances.* CA: Sage Publications.
Nonaka, I and Takeuchi, H. (1995). *The knowledge-creating company: how Japanese companies create the dynamics of innovation.* New York: Oxford University Press.
Okada, A. (2004). The collective building of knowledge in collaborative learning environments. In Roberts, T. S. (ed) *Computer-Supported Collaborative Learning in Higher Education.* Hershey, PA: Idea Group. Available online at: http://oro.open.ac.uk/11811/1/06okada_ROBERTS2005.pdf (accessed 3 November 2008).
Piaget, J. (1975). *The equilibration of cognitive structures: the central problem of intellectual development.* Chicago: University of Chicago Press.
Plass, J. L. and Salibury, M. W. (2002). A living-systems design model for web-based knowledge management systems. *Educational Technology Research and Development* 50 (1): 35–56.
Polanyi, M. (1958). *Personal knowledge, towards a post-critical philosophy.* Chicago: University of Chicago Press.

Porter, A. (1969). *Cybernetics simplified.* London: English University Press.

Prigogine, I. (1967a). Dissipative process, quantum states and field theory. XIVe Conseil de Physique Solvay, Brussels, October 1967.

Prigogine, I. (1967b). *Introduction to thermodynamics of irreversible processes* (3rd ed.). New York: Wiley.

Prigogine, I. (1967c). Quantum theory of dissipative systems and scattering processes. *Nobel Symposium 5* (pp. 99–129). Stockholm: Interscience Publishers.

Prigogine, I. (1976). Order through fluctuations: self-organization and social systems. In E. Jantsch and C. H. Waddington (eds) *Evolution and consciousness: human systems in transition* (pp. 93–133). Reading, MA: Addison-Wesley.

Prigogine, I. (1980). *From being to becoming: time and complexity in the physical sciences.* San Francisco: Freeman.

Prigogine, I. and Lefever, R. (1973). Theory of dissipative structures. In H. Haken (ed.) *Synergetics cooperative phenomena in multi-component systems: proceeding of the Symposium on Synergetics, from April 30 to May 6, 1972, Schloss Elmau.* Stuttgart: B. G. Teubner.

Prigogine, I. and Nicolis, G. (1989). *Exploring complexity: an introduction.* New York: Freeman.

Prigogine, I. and Stengers, I. (1984). *Order out of chaos: man's dialogue with nature.* New York: Bantam.

Pöyhönen, A. (2004). Renewal ability of organizations: synthesis of theoretical literature and suggestions for measurement. In M. Hannula and P. Ståhle (eds) *New directions of intellectual capital management.* Lappeenranta: Lappeenranta University of Technology.

Rangel, O. and Jose, A. (2005). The systemic theory of living systems and relevance to CAM: the theory (Part III). *Evidence-based Complementary and Alternative Medicine,* 2(3) (September 2005): 267–75.

Rapoport, A. (1986). *General systems theory: essential concepts and applications.* Tunbridge Wells: Abacus Press.

Ratcheva, V. (2007). Redefining multidisciplinary team boundaries in resolving heterogeneous knowledge dilemmas. *International Journal of Intelligent Enterprise* 1 (1): 81–97.

Reynolds, S. (2003). Higher education administration in a dynamic system. Working document for the PaVie 2003 Research Colloquium, Lausanne, Switzerland, 9–11 October 2003. Available online at: http://www2.unil.ch/pavie/documentation/workingdocument.pdf

Senge, P. M. (1990). *The fifth discipline: the art and practice of the learning organization.* London: Century Business.

Spinardi, G. (1998). Nuclear weapons experts: bomb building inside and outside the laboratory. In R. Williams, W. Faulkner and J. Fleck (ed.) *Exploring expertise: issues and perspectives* (s. 245–264). London: Macmillan.

Ståhle, P. (1998). *Supporting a system's capacity for self-renewal.* Helsinki: Yliopistopaino.

Ståhle, P. and Grönroos, M. (2000). *Dynamic intellectual capital: knowledge management in theory and practice.* Porvoo, Helsinki, Juva: WSOY.

Ståhle, P., Ståhle, S. and Pöyhönen, A. (2003). Analyzing dynamic intellectual capital: system-based theory and application. *Acta Universitatis Lappeenrantaensis* 152. Lappeenranta: Lappeenranta University of Technology.

Thompson, E. (2004). Life and mind: from autopoiesis to neurophenomenology. A tribute to Francisco Varela. *Phenomenology and the Cognitive Sciences* 3 (4): 381–98.

Tsytovich, V. N., Morfill, G. E., Fortov, V. E. and Gusein, N. G. (2007). From plasma crystals and helical structures towards inorganic living matter. *New Journal of Physics* 9 (August 2007): 263.

Varela, F. J. and Johnson, D. (1976). On observing natural systems (interview by Donna Johnson). *Co-Evolution Quarterly* 11 (Summer): 26–31.

von Bertalanffy, L. (1967). General System Theory. In N. J. Demerath and R. A. Peterson (eds) *System, change, and conflict* (pp. 115–29). New York: The Free Press.
von Bertalanffy, L. (1972). The history and status of General Systems Theory. In G. J. Klir (ed.) *Trends in General Systems Theory* (pp. 21–41). New York: Wiley-Interscience.
von Bertalanffy, L. (1975). *Perspectives on general systems theory: scientific-philosophical studies.* New York: Braziller.
Wegner, D. (1986). Transactive memory: a contemporary analysis of the group mind. In B. Mullen and G. R. Goethels (ed.) *Theories of group behaviour* (pp. 185–208). New York: Springler-Verlag.
Weick, K. and Roberts, K. H. (1993). Collective minds in organizations: heedful interrelating on flight decks. *Administrative Science Quarterly* 38:357–81.
Weick, K. and Sutcliffe, K. (2001). *Managing the unexpected: assuring high performance in an age of complexity.* San Francisco: Wiley.
Wheatley, M. J. (1999). *Discovering order in a chaotic world.* San Francisco: Berrett-Koehler Publishers.
Wiener, N. (1948). *Cybernetics, or control and communication in the animal and the machine*. New York: John Wiley and Sons.
Wiener, N. (1950). *The human use of human beings*. Boston: Houghton Mifflin.
Zeleny, M. (ed.) (1981). *Autopoiesis: a theory of living organization.* New York: Elsevier-North Holland.

8 Applying KVA analysis, risk simulation and strategic Real Options

The shipyard case

Thomas Housel, Sandra Hom, Johnathan Mun and Christine L. Komoroski

Special thanks to Rear Admiral (retired) Jim Greene and the Acquisitions Program at the Naval Postgraduate School for his generous support of this research project.

Disclaimer: The views represented in this report are those of the author and do not reflect the official policy position of the Navy, the Department of Defense, or the Federal Government.

Introduction

Defense leaders must maintain and modernize the United States Armed Forces to retain technological superiority while balancing defense budget constraints and wide-ranging military operational commitments, in addition to navigating an intricate information technology (IT) acquisition process. The Department of Defense (DoD) spends more than $63 billion annually – 14 percent of its total budget – on defense maintenance programs spanning major depots, shipyards, and intermediate and organizational units throughout the world (Office of the Deputy Under Secretary of Defense (Logistics and Material Readiness), 2005). A broad range of defense maintenance capabilities and programs supporting approximately 280 ships, 14,000 aircraft, 900 strategic missiles and 330,000 ground combat and tactical vehicles are provided by nearly 680,000 personnel and several thousand commercial firms (Office of the Deputy Under Secretary of Defense (Logistics and Material Readiness), 2005).

To evaluate and select projects returning maximum benefits, measurement tools are essential to define, capture and measure the total value of IT acquisitions. These tools must capture data across a spectrum of organizations to compare processes, capabilities, costs, revenues and other benefits. Moreover, they must incorporate and analytically quantify elements of uncertainty and risks inherent in predicting the future, include ways to mitigate these risks through strategic options, and analytically develop and allocate budgets to optimize project portfolios. Understanding uncertainties and mitigating the potential impact of risks can significantly improve the likelihood of success in acquisition decisions.

The Naval Postgraduate School (NPS) developed the Knowledge Value Added/ Real Options (KVA+RO) valuation framework to address these issues. KVA+RO analysis is designed to support IT portfolio acquisitions and to empower decision-makers by providing performance-based data and scenario analysis. Analyses like Return on Investment (ROI) on individual projects, programs and processes within a portfolio of IT acquisitions can be derived through KVA methodology. With historical data provided by KVA, potential strategic investments can then be evaluated with Real Options analysis. The analysis applied is a robust and analytical process incorporating risk identification (applying various sensitivity techniques), risk quantification (applying Monte Carlo simulation), risk valuation (Real Options analysis), risk mitigation (Real Options framing), and risk diversification (analytical portfolio optimization).

This paper introduces the KVA+RO valuation framework. It begins with a discussion of the DoD's Portfolio Management mandate, requiring measurement of portfolio investments. It then briefly reviews performance measurement tools used by profit and non-profit organizations. In the third section, "Measuring value", core concepts of the KVA+RO Valuation Framework, along with underlying assumptions, metrics and potential applications, are presented. The fourth section "Methodology proof-of-concept" applies KVA+RO Valuation Framework to naval maintenance processes in a case study analyzing the potential impact of Commercial-off-the-shelf (COTS) technology. COTS technology could improve maintenance processes and substantially reduce costs over the 20-, 30- and 50-year life cycle of Navy ships. In particular, three-dimensional (3D) laser scanning technology and collaborative Product Lifecycle Management (PLM) solutions are evaluated under three scenarios: current "As Is," potential "To Be," and "Radical To Be." Results from our case analysis indicate that these technologies have the potential to:

- reduce maintenance costs for ships by expediting maintenance work in shipyards
- decrease maintenance costs by eliminating or reducing DoD planning yard labor costs
- provide an opportunity to improve fleet utilization and/or reduce fleet inventory requirements through reduced cycle-time
- improve productivity in current shipyard planning processes, allowing for increased shipboard modernization

This section also identifies cost savings and areas of process improvements. In the fifth section, Real Options analysis is conducted to determine the prospective value of the three strategic options over a three-year period using KVA data as a platform. The paper concludes with specific recommendations.

Defense maintenance and technology acquisitions

The nation's leaders are committed to maintaining force operational readiness, superior technological edge, and quality material condition of military assets. DoD maintenance activities span a broad range of capabilities and programs, ranging from major depots and shipyards to intermediate and organizational level units throughout the world. Maintenance activities, performed at several levels of complexity, range from the rapid removal and replacement of components to complete overhaul or rebuilding of a weapon system.

The DoD has also been transforming itself towards capabilities-based planning, resource allocation and acquisition, based on principals of joint interoperability and network-centric warfare. IT resources were traditionally managed and acquired as stand-alone systems, resulting in duplicative investments in systems or platforms to deliver the same or similar capabilities, focusing on system or platform capabilities rather than on mission capabilities, and limiting the ability to share information. Legislation like the Clinger-Cohen Act of 1996 and the Information Technology Management Reform Act required federal agencies to implement an IT investment capital planning process. Directive 8115.01, issued in October of 2005, further mandates the management of IT investments as portfolios within the DoD enterprise. A portfolio is identifed by the DoD as the group of capabilities, resources, management, and related investments required in accomplishing a mission-related or administrative outcome.[1] A portfolio includes outcome performance measures (mission, functional or administrative measures) and an expected return on investment (Department of Defense, 2005, October).

The Portfolio Management process emphasizes overall mission capability from individual systems and is a comprehensive strategy for making decisions based on enterprise strategic planning, integrated architectures, and outcome-based performance measures to achieve desired mission capabilities. It is an ongoing, collaborative, cross-cutting, and flexible process that is performed by stakeholder teams representing all life cycle activities (e.g. capabilities, resources, acquisition, operations, deactivation, and retirement/reutilization or demilitarization). Driven by mission outcomes to produce end-to-end IT capabilities, Portfolio Management provides the "glue" linking systems and the DoD's principal decision support processes: Joint Capabilities Integration and Development System (JCIDS), Planning, Programming, Budgeting and Execution (PPBE), and the Defense Acquisition System (DAS).

To manage IT portfolios, the DoD uses four continuous integrated and iterative activities: analysis, selection, control, and evaluation. As an iterative process, results are fed back into the system to guide future decisions.

Each activity in the Portfolio Management process has a specific function:

- ***Analysis:*** performance goals established, gaps and opportunities identified; continuous improvement measures implemented; functional and technical options documented "as-is" and future architectures are further explored (Department of Defense, 2005, October); Addresses front-end requirements for legislation requiring strategic planning, performance and results management, benchmarking, elimination of unnecessary functions, process improvement, and definition of capabilities and gaps.
- ***Selection:*** best mix of investments to achieve Enterprise, Mission Area, Sub-Portfolio, and Component outcomes to meet integrated strategic goals,

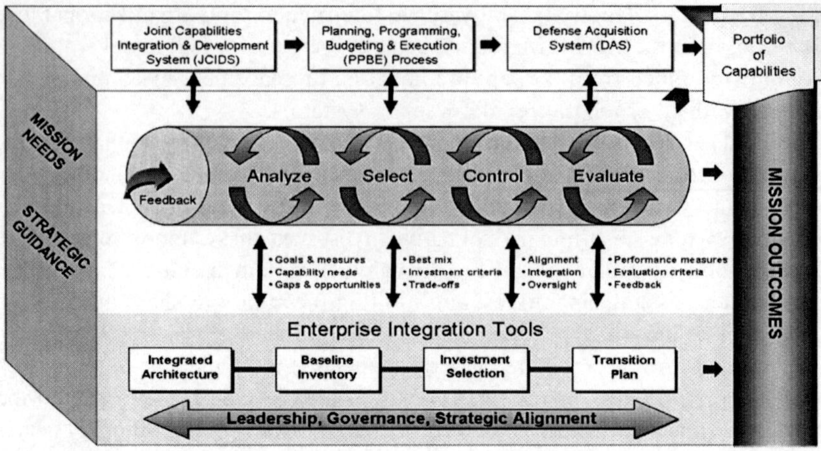

Figure 8.1 DoD IT portfolio management decision-support interactions.
Source: Department of Defense, 2005, October

architectures, programmatic and technical criteria, achieve results and maximize outcome.

- ***Control:*** capabilities selected for portfolio are acquired. Consists of acquisition and oversight activities at the portfolio level complementing and supplementing traditional single-system, single-platform acquisition and oversight activities.
- ***Evaluation:*** focuses on measuring and assessing outcomes of portfolio investments to determine whether expected benefits are achieved. Mechanisms for evaluation are post-implementation reviews and other operational assessments (e.g. after-action reports from military exercises). Evaluation results feed back into other phases of Portfolio Management to guide all investment decisions.

Key to the Portfolio Management process are tools measuring performance, outcomes, and overall value. Yet, the DoD, as a non-profit organization, cannot measure returns in strictly monetary terms and must evaluate investments on the overall "value" received from investments. It cannot establish monetary benefits for the value added from combat effectiveness, operational readiness, and national defense.

What does value translate into in the public sector? What capabilities deliver the greatest value in services provided to citizens? Government and industry-sponsored initiatives have been launched, over the past several years, to develop frameworks to define "value" in the public sector and identify high-performance capabilities, enabling government agencies to create the greatest "value." Nearly 70 percent of public sector executives around the world plan to measure social returns on IT initiatives to their citizens and stakeholders over the next five years, according to a 2005 *Economist* study.

The consultancy firm Accenture created a Public Sector Value model to calculate the value of IT projects to government organizations in 2003. Market research firm Gartner established a consulting practice around the "Public Value of IT" to measure how government IT investments/programs contribute to improved operational efficiency, improved constituent service and political return. Computer software manufacturer SAP unveiled its collaborative "Public ROI" project to develop a methodology for defining, measuring, and communicating economic, social and political returns of government and public services programs in 2005. Beyond these specific corporate initiatives are models that have been developed to measure value derived from today's knowledge-based economy.

Measuring value

Intangible assets have supplemented tangible assets as the key drivers in the economy during the past 25 years, according to Accenture. As one indicator, accounting book value of the S&P 500 declined from approximately 80 percent of total enterprise value in 1980 to approximately 25 percent in 2002 (Ballow, Burgman, and Burgoz, 2004, October). Figure 8.2 shows unexplained market value (intangible value) is a long-term business trend transcending business cycles (Ballow, Burgman, and Burgoz, 2004, October).

Further indicators include two of the largest corporate acquisitions in 2005, involving intangible assets valued at above 50 percent of the total purchase price (Neils, 2006, April 6). In SBC's $14.5 billion purchase of AT&T, $8.2 billion or 53 percent of the purchase price was allocated to intangible assets. With Procter & Gamble's $53.5 billion acquisition of Gillette, $31.5 billion or 59 percent of the total purchase price was allocated to intangible assets (Neils, 2006, April 6).

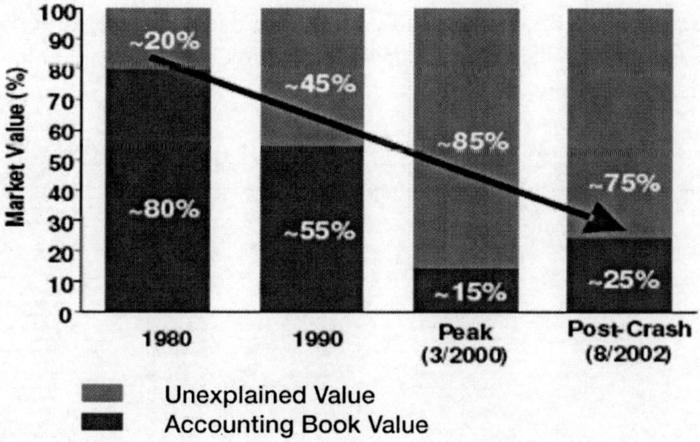

Figure 8.2 Market value vs. book value over time (S&P 500).

Source: Ballow, Burgman, and Burgoz, 2004, October; Adapted from Lev, 2001; Lev, 2003, September

Traditional accounting methods remain focused on tangible assets; therefore, a significant portion of corporate assets go unrecognized and underreported, as seen in Figure 8.3 (Ballow *et al.*, 2004).

Recognizing the significance of intangible assets to the overall value of an organization, the European Union recently implemented IFRS3 (International Financial Reporting Standards No. 3 on Business Combinations). IFRS3 stipulates that companies must measure, disclose and monitor intangible assets. It requires all acquired intangible and tangible assets be recognized on the balance sheet and priced at fair market values; intangible assets with indefinite lives also need to be tested annually for loss in value.

Given the economic importance of intangible assets, it is critical to properly report and manage them. A number of performance measurement models have been developed in an attempt to capture non-financial, intangible value, as seen in Table 8.1. Although valuable, these models have several limitations:

- revenues cannot be allocated at sub-corporate levels
- advanced techniques, such as project flexibility as accounted for in Real Options, cannot be conducted for further analysis
- risk and uncertainty quantification, mitigation, and management are not considered
- project and program interactions and interconnectivity within a portfolio are not considered

Performance measures often fail to capture the complete benefit stream produced by organizations, processes or assets to beneficiaries or stakeholders such as taxpayers, program managers and government sponsors. Measurement of ROI on how public monies are used, along with how benefits are received, is critical given increased regulations and pressures for increased accountability and transparency. DoD Directive 8115.0, as discussed earlier, mandates the use of performance metrics based on outputs with ROI analysis required for all current and planned IT investments.

Asset Recognition	Asset Type: Traditional Accounting Assets		Asset Type: Intellectual capital Assets		
	Monetary	Physical	Relational	Organizational	Human
Tangible	• Cash • Investments • Receivables/ debtors • Payables/creditors	• Property • Plant • Equipment • Inventory – Finished goods – WIP – Parts/ raw materials	• Customer contacts • Formal alliances, JVs, supply agreements	• Systems • Formalized processes • Codified knowledge • Patents • Brands	• Management contracts • Documented accessible skills inventories
Intangible	• Credit ratings • Undrawn facilities • Borrowing capacities (relative to like companies, based on character) • Receivables certainty • Accruals convertability	• Plant flexibility • Plant modernity • Infrastructure surrounding plants • Access rights • Balance sheet strength • Inventory (good and usable, obsolete, redundant)	• Customer loyalty – Behavioral – Attitudinal • Quality of supply contracts • Right to tender, right to design • Strength of stakeholder support (including opinion leaders) • Networks	• Structural appropriateness • Informal processes • Organizational reputation • Productivity of R&D process • Quality of corporate governance • Tacit knowledge	• Top management quality • Top management experience • Ability to execute on strategy • Leadership capabilities • Problem-solving ability • Employee loyalty – Behavioral – Attitudinal • Personnel reputation • Workforce adaptability • Employee engagement

☐ Traditional scope of accounting/financial reporting

Figure 8.3 Classification of assets.

Source: Asseteconomics Holdings, Accenture, 2004

How can the value of intangible assets be defined? How can any organization define the value of intangible assets, particularly hard-to-quantify intellectual capital assets? Benefits may result in many forms, including improved market competitiveness, expanded markets, new capabilities, or increased efficiency. NPS professors Dr Thomas Housel and Dr Johnathan Mun have developed an analytical tool to facilitate strategic, performance-based investment decisions. The KVA+RO Valuation Framework measures the value of intangibles provided by human capital assets like intellectual capital (e.g. training, knowledge, skills) critical to the completion of final outputs (yet difficult to quantify), as well as the risks and uncertainties involved with such assets; the Framework also includes ways to mitigate and manage these risks.

Measuring value: the KVA + RO valuation framework

The KVA+RO valuation framework measures operating performance, cost-effectiveness, return on investments, risk, Real Options (capturing strategic flexibility), and analytical portfolio optimization. The framework facilitates regulatory compliance and applies portfolio management techniques to evaluate programs and risks, taking into account uncertainty in estimating future benefits. Large, complex organizations ranging from publicly traded *Fortune 500* firms to public-sector entities can use the KVA+RO framework. Its focus on core processes, sub-processes, and outputs provides several advantages:

- Quantifies value of specific processes, functions, departments, divisions, or organizations in common units
- Provides historical data on costs and revenues of specific processes and tasks of specific programs or organizations
- Facilitates regulatory compliance in the public sector (with legislation such as the Clinger-Cohen Act of 1996) mandating portfolio management for all federal agencies. In the private sector, facilitates compliance with Sarbanes-Oxley by making performance among corporate entities more transparent.
- Highlights operational efficiencies/inefficiencies, and
- Leverages current and potential portfolio investments by estimating potential total value created.

Organizations can drill down to understand specific processes involved in the production of an output, the cost of each process and its contribution to the bottom line with the KVA+RO framework. Government entities can use the framework to enhance existing performance tools, while on the corporate side, the framework can be used to value specific divisions or operating units to determine division profitability or shareholder value.

Table 8.1 Performance measurement models

Model	*Origin*	*Rationale*	*Purpose*	*Approach*	*Advantages*	*Disadvantages*
The Balanced Scorecard	Introduced in 1990s by Kaplan and Norton.	Companies need system of leading and lagging, internal and external indicators.	Measures and manages execution of strategy Includes financial and non-financial perspectives Serves as a management tool reflecting the whole business (holistic).	BSC organizes its measurement system into four perspectives: financial, customer, internal business, and growth Cause-and-effect relationships link the four scorecard perspectives.	Powerful logic Clear correlation between indicators and financial performance Cause-and-effect linkages Can be deployed into a system for managing intellectual capital Well-developed and consistent literature In practice, often used to formulate strategy and gain internal commitment.	Rigid; static; no consideration of dynamics Four perspectives limiting; insufficient consideration of human assets and knowledge-creation processes Limited treatment of external environment (i.e. focus exclusively on customers) Internal use only; external comparisons are difficult.
Economic Value Added	Introduced in 1994 by Stern, Stewart & Co., as a tool to assist corporations in pursing their prime financial directives by aiding in maximizing the wealth of their shareholders.	The purpose of a company is to maximize shareholder value, and maximize the effective use of capital – a purpose that should be reflected in every decision, at all levels of the organization.	Develops a performance measure that properly accounts for all ways in which corporate value could be added or lost.	EVA is net sales minus operating expenses minus taxes minus capital charges, where capital charges are calculated as the weighted average cost of capital multiplied by the total capital invested. In practice, EVA is increased if weighted average cost of capital is less than the return on net assets, and vice versa.	Correlates well with stock price Ties budgeting, financial planning, goal setting, and incentive compensation together Provides a common language and benchmark for managers to discuss value creation.	Complicated adjustment procedures Trade-off between accuracy and complexity Based on net assets versus market value of assets Weak additional explanatory power Assumes governance structure in the interest of shareholders only.

continued on next page

Model	*Origin*	*Rationale*	*Purpose*	*Approach*	*Advantages*	*Disadvantages*
Intellectual Capital (IC) Approaches	Introduced in 1997 by Bontis, Edvinsson, Malone, Roos and Roos.	A good part of the value generated by a company comes from intangible resources, which also should be measured and monitored. However, intangibles do not obey conventional laws of diminishing returns and, therefore, needed a new approach to being measured, managed, and reported.	Measures IC in an integrated framework Combines financial capital with IC Provides new insights into value creation by revealing and measuring the contribution of IC Achieves innovative external reporting.	IC includes all the intangible resources that contribute to the creation of value for the organization (monetary, physical, human, relationship, and organizational) Approach measures IC in conjunction with financial capital Presents sophisticated methodology to calculate overall IC index.	Flexible Dynamic model Applicable to non-profit organizations IC index could allow for external comparison between companies and across industries Begins to address question of value creation being based on the use of resources (flows), not their mere existence (stocks).	Elusive and complex More metric development needed Some argue too much emphasis on stocks versus flows Diversity between organizations (and thus context specificity) hinders any possible comparison between companies Provides measures of performance rather than absolute values – so lends itself to reporting of processes rather than value.
Value Explorer®	Originated in 2000 by Andriessen and Tissen.	Provides insight into the future potential of intangible assets by looking at: Added value for customers Competitiveness Potential for new opportunities Sustainability Robustness	Helps organizations understand and measure value of core competencies.	The core of the approach is a methodology to: Identify core competencies/ intangible assets that are of strategic importance Assess the relative strengths and weaknesses of intangibles with regards to future potential Allocate the organization's income stream across the core competencies.	Identifies core competencies of the organization Relatively simple and practical tool and process involved Provides practical guidelines for strategic decision-making and prioritization of intangibles that help develop the strategic agenda Concepts are similar to financial terminologies.	Dependent on subjective data for valuations Provides a measure of value, not performance of underlying processes Requires a thorough analysis of the hidden driving forces of the company.

continued on next page

Model	*Origin*	*Rationale*	*Purpose*	*Approach*	*Advantages*	*Disadvantages*
Human Resource Accounting	Since Hermanson's (1964) classic study several decades ago, the topic of how and whether to value human assets has been debated by accountants and human resource theorists.	The value of human capital, as expressed in financial terms, should be capitalized on balance sheets instead of expensed on the income statements.	Quantifies economic value of people to organizations in order to provide input for managerial and financial decisions.	Researchers have proposed three types of HRA models: Cost models that consider historical, acquisition replacement, or opportunity cost of human assets HR value models that combine non-monetary behavioral models with monetary economic models Monetary emphasis models that calculate discounted estimates of future earnings or wages.	Calculated in financial terms Extensive internal use in certain service industries.	Too many assumptions must be made, some of which cannot hold Subjective and uncertain Lacks reliability in that measures cannot be audited with any assurance.
Value Chain Scoreboard	Originated in 2001 by Baruch Lev, Philip Bardes, Professors of Accounting and Finance with the Stern School of Business at New York University.	As innovation becomes central to achieving a dominant competitive position, corporations will need to invest more heavily in intangible assets and monitor them closely. But, the amount of information available on intangibles lags behind. These information inefficiencies result in economic and societal damage.	Improves reporting on investments in innovation.	Scoreboard uses a "value chain" consisting of three phases: discovery of new products or services or processes, establishment of technological feasibility, and commercialization of new products and services Three categories in each phase that contain a number of indicators.	Based on thorough scientific research on the relationship between intangibles and company market value Based on research of the information needs of analysts and other stakeholders Simple and comprehensive.	Only focused on innovation Seems primarily suitable for technology companies investing strongly in R&D Strongly focused on external reporting Weak additional explanatory power.

Source: KPMG, 2001. Adapted from materials developed by Bontis, N., Dragonetti, N.C., Jacobsen, K., and Roos, G., 1999; Andriessen, D. and Tissen, R., 2000; Lev, B., 2001. Also see the Ricardis Report: that can be downloaded from the New Club of Paris web site: www.the-new-club-of-paris.org for additional performance measurement models pertinent to this area of research.

Overview of KVA+RO framework

KVA+RO is designed to help organizations manage IT investments and mitigate risk. The framework's three components of data collection, KVA methodology, and Real Options analysis collectively provide performance-based data and analyses on individual projects, programs, and processes within a portfolio of IT investments.

The first step under the framework is data collection on processes and sub-processes required to produce an output. Once all process data are accurately documented, they are supplemented by market research to compare cost and revenue data to establish baseline information. KVA methodology is then applied to uncover value and historical costs for each process. Cost per unit of output calculated by KVA, in conjunction with price-per-unit estimates, provides raw data required for ROI analysis. In the final step of the framework, risk-based simulation and Real Options analysis are conducted to estimate the value and risks of potential investments as well as the best strategic pathway to proceed. Alternative scenarios are run, enabling decision-makers to assess risk, leverage uncertainty and limit downside risk. Principles of KVA and RO are discussed further in the next sections.

KVA+RO framework: Knowledge Value Added methodology

A new paradigm in sub-corporate performance analytics, KVA measures the value provided by human capital assets and IT assets by analyzing an organization, process or function at the process level. It provides insights into each dollar of IT investment by monetizing the outputs of all assets, including intangible knowledge assets. By capturing the value of knowledge embedded in an organization's core

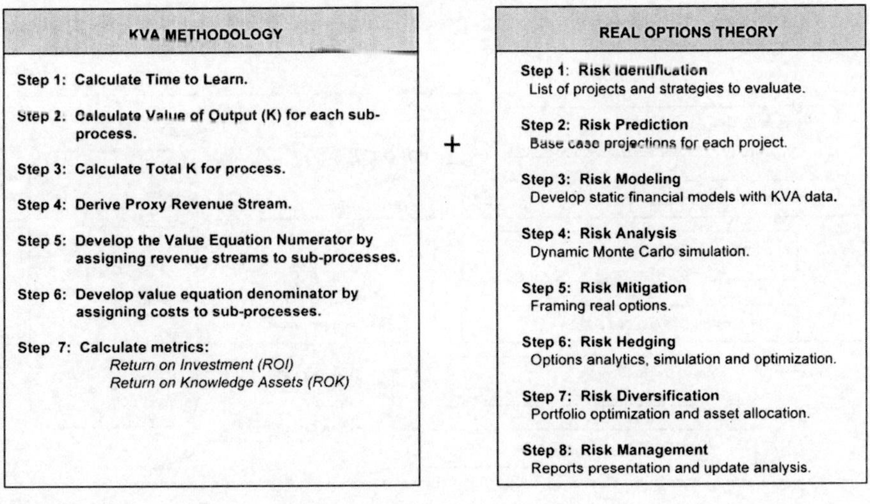

Figure 8.4 NPS valuation framework.

processes, employees and IT, KVA identifies the actual cost and revenue of a product or service. Because KVA identifies every process required to produce an output and the historical costs of those processes, unit costs and unit prices of products and services are calculated. An output is defined as the end result of an organization's operations; it can be a product or service, as shown in Figure 8.5.

KVA has been applied in over 100 organizations in the public and private sectors, ranging in size from under 20 employees to thousands, for the past 15 years. The methodology has been applied in 35 areas within the DoD, from flight simulation applications to maintenance and modernization processes. As a performance tool, the methodology:

- Compares all processes in terms of relative productivity
- Allocates revenues to common units of output
- Measures value added by IT by the outputs it produces
- Relates outputs to cost of producing those outputs in common units, and
- Provides common unit of measures for organizational productivity.

Based on the tenets of complexity theory, KVA assumes that humans and technology in organizations add value by taking inputs and changing them into outputs through core processes (Housel and Bell, 2001, pp. 92–93). The amount of change an asset or process produces can be a measure of value or benefit. Additional assumptions include:

- Describing all process outputs in common units (i.e. the knowledge required to produce the outputs) allows historical revenue and cost data to be assigned to those processes at any given point in time.
- All outputs can be described in terms of the time required to learn how to produce them.
- Learning Time, a surrogate for procedural knowledge required to produce

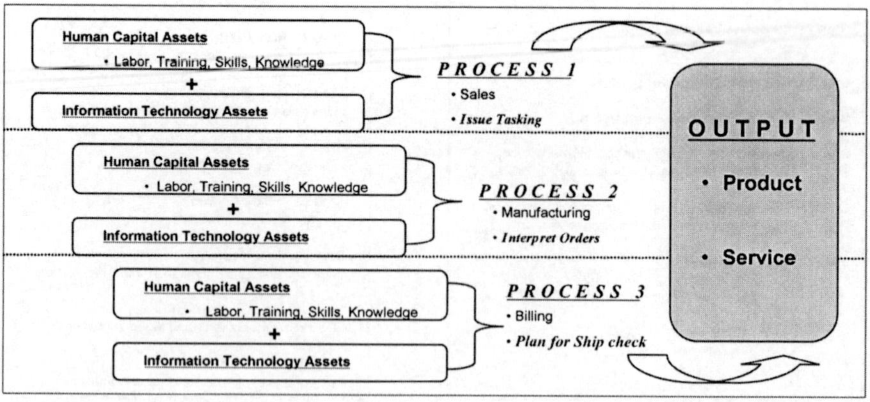

Figure 8.5 Measuring output.

process outputs, is measured in common units of time. Consequently, Units of Learning Time = Common Units of Output (**K**).

- Common unit of output makes it possible to compare all outputs in terms of cost per unit as well as price per unit, because revenue can now be assigned at the sub-organizational level.
- Once cost and revenue streams have been assigned to sub-organizational outputs, normal accounting and financial performance and profitability metrics can be applied.

Describing processes in common units also permits market-comparable data to be generated, particularly important for non-profits like the US Navy. Using a Market Comparable approach, data from the commercial sector can be used to estimate price per common unit, allowing for revenue estimates of process outputs for non-profits. This also provides a common-units basis to define benefit streams regardless of process analyzed.

KVA differs from other nonprofit ROI models because it allows for revenue estimates, enabling the use of traditional accounting, financial performance and profitability measures at the sub-organizational level.

KVA can rank processes by the degree to which they add value to the organization or its outputs. This assists decision-makers in identifying what processes are really value-added – those that will best accomplish a mission, deliver a service, or meet customer demand. Value is quantified in two key metrics: Return-on-knowledge (ROK) and Return-on-knowledge Investment (ROI).

KVA analysis can be conducted through three methods, as shown in Table 8.3.

Traditional Accounting		KVA Process Costing	
Compensation	$5,000	Issue Task	$1,000
Benefits/OT	1,000	Interpret Orders	1,000
Supplies/Materials	2,000	Shipcheck Planning	1,000
Rent/Leases	1,000	Conducting Shipcheck	5,000
Depreciation	1,500	Report Assembly	600
Admin and Other	900	Revise Schedule	900
Total	**$11,000**	Generate Drawings	1,500
		Total	**$11,000**

Explains what was spent (left) — *Explains how it was spent* (right)

Figure 8.6 Comparison of traditional accounting versus process-based costing.

Traditional Accounting/ Finance Measure		KVA Process Value Measure
Sales / Revenues	→	Common units of output
Rent Receipts	→	Market comparables: Price per unit of output
Total Revenues	→	Total units of output X price per unit = total revenue surrogate

Figure 8.7 Comparison of outputs traditional accounting benefits (revenues) versus process-based value.

Table 8.2 KVA metrics

Metric	*Description*	*Type*	*Calculation*
Return-on-Knowledge (ROK)[1]	Basic productivity, cash flow ratio	Sub-corporate, process-level performance ratio	Outputs-benefits in common units/cost to produce the output
Return on Investment (ROI)	Same as ROI at the sub-corporate, process level	Traditional investment finance ratio	(Revenue-investment cost)/investment cost

Notes:

1 ROK was used extensively in the thesis research on which this white paper is based because market comparables had not been applied to derive revenue surrogates to enable generation of the ROI metric.

KVA+RO Framework: Real Options analysis

Real Options analysis incorporates strategic planning and analysis, risk assessment and management, and investment analysis. As a financial valuation tool, Real Options allow organizations to adapt decisions to respond to unexpected environmental or market developments. As a strategic management tool, Real Options are a strategic investment valuation tool affording decision-makers the ability to leverage uncertainty and limit risk. Real Options can be used to:

- Identify different corporate investment decision pathways or projects that management can consider in highly uncertain business conditions;
- Value the feasibility and financial viability of each strategic decision pathway;
- Prioritize pathways or projects based on qualitative and quantitative metrics;
- Optimize strategic investment decisions by elevating different decision paths under certain conditions or determine how a different sequence of pathways can lead to the optimal strategy;
- Time effective execution of investments and find the optimal trigger values and cost or revenue drivers; and

Table 8.3 Approaches to KVA calculation

Steps	*Learning Time*	*Process Description*	*Binary Query Method*
1		Identify core process and its subprocesses.	
2	Establish common units to measure learning time.	Describe products in terms of instructions required to reproduce them, and select unit of process description.	Create set of binary yes/no questions such that all possible outputs are represented as sequence of yes/no answers.
3	Calculate learning time to execute each subprocess.	Calculate number of process instructions pertaining to each subprocess.	Calculate length of sequence of yes/no answers for each subprocess.
4		Designate sampling period long enough to capture representative sample of core process's final product/service output.	
5	Multiply learning time for each subprocess by number of times subprocess executes during sample period.	Multiply number of process instructions used to describe each subprocess by number of times subprocess executes during sample period.	Multiply length of yes/no string for each subprocess by number of times this subprocess executes during sample period.
6		Allocate revenue to subprocesses in proportion to quantities generated by Step 5, and calculate costs for each subprocess.	
7		Calculate ROK, ROI, and interpret results.	

Source: Housel and Bell, 2001

- Manage existing or develop new options and strategic decision pathways for future opportunities (Mun, 2005).

Options are used in a variety of ways across a number of industries.

Although there are many approaches, the methodology used in the KVA+RO valuation framework is developed by leading expert Dr Johnathan Mun. Dr Mun's Real Options approach consists of eight steps, as shown in Figure 8.8, called the Integrated Risk Analysis Approach.[2]

The Approach involves the following eight procedural steps:

1. Qualitative management screening
2. Forecasting and prediction
3. Base-case KVA net present value and ROI analysis
4. Risk-based Monte Carlo simulation
5. Strategic Real Options problem framing and courses of action
6. Real Options modeling and analysis
7. Analytical portfolio and resource optimization
8. Reporting and update analysis.

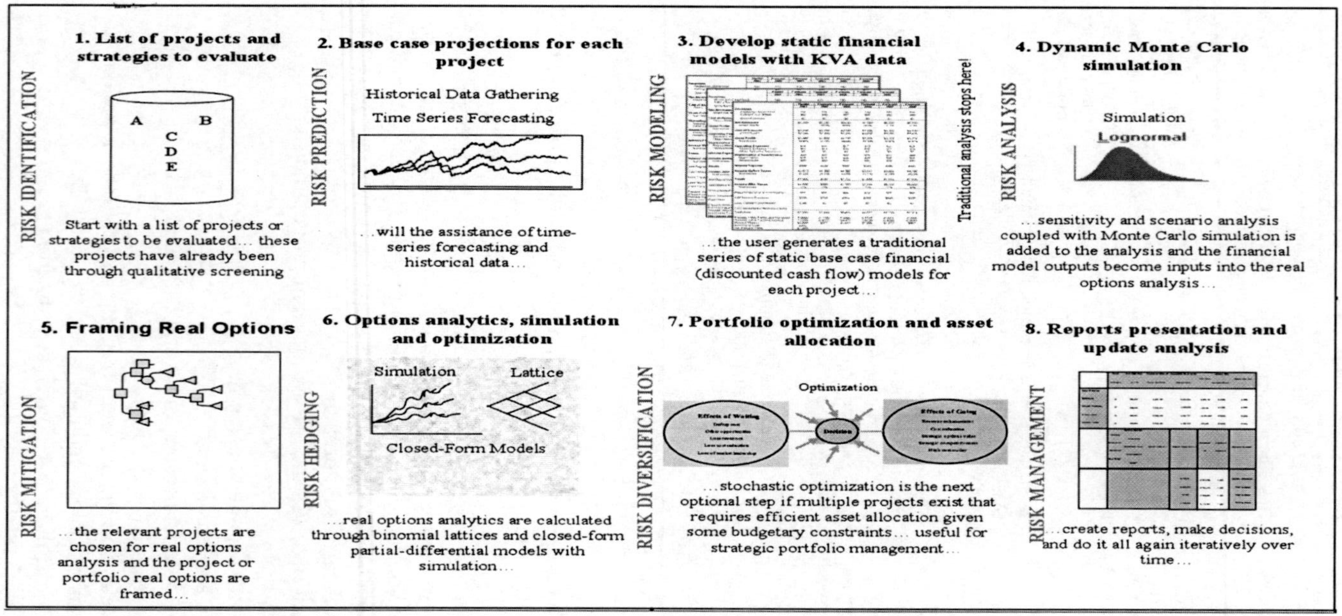

Figure 8.8 Integrated Risk Analysis.

Qualitative management screening is the first step in the integrated risk analysis process. Decision-makers have to decide which projects, assets, initiatives, or strategies are viable for further analysis, in accordance with the DoD's mission, vision, goal, or overall strategy. That is, the initial list of projects should be qualified in terms of meeting the DoD's overall agenda. The most valuable insight is often created as decision-makers frame the complete problem to be resolved. This is where the various risks to the organization are identified and fleshed out.

The future is then forecasted using time-series analysis, simulation, multivariate regression analysis, econometric models, or forecasting heuristics if historical or comparable data exist. Otherwise, other qualitative forecasting methods may be used (subjective guesses, growth-rate assumptions, expert opinions, Delphi method, and so forth). In a financial and KVA context, this is the step where future proxy benefits and cost drivers are forecasted.

For each project that passes the initial qualitative screens, a KVA-based discounted cash flow and ROI model is created. This model serves as the base-case analysis where a net present value (NPV) and ROI are calculated for each project, using the forecasted values in the previous step. This step also applies if only a single project is under evaluation. This ROI and NPV are calculated using the traditional approach of utilizing the forecast revenues and costs, and discounting the net of these revenues and costs at an appropriate risk-adjusted rate. The return on investment and other metrics are generated here.

Because the static KVA ROI and discounted cash flow models produce only single-point estimate results, there is often little confidence in their accuracy, given that future events affecting forecast cash flows are highly uncertain. To better estimate the actual value of a particular project, Monte Carlo simulation should be employed next. Usually, a sensitivity analysis is first performed on the model; that is, setting the ROI or net present value as the resulting variable, we can change each of its precedent variables and note the change in the resulting variable.

Precedent variables are those which ultimately flow through the model to affect the ROI or net present value figure. By tracing back all these precedent variables, we can change each one by a preset amount and see the effect on the resulting net present value. A graphical representation can then be created, which is often called a tornado chart (the Risk Simulator software is used to run simulation analysis as well as these sensitivity tornado charts and spider charts) because of its shape, where the most sensitive precedent variables are listed first, in descending order of magnitude. Armed with this information, we can then decide which key variables are highly uncertain in the future and which are deterministic. The uncertain key variables that drive the NPV and, hence, the decision, are called critical success drivers. These critical success drivers are prime candidates for Monte Carlo simulation using Risk Simulator.[3] Because some of these critical success drivers may be correlated, a correlated Monte Carlo simulation may be required. Typically, these correlations can be obtained through historical data. Running correlated simulations provides a much closer approximation to the variables' real-life behaviors.

After quantifying risks in the previous step, the question is, "What next?" The risk information obtained somehow needs to be converted into *actionable intelligence*. Just because risk has been quantified to be such-and-such using Monte Carlo simulation, so what? And what do we do about it? The answer is to use Real Options analysis to hedge these risks, to value these risks, and to position the project to take advantage of or to mitigate the risks. The first step in Real Options is to generate a strategic map through the process of framing the problem. Based on the overall problem identification occurring during the initial qualitative management screening process, certain strategic optionalities would have become apparent for each particular project. The strategic optionalities may include, among other things, the option to expand, contract, abandon, switch, choose, and so forth.

Through the use of Monte Carlo simulation, the resulting stochastic KVA ROI model will have a distribution of values. Thus, simulation models, analyzes, and quantifies the various risks and uncertainties of each project. The result is a distribution of the ROIs and the project's volatility. In Real Options, we assume that the underlying variable is the future benefit minus the cost of the project. An implied volatility can be calculated through the results of a Monte Carlo simulation previously performed. Usually, the volatility is measured as the standard deviation of the logarithmic returns on the free net benefit stream. The Real Options valuation is then performed using the Real Options SLS software.[4]

Portfolio optimization is the next optional step in the analysis. If the analysis is done on multiple projects, decision-makers should view the results as a portfolio of rolled-up projects, because the projects are, in most cases, correlated with one another; viewing them individually will not present the true picture. As organizations do not only have single projects, portfolio optimization is crucial. Given that certain projects are related to others, there are opportunities for hedging and diversifying risks through a portfolio. Because firms have limited budgets, time, people, and resources, in addition to requirements for certain overall levels of returns, risk tolerances, and so forth, portfolio optimization takes all such factors into account to analytically and robustly create an optimal portfolio mix. The analysis will provide the optimal allocation of investments across multiple projects. Portfolio optimization is performed using the Risk Simulator software.

The analysis is not complete until reports can be generated. Not only are results presented, but the process should also be shown. Clear, concise, and precise explanations transform a difficult black-box set of analytics into transparent steps. Top decision-makers will never accept results coming from black boxes if they do not understand where the assumptions or data originate and what types of mathematical or financial massaging takes place.

Risk analysis assumes that the future is uncertain and that decision-makers have the right to make midcourse corrections when these uncertainties become resolved or risks become known; the analysis is usually done ahead of time and, thus, ahead of such uncertainty and risks. Therefore, when these risks become known, the analysis should be revisited to incorporate the decisions made or to revise any input assumptions. Sometimes, for long-horizon projects, several iterations of the Real Options analysis should be performed in which future iterations are updated with the latest data and assumptions. Understanding the steps required to undertake an integrated risk analysis is important because it provides insight, not only into the methodology itself, but also into how it evolves from traditional analyses, showing where the traditional approach ends and where the new analytics start.

Potential applications of KVA + RO framework

The strategic value of Real Options for the DoD is that it offers decision-makers alternative decision pathways or courses of action, something that the military has been accustomed to for decades. In a dynamic and uncertain environment where investment decisions must be flexible and fluid, strategic Real Options offers insights into alternative paths and how they relate to unique DoD requirements. A tool to augment existing performance tools, KVA+RO can be applied in many areas.

Methodology proof-of-concept

Implementation of 3D laser scanning and collaborative PLM solutions has resulted in significant cost savings, optimized maintenance schedules, increased quality, improved safety and reduced re-work in several industries. In this proof-of-concept case study, we examine the hypothesis that if these technologies are applied to ship maintenance procedures, similar benefits could be derived:

- decreased cycle-time for US Navy ships by minimizing downtime in shipyards
- lowered maintenance cost by eliminating or reducing DoD planning yard labor costs
- reduced fleet inventory requirements through reduced cycle-time
- improved productivity (increased ROI) in current shipyard planning processes to facilitate faster and cheaper shipboard modernization.

Table 8.5 Potential DoD applications of KVA and Real Options

	Application
Activity-based Costing (ABC) Enhancement	KVA provides a way to define common units of output of former overhead functions. RO/KVA provides a way to compare outputs-per-cost value flows.
OMB Circular A-76 Comparisons	RO/KVA could enhance outsourcing comparisons between the Government's Most Efficient Organization (MEO) and private-sector alternatives.
JCIDS and DAS	RO and RO/KVA present themselves throughout JCIDS requirements generation and the Defense Acquisition System (e.g. DOTMLPF vs. New Program/Service solution, Joint Integration, Analysis of Material Alternatives (AMA), Analysis of Alternatives (AoA), and Spiral Development)
SHIPMAIN	RO/KVA theory applies to cost/benefits analysis for the various modernization options, as well as a way to measure the risks/valuation necessary in managing the portfolio of options.

To test our hypothesis, we apply the KVA+RO framework with data compiled from interviews and conversations with a select group of Subject Matter Experts (SMEs) from the Puget Sound Planning Yard (Puget Sound).[5] Using KVA methodology, we compared three scenarios on that one aspect of maintenance processes, ship planning yards:

- "As Is": Current labor-intensive process.
- "To Be": Introduction of 3D laser scanning and data capture and storage technology into the shipyard planning processes, enabling management and re-use of data. These technologies result in limited re-engineering.
- "Radical To Be": Several technologies introduced, including laser scanners, 3D digital imaging, data warehousing, a robust database management system (DBMS) and PLM. These technologies result in substantial redesign of current processes.

We also explore the question of how data capture and storage technologies, in conjunction with collaborative data-sharing technologies, could contribute to productivity of Navy organizations outside the planning yard. Could these technologies impact downstream processes, particularly in the public/private-sector shipyards performing maintenance, modernization and repair work on Navy vessels? Could reengineering the shipyard planning process affect the Navy's overall maintenance and modernization efforts?

The challenge

The US Navy must be extremely diligent with its maintenance policies to ensure that ships and submarines meet national defense objectives. Maintenance Policy for Navy Ships delineates maintenance and modernization efforts as those aimed "to define and manage the material condition requirements and the configuration of Navy ships." Consequently, maintenance and modernization policy is carefully designed to keep Navy ships operating at the maximum level of material readiness possible (OPNAVINST 4700.7K). This requirement is carefully balanced with the expectation of asset availability to Fleet Commanders since naval vessels undergoing repair, maintenance, or modernization in an industrial activity facility are unavailable for operational tasking until scheduled work is complete.

Maximizing the Navy's readiness requires continuous process improvement and innovation, as well as capitalization on technological advances to reduce costs and increase efficiency. Navy ships are expensive to operate and maintain, and can remain in service for many years; the life cycle for a small combatant is 20 or more years, 30 or more years for an attack submarine or larger surface combatant, and up to 50 years for an aircraft carrier (O'Rourke, 2005, June 23).

In the fiscal year 2005, the Navy spent $3.9 billion on maintenance and modernization efforts. There are many challenges to maintenance activities, including labor-intensive and costly ship checks, currently involving manual measurement methods. In addition, many of the Navy's ships were designed and fabricated in the 1970s and 1980s, in primarily 2D work processes with no comprehensive, centralized source documenting all maintenance and modernization efforts (Greaves, 2005, October 11).

COTS like 3D terrestrial laser scanning and PLM technologies could improve maintenance processes and substantially reduce the costs of Navy ships. COTS could complement current naval maintenance initiatives, including "one shipyard for the nation" and SHIPMAIN. Launched in 2002, SHIPMAIN's goal is to ensure that all shipyard processes are redesigned, with consistency among different maintenance facilities, to preserve ship quality and lifespan within schedule constraints. It is anticipated that SHIPMAIN will ultimately reduce the overall cost of ship maintenance and modernization by installing a common planning process for surface ship alterations. By installing a disciplined management process with objective measurements, SHIPMAIN strives to increase the efficiency of the process without compromising its effectiveness. Finally, the initiative will institutionalize the process, and implement a continuous improvement method.

Terrestrial three-dimensional technology

Terrestrial three-dimensional (3D laser) technology has moved from early adopter acceptance to mainstream markets since its introduction in the late 1990s. The terrestrial 3D laser scanning market is forecast to reach $180 million in sales in 2005, up 45 percent from the previous year (Greaves, 2005, October 11).[6]

Use of 3D laser scanning technology has resulted in significant cost savings, optimized maintenance schedules, increased quality, improved safety and reduced re-work. Commercial applications range from maritime and space applications to manufacturing and production. Driving the industry's growth is increasing recognition

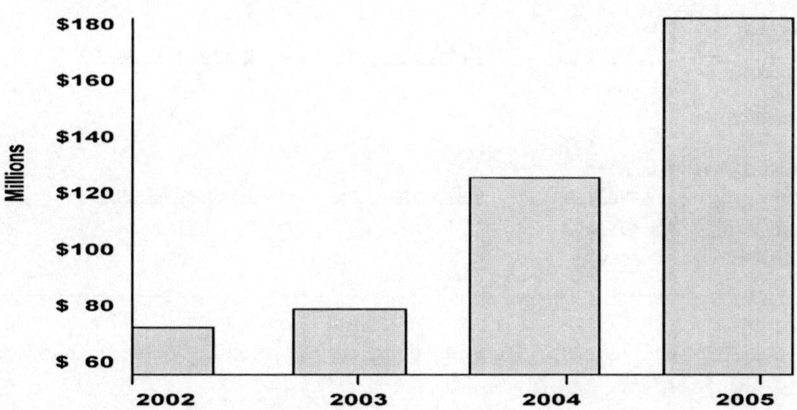

Figure 8.9 Terrestrial 3D laser scanning market forecast (hardware, software and services). Forecast October 11, 2005.

Source: Spar Pont Research LLC, 2005

that 3D aids in the design, fabrication, construction, operations and maintenance processes, according to industry analysts (Greaves, 2005, October 11).

The industry is poised for further growth with companies making large R&D investments. Laser-scanning solution providers offer every potential business model: software, hardware, software/hardware, hardware/services, software/services, software/hardware/services. Vendors include: CALLIDUS Precision Systems GmbH, FARO Technologies Inc., I-SiTE Pty Ltd., Leica Geosystems HDS, MDL (Measurement Devices Ltd), Optech Incorporated, RIEGL Laser Measurement Systems GmbH, Spatial Integrated Systems, Inc. (SIS), Trimble Navigation Limited, Visi Image, Inc. and Zoller+Frohlich GmbH. Although the industry is dominated by a few large players, emerging companies like SIS are rapidly becoming key competitors. SIS develops and implements digital 3D data capture, imaging, modeling and visualization technologies integrated with commercial off-the-shelf software to provide engineering design, collaboration and PLM solutions.

Ship Check Data Capture 2005 project

Recognizing the potential of new technologies on the ship check process in the US shipping industry, NSRP funded the Ship Check Data Capture project in 2005. Laser scanning, close-range photogrammetry and other technologies capturing as-built ship conditions in digital format to create 3D electronic models were evaluated. The project's goals were to determine potential technology synergies producing cost-effective solutions and prototype a ship check data capture process that could be used by the US shipbuilding industry. It is also anticipated that archived digital data would provide a cost-effective solution to the life cycle cost management of ships.

SMALL SHIP CHECK:

	Traditional	Laser Scanning	Realized Savings
Cost	$9,351	$6,398	32%
Labor Hours	112	72	36%

LARGE SHIP CHECK:

	Traditional	Laser Scanning	Realized Savings
Cost	$47,650	$26,465	44%
Labor Hours	660	336	49%

Figure 8.10 NSRP Ship Check Data project preliminary results cost/time savings.

Source: NSRP ASE, 2005, December 8

Notes

1 Project time savings are close to project goal of 50 percent.
2 Savings shown are only for first ship check and do not include elimination of future ship checks for the same space.
3 Please see Appendices for full cost savings.

With laser scanning technologies, preliminary results were encouraging, given a 32 percent cost savings over the traditional ship check process for a small ship; cost savings were even greater for a large ship, at 44 percent.

Specific benefits from the software and hardware tested include:

- Creation of as-built 3D models and validation of as-built models to design models
- Reduction of costly design changes, improved design capability
- Reduced construction rework
- Accurate factory-fabricate in lieu of field-fabricate
- Reduced ship check costs: fewer days, fewer personnel
- Elimination of return visits to the ship for missed measurements
- Obtaining measurements which are difficult or unsafe for human reach (NSRP ASE, 2005, December 8).

Spatial Integrated System (case example)

SIS's 3DIS (3DIS) is the solution used in the current case study. 3DIS is employed as a 3D image and data capture system (Figure 8.11). Upon its setup and execution, 3DIS works by scanning its predetermined environment: a compartment, or selected area within that compartment, with a pinpoint of laser light to quickly and accurately capture the digital space and distance information of that space or area. At the same time, an embedded wide-angle digital camera captures a photo image of the target.

Once data is captured, the technology automatically implements image-processing algorithms, and a digital point cloud results. The graphical user interface (GUI) of the system portrays this point cloud as faint lines outlining the images within that space. The actual file created is a long list of raw data in the form of (x,y,z) coordinates, and, as an added feature, each point retains its original color

Figure 8.11 SIS laser scanning equipment.

Source: Strategic Integrated Systems, Inc., www.sisinc.org/index.asp?id=12, 2006

Figure 8.12 Sample point cloud image (USNS ship exterior).

information. These data points can then be connected and enhanced to create a realistic, 3D model (Figure 8.12).

The file format used in the 3DIS system can be exported for further processing, such as 3D CAD analysis and modeling. The process for modeling the captured point cloud is more complex and can be accomplished several different ways. This path is typically used for a whole compartment or topside area. The complete process involves:

1 Point cloud captured and saved by 3DIS Imager, the scanner software.
2 Point cloud is viewed via 3DIS Viewer for quick check of data and point-to-point measurements.
3 Captured point clouds are registered to one another using Imageware, point-processing application.
4 Surface model is constructed from the point-cloud data.
5 Surface model created is imported into CAD system and an assembly model of space and components is completed.
6 Files are exported to AUTOCAD, as required.
7 Detailed information, such as engineering notes and dimension call-outs, are added in AUTOCAD.[7]

Completion of this process provides a workable, 3D model of the captured area or compartment. From this model, prospective alterations can be visualized, accurate dimensions can be ascertained, and most importantly, the model may be reused many times over the life cycle of the naval vessel, and for vessels of the same class. Figure 8.13 shows the completed 3D model created from a captured point cloud (Figure 8.12).

SIS technology has been used in several projects, including:

Figure 8.13 Digital 3D model of USNS superstructure.

- **USS San Francisco damage assessment.** Damaged areas of the USS San Francisco (SSN 711) were scanned when the submarine collided at high speed with an undersea mountain south of Guam.
- **USS Abraham Lincoln ship check.** 3D laser scanning services were provided for ship check of a 3-story hangar bay on the USS Abraham Lincoln (CVN 72) in 2005. Hundreds of hours of labor were saved by scanning the HVAC, piping, fuel storage tanks and other structures. Engineers were also able to conduct multi-discipline "what if" scenarios to avoid clashes in the installation of a new deck (Greaves, 2006, January 17).

Collaborative technology

Product Lifecycle Management (PLM) is technology and a strategic approach applying business solutions to support collaboration, management, dissemination and use of product definition information across the extended enterprise from concept to end of life – integrating people, processes, systems and information.[8] Worldwide sales for PLM software and services in 2005 grew 8.7 percent to $18.1 billion, with sales estimated to reach $26.3 billion by 2010 (CIMdata, 2006, April 5).

The fastest growing segments of PLM solutions are collaboration, management and product-related sharing tools. These tools include technologies that support data exchange, portfolio management, digital manufacturing, enterprise application integration, and workflow automation. A range of industries have invested in PLM solutions, including those involved in aerospace and defense, automotive and other transportation, utilities, process manufacturing, and high-tech development. The PLM market is poised for further growth, with vendors expanding product offerings as the industry evolves. Figure 8.15 indicates the evolution of PLM applications, illustrating their stages before reaching the "plateau of productivity" in the mainstream market.

Some vendors in the PLM space are focused on specific niches within the marketplace, while a handful of companies are distinguishing themselves as "PLM

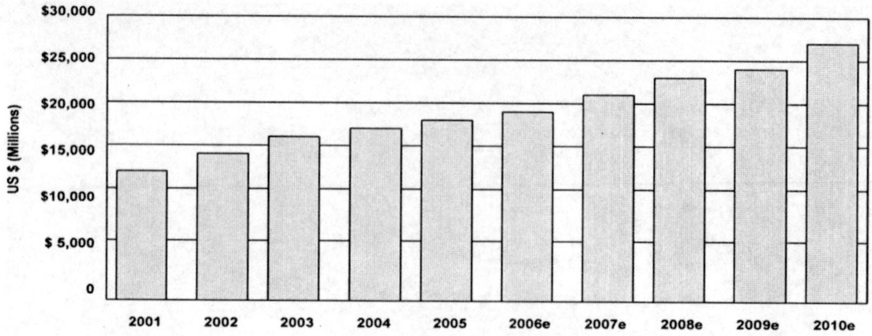

Figure 8.14 Overall PLM market growth history and forecast.

Source: CIMdata, 2006, April 5.

Note: Estimates for 2005 to 2010.

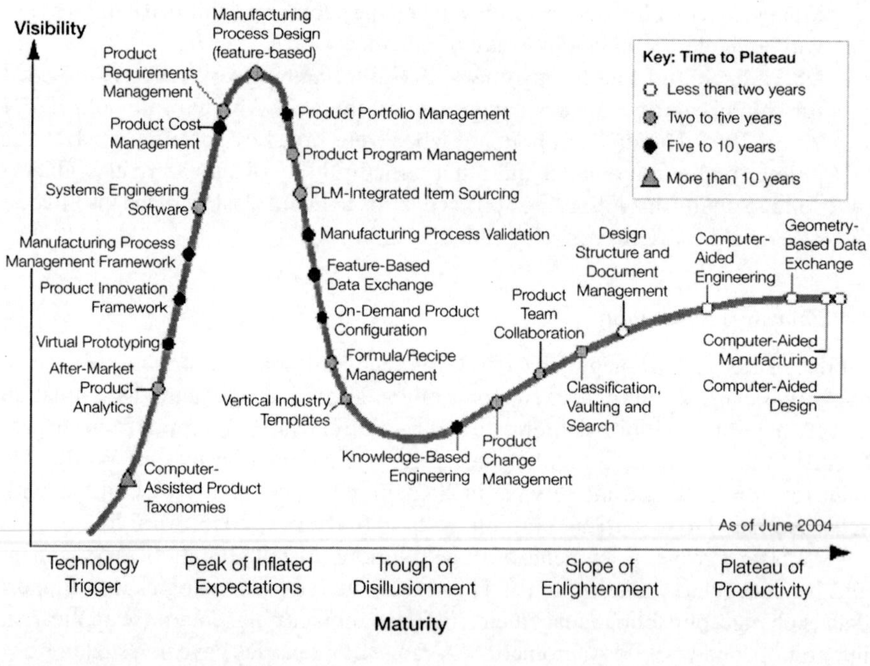

Figure 8.15 Evolution of PLM.

Source: Gartner Group, Inc. Report: Halpern, Michael and Smith, Michael, "Total Value of Opportunity Analysis Exposes Value of PLM", 29 December, 2004.

Mindshare Leaders." This select group, at the forefront of the market in terms or revenue or thought leadership, offers broad-based capabilities supporting full life cycle-focused solutions. PLM Mindshare Leaders include UGS, SAP, Agile and IBM/Dassault Systemes (CIMdata, 2006, April 5). UGS appears to be leading the segment by solidifying its leadership position with strategic acquisitions and key customer wins, including Northrup Grumman Ship Systems (NGSS), in shipbuilding. After an extensive benchmarking study, NGSS selected UGS's solutions for digital manufacturing of ships (UGS, 2006, May 11).

Planning yards

America's naval shipyards went through a major transformation during the 1990s, with numbers decreasing to four public-sector shipyards and six private-sector shipyards.[9] The Puget Sound Planning Yard in Washington State is one of the four public-sector Navy planning yards remaining in the US; other shipyards are situated in Virginia, Maine and Hawaii. Puget Sound is responsible for planning the maintenance and modernization ship alteration jobs scheduled for the aircraft carriers stationed on the West Coast and Japan, along with the minesweeper force based in Texas.

Planning yards serve an essential role within the larger framework of the Navy's Fleet Modernization Program, supporting shipyards and other customers. For every ship maintenance or modernization task mandated by the Department of the Navy (DoN), the planning yard receives funding through the Design Services Allocation (DSA), along with technical guidance and tasking orders to prepare the shipyard to complete that task. The DSA is a funding line with provisions for design and SHIPALT development work, including Ship Alteration Requests (SAR), Ship installation drawings (SID), MDS, Liaison Action Requests (LAR), and Ship Service Request (SSR) updates including Configuration Overhaul Planning (COP). SHIPALTS constitute an order mandating the introduction, design, or installation of changes to naval vessels.

Planning yards must compile all applicable data and job-related information for its end-users, which can then be used for some form of industrial activity. End-users may be the shipyard itself, a private-sector shipyard, or an entity independent of the planning yard and shipyard. This work is necessary so that physical work required to accomplish a SHIPALT may be planned and accomplished with minimal system or human conflict. All system interferences, problems, or conflicts relating to assigned SHIPALTS will be resolved by the planning yard. Planning yards strive to achieve these tasks, create quality installation drawings and retain experienced employees. Planning yards are overseen by a Chief Engineer and supported by staff, typically in four divisions: Electrical/Electronics, Mechanical/Marine, Logistics/Material, and Structural/Naval.

Planning yard processes and outputs

Planning yard activities involve essentially a chain of seven sequential core processes: issue tasking, interpret orders, plan for ship check, conduct ship check, report assembly, revise schedule, and generate drawings.[10] This chain of core processes is executed for every naval vessel as it approaches its shipyard availability period and involves several sub-processes, as seen in Figure 8.16.

The schedule, timeline and location for ship availabilities are established by Navy leadership far in advance, but calendar dates and work assigned may be constrained by budget allowances and other prioritization factors. Availability schedules may also be affected by specific trigger events or unanticipated demand for operational naval assets. For example, the terrorist attacks of September 11, 2001, and Operation Iraqi Freedom prompted major changes in the deployment of naval forces. These events resulted in an ultimate surging to deploy seven carrier battle groups, and the largest Amphibious Task group assembled since World War II. The Navy implemented the Fleet Response Plan in May of 2003 to enhance its operational readiness, extending scheduled time between ship availabilities from 24 months to 27 months (www.gao.gov, 2004).

Standard documents considered to be planning yard products or "outputs" include two-dimensional (2D) detailed AUTOCAD drawings of ship compartments or installation areas, equipment removal routes, and material lists. Less tangible outputs include ship's force/shipyard accord in regard to equipment configuration,

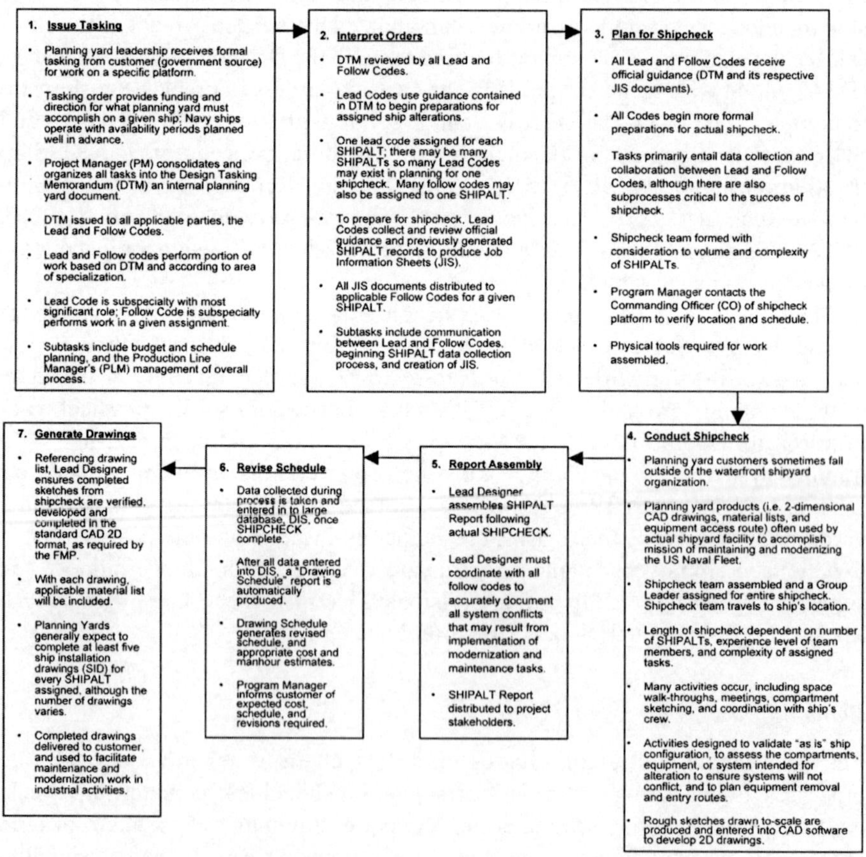

Figure 8.16 Planning yard core processes.

and the assurance that alteration-specific capacities (such as sufficient chill water or electrical capacity for certain alterations) meet the requirements for a given SHIPALT.

The introduction of 3D laser scanning technology, in combination with the ability to improve collaboration among the multiple parties involved in the process, promised to greatly improve the overall performance of the processes. This study focused on estimating the potential of these two technologies in improving the return on investment (ROI) of these core processes and the value and risk of the options these technologies would provide Navy shipyard planning process leadership. For this purpose, we applied the KVA+RO Framework.

KVA methodology: data collection

The first step in the KVA+RO Framework is to conduct KVA data-gathering meetings. As a result of these meetings, aggregated data was compiled based on input received from Subject-matter Expects (SME) as well as historical data presented at the meetings.[11] Interview data was augmented by additional research data to derive several key assumptions used for this case study.

Table 8.6 Discussion of KVA methodology used in case study

- Learning Time method used to estimate value of subprocesses.
- SMEs achieved consensus on core planning yard processes, inputs and outputs of those processes, and frequency of subprocess iterations.
- SMEs subsequently defined seven subprocesses, describing each in great detail. Each subprocess requires a given level of knowledge in one or more of the following areas: administration, management, scheduling, budgeting, basic computer skills, drafting, engineering, shipboard systems, or AUTOCAD drafting and drawing development.
- SMEs analyzed amount of knowledge embedded in each subprocess and provided learning time estimates for each.
- Established baseline level of knowledge for all estimates was a GS-7 employee with a college degree (no field specified).
- SMEs provided learning-time and rank-order estimates to establish reliability level on actual learning-time (ALT) figures.
- Preliminary analysis of initial learning time estimates resulted in an insufficient level of correlation between learning time estimates and rank order (based on difficulty to learn) estimates. Greater detail was gathered to evaluate each core planning yard process.
- To improve reliability of estimates, SMEs were asked to break each subprocess down into its component tasks and provide better estimates for the overall core process ALT by summing up new values.
- The resulting ALT estimates for the subprocesses were derived from the developed process instructions, and a correlation of greater than 80 percent was attained.

Table 8.7 Case analysis – baseline data assumptions

"As Is" Data Assumptions

Head Count

- Average ship check team is composed of 35 people (including all Lead and Follow Codes).

Times Fired

- Values derived from statistical information for fiscal years 2003, 2004, and 2005, and by SMEs.
- Fiscal year 2003 – 95 ship and submarine maintenance availabilities.
- Fiscal year 2004 – 3 maintenance availabilities were funded, with additional funding granted to perform depot- and intermediate-level maintenance on 42 additional ships.
- Fiscal year 2005 – 85 planned availabilities. To remain conservative, and to properly account for planning yard work outsourced to private industry, this study approximates that work across the four public planning yards amounts to 40 planning yard process executions per year.
- 100 SHIPALTS occur per planning yard process:
  - 25 low-complexity alterations (a modification to a component or set of components)
  - 25 high-complexity alterations (a modification to a major system)
  - 50 medium-complexity alterations (a modification to a subsystem).
- Estimates for SHIPALTS are of medium-complexity, the likely mean and most common SHIPALT performed.

Actual Learning Time

One year = 230 work days. One month = 20 work days. One week = 5 work days. One day = 8 hours.

Costs

- Salary figures based on midpoint average pay of GS-12 planning yard employees ($62,353/year) and GS-11 employees ($52,025/year).
- Because basic computing hardware and software is utilized in every scenario, IT cost is not included in the "as is" analysis. It is assumed that each employee in this process has an e-mail account, laptop or desktop computer with identical software, and access to a printer. Material, travel, and other miscellaneous costs are not included in this analysis in order for labor cost to be isolated.

Other

- 40 ship checks are accomplished between the four public-sector planning yards. Other naval ship checks are outsourced to private planning yards.
- The level of effort for each ship check is 100 SHIPALTS.
- All estimates assume a SHIPALT of medium-complexity.
- Each ship check team averages 35 personnel.
- Duration of a ship check is 10 work days, with a travel day at each end.
- A minimum of five sketches/drawings are created for each SHIPALT.
- Approximately 10 digital photographs are captured for each SHIPALT.
- Each ship check will have five Lead Codes, and many Follow Codes.

"To Be" Data Assumptions

Cost of IT

- Cost for laser scanning equipment and all applicable IT was provided by the Improved Engineering Design Process (IEDP) Project Manager for SIS.

continued on next page

- Cost for IT amortized for a 10-year period.
- Given an initial cost of $88,000 for one 3DIS scanner plus its applicable software suite, a maintenance/upkeep annual cost estimate of 20 percent, a use estimate of 200 days per year, and a lifespan estimate of 10 years, the resulting cost per day is: $132.00.
- For analysis of the "to be" KVA, this cost is absorbed by the actual scanning process, and not distributed evenly among the processes that utilize the software suite for modeling. This cost is based on the logistical ideal that one 3DIS scanner is shared between two planning yards.

Table 8.8 Core planning yard process overview

"AS IS" Planning Yard Process Overview Values Reflect Estimates for all U.S. Public-Sector Planning Yards															
Core Process	Process Title	# Org	Est. # Shipcheck per Org	Head Count per Shipcheck	Daily Salary	Times Fired per Shipcheck	Time (days)	ALT	K in IT	Total Learning Time	Rank Order	Total Benefits	Total Cost	ROI
1	Issue Tasking	4	10	2	$271.10	1	8	690	208	898	5	35984	$173,500.00	-69%
2	Interpret Orders	4	10	5	$226.20	100	10	470	66	536	4	2142000	$520,000.00	518%
3	Plan for Shipcheck	4	10	35	$226.20	1	6	238	12	250	3	9984	$1,655,000.00	-99%
4	Conduct Shipcheck	4	10	35	$271.10	1	10	1150	173	1323	6	11327940	$2,604,500.00	552%
5	Report Assembly	4	10	1	$226.20	1	6	405	21	426	2	1383240	$235,000.00	783%
6	Revise Schedule	4	10	1	$226.20	1	3	232	94	326	1	1288144	$131,000.00	1375%
7	Generate Drawings	4	10	110+	$226.20	500	18	750	80	830	7	16590000	$39,386,000.00	-37%
					"AS IS" PROCESS TOTALS:							32777292	$44,705,000.00	10%

KVA analysis

To understand the value of technology on shipyard planning processes on US Navy fleet maintenance activities, KVA methodology was applied to three scenarios: "As Is," "To Be," and "Radical To Be." Although initial data estimates were compiled from Puget Sound Planning Yard sources, overall analysis and data values have been aggregated to reveal information relevant to all four public-sector planning yards. All estimates contained in this analysis are as conservative and accurate as possible. Table 8.8 summarizes KVA analysis for baseline data of current planning yard subprocesses.

The actual number of times each planning yard subprocess executes can be documented with historical data. The numbers used in this analysis are based on historical averages derived from SME estimates. Regardless of the actual number of overall process operations or firings per year, the relative orders of magnitude among the resulting ratios would be the same because the number of firings represents a constant across all estimates.

Under the "To Be" scenario, SIS's 3DIS laser scanner system and 3D data-capture technology was introduced in terms of the estimated impact on process parameters. Implementation of this system into the planning yard process would result in process outputs changing from static installation drawings delivered on paper to 3D digital images and models that are more accurate and precise. An added third dimension also provides greater value to end-users. To account for this added value, potential outputs of the "To Be" process affected by the technology were assigned a conservative increase of 20 percent.[12] In the final “Radical To Be” scenario, both 3D and collaborative information technology are fully maximized with deployment of laser scanners, 3D digital imaging, data warehousing, a robust database management system (DBMS), and PLM collaborative environments.

KVA results

Results from KVA analysis reveal that digital 3D data capture with its high-quality, accurate, and reusable outputs, alongside the information storage and sharing capabilities of a PLM collaborative environment, may prove beneficial in naval ship maintenance and modernization planning and production efforts. Specific findings include:

Substantial cost savings

The DoD spends nearly $45 million to complete the shipyard planning process cycle an estimated 40 times per year.[13] With the introduction of 3D laser scanner system and 3D data-capture technology, costs would drop a substantial 84 percent – to nearly $8 million as seen in Table 8.9. Over the longer term, implementation of 3D and collaborative technologies could potentially reduce costs by $40 million per year.

Introduction of 3D technology in the “To Be” scenario results in cost savings of nearly $37 million, derived through three subprocesses: process 3, 4 and 7. In the “Radical To Be” scenario, cost savings of $40 million are anticipated from five of the seven subprocesses (process 2, 3, 4, 5 and 7).

Table 8.9 KVA results – analysis of costs

	Process Title	*"AS IS"*	*"TO BE"*	*"RADICAL TO BE"*	*"AS IS" & "TO BE" Cost Savings*	*"AS IS" & "RADICAL" Cost Savings*
1	Issue Tasking	$173,500	$173,500	$173,500	$0	$0
2	Interpret Orders	$520,000	$520,000	$328,000	$0	$192,000
3	Plan for Ship Check	$1,655,000	$714,000	$374,500	$941,000	$1,280,500
4	Conduct Ship Check	$2,604,500	$1,364,000	$1,041,000	$1,240,500	$1,563,500
5	Report Assembly	$235,000	$235,000	$122,000	$0	$113,000
6	Revise Schedule	$131,000	$131,000	$131,000	$0	$0
7	Generate Drawings	$39,386,000	$4,716,000	$2,319,000	$34,670,000	$37,067,000
	TOTALS	$44,705,000	$7,853,500	$4,489,000	$36,851,5000	$40,216,000

Improved process performance

Several sub-processes that **will be** impacted greatly include "conduct ship check" and "generate drawing." Figure 8.17 shows the potential reduction from 286 days to 113 total work days required between the four public-sector planning yards to complete 40 ship checks.

More dramatic manpower reductions are seen in the "generate drawings" core process. Because a once manual effort is largely replaced by a more automated digital capture, and the subsequent creation of a 3D model capable of producing many, reusable 2D or 3D ship installation drawings, the requirement for a large workforce is minimized. An annual requirement of roughly 20,000 installation drawings for 40 ship checks, with 100 SHIPALTS each, can be reduced from 3,960 paid work days (regardless of the number of workers) to only 256 paid work days. Figure 8.18 depicts this reduction.

As currently executed, the "generate drawings" process is very labor-intensive because the majority of the process is manual, translating from a sketch on paper, or a pencil-marked revision to a previous SID, to a two-dimensional AutoCAD paper drawing. As evident in Figure 8.18, through automation of the SID, manpower requirements are significantly reduced.

Optimized operational efficiency

The ROI metric identifies the productivity of specific processes. KVA analysis reveals that the implementation of new technology greatly impacts four of the seven core shipyard planning subprocesses.

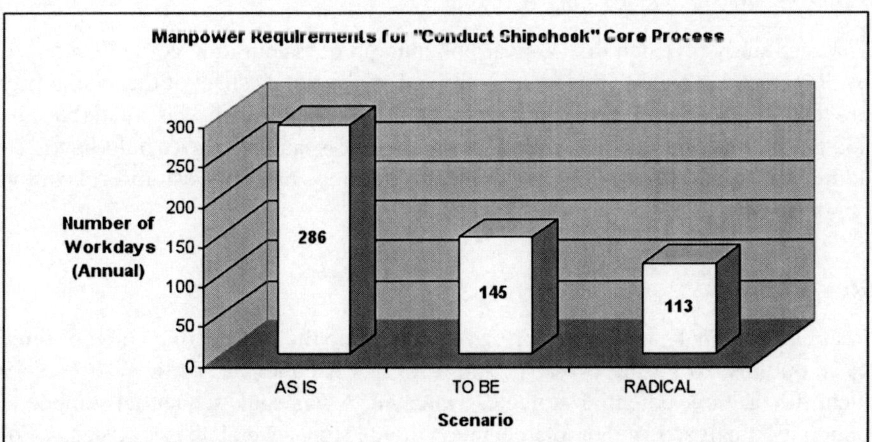

Figure 8.17 Potential reduction of work days for "Conduct ship check" process.

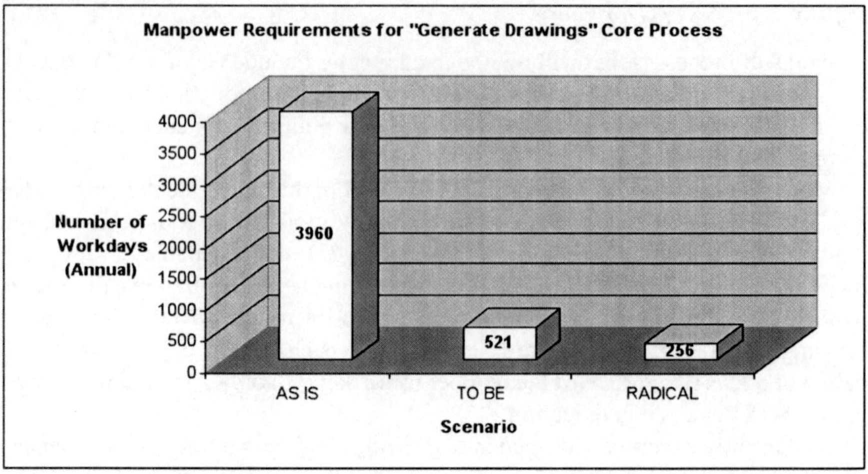

Figure 8.18 Potential reduction of work days for "Generate Drawings" process.

Reduced inventory and expanded capability

Expediting the planning yard process creates a ripple effect through all industrial activity for maintenance and modernization of naval assets. Reducing the duration of ship availabilities and providing more operational availability of naval assets could provide leadership options in deploying more ships or reducing the size of the fleet. Leadership could schedule increased time gaps between new ship acquisitions or allow ship decommissioning to occur at an earlier, more realistic phase of its current expected life cycle.

Reduced Navy fleet cycle-time

The case study revealed that shipyard planning process duration could be reduced by 50 percent. Although this value is limited to a specific aspect of the availability process (the planning yard), if every operational Navy ship was available one additional week for tasking, over a two-year time-span the DoN would have 280 additional weeks for tasking assignments, training, or crew rest and relaxation opportunities.

Real Options

Real Options analysis was performed to determine the prospective value of three basic options over a three-year period using KVA data as a platform. Figure 19 identifies the three potential strategies evaluated. A stage gate sequential compound option was analyzed, with implementation divided into several phases or stages. For example, instead of implementing a complete 3D scanning technology immediately, a proof-of-concept stage was first applied at the Puget Sound shipyard.

Table 8.10 KVA results – analysis on ROI

Core Process	*Process Title*	*"AS IS" ROI*	*"TO BE" ROI*	*"RADICAL TO BE" ROI*
1	Issue Tasking	–69%	–69%	–68%
2	Interpret Orders	518%	881%	1168%
3	Plan for Ship Check	–99%	–96%	–92%
4	Conduct Ship Check	552%	1785%	2530%
5	Report Assembly	783%	783%	1601%
6	Revise Schedule	1375%	1375%	1373%
7	Generate Drawings	–37%	2169%	4515%

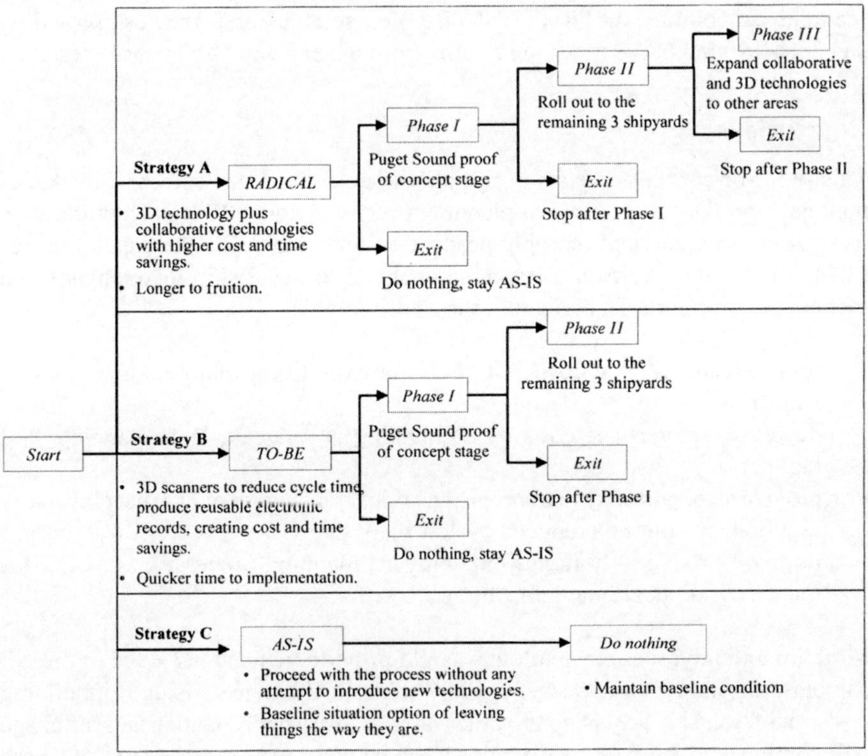

Figure 8.19 COA strategic options.

Only if the implementation is successful will the process be implemented at the remaining three shipyards; otherwise, the technology will be abandoned. These options to abandon and options to defer capital investments until more information is obtained and after the risks and uncertainties have been resolved over the passage of time, actions and events, creates a higher value than a direct risky implementation. The additional value exists as the risky, or downside, values in the implementation are mitigated (the maximum loss is the cost of a single implementation rather than 4 shipyard implementations simultaneously), thereby reducing the risks and enhancing the value of the project through a first-stage proof-of-concept.

Further, in the "Radical To Be" approach, the 3D scanning technology, coupled with collaborative technologies, can be applied to an additional 10 private shipyards across the US. These technologies can also be expanded into various other areas where 3D-collaborative efforts can be employed. This provides additional expansion and growth options that further increase the value of this strategic path.

After running the different scenarios, "To Be" and "Radical To Be" provide highest overall total strategic value, with little difference between the two (19.51 to 20.49 times improvement over the baseline "As Is" option). However, when considering all the downstream options available from collaborative technologies with 3D scanning capabilities, the "Radical To Be" course of action is the best, providing an overwhelming 68.88 times the returns from the existing "As Is" base case.

Conclusions

This proof-of-concept case study reveals the potential value select IT resources may have on the Navy shipyard planning process. Digital 3D data capture, with its quality, accurate, and reusable product outputs, alongside the capabilities of PLM collaborative software, appears beneficial to naval ship maintenance and modernization efforts. In particular, these technologies:

- reduce maintenance costs for ships by expediting maintenance work in shipyards
- decrease maintenance costs by eliminating or reducing DoD planning yard labor costs
- provide an opportunity to improve fleet utilization and/or reduce fleet inventory requirements through reduced cycle-time
- improve productivity in current shipyard planning processes, allowing for increased shipboard modernization.

More importantly, these technologies could provide tremendous value in the US shipbuilding and repair industry. Given war-strained budgets, rising shipbuilding costs, and fewer ship acquisitions by the Navy, industry consolidation and shrinkage will continue, which will greatly impact the nation's security strategy.[14–16] These technologies present an opportunity to help the US maintain its naval national security requirements and allow the industry to remain competitive in the global arena.

There has been anecdotal evidence from contacts within the Navy that this research has helped the top Navy executives in making the decision to acquire the technology that was assessed. The methodology is new to the Navy and it will take some time to make it a routine part of their decision-making process. However, they

Table 8.11 Summary of Results

Maturity (Years)	5		
Risk-Free Rate (%)	5.00%		
Strategic Option Valuation			
	AS-IS	**TO-BE**	**RADICAL**
Benefits	$ 49,175,536.83	$ 93,344,192.00	$ 95,097,452.00
Costs	$ 44,705,033.48	$ 7,854,206.09	$ 4,488,887.70
Volatility	N/A	8.04%	9.81%
Total Strategic Value	$ 4,470,503.35	$ 87,227,330.00	$ 91,601,502.00
Factor Increase		19.51	20.49
Expansion Valuation on Stage-Gate Options			
Maturity (Years)	10	10	10
Factor Increase	3	3	10
	AS-IS	**TO-BE**	**RADICAL**
Benefits	$ 147,526,610.48	$ 280,032,576.00	$ 950,974,520.00
Costs	$ 134,115,100.43	$ 23,562,618.26	$ 44,888,876.96
Volatility	N/A	25.43%	31.02%
Long Term Total Strategic Value	$ 13,411,510.04	$ 265,742,275.00	$ 923,752,800.00
Factor Increase		19.81	68.88

are beginning to recognize it and there is a move to acquire the GaussSoft (KVA) software necessary to routinely assess the performance of systems and processes in the intelligence collection area and to monitor rapid acquisition processes.[17]

A more general conclusion from this case is that it is possible to measure the contributions of technology, enabling new ways of performing processes that can add significant (e.g. super-normal returns) value to a firm's organizational capital.[18] The two technologies explored in this study, when combined with the improvements in processes they enable, represent a significant potential contribution for any firm that employs same in similar processes. Further, real options analysis can uncover the potential such technology options enable in building future organizational capital. Thus, the real options valuation technique, when combined with historical KVA data, can be used to monitor and adjust options over time. This promises to increase the probability that firms' leadership will continue to build inimitable organizational capital, sustaining their competitive advantages by rapidly adapting their processes and supporting technology to take advantage of changes in the marketplace.

Notes

1 "Resources" include people, money, facilities, weapons, information technology, other equipment, logistics support, services, and information. "Management" includes strategic planning, capital planning, governance, process improvements, performance metrics/measures, requirements generation, acquisition/development, and operations.

2 Dr Johnathan Mun is a Research Professor at the Naval Postgraduate School and teaches public seminars on risk analysis, strategic real options, analytical portfolio management, forecasting and statistical analysis, where successful participants will obtain the Certified Risk Management (CRM) designation. For more information, visit www.realoptionsvaluation.com.

3 Risk Simulator is a risk-based Monte Carlo simulation, forecasting, optimization, and statistical software used in the analysis, and was developed by Dr Johnathan Mun (www.realoptionsvaluation.com). See Mun (2006) for details on using the software, applying the Integrated Risk Analysis approach, as well as multiple case studies.

4 The valuation is performed using the Real Options SLS software developed by Dr Johnathan Mun. (www.realoptionsvaluation.com).

5 Input from SMEs was analyzed and verified by independent sources; cost and process information was then aggregated to reflect data for all US public planning yard facilities.

6 Based on estimates concluded from interviews conducted with software and service providers and laser scanner manufacturers, who report increasing activity in a wide variety of markets, including civil infrastructure, ship and boat building, and automobile manufacturing.

7 Information on the operation of the laser scanning equipment and its proprietary software, including these seven steps listed here, was provided by Spatial Integrated Systems Subject Matter Experts.

8 For the purposes of this report, we are using CIMdata's definition of PLM.

9 The remaining private-sector shipyards are owned by two companies.

10 The planning yard process chain was developed by conducting interviews with subject-matter expects at the Puget Sound Planning Yard. It is assumed that operations at alternate public planning yards are comparable in scope, duration, and knowledge requirements.

11 Meetings were conducted in group settings. At the initial meeting, five planning yard SMEs with expertise in several areas and current Puget Sound employees were present. Each SME possessed over 20 years experience in the planning yard industry and a high degree of expertise in his/her affiliated discipline.

12 An important note is that although the output is in 3D, the 2D drawing currently required by FMP policy is easily modified. Because appropriate stakeholders would still benefit from the 3-dimensional models, the value is conserved, while downstream shipyard processes which require 2D drawings would be supported until a new policy and IT-based infrastructure supporting 3D digital imagery is implemented.

13 Cost estimate based solely on labor rates and excludes expenses such as travel and material. This figure consists of ship checks conducted by only the four public-sector planning yards.

14 The Navy's 2006–2001 budget calls for cutbacks in various ship programs.

15 There are six remaining private shipyards in the US, which are owned by two companies.

16 In a 2005 analysis of Shipbuilding Programs, the GAO found that the Navy used "prior year completion" funding to pay for cost overruns. Increases in labor hours and material costs accounted for 77 percent of the cost growth of the eight ships studied. Design modifications, the need for additional and more costly materials, and human capital expenditures were the primary causes of cost growth.

17 There is an ongoing three year effort to assess and implement the GaussSoft (KVA) software to routinely monitor the performance of intelligence collection systems and processes. The goal of the program is to implement the KVA methodology via the software in order to provide management with routine performance information, allowing them to better manage their processes and acquisitions of their crytologic systems.

18 See B. Lev and S. Radhakrishnan (June 2004), "The Valuation of Organizational Capital", www.wren-network.net/resources/2006-02-27.lev_and_radhakrishnan2005.pdf for a more complete discussion of organizational capital and methods for estimating its value.

References

Ballow, J. J., Burgman, R., and Burgoz, S. (2004). *Enhanced business reporting: a formal joint proposal to the AICPA from Accenture LLP & Asset Economics, Inc. October 2004.* White Paper, p. 5. Available at: http://www.ebr360.org/downloads/exchange.pdf

Ballow, J. J., Thomas, R. J. and Roos, G. (2004) Future value: the $7 trillion challenge. *Accenture Outlook* Issue 1, p. 32. Available at: http://www.accenture.com/Global/Research_and_Insights/By_Subject/Strategy/Corporate_Strategy/FutureChallenge.htm

CIMdata. (2006). CIMdata reports PLM market exceeds forecasts. Press release, April 5. Available at http://www.contact.de/news/archive/news2006/LP12-05-06.

Greaves, T. (2005). 3D Laser scanning market red hot: 2005 forecast raised to $178 million: 45% growth projected. *SparView* 3(31) (October 11), p. 1.

—— (2006). US Navy improves readiness with 3D Laser scanning. *SparView* 4(2) (January 17), p. 1.

Housel, T., and Bell, A. (2001). *Measuring and managing knowledge.* Boston: McGraw-Hill.

KPMG LLP (2001). *Achieving measurable performance improvement in a changing world: the search for new insights*, pp. 17–18. Available at: http://www.kpmg.com.au/aci/docs/measure-performance.pdf

Lev, B. (2001). *Intangibles: management, measurement, and reporting*. Washington, DC: Brookings Institution Press.

Lev, B. (2003). Remarks on the measurement, valuation, and reporting of intangible assets. *Economic Policy Review*, 2003 (September): 17–22.

Lev, B. and Radharkrishnan, S. (2004). The valuation of organizational capital. Available at: http://pages.stern.nyu.edu/~blev/docs/TheValuationOfOrganizationCapital.pdf

Mun, J. (2006). *Modeling risk: applying Monte Carlo simulation, Real Options analysis, forecasting, and optimization*. Hoboken, NJ: Wiley Finance.

Mun, J. (2005). *Real Options analysis: tools and techniques*. Hoboken, NJ: Wiley Finance.

Neils, E. (2006). Intangible assets create majority of acquisition value. Intangible Business, April 7. Available at: http://www.intangiblebusiness.com/Brand-services/Financial-services/News/Intangible-assets-create-majority-of-acquisition-value~419.html

Peters, K. and Thiyagarajan, R. (2005). Ship check follow-on project. Presentation given at the Joint Meeting of Shipyard Production Process Technologies, Business Process Technologies, System Technology and Facilities, Tooling and Risk Management Panels, December 8, pp. 139–144. Available at: http://www.nsrp.org/Ship_Production_Panels/Business_Process/downloads/121206_Ship_Check_Thiyagarajan.pdf

O'Rourke, R. (2005). *Navy ship acquisition: options for lower-cost designs – issues for Congress.* CRS Report for Congress RL32914. Washington, DC: CRS, p. 20. Available at: http://www.fas.org/sgp/crs/weapons/RL32914.pdf

Spatial Integrated Systems, Inc. (SIS), www.sisinc.org

UGS (2006). Northrop Grumman Ship Systems standardizes on UGS Tecnomatix digital manufacturing solution. Press release, May 11. Available at: www.plm.automation.siemens.com/about_us/press/press.shtml?id=4646

US Department of Defense. (2005, October). Instruction on IT Portfolio Management (Draft). Number 8115.bb. Washington, DC.

—— Office of the Deputy Under Secretary of Defense (Logistics and Material Readiness) (2005). *DoD maintenance policy, programs and resources fact book.* Washington, DC, p. 2. Available at: http://www.acq.osd.mil/log/mrmp/factbooks/Fact_Book_2005_FINAL_10_06_05.pdf (accessed June 2006).

US Department of the Navy, Chief of Naval Operations (2003). OPNAVINST 4700.7K. July 11.Available at: http://www.combatindex.com/mil_docs/pdf/opnav/4700/4700-7K.pdf

US General Accounting Office (2004). Defense logistics: GAO's observations on maintenance aspects of the Navy's Fleet Response Plan, pp.1–3. Available at: http://www.gao.gov/new.items/d04724r.pdf

US Government Accountability Office (2005). *Best practices: better support of weapon system program managers needed to improve outcomes*. Washington, DC, pp.1–12. Available at: http://www.gao.gov/new.items/d06110.pdf

9 When IT does matter

Setting up "value contracts" between stakeholders

Yves Caseau

Introduction

Nicholas Carr's book *Does IT Matter?* has become a instant classic in the professional world of IT. This is indeed a great book, quite thought-provoking and relevant to the everlasting debate about the value that is produced by IT, if any. It is based, as its premise, on the following economic analysis: IT has become a mature industry, technology has become commonplace and IT is today a commodity. What used to be a differentiation factor is now a common business practice for any decent modern company. Actually, many competing corporations use similar tools and software solutions to perform similar tasks. One of Carr's most provoking ideas is that the biggest risk, from an IT perspective, is to overspend.

The reference to Carr's book is an introduction to a more complex issue that we shall consider in this chapter. What form of value creation may be associated with the portfolio of existing IT services? In many companies, everyone focuses their interest on the new projects, the new technologies. It is already a difficult endeavor to produce a business case for a project (the famous ROI); it is even more complex to continuously manage the value that is produced by IT services.

The issue of value creation is a "landmark" of IS management. It is a dual question from the issue of IT cost management: it is impossible to ask oneself questions that relate to costs without wondering about the associated value creation. This a complex, nested, multi-level question:

- What is value creation? Does value concern present or future? How does it take uncertainty into account and introduce some form of risk-related depreciation? How does one account for intangible value, such as brand, reputation, human capital? This sole topic has prompted many books. It will be evoked briefly in the next section.
- How is value creation measured? At the enterprise level? For a given business function? For a project? Project-related measure is simpler in the sense that one may compare amongst two scenarios: with or without the benefits from the project. Assigning value between different business processes or functional roles is much more difficult.
- How does one identify IT contribution? It is a common practice to assign the benefits of a new software application to the IT project, as part of the business

case that is built to justify the project. However, there exist multiple success factors that are not related to IT and that are equally important.

Our thesis in this chapter[1] is to accept the difficult and subjective nature of this issue: assigning value is a management act, as is the validation of a business plan. We encounter here a common idea from the business management literature: a manager's role is to take decisions about questions that cannot be solved.[2] This approach avoids getting into a common paradox of analytical methods, where the easy part of the problem is over-engineered and analyzed *ad libitum*, while the complex part is simply left aside. Once the subjectivity is accepted, value analysis is a decision-aid method; it is no longer a holy grail.

The experience of any seasoned IT manager shows that there exists no mechanical or linear formula to evaluate the value which is brought by a project. It is possible to create a lot of value with small well-crafted projects and to only create little value with large applications that were poorly deployed or poorly used. Nicholas Carr's book is built upon a statistical observation known as Solow's paradox: there is no visible correlation between IT investment (as a share of revenue) and productivity gains.[3] The suggested consequence from the absence of correlation is that IT does not participate to productivity gains. Since then, this thesis has been disproved by many authors; however, we can use the information to our own advantage and observe that the absence of correlation only shows that it is not enough to spend on IT to produce value, and that Information Systems is not a commodity market.

The first issue we will address deals with the nature of value creation. We will take a tour of different existing approaches and show why simplicity is a virtue when the purpose is the economic analysis of the information system. Instead of considering the practice of ROI as the accounting demonstration of the project interest, we propose to take it as a tripartite contact between the IT division, the management board and the operational division that sponsors the project. This viewpoint entails that the simpler the contract is, the easier it is to monitor and to enforce.

Next, we shall focus on our proposal to use this type of value management as a framework for the application portfolio management. This section contains our main contribution to this issue, which has inspired this chapter's title. The key concept of "value contract" is inspired by "service contracts." Managing quality of service is equally difficult and may be seen as subjective. Using "service level agreements" and contacts between the different stakeholders has helped considerably to establish a mature management practice. Our claim is that managing the "value which is produced by IT" should follow the same path.

Since this management relies on the "project contracts," which themselves include non-financial arguments, we shall address in the next section the issue of intangible value for the information system.

Project analysis and value creation

Which Value?

This first section will attempt to tackle this question in a top-down approach, which will yield an analysis framework as well as the outline of this chapter. Our first axis of analysis is to separate between marginal (incremental) value and global value:

- The *incremental value* is the value which may be linked to an evolution of the information system, that is, a project. The incremental aspect makes the analysis simpler since we may rely on before/after comparisons.
- The *global value* is the one that is produced by the system as a whole, that is, the cumulated value produced by the portfolio of existing services.

The second axis for this investigation is the separation between financial and intangible value.

- *Financial value* is what may be measured by the accounting department, whether it is an increase in revenue or a reduction of expenses. Financial value usually is a direct consequence from the financial hypothesis that is put together in the project business plan – namely, the list of positive and negative gains that are expected for each future time period.
- *Intangible value* is, on the contrary, what cannot be taken into account in the discounted cash flows,[4] but still contributes to the "market value" of the enterprise. This is commonly referred to as the "goodwill." In this second category may be found the human capital value, the public image of the company, the customer satisfaction, and so on. The separation between the two is not absolute; it is often possible to place a financial value onto an intangible asset. However, the methods for doing so are, by nature, prone to debate and refutation.

Numerous books have been written about the measure of a project's financial value. Our thesis, which will be further developed in the next section, is that the choice of the method is not the most important issue concerning the value that is generated by IT. With a fair amount of simplification, we may distinguish the following different approaches, in an increasing order of sophistication:

- The computation of "pay-back," which is the moment when the cumulative gains offset the total cost.
- The computation of "ROI" (return on investment) *over a given period of time*. The ROI yields a synthesis of all cumulated gains with respect to the total expenses, expressed as a return rate.
- The ROCE (*Return on Capital Employed*) is a measure of the profitability of the project. It evaluates the net results associated to the project with respect to the invested capital. The separation between capital expenses (CAPEX) and

operational expenses (OPEX) makes this approach more sophisticated than the simpler computation of a ROI.

- The DCF[5] (*Discounted Cash Flow*, called VAN in French) introduces the depreciation of money into the temporal sequence of net results.
- Last, the EVA (Economic Value Added) analysis introduces the cost of capital into an ROCE. Taking the WACC (*Weighted Average Cost of Capital*) into account is important to compare the value of an IT investment against other alternatives.

It is not necessary to use sophisticated methods to tackle the issue of value creation. A proper usage of ROI is amply adequate.[6] One may leave the topics of capital costs and profitability threshold to the CFO and his team. The question of the appropriate practice of the ROI will reappear in Chapter 9. To summarize, we may say that it is necessary:

- To establish the earning reports for the next five years of the project. It is important to work on such a long time horizon to ask oneself the relevant questions about durability, replacement, clean-up.
- To compute and to justify total costs of ownership (TCO). This must be expressed with cost drivers (prices and quantities).
- To compute a ROI over a three-year period, together with an assessment of the risk level (computing a pay-back is not enough). With some very rare exceptions, a project without a positive ROI over three years should be cancelled.

"Intangible value" should be measured in a separate way,[7] as we shall see below. Value analysis may be part of the regular procedure to assess a project; the final evaluation to launch is still a management act, which cannot be expressed as the result of sorting a spreadsheet.[8]

We may now return to our initial question about the global value produced by the information system. A first simple approximate answer exists: the value of the "service stack" is the sum of the values of the projects that were completed to build this stack. Two caveats apply to this proposition:

- Business conditions constantly change; the financial hypotheses that were used to establish a business plan when the projects were launched need to be monitored regularly. We shall examine this issue below.
- An information system is not reducible to a sum of projects: the accumulation of transformations produces mutations that deteriorate traceability between services (which produce benefits) and software applications (which generate costs).

However, grounding the value analysis of the complete information system into the information that is gathered to launch projects has the huge benefit of relying on data that is shared and known by all the stakeholders.

Different approaches yield different limits

A short bibliographic survey about information system value analysis produces numerous methods – and numerous debates. Alan Fustec and Bruno Ghenassia rightly use the term "religious debates."[9] Against the group that advocates complex and rigorous analysis, another group of skeptics declare – no less vehemently – that information systems value analysis is a dead end. As was mentioned earlier, value analysis may become a truly complex topic if precise and indisputable metrics are required. My own opinion is that the search for a management (decision making) method based on value analysis is hopeless; its application to information systems should be qualified as decision-aid, in the sense that it promotes balanced thinking. I have categorized my own bibliographic search into four categories:

1 *Analyzing the "market value" of the IT organization*: how to measure, in a way that is as objective as possible, the value that is produced by the IT division with respect to the open market for IT services and integration.[10] Its principle is to compare the IT activities with those of a virtual ISV (Independent Software Vendor), whose ability to create value has been established statistically from financial statements of existing ISV. This comparative evaluation relies on performance and maturity metrics, taken from reference standards such as COBIT, CMMI or ITIL. This is a promising method, although it is more a form of benchmarking than a true technique for measuring the creation of value by the information system itself. Indeed, it is possible to create a lot of value with IT projects that were poorly executed (as far as their maturity and their respect of software standard practices are concerned), while superbly executed projects (as far as the development is concerned) may turn out to be useless.

2 *Financial methods* extend the classics of value analysis, applied to business activities, to the field of IT projects and services (although the former is more common than the latter). They draw from the previously mentioned techniques of ROCE, DCF or EVA; they also include risk evaluation formulas, especially from a project portfolio perspective. The portfolio framework has been extensively adapted to the management of IT projects, mostly for risk management. Here, positive risk means that the benefits of the project depend on uncertain grounds that require some probabilistic evaluation, or that the project may reduce an existing risk of a loss-producing incident. Similarly, a negative risk is either a "chance" to reduce revenue or to incur an additional loss.

3 *Scoring methods* are popular in the project management literature. Their goal is to re-introduce intangible benefits, which are often labeled as "strategic," into accounting tables. These methods rely on questions/answers forms, with a subtle interplay of qualitative scoring and *ad hoc* multiplying factors.[11] The obvious reproach that pragmatics make to these methods is their subjectivity; nothing validates the stability or the universal relevance of the criteria or the formulas.

4 A last approach is to *assign value creation to business process* and then to evaluate the contribution of IT services. This method is directly inspired by the concept of value-chain, developed by M. Porter (1979).[12] A value chain analysis builds a model of the creation of value from the customer point of view. Business processes are introduced as "strands" of the value chain. Value analysis requires disassembling each process step by step, in order to assign a share of the process value to each step. It is a difficult task, which is most often felt as subjective, especially when one tries to identify the precise contribution of IT to each step. The most common method is to use "what-if" scenarios (what would happen without this step, without this software application, and so on). As far as orders of magnitude are concerned, this method succeeds to assign a share of the business process value to the IT services. However, this evaluation can only be offered as "food for thought," and may not be proven nor established in an indisputable manner.

Most such approaches may be qualified as "theoretical." To stay away from any "religious" debate, I would advocate distinguishing amongst two analysis levels:

- The "enterprise common ground" – what must be shared among the stakeholders – is necessarily built upon a simple, clear and measurable method. This is the reason why I advocate the "simple use" of ROI for all projects.
- Decision-aid methods for different roles in the company (CFO, CIO) may include more specialized methods. Everyone is free to follow the method of her/his choice, as long as she/he remembers that, when applying such a method, the process of application is more important than the result itself.

This last point is especially critical: as soon as a complex method is picked, convincing the other stakeholders about the results produced by the method becomes an illusion. What matters is no longer the ending destination (the result) but the journey itself (the framework and the questions that are produced by the method). To summarize, information system value analysis is a tool for better thinking.

Dynamic follow-up of ROI

In every company, the usage patterns and the overall business context of software applications evolve in a continuous way. The parameters that relate to customer usage, such as usage rate, average amount for transactions, average duration, etc., change over time. In a similar way, usage patterns evolve and software applications become obsolete. Some forecasts may be missed, either because they were too optimistic or because the market has changed.

"Keeping an eye on the ROI business case" is the best practice for the continuous improvement of the IT development process. In its simplest form, it is the application of the well-known principle that post-checking forecasts gradually improve their accuracy. However, this is not the most compelling reason; the follow-up of ROI is crucial to monitor and evaluate the application portfolio. Even in a company where investment decisions are carefully studied, usage conditions often evolve rapidly with respect to the application life cycle.

Follow-up (long-term monitoring) means to re-evaluate the following at a constant rate (e.g. yearly):

- Do the expected benefits and savings still occur?
- Do the hypotheses that were made on the business process operations still apply? (Maybe the benefits are still there, but for another reason.)
- Is the utilization ratio for the applications similar to what was anticipated?
- Is the Quality of Service in line with the project objectives?
- Does the cost of ownership, including the operation costs, comply with the business case hypothesis?

This evaluation will, most often, be undertaken by employees different from the original project team. Hence, it is necessary to use simple measures:

- Business hypotheses should be expressed with the KPIs that are associated with the business processes. KPIs (Key Performance Indicators) are evaluated regularly, in a stable manner, by the business process owners.
- Quality of service must be expressed according to the SLA (Service Level Agreements) that are set up in the service contracts.
- The assessment of gains, savings and costs become difficult after a few years (cf. next section). Therefore, the project contract needs to state clearly how the benefits and savings are made, and how they relate (how to evaluate them) to the previously mentioned KPIs.

The project investment case (which was called "ROI business case" earlier) is, therefore, a contract between three parties:

- The business division, which makes a commitment about the business case hypotheses.
- The IT division, which commits on the operation costs and the quality of service.
- General management, who – with the help of the CFO team – validates and then asserts the value assigned to the project, from the business case.

This is a true commitment, which binds all three parties to a common objective. General management, as long as the business goals are met, commits to support the business division as far as resource allocation is concerned and to support the IT division as far as the total cost of the "service stack" is concerned.

We implicitly referred to the concept of "service contract," which collects all operating requirements associated with a software application or a group of applications. A service contract is a synthesis of multiple requirements that are expressed with availability and performance metrics, which are themselves defined in different IT projects. In a similar way, we may define a "value contract," which collects all business hypotheses that belong to project investment cases, from IT projects that either set up or modify a piece of the application portfolio. This concept allows us to summarize the content of this chapter into a simple sentence: the value analysis of the information system is the long-term monitoring of value contracts.

Managing information system value

Projects and maintenance: sedimentation and sharing

Transforming the project investment case into a contract that relies on straightforward and measurable indicators is not only about ensuring the commitment of the stakeholders. As was mentioned earlier, the integration, over time, of multiple projects into the information system, including upgrades that become mandatory, makes it very difficult to ensure value traceability. This means that, after a few years, one no longer knows which application or IT service is really contributing to which benefit or which savings. Two natural transformations occur during the application life cycle:

- Sharing: as we saw in the first chapter, evolutions that impact the same technical system are grouped into a common project. This gathering offers the dual benefit of reducing the overall cost and ensuring more easily the coherence of the technical system as a whole. However, after a few such iterations, it becomes difficult to trace and assign operation costs to original projects.
- "Sedimentation": each update partially removes changes that were made with previous updates. There is a gradual merging between the successive "software layers," which also translates into making traceability more difficult.

Because of these two transformations, value analysis of project cases has to be performed globally, as part of an "asset management practice" for the application portfolio. It may be divided into functional domains (hence the concept of "value contract"), but is still a matter of judgment, requiring one to stand back and to take a look at "the big picture." The idea that a project investment case could be validated line-by-line 5 years later is pure utopia.

Following up on maintenance expenses is another activity that is bound to the concept of value contract. It is neither necessary nor advisable to produce investment cases for each maintenance operation because:

1 It would rapidly become fastidious. Maintenance cost needs to be included in the total cost of a new project to avoid this useless complexity
2 Continuously updating a software application is part of a typical life cycle. It is necessary so that the services which are delivered by the application keep their relevance across time.

However, application owners need to ensure that legitimate evolutions do not conflict with the original business hypotheses from the original project investment case. It may occur that these evolutions significantly change the utilization process, up to the point where the application is no longer relevant from an economic point of view. For instance, this may happen when security requirements are strengthened.

What is true for a maintenance operation also applies to a new project. What would happen if a new project invalidates the profitability of a previous IT project? This is more frequent than one might think and is not necessarily a problem. However, the management of the "value contract" is precisely designed to catch such situation and to take this trade-off into account when building the business case for the new project.

Managing "value contracts"

To summarize, setting up and following up ROI figures as part of the project investment case first, then as part of the value contract later, fulfills three requirements of information systems governance:

1 *To choose the right projects so that the information system delivers the most relevant services with respect to the company goals.* This is a double requirement. ROI is both a ranking criteria and a method to validate incrementally the amount of investment. The use of ROI for ranking may be seen as a method to manage a project portfolio, when we select projects with higher profitability first. On the other side, since there does not exist an analytical formula that would tell the proper amount of IT investment, this amount is validated incrementally from the last project that gets accepted.

2 *To continuously validate the relevance of the software assets (at least, regularly) and check that their business benefits are still current.* This practice avoids ending up with an "IT service stack" that is perceived as a dead weight, a cost burden. It does not, in any way, mean that one should not try to reduce IT costs as much as possible. On the contrary, since the installed service stack yields the most significant part of IT costs, the management and reduction of this stack is mandatory. This practice, however, prevents taking dramatic and inappropriate reduction measures, because one no longer understands the value produced by existing IT services. It is also an opportunity to monitor and evaluate continuously the size of the software portfolio.

3 *When appropriate, to simplify the software assets by removing software applications that are no longer profitable.* Since application "cleaning" is the most efficient lever to reduce IT cost, a method is needed as opposed to simply removing what is no longer necessary. One needs to proactively assess usage conditions to perform software application "euthanasia" once the "value contract" is no longer respected.

Project ROI is only a tool. Although it is a useful one, it also suffers from various drawbacks and is not a foolproof method for project management:

- Regardless of how much care is taken when setting up the balance sheet for the project future operations, it remains an approximation.
- One needs to keep a global perspective on the information system as a whole. This is why the concept of project portfolio has become so popular. This is also why we refer to software asset management.
- There are many other aspects in selecting a project other than value or finance. Some of them will be dealt with in the next section. As mentioned earlier, selecting a project portfolio is a management decision that is a commitment from all the stakeholders.

Information system's "*goodwill*"

The economic impact of a poor QoS

This chapter will end with a short look at three components of "intangible value," which must be taken into account when measuring the value of an IT project or the value of the complete information system. It would be possible to assign a monetary value to each, but it would be difficult to do so convincingly. The models required are both difficult to explain and to calibrate (which means finding the proper statistical series from which a justification may be drawn).

Quality of Service (QoS) is the first dimension of an information system that yields intangible value. QoS generates a "compensation" value, which can be measured when it is not there. More precisely, we may distinguish between:

- *Usage value*: when a software application is not available or does not perform correctly, it no longer contributes to the value that is produced by one or many business processes.
- *Image value*: quality of service is part of customer satisfaction and contributes to the positive brand image of the company.
- *Efficiency value*: each company optimizes the continuous operation of its processes; QoS degradation yields a deviation from the standard behaviour, which in turn generates a loss of efficiency and higher costs. This principle is the essence of Six Sigma quality management.

Experience shows that each company understands and takes into account the first form of QoS value. This is precisely how service contracts are built. The second form of value loss is twice as difficult to evaluate. On one hand, it is difficult to distinguish between the different motives for customer (non-)satisfaction. On the other hand, it is also hard to relate value-creating usage and satisfaction. In some cases, customers tolerate multiple QoS issues while keeping their usage, and in some others (depending on competition, substitution, etc.) a minor problem will have a huge impact. This is why image value is often considered as a modulation factor of the usage value, which is used by operations management to soften or strengthen the requirements for the service contract.

The last form of value is known by everyone in each enterprise, but is rarely

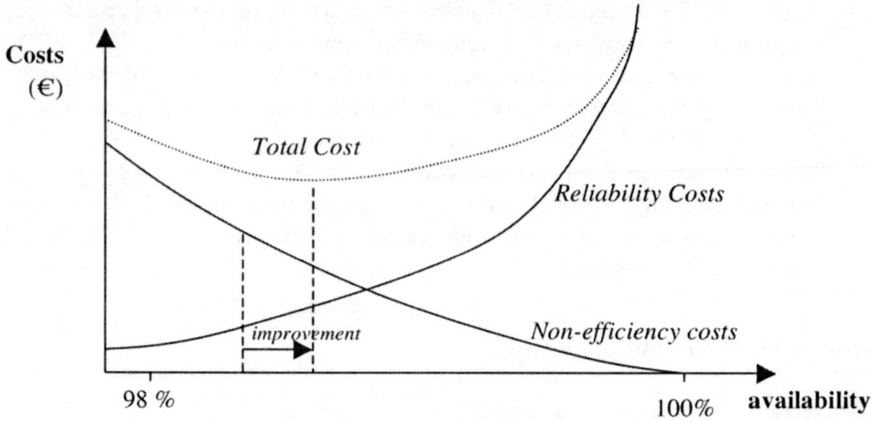

Figure 9.1 Efficiency value related to quality of service.

analyzed and taken into account. When an incident occurs, everyone complains about the negative consequences for all divisions processes, whether it is inside the IT organization or outside. Exception handling that is associated with incident management significantly degrades everyone's productivity. Figure 2.5 shows the reliability costs – necessary to increase the application(s) availability – and the losses that are caused by the non-quality of service. On a first approximation, losses are proportional to incident duration. On the opposite, reliability costs grow inversely exponentially. (Gaining a new digit in availability requires a similar effort.) In this example, the starting point for availability (98%) is arbitrary – a higher figure could have been used. What matters is that it is indeed possible to measure the loss of efficiency caused by incidents. It is tiresome work, but it yields a relevant-though-approximate measure of the efficiency value, which in turn is the basis for managing the proper amount of reliability investment.

Quality of service is an active asset from the enterprise, which deserves to be monitored and maintained proactively. All companies perform the necessary reliability investments once a crisis has occurred. Few elect to invest regularly according to the findings obtained from the analysis of regular minor incidents. This is one issue on which there is a complete agreement between Nicholas Carr and most CIOs.

Value as a tool to balance risks?

The opposite of "Quality of Service" may be many things. It may be the occurrence of minor incidents, which we have just talked about. It may also take the form of a major accident, which is much more unlikely, but with a much larger impact. This is not, obviously, a binary separation but rather a continuous one; from recurring incidents that generate (tolerated) "micro-interruptions" of service, up to disasters, for which a DRP (*Disaster Recovery Plan*) must have been prepared. However, it makes sense to distinguish between incident management, which is part of quality of service and operations management (incidents have a high probability of occurrence over a time span of many years); and risk management (accidents whose probability of occurrence is very small).

It would be logical to expect that a probabilistic approach might cover this type of issue from an economic perspective (one would multiply the value – gain or loss avoidance – by the occurrence probability). In practice, this approach is not relevant for two reasons:

1 One may not speak about value, in the context of risk analysis, without introducing the utility concept. Utility represents the company's own stand with respect to risks, according to its capacities and its responsibilities. Utility is subjective (it varies from one company to the other) and is non-linear.[13] The consequence is that computing the impact associated with a risk cannot be reduced to a mathematical expected value (a product value X probability).
2 Occurrence probabilities are actually unknown. Even though they are approximated with confidence intervals or orders of magnitude, they most often remain inaccurate.[14]

As a consequence, a better approach is to use an "abstract" risk evaluation method, using symbolic scores (associated with categories) to measure the impact and the plausibility of each risk. A similar method is also what works best for managing the complete risk portfolio at the whole enterprise scale. Even though a "symbolic" measure is used, the "value" associated with a risk may be very significant. Hence a regular appraisal is required, with the possible help of an "outside eye" (the "eye" of someone who is as neutral as possible). This is why the concept of a "major risk management unit" is popular in many companies.

Another consequence is that risk evaluation is a matter of judgment and a management responsibility. Tools may be used to sort and analyze a risk portfolio, but the proper decisions may not be drawn from the use of a spreadsheet.

IT readiness to future opportunities

The previous section about negative risks will now be followed by a short comment about positive risks, which are the occurrence of future events that would create additional value. Our topic in this section is not "how to find an (electronic) crystal ball" to foresee opportunities, but rather to evaluate how is the information system ready (or not) to transform such an opportunity, should it occur, into value. To put it differently, is it possible to assign a value to IS properties such as flexibility and adaptability?

1 Obviously, we are not talking about an exact measure, for the same reasons that were given previously. However, there is a large difference with risk management: we only focus on events which are definitely possible (extremely rare events are of no interest here). The question is the evaluation of the different evolutions, as far as the information system is concerned, that

would become necessary for different plausible scenarios. There is, actually, no other method than the study of different scenarios, with the possible help of a quantitative model when precise results are expected. This is both time-consuming (working out the evolution scenario) and incomplete (one cannot evaluate all relevant scenarios) but definitely provides a useful approach to grasp something (flexibility) that might remain a keyword on a PowerPoint.

As a matter of fact, flexibility is a popular concept. Everyone agrees that a new software application or infrastructure should be "agile"/flexible, or that long-term business evolutions should be taken into account when selecting a software solution. Indeed, it makes a lot of business sense to measure this "flexibility value," especially when launching an IT project with a long life expectancy. *This requires the definition of a set of scenarios that correspond to different evolution strategies*. It is not necessary to place a quantitative value on the probability of each scenario, nor to verify that the scenario portfolio is thorough. As for any "intangible value" method, the goal is to provide support to the decision-making process, to entice thinking. Plausibility of the scenarios is sufficient to make this approach interesting. Each scenario may yield a balance sheet with two columns (what would be necessary with and without the project/infrastructure that is being considered), from which "a value addition" may be derived.

This approach may sound speculative or theoretical. It happens to be necessary, nevertheless, to justify large-scale information system investments such as:

- Deploying an integration infrastructure (a "software bus") as part of "enterprise architecture" re-engineering.
- Deploying a "service oriented architecture" (SOA), which requires the construction of a "shared services" common, whose value is only justified by their future "reuse."

Such programs are expensive. Their main interest is to increase the flexibility (and the reactivity) of the information system. (Flexibility measures what may be added and reactivity measures how fast it may be added.) To quantify such gains against the costs, it is necessary to formulate hypotheses about the types of evolutions that will occur in the future of the information system.

What conclusions may we draw from these ideas concerning the value of flexibility? CSC, in its document entitled *Using IT Portfolio Management to Improve the IT Contribution to the Business*, says that the value of flexibility only exists if future is uncertain. Investing money to "prepare the future" has always been a trademark of good managers. Evaluating the information system through a scenario portfolio is suggested, when a large-scale investment is at stake, to transform intuition into analysis.

Conclusion

The heart of the matter, when we analyze what value may be produced by IT, is that Nicholas Carr is right as far as technologies are concerned: Information Technologies are becoming commodities based on standards. However, he is far too optimistic as far as whole systems are concerned. Building a reliable information system that is aligned with the enterprise business objectives is not a mature industrial discipline yet, nor a service that one could buy in a catalog. Software application integration, even though standard and efficient technologies are available, still remains a difficult topic, as soon as there are a large number of demanding users. If you consider the "failed" projects that everyone is mentioning in the newspapers, they often use the same tools and the same technologies as successful projects. What really matters today, as far as the success of an integration project is concerned, is the quality of the software engineers. It is still a skill issue – *IT excellence does matter*.

Our conclusion is that Information Systems "value analysis" has two requirements: on the first hand, to construct return-on-investment (ROI) cases from business processes KPI, over a period of three years; and on the second hand, to follow up these cases during the software application lifetime. Usage conditions for software applications evolve over time, so the software application portfolio needs to be reassessed regularly. The business conditions that make each application worthwhile need to be evaluated each year.

A project investment case should be considered as a contract between the operational division, the IT division and general management. Following up should be regrouped by domains into "*value contracts*," which tie together all business performance indicators. These indicators validate the investment that was made on the domain's IT. "Value contract" follow-up yields a proactive software application clean-up program, which is the best way to reduce IT operational costs.

Last, we have seen that the value that is linked to the flexibility of the information system (i.e. its ability to take advantage of future opportunities) may be analyzed through a scenario portfolio. This approach is recommended for large-scale (e.g. infrastructure) investments.

Notes

1 This text has been extracted and translated from the author's book *Performance du Système d'Information*. Dunod, Paris, 2006.
2 The same idea was found much earlier in books about the theory of political action. For instance, Carl Schmitt starts his book *Political Theology* (1922) with the statement that the one who has the power is the one who decides in exceptional circumstances, that is, when ordinary rules are no longer sufficient.
3 A complete list of reference about the paradox from Robert Solow (which appeared in 1987) would be too long to consolidate. A really nice introduction may be found in *Mirages et miracles des technologies de l'information* from F. Meston, H. Nora and P. Rosé (cf. p. 43). To read a more thorough analysis, one should look at *The trouble with computers* from T. Landauer, as well as – obviously – N. Carr's book. The most brilliant counter-argument against the idea of "commodity IT" that I know may be found in P.

Keene's book, *Shaping the Future*, which was published 10 years earlier than the first article from N. Carr.

4 A more detailed introduction to the application of value analysis to information technology may be found in J. Michel's book *Pratique du Management de l'information: Analyse de la valeur et résolution de problèmes*. The difference between financial and immaterail value is discussed in the book *Votre informatique est-elle rentable?* from A. Fustec & B. Ghenassia. To better understand the concept of intangible value and intellectual capital, see A. Bounfour's book *The Management of Intangibles, The Organisation's Most Valuable Assets,* Routledge, London & New York, 2003, as well as his coedited book with Leif Edvinsson, *Intellectual Capital for Communities*, Elsevier Butterworth-Heinemann, Burlington, 2005.

5 This topic is covered in the excellent book from Jean-Louis Peaucelle, *Informatique rentable et mesure des gains*, in its fourth chapter.

6 This does not imply that companies who practice ROCE, DCF or EVA analysis are misled. These methods are indeed more precise and more relevant than simpler ones. What I mean is that one should focus on the proper target. The issue really is the validation and the long-term follow-up for all the business plan hypotheses, much more than the level of precision of the figures in this business plan. Measuring value must not become a dogma with an elaborate vocabulary and many abstract concepts that precisely shut away any possible discussion. As will be emphasized below, the key issue is to build a contact between the stakeholders, which requires complete communication and understanding.

7 A very similar remark could be made here: there exist many sophisticated methods which enable taking intangible value into account within a finance equation. However, their complexity is precisely opposed to our goals of sharing ideas and setting transparent governance.

8 There exists a subliminal message within those lines: beware of methods that replace thinking with mechanical use of formulas and criterions. This message is well explained in an online article from E. Monnoyer and P. Wilmott, *What IT Leaders do – Companies that rely on IT governance systems alone will come up short* (The McKinsey Quarterly, August 2005).

9 Their book starts with a discussion of the profitability of IT investment, where they distinguish between believers, unbelievers and agnostics. Such words, drawn from the religious vocabulary, may surprise the reader, but they convey the importance of beliefs (and their counterparts – doubts) in a domain as complex as value analysis.

10 This method is one of the approaches that have been applied by a workgroup from the CIGREF, under the direction of A. Bounfour (IC-dVal® method). For instance, see his article 'The IC-dVal approach' in *Journal of Intellectual Capital*, Vol. 4, No. 3, 2003, and reprinted in his co-edited book with Leif Edvinsson, Chapter 7. For a more detailed presentation of the method, see: A. Bounfour, G. Epinette. *Valeur et Performance des SI, une nouvelle approche du capital immaterial de l'entreprise.* Dunod, Paris, 2006.

11 Refer to the third chapter of the book by A. Fustec and B. Ghenassia.

12 A more practical introduction to value analysis may be found in the previously quoted book by J. Michel. For someone who wishes to move from theory to practice, I recommend *Design for Six Sigma for Service* by Kai Yang, especially the third and seventh chapters.

13 This is why industries such as gaming and insurance exist.

14 One must remember one of the foremost principles of risk analysis: one always underestimates her/his own ignorance. Amongst the different books which illustrate this point, I strongly recommend the wonderful book of P. Bernstein *Against the Gods, the remarkable story of risk.* It contains brilliant passages about the utility concept, as well as risk as opposed to uncertainty.

References

Bernstein, P. L. (1996). *Against the Gods: the remarkable story of risk.* New York: Wiley.

Bass, L., Clemets, P. and Kazman, R. (2003). *Software Architecture in Practice*. New York: Addison-Wesley.

Boehm, B., Abts, C., Winsor Brown, A., Chulani, S., Clark, B., Horowitz, E., Madachy, R., Reifer, D. and Steece, B. (2000). *Software Cost Estimation with COCOMO II.* New Jersey: Prentice Hall.

Brisse, L., Cabot, J., Laborderie, G., Pezziardi, P. and Thibault C. (2006). *Une Politique pour le Système d'Information: Descartes – Wittgenstein – (XML).* Paris: Octo Technology.

Bounfour, A. (2003). *The Management of Intangibles: the organisation's most valuable assets.* London and New York: Routledge.

Bounfour, A. and Edvinsson, L. (2005) *Intellectual Capital for Communities, Nations, Regions and Cities.* Burlington, MA: Elsevier Butterworth-Heinemann.

Bounfour, A. and Epinette, G. (2006). *Valeur et Performance des SI: une nouvelle approche du capital immatériel de l'entreprise.* Paris: Dunod.

Brooks, F. P. (1995). *The Mythical Man-Month.* Reading, MA: Addison-Wesley.

Burlton, R.T. (2001). *Business Process Management.* Indianapolis: Sams.

Carr, N. G. (2004). *Does IT matter? Information technology and the corrosion of competitive advantage.* Boston: Harvard Business School Press.

Caseau, Y. (2007). *Performance du SI: analyse de la valeur, organisation et management.* Paris: Dunod.

Chamfrault, T. and Durand, C. (2006). *ITIL et la Gestion des Services: méthodes, mise en œuvre et bonnes pratiques.* Paris: Dunod.

Chrissis, M. B., Konrad, M. and Schrum, S. (2003). *CMMI: guidelines for process integration and product improvement.* New York: Addison-Wesley.

Cummins, F. (2002). *Enterprise Integration: an architecture for enterprise application and system integration.* New York: Wiley Computer Publishing.

DeMarco, T. (1995). *Why Does Software Cost So Much? And other puzzles of the information age.* New York: Dorset House Publishing.

DeMarco, T. and Lister, T. (1999). *Peopleware, Productive Projects and Teams.* New York: Dorset House Publishing.

Jones, C. (1996). *Applied Software Measurements.* New York: McGraw Hill.

Keen, P. (1991). *Shaping The Future: business design through information technology.* Boston: Harvard Business School Press.

Landauer, T. K. (1995). *The Trouble with Computers.* Cambridge, MA: The MIT Press.

Michel, J. (and Sutter, E.) (1992). *Pratiques du Management de l'Information: analyse de la valeur et résolution de problèmes.* Paris: ADBS.

Messerschmitt, D. G. and Szyperski, C. (2003). *Software Ecosystem: understanding an indispensable technology and industry.* Cambridge, MA: The MIT Press.

Paucelle, J.-L. (1997). *Informatique Rentable et Mesure des Gains.* Paris: Hermes.

Perry, W. (1995). *Effective Methods for Software Testing.* New York: Wiley & Sons.

Porter, M. (1980). *Competitive Strategy: techniques for analyzing industries and competitors.* New York: The Free Press.

Porter, M. (1985). *Competitive Advantage: creating and sustaining superior performance.* New York: The Free Press.

Putnam, L. H. and Myers, W. (2003). *Five Core Metrics: the intelligence behind successful software management.* New York: Dorset House Publishing.

Volle, M. (2006). *De l'Informatique: savoir vivre avec l'automate.* Paris: Economica.

Yang, K. (2005). *Designing for Six Sigma for Service.* New York: McGraw Hill.

10 Mapping value creation of organizational capital

Bernard Marr

There is immense confusion about the definition, role and importance of organizational capital.[1] One powerful tool to clarify the role and importance of the various components of organizational capital is to visually map the strategic value creation in organizations.[2] Such maps allow organizations to picture how they create value and most importantly what elements of organizational capital they require to do so.[3] This in turn provides them with a blueprint of what to focus on, what to manage and what to measure. The aim of this chapter is to introduce the reader to the concept of mapping value creation, discuss various approaches and provide actual application examples to illustrate how this can be done in practice.

Conceptual model

The analogy often used to illustrate the importance of organizational capital is an apple tree.[4] If we compare your organization to an apple tree then we have to try to answer questions such as:

- What kind of apples (products or services) can this tree produce?
- What does the trunk, which holds the tree up, look like? i.e. what are we good at? What are our competencies and capabilities?
- What does the root system (our resource architecture) look like?
- How do our roots (resources) combine to give us our capabilities?
- Which are the major roots (our key resources)?

The apple tree analogy is powerful as it captures the value creation with all its major components, which can then be used as the basis for a mapping exercise. In this analogy the organizational capital is in the roots and the trunk of the tree.

Organizational capital

The roots of the tree represent the organizational resource architecture. Resources are critical building blocks of strategy because they determine not what an organization wants to do, but what it can do.[5] Even though economists started to make a strong case for the significance of intangible resources as an important production factor in the early part of the nineteenth century,[6] organizations have traditionally looked at only their financial and physical resources and, by doing so, often overlooked their intangible resources as a source of competitive advantage. Today, most executives do see the critical importance of intangible resources as the drivers of performance.[7] Based on this, we can classify organizational resources into three principal categories (see Figure 10.2).[8] These are: monetary resources, physical resources, and intangible resources.

Monetary resources are simply the amount of cash available – from various sources (cashflows, borrowings, asset sales, equity stakes, etc.) – to invest in the maintenance and development of either physical or intangible resources. Physical resources consist of such items as factories, information and communication technology infrastructure, R&D facilities, plant and equipment, premises or land, and, in some cases, owned natural resources. Intangible resources are non-physical sources of value such as knowledge and skills of employees, brand image, reputation, relationships with suppliers, organizational culture, best practices, or patents.

Here, intangible resources are defined as non-tangible resources that are attributed to an organization and which support an organization's competencies and therefore contribute to the delivery of the organizational value proposition to its various stakeholders. Intangible resources can be split into three component classes: these are human resources, structural resources, and relational resources – see Figure 10.3.

Human Resources refer to the workforce and their skill-sets, depth of expertise and breadth of experience. Human resources can be thought of as the living and thinking part of the intangible resources.[9] Relational resources are the relationships that exist between an organization and any outside party, both with key individuals and other organizations. These can include customers, intermediaries, employees, suppliers, alliance partners, regulators, pressure groups, communities, creditors, or investors. A firm's structural resources cover a broad range of vital factors.

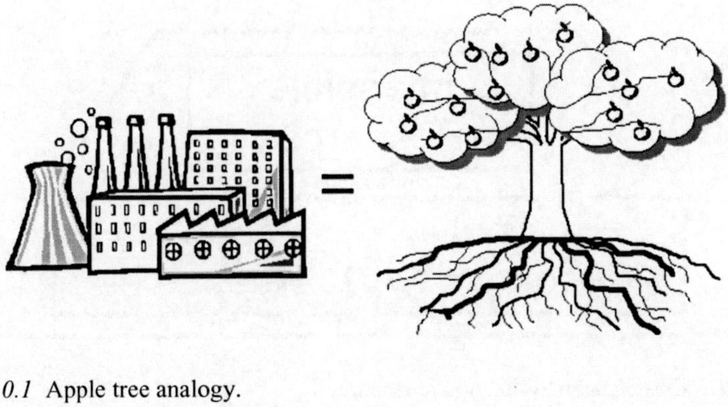

Figure 10.1 Apple tree analogy.

Source: Marr, 2006

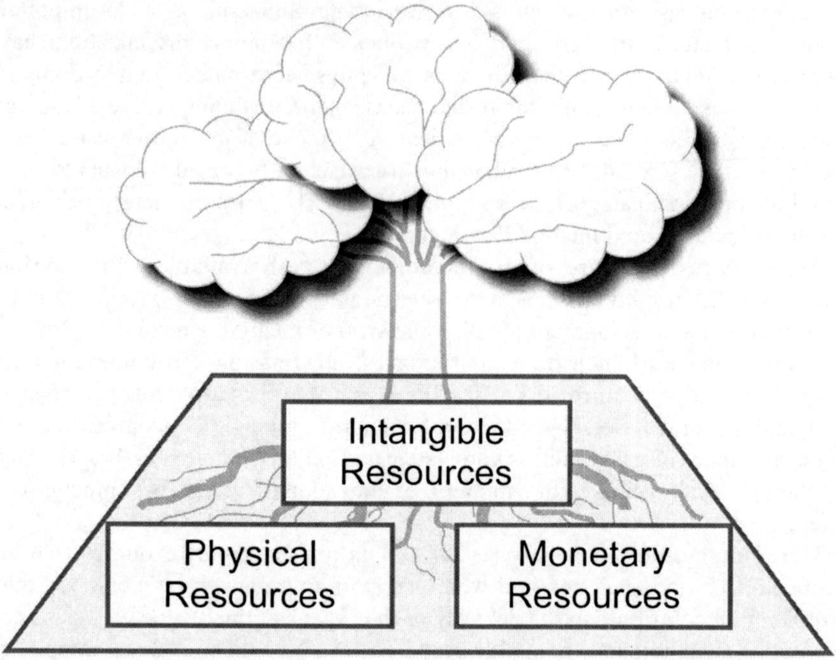

Figure 10.2 Organizational resources.

Source: Marr, 2006

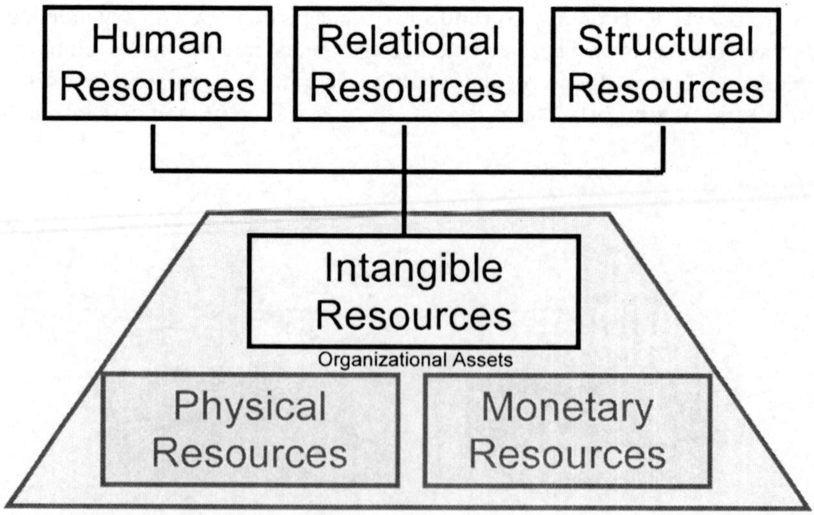

Figure 10.3 Classification of intangible resources.

Source: Marr, 2006

Foremost among these factors are the organization's essential operating processes, the way it is structured, its policies, its information flows and the content of their databases, its leadership and management style, its culture, and its incentive schemes; but it also includes the intangible resources that are legally protected.

No discussion about organizational resources would be complete without a view of how the individual resources interrelate with each other to create vital capabilities and core competencies. Resources are bundled together to form capabilities and competencies.[10] Therefore, in order to be valuable, organizational resources have to be transformed, through core competencies, into products or services that deliver value. Resources are often referred to as performance drivers, reinforcing the notion of causal relationships between the resources and organizational value creation. Intangible resources such as employee skills and customer relationships often deliver customer satisfaction and loyalty, which in turn delivers shareholder value.[11]

In summary, organizations own resources or organizational capital, both tangible and intangible, which interact with and depend on each other to form the basis for capabilities and core competencies. Organizations, therefore, require tools to help them understand their resource architecture, capabilities, core competencies, and value creation. This is where strategic maps or value creation maps come in.

Mapping value creation

Without an explicit understanding of strategy and value creation, the effective management of an organization will never be possible. Today, one of the biggest barriers to successful performance management is that strategy is often communicated in cryptic or incomplete ways, with the hope that employees will understand how it all fits together.[12] In most cases they don't! The primary function of strategy or value creation maps is to communicate information so it can become meaningful. Our human brain is there to interpret incoming information to create meaning. The work of Nobel Prize winners Roger Sperry and Robert Ornstein discovered that the brain is divided into two halves, or hemispheres, and that different kinds of mental functioning take place in each.[13] Thus, the left hemisphere operates sequentially and deals largely with "academic" activities, such as reading, arithmetic and logic. By contrast, the right hemisphere operates holistically and deals more with synthesizing and "artistic" activities, such as art, music, color, and creativity. It is therefore easier for our brain to make meaning of complex information when it is presented in visual formats. Visual maps are processed in our right hemisphere, which is better equipped to deal with complex and holistic information. This is why a picture can be worth a thousand words.

Maps have long been used in strategic management to visualize complex relationships and knowledge.[14] Napoleon, for example, was a great advocate of their use. More recently, Robert Kaplan and David Norton have made strategic mapping part of their Balanced Scorecard (BSC) model, and have therefore significantly contributed to the widespread usage of mapping tools in modern organizations.[15] Strategy maps are visual representations of the causal linkages assumed between strategic objectives in the following Balanced Scorecard perspectives: financial – traditional financial metrics; customer – customer value proposition (operational excellence, customer intimacy, product leadership); internal processes – manage operations, manage customers, manage innovations, manage regulatory and social processes; learning and growth – human capital, information capital, organizational capital. This visual representation of cause-and-effect relationships between distinct strategic objectives was first introduced into the BSC in 1996 and then extended in 2000. Kaplan and Norton argue that strategy maps show how an organization will convert intangible resources into tangible outcomes.[16] The Balanced Scorecard strategy map template is depicted in Figure 4.

However, generic strategy maps have been criticized for being too narrow and too prescriptive.[17] The overall goal of financial performance and shareholder value, for example, doesn't work for public sector or not-for-profit organizations, where finance is primarily an input resource that has to be managed as effectively and efficiently as possible, rather than as an outcome that has to be maximized.[18] Key criticisms of the Balanced Scorecard are that it mainly addresses the needs of shareholders, as opposed to a broader set of stakeholders, and that its resource classification is incomplete.[19] It is argued that the Balanced Scorecard fails to adequately highlight the contributions that, for example, employees and suppliers make to help the organization achieve its objectives, and that it fails to include monetary, physical and relational resources.[20]

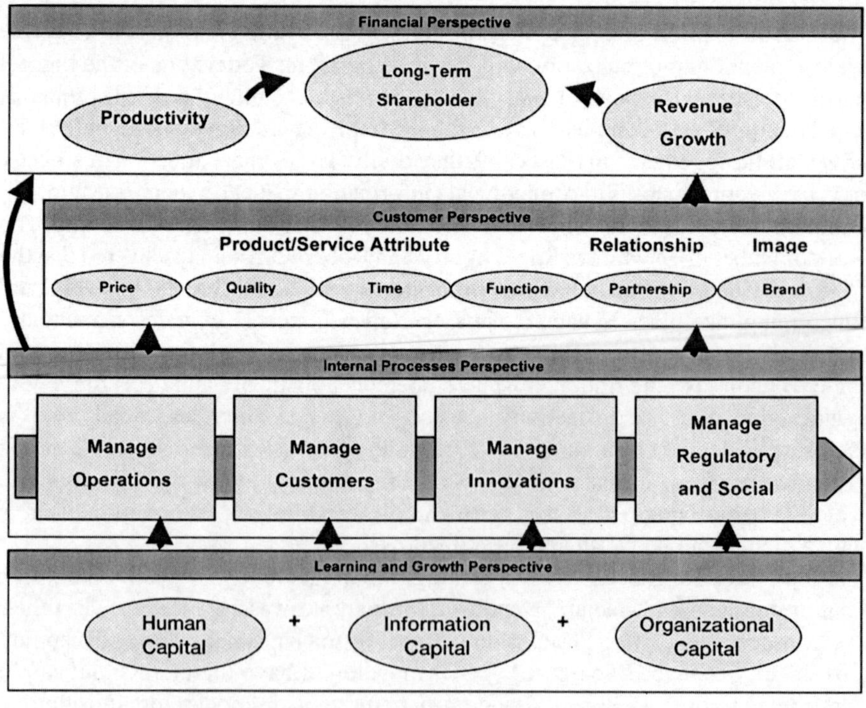

Figure 10.4 Kaplan and Norton's strategy map template.

However, in order to map the organizational value proposition, the core competencies and the underlying resource architecture, as outlined in this chapter, a more generic tool can be used without prescribing specific perspectives. The value creation map outlined below is such a generic template.

Value creation maps

A value creation map is defined as a visual representation of the organizational strategy that includes the most important components that exist within this strategy (namely stakeholder value proposition, core competencies, and key resources) and places them in relationships with each other. It therefore establishes a shared understanding and facilitates communication of strategy.[21] Such shared understanding of the organizational strategy can then be the starting point to assess, implement, and continuously manage the strategy. Someone looking at a value creation map should be able to answer the following questions:

- Who are the key stakeholders of this organization and what value is the organization delivering to them? Basically, why does this organization exist and what are its roles and deliverables?
- What must therefore be the core competencies of the organization so it can deliver the above value proposition? Basically, what are the few vital things the organization has to excel at?
- What are the key resources that underlie the above core competencies? Basically, what are the building blocks of these competencies, in terms of monetary, physical, and intangible resources?

The basic template of a value creation map is shown in Figure 10.5. The top box shows the stakeholder value proposition or the output deliverables. As discussed earlier, these are either prescribed (in the case of public sector organizations or business units), derived from the external analysis, or developed based on the core competencies and resource architecture. In the middle are the core competencies. In this template, I have depicted core competencies – usually organizations would have between one and five core competencies. In the bottom box are the organizational resources. The way the resources are visualized can vary depending on preferences, levels of understanding, and available data. The most basic visualization does not show any causal relationships or individual interdependencies between individual resources. By showing overlap between the relatively sized bubbles, it indicates that these different resources are interdependent and, as a bundle of resources, provide the outlined core competencies.

The value creation map template can, for many private sector organizations, be similar to the classic Balanced Scorecard Strategy Map template, as the underlying logic is the same (see Figure 10.6). However, the advantage of using the value creation map logic is that it is appropriate for any form of organization, be it a corporation, a not-for-profit organization, a government agency, or any other form of organization.

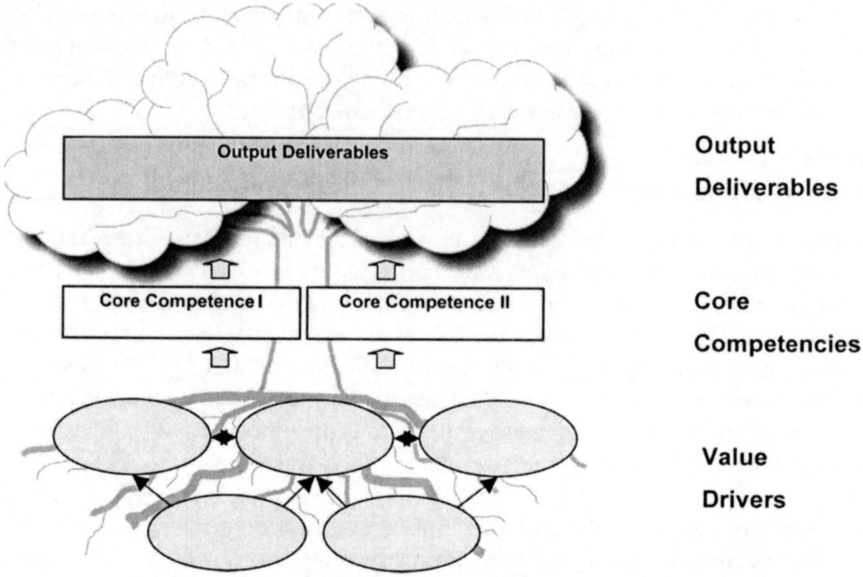

Figure 10.5 Value creation map template.
Source: Marr, 2007

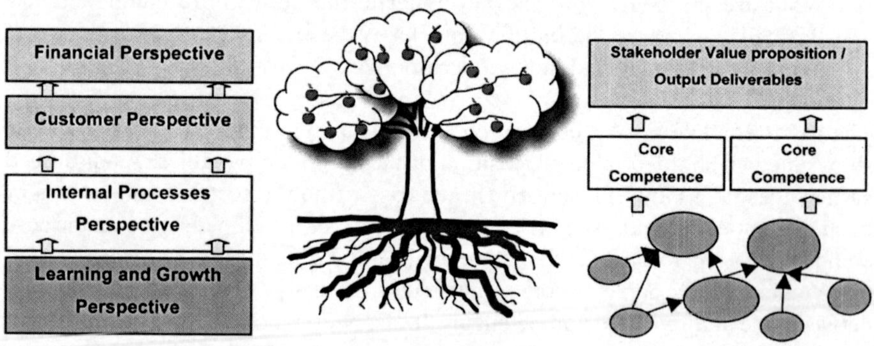

Figure 10.6 Value creation map vs. Balanced Scorecard.
Source: Marr, 2007

A value creation map visualizes the strategy of an organization at a single point in time. Organizations continuously evolve and change. The external and internal environments evolve, and so the strategy needs to evolve, too. This means that the value creation map needs to be revised on a regular basis in order to ensure that it reflects a current view of the strategy. How often these revisions take place depends on the speed of change in the industry the organization is part of. It is usually a good idea to align the revisions of the value creation map with the strategic planning cycles and, for many organizations, an annual revision is adequate. However, in some emerging or fast moving industries this revision cycle can be accelerated.

Value creation maps in practice

Value creation maps have been implemented by many organizations around the globe. They have proven successful for a very diverse group of organizations, from leading international blue-chip corporations to very small and medium sized companies, as well as many public sector and not-for-profit organizations, including central and local government institutions, schools, and charities. It is important to highlight, however, that every organization takes their own journey, with their own interpretations of the tools and techniques.

Below I will discuss how Novo Nordisk, a focused health care company and a world leader in diabetes care, applied this tool. The company has its headquarters in Denmark and is active in 179 countries, with production facilities in six countries and affiliates in 78 countries. Novo Nordisk has over 21,000 employees and a sales turnover of over 3,900 million EUR.[22]

The project to develop a value creation map was part of a wider Knowledge Strategy initiative in Novo Nordisk to identify and prioritize a set of strategic value drivers that can be influenced in order to increase future value creation.

Overall, Novo Nordisk's promise is to be "leading the fight against diabetes. Defeating diabetes is our passion and our business." To be able to deliver on this promise it must continuously develop innovative products, processes, and services. The key knowledge-based elements to achieve this are good collaboration and creativity, facilitated by the best skilled, committed and motivated people that are able to leverage external relationships.

People in Novo Nordisk are a cornerstone of its performance, and Novo Nordisk's people strategy aims to improve their ability to address business challenges across borders. A key driver of performance is having the best skilled and knowledgeable people with the capabilities needed to perform their jobs. This means recruiting the best people, as well as developing high performers internally.

In order to collaborate and be creative, people have to be committed and motivated. A key driver for commitment and motivation in Novo Nordisk is that people feel passionate about what they do and are engaged and feel pride in their jobs. Engagement and pride derive from sharing a meaningful purpose with the organization. This is further supported by the fact that Novo Nordisk has a strong brand reputation and history, which also makes people feel good about their jobs.

The values and commitments of Novo Nordisk are key foundations for its performance. The key values are "accountable," "ambitious," "responsible," "engaged with stakeholders," "open and honest," and "ready for change." The company is committed to pursuing its objectives in ways that consider the Triple Bottom Line – a business principle that requires balancing social, environmental and financial responsibility in every decision and action. This business principle influences Novo Nordisk's reputation, enables Novo Nordisk to build and maintain

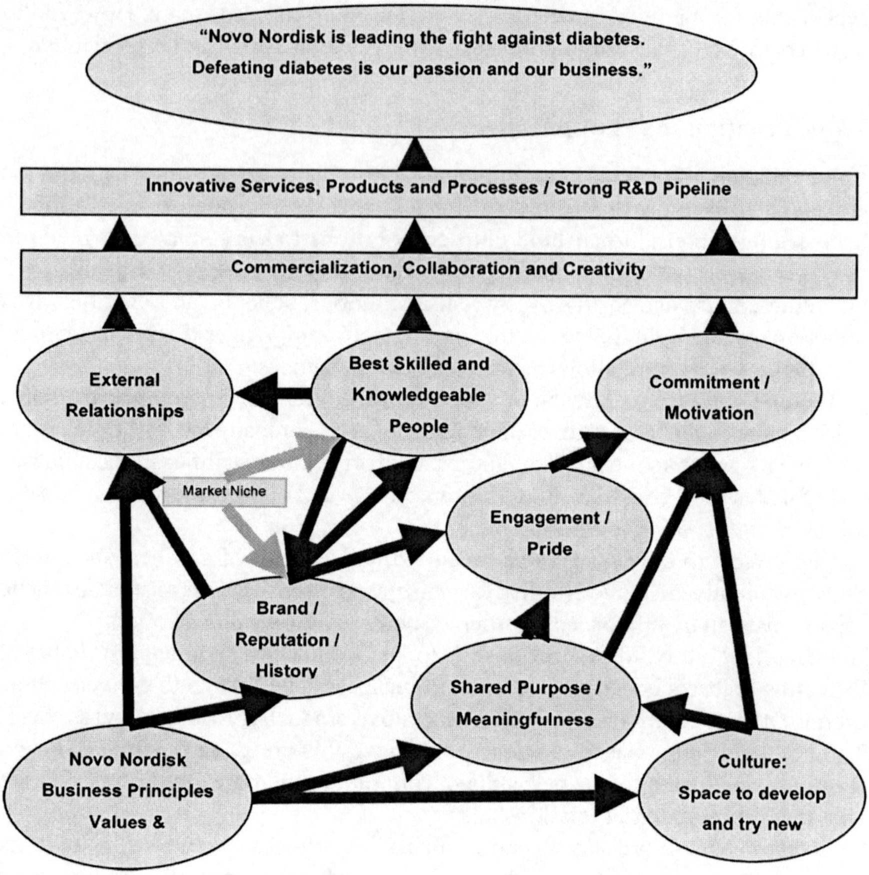

Figure 10.7 Value creation map for Novo Nordisk.

external relationships, fosters a shared sense of purpose, and creates a culture in which employees are valued and empowered to develop and try new things. This in turn motivates people.

The organization's market position as a leading player in a niche market, as well as its values and open and honest communication, helps to create the brand needed to facilitate the development of external relationships, and also helps to attract the best people, who are then able to flourish and deliver the innovations needed for a sustainable future performance.

Today, the value creation map is at the heart of a new prototype performance management report called "Foresight" (see Figure 10.8). The aim of this new report will be to provide senior management with an overview of the key drivers of performance. The objectives are to offer (1) strategic guidance and performance monitoring; (2) qualitative assessment and data analysis/interpretation; and (3) indicators that are then available for external reporting and benchmarking. Once

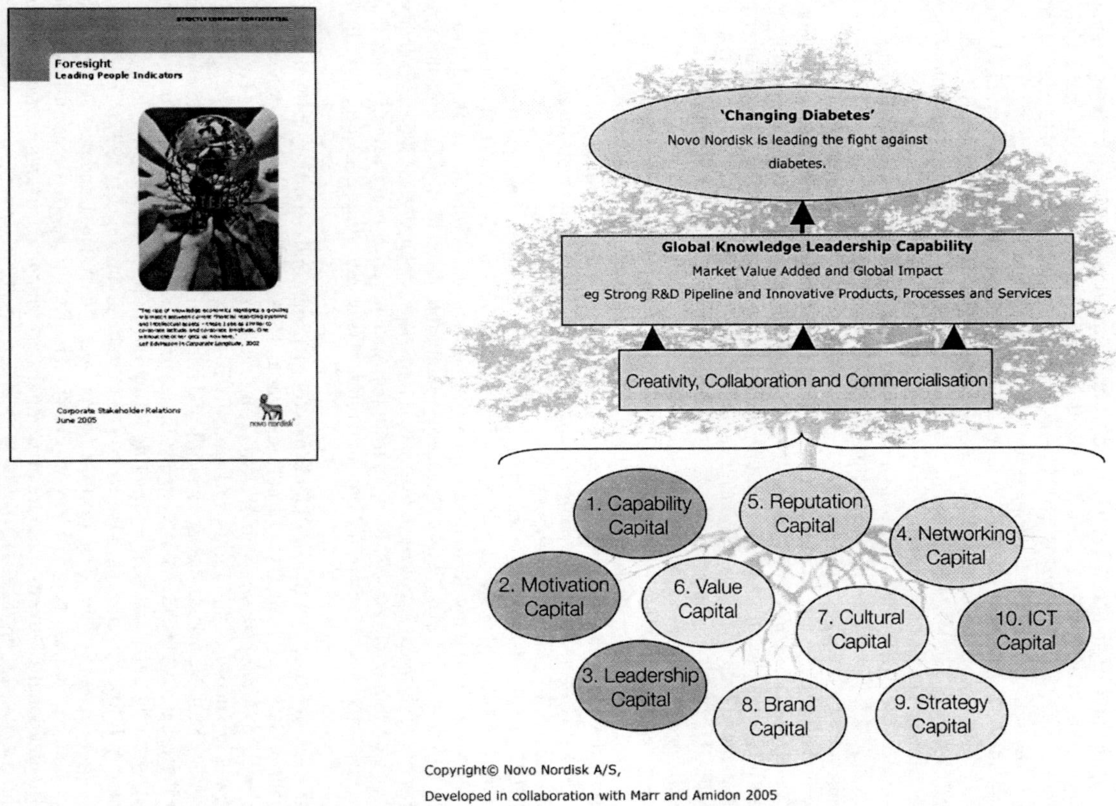

Figure 10.8 Value Creation Reporting in Novo Nordisk.

fully implemented, the report will not only describe the value creation and identify the performance drivers but also provide performance assessments and indicators for each of the performance drivers.

Notes

1 Marr, B. and Chatzkel, J. (2004) 'Intellectual Capital at the Crossroads: managing, measuring, and reporting of IC', *Journal of Intellectual Capital* (editorial), Vol. 5 No. 2, pp. 224–229; Marr, B. (2004) Measuring Intangible Assets – The State of the Art, *Measuring Business Excellence* (editorial), Vol. 8 No. 1, pp. 3–5.

2 Kaplan, R. S. and Norton, D. P. (2000b) 'Having Trouble With Your Strategy? Then Map It', *Harvard Business Review*, Sept-Oct, pp. 167–176 and Marr, B., Schiuma, G. and Neely, A. (2004) 'The Dynamics of Value Creation – Mapping Your Intellectual Performance Drivers', *Journal of Intellectual Capital*, Vol. 5, No. 2.

3 Marr, B. (2006) *Strategic Performance Management: Leveraging and Measuring Your Intangible Value Drivers*. Oxford: Butterworth Heinemann.

4 This analogy has been used on various occasions – one of the most convincing was by Prahalad, C. K. and Hamel, G. (1990) 'The Core Competence of the Corporation', *Harvard Business Review*, Vol. 68, No. 3, May/Jun, p. 79. However, tree diagrams can be traced back to the third-century Syrian philosopher's diagram named after its developer, 'Tree of Porphyry', based upon the work of Aristotle.

5 Collis, D. J. and Montgomery, C. A. (1997) *Corporate Strategy – Resources and the Scope of the Firm*, p. 9. Boston: McGraw-Hill.

6 See for example: Senior, N. W. (1836), *An Outline of the Science of Political Economy*, London: Longman; or Marshall, A. (1890), *Principles of Economics*, London: Macmillan. Volume I (1982), *Knowledge and Knowledge Production*, Volume II (1982), *The Branches of Learning,* Volume III (1984), *The Economics of Information and Human Capital* (Posthumous).

7 Hall, R. (1989), 'The Management of Intellectual Assets: A New Corporate Perspective', *Journal of General Management*, Vol. 15, No. 1, pp. 53. Hall, R. (1992), 'The Strategic Analysis of Intangible Resources', *Strategic Management Journal*, Vol. 13, No. 2, pp. 135–144. Marr, B. (2004), 'Measuring Intangible Assets – the State of the Art', *Measuring Business Excellence*, Vol. 8, No. 1, pp. 3–5. Molnar, M.J. (2004), 'Executive Views on Intangible Assets: Insights from the Accenture/Economist Intelligence Unit Survey', *Accenture Research Note 'Intangible Assets and Future Value'*, Vol. Issue one, April.

8 MERITUM Guidelines (2002), 'Guidelines for Managing and Reporting on Intangibles', Madrid. Barney, J. B. (1991), 'Firm Resources and Sustained Competitive Advantage', *Journal of Management*, Vol. 17, No. 1, pp. 99; Rumelt, R. P. (1984), 'Towards a Strategic Theory of the Firm', in Lamp, R. B. *Competitive Strategic Management*, Prentice Hall, New Jersey; or de Haas, M. and Kleingeld, A. (1999), 'Multilevel Design of Performance Measurement Systems: Enhancing Strategic Dialogue Throughout the Organization', *Management Accounting Research*, Vol. 10, pp. 233–261.

9 See e.g. Roos, J., Roos, G., Dragonetti, N. C. and Edvinsson, L. (1997), *Intellectual Capital: Navigating the New Business Landscape*, Macmillan, London.

10 See e.g. Carmeli, A. and Tishler, A. (2004), 'The Relationships Between Intangible Organizational Elements and Organizational Performance', *Strategic Management Journal*, Vol. 25, pp. 1257–1278.

11 See e.g. Rucci, A. J., Kirn, S. P. and Quinn, R. T. (1998), 'The Employee-Customer-Profit Chain at Sears', *Harvard Business Review*, Vol. 76, No. 1, pp. 83–97; and Ittner, C. D. and Larcker, D. F. (1998b), 'Are Nonfinancial Measures Leading Indicators of Financial Performance? An Analysis of Customer Satisfaction', *Journal of Accounting Research*, Vol. 36, pp. 1–35.

12 Marr, B. (2004) *Business Performance Management – The State of the Art*, Research Study for Hyperion Solutions.

13 Springer S. P. and Deutsch, G. (1998), 'Left Brain, Right Brain', in W.H. Freeman, New York Gardner, H. (1996), *Leading Minds – An Anatomy of Leadership*, BasicBooks, New York.

14 For a good overview of how mapping is used in strategic management see Huff, A. S. and Jenkins, M. (2002), Mapping Strategic Knowledge, Sage, London.

15 See for example: Kaplan, R. S. and Norton, D. P. (2000b), 'Having Trouble With Your Strategy? Then Map It', *Harvard Business Review*, Sept-Oct, pp. 167–176; Kaplan, R.S. and Norton, D.P. (2004a), 'Strategy Maps – Converting Intangible Assets into Tangible Outcomes', Harvard Business School Press, Boston, MA; Kaplan, R.S. and Norton, D.P. (2000a), *The Strategy Focused Organization: How Balanced Scorecard Companies Thrive in the New Business Environment*, Harvard Business School Press, Boston.

16 Kaplan, R.S. and Norton, D.P. (2000b), 'Having Trouble With Your Strategy? Then Map It', *Harvard Business Review*, Sept-Oct, pp. 167–176; Kaplan, R. S. and Norton, D. P. (2004b), 'Measuring the Strategic Readiness of Intangible Assets', *Harvard Business Review*, Vol. 82, No. 2, Feb, pp. 52–63.

17 Marr, B. and Adams, C. (2004), 'The Balanced Scorecard and Intangible Assets: Similar Ideas, Unaligned Concepts', *Measuring Business Excellence*, Vol. 8, No. 3, pp. 18–27.

18 Irwin, D. (2002), 'Strategy Mapping in the Public Sector', *Long Range Planning*, Vol. 35, No. 6, pp. 637–647.

19 See for example: Atkinson, A. A., Waterhouse, J. H. and Well, R. B. (1997), 'A Stakeholder Approach to Strategic Performance Measurement', *Sloan Management Review*, Spring, pp. 25–37; Maltz, A. C., Shenhar, A. J. and Reilly, R. R. (2003), 'Beyond the Balanced Scorecard: Refining the Search for Organizational Success Measures', *Long Range Planning*, Vol. 36, No. 2, pp. 187–204; Ahn, H. (2001), 'Applying the Balanced Scorecard Concept: An Experience Report', *Long Range Planning*, Vol. 34, No. 4, pp. 441–461; Marr, B. and Adams, C. (2004), 'The Balanced Scorecard and Intangible Assets: Similar Ideas, Unaligned Concepts', *Measuring Business Excellence*, Vol. 8, No. 3, pp. 18–27.

20 Ibid.; Neely, A., Adams, C. and Kennerley, M. (2002), *The Performance Prism: The Scorecard for Measuring and Managing Business Success*, FT Prentice Hall, London.

21 The definition of a value creation map was facilitated by the definition of a map, provided by Huff, A. S. and Jenkins, M. (2002), *Mapping Strategic Knowledge*, Sage, London (pp. 2–15).

22 These figures are as per 2005, based on the 2004 Annual Report.

11 Attention management in organizations

Four levels of support in information systems

Claudia Roda and Thierry Nabeth

Introduction

The advent of modern Information and Communication Technologies (ICT) has radically changed access and communication of knowledge within organizations. Nowadays, knowledge workers have wide access to both formalized (e.g. information repository) and informal (e.g. contacts with experts) knowledge resources. The problem faced most often by knowledge workers is not related anymore to the scarce access to knowledge, but rather to the choice they have to make in the allocation of their limited cognitive abilities to a wide variety of knowledge sources. Management of *attention* has thus become the issue that needs to be addressed. This state of things directly impacts processes of knowledge creation, which demand careful management of individual and collective attentional resources (Belmondo, 2006). New methodologies and tools are needed for managing the wide range of data, knowledge, and opportunities that have become available. It is increasingly recognized that ICT, whilst providing access to information and communication, should also support human limited cognitive abilities in the selection of the most relevant information and tasks. Such support, by facilitating human attentional processes, may represent a critical factor in fostering innovation.

Knowledge workers are faced with situations in which: (1) they have access to a very large amount of, mostly de-contextualized, information; (2) they need to collaborate or communicate with colleagues of whom they may know very little; and (3) they may have to attend to several tasks at once (multitasking).

In modern organizations, many interactions take place in shared virtual environments that allow knowledge workers to access information and people necessary for the achievement of various goals. However, shared virtual environments (such as virtual communities and other collaborative systems), whilst supporting increasingly complex interactions (Nabeth and Roda, 2006; Schroeder and Axelsson 2006), enable new interruption channels, which have become an almost constant factor in many working environments. Although interruptions may bring to one's attention information possibly useful for the primary (current) task, it has been widely reported that such interruptions increase the load on attention and memory (Gillie and Broadbent, 1989), may generate stress (Bailey *et al.*, 2001; Zijlstra *et al.*, 1999), and compromise the performance of the primary task

(Franke *et al.*, 2002; McFarlane and Latorella, 2002; Nagata, 2003; Speier *et al.*, 2003). In order to cope with these new dynamic and far-reaching environments, a certain number of practices have been developed to improve the effectiveness of information acquisition and communication, and the interaction with others. Such practices have been often explicitly stated (an online search for "netiquette" will result in a large number of such statements) and are normally accepted amongst ICT users. However, whilst the appropriate use of ICT tools by individuals may reduce the attentional effort required of the community for accessing and managing knowledge, ICT tools themselves represent an important mean to support people's attention.

Within the study of modern management processes Goldhaber (1997) and Davenport and Beck (2001) have stressed that attention is the element that counts the most in the information economy, as it is the scarcest resource and it is critical to organizations' success. In the context of work and business, attention is defined as a "focussed mental engagement on a particular item of information", and can be considered both at individual and at organizational level (Davenport and Beck, 2001). For individuals, the focus of attention corresponds generally to the activity they are currently engaged with (such as writing a report, or having a conversation). For the organization, attention represents the number of strategic items that have the focus of the employees within the organization. It has to be noted that, as for an individual, an organization can only focus its attention on a limited number of items. Several studies have been conducted and systems have been proposed to address the alignment of the individuals' goals and the company's goal (and ensure that the attention of the employees is properly oriented toward items relevant to the strategic objectives of the organization). For instance, Wright and Snell (1998) propose a unifying framework for strategic human resource management addressing the fit of people and organization. Goal alignment, appraisal, or performance systems (Summers and Dahod, 2003) have also been designed as tools for helping to enforce the focus of the employees on items that are the most critical to the organization. However, information systems helping to align the individual and the organizational attention, and more generally, Human Resource Management systems, remain very primitive and largely underdeveloped (Chew, 2003).

Attention also represents an important element for businesses in their interaction with the external world. Organizations need to manage effectively their communication to "get the attention" of their customers and of their potential business partners, since this visibility is increasingly difficult to obtain in a world flooded with information. Managing this communication represents a domain that is, however, well known and occupied by the media and advertising industry, even if it is facing major transformation (following the advent of the Internet). Although we will not address here the communication dimension of attention in management, this dimension has an important impact on knowledge workers, who are both more solicited (and therefore must establish effective filtering strategies) and also must ensure that their messages obtain the proper level of attention from receivers without overwhelming them.

In this paper, after briefly discussing the conflict between human bounded cognitive abilities and the increasing demands imposed on knowledge workers, we propose that such conflict may be, at least partially, addressed by appropriately supporting attentional processes in digital environments, and we detail four possible levels of interventions: support to perception, support to deliberation, support to operation, and support to meta-cognition.

Reaching the limits of human and organizational bounded cognitive capabilities and capacities

The advent of the knowledge-based economy has radically transformed the nature of work and business in organizations. Employees, who once used to fulfil relatively routine tasks in stable environments, have now transformed into autonomous knowledge workers who are engaged into rich, diverse, changing, and creative activities in which information processing and participation in virtual community environments play a central role. Learning organizations (Argyris and Schon, 1978; Dodgson, 1993) operate in a continuously changing world, and focus on supplying a large diversity of services, highly customized to the needs of a multitude of customers. These organizations must rapidly adapt to open, complex, and ever changing environments involving the interaction with a variety of actors and stakeholders. Success factors for these organizations include their capability to listen to their customers, to constantly innovate (Nonaka and Takeuchi, 1995), and to compete with others, often by reinventing themselves (Senge, 1994).

For the employees, these new conditions have translated into the acceleration of time, the multiplication of projects in which they are involved, and the increased number of collaborations, often based on digital interactions. They have to process a considerably larger amount of information and solicitations than in the past (Heylighen, 2004), originating from a multitude of sources and tools. They also must interact with a variety of people, with different functions, cultural backgrounds (Nisbett, 2003), and from different organizations. These interactions increasingly include less formal forms of communication, for which the filtering strategies are more fuzzily defined (for instance, Nardi *et al.* (2000) indicate that social networks, as filtering mechanisms based on the social process, have become a key source of labour and information).

Yet, humans have not radically changed: people have still very limited capacities for manipulating more than a few concepts at a given time, have difficulties with multitasking, and can only maintain relationships with a limited number of people. For example, Miller's (1956) work on short term or working memory indicates that human beings have a maximum capacity to manipulate 7 +/– 2 chunks of information at one time; Rubinstein *et al.* (2001) have experimentally demonstrated the high cost of switching from one task to another, making multitasking a not very effective strategy when one wants to be more productive; and Dunbar (1993) identifies "a cognitive limit to the number of individuals with whom any one person can maintain stable relationships" and evaluates this limit at 150 people. (Dunbar's principle has, for instance, been applied by the Goretex company to define the maximum number of employees in a factory (Gladwell, 2000).)

Notwithstanding these limitations, increased competition and pressure to augment shareholders value has conducted many organizations more frequently to downsizing rather than to expanding manpower: people are asked to do more in less time. Besides, as indicated previously, they are engaged for completing their work with interactions with a larger number of people than in the past.

How to address the productivity challenge in the information economy, with activities that cannot be really automated, and without having the possibility to increase the number of employees in the organization or their cognitive performance?

We propose in the next section that better support to attentional processes in general, and in particular in the context of shared virtual environments, may help organizations and individuals in addressing such a challenge. We also briefly indicate the work already done towards the development of systems capable of supporting users in their attentional choices (Roda and Nabeth, 2007; Roda and Thomas, 2006).

Supporting attention

Studies in cognitive psychology have clearly established (see, for example, review in Roda and Thomas, 2006) that attention allocation depends both on perceptual and deliberative processes. At the **perceptual level**, what we perceive (e.g. see, hear, feel) impacts on what we pay attention to. At the **deliberative level** our goals, motivations, and intentions also play a role in the determination of our attention focus. Therefore, a natural way to study the support of attention is the exploration of mechanisms facilitating the perception of the environment, and the interpretation and reasoning on this information.

At a different level of observation, it is clear that actions require a varying degree of cognitive effort depending on the form and the nature of the task being accomplished. For instance, some activities may require a high level of concentration to get focussed, a higher degree of vigilance, the switching between many subtasks, or may be subject to a significant number of interruptions. Therefore, at the **operational level**, the provision of mechanisms allowing the users to be more effective, in terms of the cognitive effort allocated to fulfil an objective, represents another means of supporting attention.

Finally, we are able – as we are doing here – to reflect about our own strategies for allocating attention, and to learn more effective attention allocation strategies. Therefore, mechanisms supporting the **meta-cognitive level** elaboration and evaluation of strategies for attention allocation can be proposed as another means of supporting the user's attention.

To summarize, we propose that attention should be supported at four levels:

- At the perceptual level by, for example, facilitating access to and selection of relevant information, or presenting interruptions at the appropriate level of prominence.
- At the deliberative level by, for example, supplying tools for the control of

task priorities, by motivating individuals who are losing focus, or by giving the possibility to the user to better assess the impact of their actions.

- At the operational level by, for example, simplifying some attention-related operations, such as restoring the context of interrupted tasks, filtering incoming information, or reducing the required level of vigilance over planned activities. For instance, in the latter case, mechanisms such as watch lists or notification may release the user to regularly check for the availability of important information.
- At the meta-cognitive level by, for example, providing self-diagnostic tools, helping the acquisition of more effective attention allocation strategies.

This division in "levels of support" is obviously artificial but it is fundamental for a detailed analysis of attentional breakdowns and possible support strategies. A combination of processes at several levels normally crafts human attention allocation strategies.

Supporting attention at the perceptual level

Supporting perception means increasing both the ability to notice relevant information and to discard the irrelevant. We recognize at least four different manners in which perception may be enhanced: (1) facilitating the selection of relevant information; (2) facilitating information comprehension; (3) supporting group perception; and (4) presenting interruptions at the correct level of prominence. These four issues (information selection, information comprehension, group perception, and presentation prominence) are strongly related. Access to information, in fact, has become problematic not only because of the sheer quantity of information available, but also, and especially, because individuals have very few tools and facilities enabling them to easily perceive what the content of a resource may be, and how, when, and by whom the resource was created, edited, and accessed. Not only are more resources available, but also more people may be related to each resource. Purposely designed digital tools may, however, support individuals in their perception of resources.

Information selection may be facilitated by the use of information filtering and visualization mechanisms. The former allow the user to select, statically (i.e. once for all) or dynamically, relevant types of information. Information filtering mechanisms may be based on more or less sophisticated selection algorithms or, in the case of social filtering, may use human evaluators who classify or assign ratings to various items. Visualization mechanisms aim at representing information to the user in the most appropriate format (see Toet (2006) for a review) and they should deal with the subtle processes that regulate human perception (Healey, 2005). Our ability to "see" something, in fact, does not depend solely on what we are presented with, but also on what we are looking for, or what we expect (Egeth and Yantis, 1997; Rensink, 2000; Wolfe *et al.*, 2000). Visualization mechanisms may be coupled with, or replaced by, information presentation based on non-visual modalities (Abowd *et al.*, 2002) whereby several channels are employed in order to communicate with the user. Further, in certain situations information may be made more visible, credible, and comprehensible by being communicated by an embodied agent (Lester *et al.*, 1997; Picard, 1997; Vendatam, 2004).

Several techniques have been, or may be, used in order to facilitate *information comprehension*, and therefore reduce the cognitive load associated to selecting the most relevant pieces of information, or the most appropriate action to perform. They involve providing meta-level/abstract information about people, documents, or tasks. For instance, indicators that abstract the information related to a document may include the category of the document, the size of the document, the date of creation of the document, the author, but also the popularity of the document. Similarly, the indicators that abstract a discussion space may include the number of threads, the number of messages that have been posted in the last day, or the topics generating most debate. A recent initiative addressing the collection of attention-related metadata is *Attention.XML* (Sifry *et al.*, 2006), which targets blogs and feeds. *Attention.XML* tracks data such as what has been read, what the user has spent time on, recommendations, etc.

Extending the Attention.XML framework, Wolpers and his colleagues (Wolpers *et al.*, 2006) propose to:

> unobtrusively capture the attention of employees at the workplace (e.g. through workflow systems, knowledge management systems, human resource management systems, etc.) and use the captured information to enable a targeted steering of learning process of the employee in companies in accordance with company's and employee's aims and goals.

Abstract information may also display relationships amongst documents or tasks in the form of graphs, allowing users to quickly understand and navigate a web of interrelated items.

Bier and colleagues (Bier *et al.* 1993: 73) also use metadata information as part of Magic Lens as "filters that modify the presentation of application objects to reveal hidden information, to enhance data of interest, or to suppress distracting information."

When working or learning in a group physically co-present, the group's activity influences *group perception*, and the focus of attention of each individual, in several manners. The following are three examples of such influence. First, devoting one's attention to a given activity may be necessary in order to ensure the good functioning of the whole group (as in the case when one allocates attention to a task because the completion of the task is a prerequisite for the activity of other members of the group). Second, mechanisms of peer pressure may result in diverting one's attention from its natural course. Third, one's decision on whether to interrupt the activity of others may be guided by social cues, social rules, and knowledge about what the other person is doing.

As physical co-presence is increasingly reduced in favour of device-mediated presence, many of the cues necessary for the group activity to influence individual and group attention became fuzzier, or disappear completely. In order to enable people to appropriately allocate attention in situations such as the ones exemplified above, attention aware systems may support individual and group perception by supplying cues of others' activity, their level of involvement in the activity, their role, etc. Erikson and his colleagues (Erickson *et al.*, 2002) address this problem in their research on *social translucence.*

It is interesting to note that, whilst many of the issues discussed above are due to the introduction of device-mediated communication, Vertegaal and his colleagues (Vertegaal *et al.*, 2006) propose to introduce device mediation in co-located environments, and use information about the individual's attention in order to dynamically adapt the configuration of the work environment to different attentional needs.

Presenting interruptions at the correct level of prominence may significantly reduce load at the perceptual level. Whilst in co-located communication we have developed a vast range of interruption strategies that vary in their level of prominence (e.g. standing next to a person waiting for the previous conversation or activity to be finished, making signs to signal the intention to communicate, intrude into one's conversation or activity in a more or less polite or urgent manner), the choice of the strategy is not only based on the knowledge of the message we want to communicate, but also on some knowledge of the activity of the person we want to interrupt. In the case of device-mediated communication, knowledge workers are once again lacking half of the picture. This makes the choice of the appropriate interruption prominence much more difficult to evaluate. Notification can take a variety of forms, such as the sending of an email or an instant message, the posting of a message in a chat box, the displaying of an item in the home page of a portal, the display of a blinking icon, or the intervention of an artificial character. The most appropriate format depends on a variety of factors, including the current state of the receiver (e.g. he/she is busy and should not be disturbed, or he/she is consulting the mailbox), the amount and complexity of information that needs to be communicated, the urgency of the communication, and the relevance of the information being communicated to the receiver. Whilst it has been shown that supplying information about pending tasks improves people's ability to manage interruption (C. Y. Ho *et al.*, 2004), the notification modality may impact on the user activity at various levels: it may go completely unnoticed, it may smoothly integrate with the user's current task, or it may capture the user's attention and cause a temporary or durable focus switch. McCrickard and his colleagues (McCrickard *et al.*, 2003; McCrickard and Chewar, 2003) propose to measure the effects of visual notification with respect to four parameters: (1) users' interruption caused by the reallocation of attention from a primary task to a notification; (2) users' reaction to a specific secondary information cue while performing a primary task; (3) users' comprehension of information presented in secondary displays over a period of time; and (4) user satisfaction. They provide recommendations indicating, for example, that small sized in-place animation can be defined as best suited for goals of minimal attention reallocation (low interruption), immediate response (high reaction) and small knowledge gain (low comprehension). Bartram *et al.* (2003) propose the use of moticons (icons with motions) as an effective visual technique for information-rich displays that minimize distraction. Finally, Arroyo and Selker (2003) study the effects of using different modalities for interruption in ambient displays concentrating on the effects of heat and light channels.

Supporting attention at the deliberative level

Whilst at the perceptual level attention is influenced by external stimuli, at the deliberative level attention is influenced by one's goals, motivations, and intentions; further, these two processes (perceptive and deliberative) constantly interact to determine one's attentional state. For example, although an external stimulus may effectively attract someone's attention, a lack of motivation for the proposed focus will quickly divert his/her attention to another item. On the other hand, one may be motivated to focus on a certain item (because, for example, he/she is pursuing a certain goal) but an inappropriate presentation of the content (at the perceptual level) may hinder the establishment of the desired focus. This section analyzes how attention may be supported at the deliberative level. It considers situations in which the knowledge worker:

- Loses motivation and/or stops actively pursuing a worthwhile focus;
- Loses track of the planned sequence of activity and/or experiences difficulties in prioritising his/her activity;
- Does not make best use of time resources or loses track of time;
- Has difficulty in selecting the most effective focus for the goal of the group.

Many experiments – as well as folk wisdom – tell us that loss of motivation, together with tiredness, is one of the main reasons for losing focus of attention. Motivations may be provided in many different forms. In certain situations it may be enough to remind the knowledge worker what he/she was doing; in other cases it may be necessary to supply some help in order to encourage him/her to pursue the activity.

Support to prospective memory

Two problems often encountered in situations of heavy cognitive load and multitasking are related to the correct continuation of planned activities, and the evaluation of relative priorities of concurrent tasks. These problems have been studied in relation to *prospective memory* failures. Differently from *retrospective memory*, which allows us to remember facts of the past (e.g. people's names, the lesson studied yesterday), prospective memory allows us to remember planned activities in the future (e.g. go to a meeting, complete writing a paper, turn off the stove in 30 minutes) (Meacham and Leiman, 1982) and it is closely related to intentionality (Marsh *et al.*, 1999; Sellen *et al.*, 1996). Whilst prospective memory is essential for the normal functioning of our daily activity, prospective memory failures may account for up to 70% of memory failures in everyday life (Kvavilashvili *et al.*, 2001). Prospective memory failures have been shown to significantly hinder performance in working environments (M. Czerwinski and Horvitz, 2002) and to intervene differently depending on the age of the subjects (Kvavilashvili *et al.*, 2001).

Prospective memory doesn't simply require remembering something – it also requires remembering it at the *correct time*. Such *correct time* may be represented by an actual time (e.g. going to a meeting at 2pm) or by the occurrence of an event or a series of events (e.g. publishing the minutes once everyone has approved them). This has brought about the distinction between *event-based* and *time-based* remembering tasks (Sellen *et al.*, 1996).

One obvious way to support prospective memory is through reminder services. As the need for reminder services has become ubiquitous amongst knowledge workers, we have seen the usage of tools such as digital diaries and Personal Digital Assistants (PDAs) increase dramatically. However, these tools are still very primitive compared to the real needs of knowledge workers. Systems offering reminder services should be able to issue reminders at a specified time or at the occurrence of a given event. These reminders should also help knowledge workers remember to resume tasks that have been interrupted – a study reports that in over 40% of the cases in which tasks are interrupted, they are not resumed (O'Conaill and Frohlich, 1995). Further, resuming a task doesn't only require remembering to restart the task, but it also entails being able to somehow re-establish the context of that task. This may require a significant cognitive effort on the side of the knowledge worker. As a consequence, whilst at deliberative level a system may support task continuation via reminders, at the operational level, task resumption should be further supported by enabling individuals to easily re-establish the task context (see section headed "Support for multitasking and interruption").

Since, in some situations it isn't possible for the system (or even the user) to know the set of subtasks required to continue a resumed task, presenting the user with information about the context of the interrupted task may facilitate resumption. A few researchers have already explored this possibility by developing systems that create logs of events that may help the user to remember about the context of an interrupted task. (See Czerwinski and Horvitz (2002) for an overview of this research.)

Multitasking and interruptions not only impose the cognitive load related to remembering what one was doing when resuming a task, but also generate the problem of keeping a clear idea of what other important tasks lie ahead. In situations of multitasking, in fact, it may be difficult to keep track of relative priorities between tasks. Several mechanisms may be used to help knowledge workers in the allocation of attention to the most urgent tasks; these include the explicit definition of prerequisites or constraints for task execution, tasks deadlines, as well as interruption management. For instance, an agenda can be used to help people keeping track and organizing the execution of different tasks. Such an agenda may reduce the cognitive load by giving an overall view of the way tasks are ordered, facilitating the planning and execution of tasks, allowing individuals to limit the number of tasks executed concurrently, and reducing the need for the knowledge worker to think about a particular task until it is necessary. On the basis of the contents of the agenda, digital systems may automatically send notifications about tasks due soon, relieving the knowledge worker from remembering about these events. Task agendas may also include information enabling the automatic evaluation of the satisfaction of prerequisites for actions execution, helping people to allocate attention only to those actions whose prerequisites are fulfilled.

Another consequence of task complexity and/or multitasking is an increased difficulty in the selection of the most appropriate information or task to attend in the available time. For example, given a limited amount of time available to perform a task, and two pending tasks of similar urgency but different durations, if one of the two tasks can be completed within the available time and the other one cannot, it is often more profitable to attend the task that can be completed within the available time, rather than the other one. Knowledge workers often disregard these types of time-allocation evaluations when they work in a complex multitasking environment.

Support to group level attention

In classic, strictly structured, collaborative environments, the role of the group manager is often that of a moderator capable of identifying information and tasks that are relevant and beneficial for the whole group. This can be reflected in at least two different types of attention-related actions.

First, managers are aware about task dependencies between tasks performed by different group members, and therefore they are able to suggest to a group member to attend a certain task because that task is critical for the action of other group members. Second, managers are often aware of the overall foci of all the members of a group, and they can therefore make sure that relevant information on resources and tasks can be diffused within the group.

In more decentralized collaborative environments typical of modern organizations, collaborative groups don't always have an individual manager with control on the attention-related actions mentioned above. Digital systems could partially support group level attention by enabling individuals to take on those actions themselves. For example, by tracking access to, and actions on, documents, digital systems may be able to inform group members about those tasks that are receiving the most attention from other knowledge workers. Similarly, the most popular action sequences may be used by the system to recommend task continuation strategies. This type of system behaviour is similar to the behaviour of collaborative recommender systems (a recent review of recommender systems can be found in Adomavicius and Tuzhilin, 2005). In a similar line, such tools may make users aware of the impact of their actions on others, therefore contributing to their motivation. Indeed, as proposed by Bandura (1994) with the concept of self-efficacy, people do not usually sustain their actions if they do not believe that what they do produces the desired results. Finally, we can mention the advent of new mechanisms that have emerged as part of Web 2.0 (O'Reilly, 2005), and which aim at creating conditions facilitating the emergence of collaboration (McAfee, 2006). In particular collaborative tagging (Marlow *et al.*, 2006), which can be found in services such as *del.icio.us*, provides the possibility to display, via tag clouds, topics that are receiving the highest level of attention from the community of its users.

In relation to group level support for task dependencies, it may happen that delaying or minimising the impact of a notification message, in order to optimize the performance of one user, results in sub-optimal performance for the group as a whole (as in the case when the activity of some members of the group depends on the prompt notification and consequent response of another member). In these situations, strategies optimising individual attention allocation may not be sufficient, and the selection of the notification strategy must also take into account the state of other users. Although most of the work on the evaluation of the cost/benefits of interruptions has been done taking the point of view of the user being interrupted, some analysis also takes into account the cost/benefit to the interrupter, and the joint cost/benefit (Hudson *et al.*, 2002; O'Conaill and Frohlich, 1995).

Supporting attention at the operational level

Different approaches can be proposed to support the actions of the user in a way that is more attention effective, i.e. leading to the same result while mobilising less cognitive effort.

A first way of supporting users at the operational level is to help them to be more effective at managing several tasks. For instance, some mechanisms may make the interruption of tasks less disturbing, whereas other mechanisms may help users in recovering more easily from an interruption.

A second approach is to provide mechanisms automating some tasks that can help in reducing cognitive load. For instance, a notification mechanism or a watch list may relieve users from the need to dedicate a portion of their attention to the monitoring of a particular source of information.

Support for multitasking and interruption

As indicated previously, people are very ineffective at working on too many things at the same time because of the limited human multitasking capabilities. Rubinstein *et al.* (2001), for example, evaluated the high costs of switching from one task to another. People are also subject to burnout (Maslach *et al.*, 2001) when they are the objects of excessive overload and when they feel they are losing control of the situation.

The operational support of attention consists in providing mechanisms helping knowledge workers to efficiently allocate attention amongst many tasks and interruption sources.

In many ways, support at operational level is similar to the support we obtain by writing ourselves little notes to remind us what to do; or by hiring a secretary who acts as a filter for interruptions, helps us remember about engagements, people, or important information, and takes over the execution of certain tasks. Here we consider situations in which the knowledge worker:

- Needs to resume an interrupted task;
- Deals with frequent interruption at various degrees of urgency;
- Delegates task execution.

In situations characterized by frequent interruptions or task alternation, a significant increase in cognitive load is related to the actions necessary to *restoring the context of an interrupted task at resumption time.* A diary study, tracking the activity of knowledge workers over a week, reports that participants in the study rated as significantly more difficult to switch to those tasks that required "returning to" after an interruption, that "the *returned-to* tasks were over twice as long as those tasks described as more routine, shorter-term projects," and that "*returned-to* tasks required significantly more documents, on average, than other tasks" (Czerwinski *et al.*, 2004: 178–179). As a large part of the activity of knowledge workers happens on computers, systems capable of saving the context of interrupted tasks, and restoring this context on demand, may significantly reduce cognitive load and minimize task resumption time. Task resumption is particularly critical in the context of current desktop interfaces because such interfaces force an "application oriented" rather than "task oriented" approach to computer based activities (Clauzel *et al.*, 2006; Kaptelinin and Czerwinski, 2007; Roda *et al.*, 2006). In order to complete a task (say, write a report) the user is forced to fragment the task into subtasks (such as using a word processor to write some text, then collecting data from a spreadsheet in order to paste it in the text). This artificial fragmentation of the original task imposes an increased cognitive load on the user. An innovative approach allowing users to organize their work in a task oriented, rather than application oriented manner is presented in Clauzel *et al.*, 2006; and Roda *et al.*, 2006).

As multitasking and interruptions have become the norm in modern working environments (Czerwinski *et al.*, 2004; Gonzalez and Mark, 2004; Mark *et al.*, 2005), an obvious manner for attention aware systems to support attentional processes is to supply *personalized and adaptable notification* systems that reduce the disruption provoked by digital interruptions. Notification systems have been studied in a wide variety of application domains, including messaging systems (Cutrell *et al.*, 2001; Czerwinski *et al.*, 2000; Horvitz *et al.*, 2003), alerting in military operations (Obermayer and Nugent, 2000), shared document annotation (Brush *et al.*, 2001), and end-user programming (Robertson *et al.*, 2004). Interruption and notification management must take into account many factors (see, for example, the taxonomy in Gievska *et al.*, 2005) that span across the various levels of support for attention (from perception to meta-cognitive) and collectively contribute to making an interruption more or less appropriate or disruptive. Research on interruption management has covered many of these aspects, which include the context of interruption, the timing of the interruption, and its content.

Interruptions bring to one's attention events or information that may have different degrees of utility and may provoke more or less disruption in the current activity. Whilst it has been argued that in certain situations (simple primary tasks) interruptions may facilitate task performance (Speier *et al.*, 2003), a significant body of research reports on the negative effects of interruptions both on the effectiveness and agreeableness of task performance (Bailey *et al.*, 2001; Zijlstra *et al.*, 1999; Franke *et al.*, 2002; McFarlane and Latorella, 2002; Nagata, 2003; Speier *et al.*, 2003).

The cognitive load of the task being interrupted, as well as the level of involvement of the user with this task, are deciding factors for the effect that an interruption may have (Fogarty *et al.*, 2005). In general, the effects of interruption will depend on how well the new information is integrated in the context of the current activity. For example, Carroll and his colleagues (Carroll *et al.*, 2003), focussing on the support of collaborative activities, argue that awareness information should be related to the user's current activity. Deciding what exactly the user is doing (i.e. what the current task is) is one of the most crucial aspects in interruption management. However, in current computer-supported collaborative environments, not only it is difficult to exactly evaluate what people are doing, but it also may be a challenge even establishing whether they are at all available (Fogarty *et al.*, 2004; Horvitz *et al.*, 2002). In face-to-face situations, human beings are quite capable, in a very small time, and with a limited knowledge of people's activity, of deciding whether an interruption would be acceptable or not. Studies that have tried to replicate this human ability to evaluate interruptibility include sensor-based predictive statistical models of interruptibility (Fogarty *et al.*, 2005; Fogarty *et al.*, 2004) and methods for learning models from data that can be used to compute the expected cost of interruption for a user (Horvitz and Apacible, 2003; Horvitz *et al.*, 2004).

The exact point in time when the interruption is delivered may make a significant difference on whether and how the interruption is perceived and on how much disruption it will bring to the current task. (See, for example Rudman and Zajicek, 2006.)

One of the most influential works in notification timing proposes four design solutions to coordinate user interruptions –

> immediate, negotiated, mediated, and scheduled. Interruptions can be delivered at the soonest possible moment (immediate), or support can be given for the person to explicitly control when they will handle the interruption (negotiation). Another solution has an autonomous broker dynamically decide when best to interrupt the user (mediated), or to always hold all interruptions and deliver them at a prearranged time (scheduled).
>
> (McFarlane and Latorella, 2002, p. 5)

– and concludes that in most situations negotiation is the best choice.

More recent work, however, has aimed at a much finer-grained analysis of interruption time. In particular, several authors propose that interruptions taking place at "break points" in the user activity (e.g. when the user has finished a task and is about to start another one) are less disruptive (Bailey and Konstan, 2006; Iqbal *et al.*, 2005).

Appropriate selection of interruption time is particularly critical in wireless devices because the user may be carrying or wearing such devices in a wide variety of situations. Ho and Intille (2005) propose a context-aware mobile computing device that "automatically detects postural and ambulatory activity transitions in real time using wireless accelerometers. This device was used to experimentally measure the receptivity to interruptions delivered at activity transitions relative to those delivered at random times" (Ho and Intille, 2005: 909).

The content presented to knowledge workers with a notification mechanism may range from a notification of information availability (e.g. a flashing icon indicating the presence of email) to complex awareness mechanisms (e.g. awareness display in a distributed collaborative system), to a complete switch of context (e.g. opening of a new window with a new application).

Whilst notification modality has been often studied, few authors have directly addressed the problem of the adaptation of the message content to the attentional state of the user. An example of a system that addresses this problem is READY – a natural language interface that dynamically adapts to the user's time pressure and working memory limitations. For example, shorter messages are used if the user is under time pressure, longer ones if the user is more available (Bohnenberger *et al.*, 2002; Jameson *et al.*, 1999).

Tasks delegation, automation

Linda Stone (2006) defines the concept of *continual partial attention* as a constant state of vigilance, high alert, always on. "To pay continuous partial attention is to pay partial attention – continuously." This state of continuous awareness is not without mobilising some cognitive resource from the user, in some cases causing some stress. Mechanisms automating some processes and, for instance, supporting this state of "constant vigilance" with less effort, contribute to supporting the user at the operational level. Examples of such mechanisms include all the notification mechanisms that relieve the user from monitoring resources, such as calendar systems reminding the user just in time of particular deadlines. Portals, rss feeds, and systems aggregating information in a single place also provide operational support to attention by reducing the number of sources that the users have to monitor.

More generally, systems supporting *task delegation* reduce the cognitive effort required of the knowledge worker by reducing the complexity and the steps necessary to accomplish a task. We have already discussed above how task continuation may represent a problem in situations of frequent interruption. In that section it was proposed that the system may support knowledge workers by reminding them the continuation plan for a task at resumption time. A further support strategy consists of the (possibly partial) delegation of the action in the plan to the system itself. For example, when knowledge workers create messages that need to be distributed within a certain community, they may also be allowed to indicate the time of delivery, and the operations that should take place after delivery (for instance, the message may be archived after it has been read by all recipients, or a reminder may be sent to recipients who did not reply). The system may take charge of completing some *after delivery* actions.

Supporting attention at the meta-cognitive level

Finally, individual and group attention may be supported by fostering a better understanding of the way attention is managed. Support at this level consists in the provision of mechanisms helping knowledge workers in observing their current attention-related practices, and contributing to the learning process of more attention effective practices.

A first mechanism that can be used consists in displaying a statistical *visualization of how knowledge workers are allocating their attention*. For instance, users may be presented with a graphical representation including information such as the different activities in which they are involved, the time allocated to each activity, the distribution of their efforts over time (e.g. are knowledge workers allocating long periods or short periods of time to certain activities?), etc. Another type of graphical view may visualize statistics reflecting the number and nature of interruptions, or particular behavioural practices, such as the time between the reception of a message and the processing of this message by the knowledge worker. This is, for instance, the approach that has been adopted by Davenport and Beck (Beck and Davenport, 2001; Davenport and Beck, 2001), who have proposed a system named AttentionScape, which maps the attention allocation of the users or of the organization in different dimensions. Some of this information may be private for the individual; other information may be presented to the community at large.

A second set of mechanisms supporting attention at the meta-cognitive level consists in *diagnostic tools helping to assess the communication or working practice of the knowledge workers*, and in particular to measure their level of effectiveness. One of the simplest mechanisms may consist in the comparison of the individuals' practices with one another. More sophisticated mechanisms may consist in more intelligent diagnostic tools trying to discover patterns of behaviour and interpret them. Suggestion tools may provide guidance about how to improve a current attention-management practice.

Conclusions

Digitally-mediated collaboration and interaction in modern organizations has opened a new range of opportunities for collaboration, improved productivity, knowledge creation, and innovation. Several studies, however, demonstrate that modern Information and Communication Technologies also place an unprecedented strain on human attentional abilities by increasing considerably the amount of information and interaction the user has to process, and by inducing frequent interruptions and situations of extreme multitasking. In this paper we have argued that digital environments should have built-in support for appropriate attention allocation. both at the level of the individual and of the community. We have analyzed such support at four different levels: perceptual, deliberative, operational, and meta-cognitive; and we have discussed how computer-mediated activity in modern organizations has been, or could be, enhanced by attention-related services at these four levels.

Acknowledgement

The work described in this paper was partially sponsored by the EC under the FP6 framework project AtGentive IST-4-027529-STP. We would like to acknowledge the contribution of all project partners.

References

Abowd, G. D., Mynatt, E. D., and Rodden, T. (2002). The human experience. *IEEE Pervasive Computing* 1(1), 48–57.

Adomavicius, G. and Tuzhilin, A. (2005). Toward the next generation of recommender systems: A survey of the state-of-the-art and possible extensions. *IEEE Transactions on Knowledge and Data Engineering* 17(6), 734–49.

Argyris, C. and Schon, D. (1978). *Organizational learning: A theory of action perspective.* Reading, MA: Addison-Wesley.

Arroyo, E. and Selker, T. (2003). Self-adaptive multimodal-interruption interfaces. In *Proceedings of the 8th International Conference on Intelligent User Interfaces*. New York: Association for Computing Machinery, pp. 6–11.

Bailey, B. P. and Konstan, J. A. (2006). On the need for attention aware systems: Measuring the effects of interruption on task-performance, error rate, and affective state. *Computers in Human Behavior* 22(4), 685–708.

Bailey, B. P., Konstan, J. A., and Carlis, J. V. (2001). The effects of interruptions on task performance, annoyance, and anxiety in the user interface. In *Proceedings of IFIP INTERACT01: Human-computer interaction*, Tokyo, Japan, pp. 593–601.

Bandura, A. (1994). Self-efficacy. In V. S. Ramachaudran (ed.), *Encyclopedia of human behavior,* vol. 4. New York: Academic Press, pp. 71–81.

Bartram, L., Ware, C., and Calvert, T. (2003). Moticons: Detection, distraction and task. *International Journal of Human-Computer Studies* 58(5), 515–45.

Beck, J. and Davenport, T. H. (2001). How corporate leaders can help their companies manage the scarcest resource of all: Attention. *Outlook Point of View.* Available at: http://www.accenture.com/Global/Research_and_Insights/Outlook/By_Alphabet/HowAttention.htm (accessed June 2007).

Belmondo, C. (2006). Ressources attentionnelles and processus de creation de connaissance. In A. Bounfour (ed.), *Capital immatériel, connaissance et performance.* Paris: L'Harmattan, pp. 57–86.

Bier, E. A., Stone, M. C., Pier, K., Buxton, W., and DeRose, T. D. (1993). Toolglass and magic lenses: The see-through interface. In *Proceedings of the 20th Annual Conference on Computer Graphics and Interactive Techniques*. New York: Association for Computing Machinery, pp. 73–80.

Bohnenberger, T., Brandherm, B., Grossmann-Hutter, B., Heckmann, D., and Wittig, F. (2002). Empirically grounded decision-theoretic adaptation to situation-dependent resource limitations. *Künstliche Intelligenz* 3, 10–16.

Brush, B., Bargeron, D., Gupta, A., and Grudin, J. (2001). Notification for shared annotation of digital documents (Technical Report No. MSR-TR-2001-87). Microsoft Research, Microsoft Corporation.

Carroll, J. M., Neale, D. C., Isenhour, P. L., Rosson, M. B., and McCrickard, D. S. (2003). Notification and awareness: Synchronizing task-oriented collaborative activity. *International Journal of Human-Computer Studies* 58(5), 605–632.

Chew, J. (2003). *Helping HR apps unlock human capital.* With L. Orlov, R. Hudson, and L. Herbert. Forrester Research.

Clauzel, D., Roda, C., and Stojanov, G. (2006). Tracking task context to support resumption. In *Proceedings HCI 2006, Human Computer Interaction – Engage*, London, UK, September 12, pp. 43–54.

Cutrell, E., Czerwinski, M., and Horvitz, E. (2001). Notification, disruption, and memory: Effects of messaging interruptions on memory and performance. In *Proceedings of IFIP INTERACT01: Human-computer interaction*, Tokyo, Japan, pp. 263–69.

Czerwinski, M., Cutrell, E., and Horvitz, E. (2000). Instant messaging: Effects of relevance and time. In S. Turner and P. Turner (eds), *People and Computers XIV: Proceedings of HCI 2000, Human Computer Interaction*, Volume 2. Sunderland, UK, pp. 71–76.

Czerwinski, M. and Horvitz, E. (2002). Memory of daily computing events. In X. Faulkner, J. Finlay and F. Detienne (eds), *People and Computers XVI: Proceedings of HCI 2002, Human Computer Interaction*, Minneapolis, Minnesota, USA, pp. 230–45.

Czerwinski, M., Horvitz, E., and Wilhite, S. (2004). A diary study of task switching and interruptions. In *Proceedings of the ACM Conference on Human Factors in Computing Systems, CHI 2004, Computer-Human Interaction*, April 24–9, Vienna, Austria, pp. 175–82.

Davenport, T. H. and Beck, J. (2001). *The attention economy*. Boston: Harvard Business School Press.

Dodgson, M. (1993). Organizational learning: A review of some literatures. *Organizational Studies* 14(3) 375–94.

Dunbar, R. I. M. (1993). Coevolution of neocortical size, group size and language in humans. *Behavioral and Brain Sciences* 16(4), 681–735.

Egeth, H. and Yantis, S. (1997). Visual attention: Control, representation, and time course. *Annual Review of Psychology* 48, 269–97.

Erickson, T., Halverson, C., Kellogg, W. A., Laff, M., and Wolf, T. (2002). Social translucence: Designing social infrastructures that make collective activity visible. *Communications of the ACM* 45(4), 40–4.

Fogarty, J., Hudson, S. E., Atkeson, C. G., Avrahami, D., Forlizzi, J., Kiesler, S., Lee, J. C., and Yang, J. (2005). Predicting human interruptibility with sensors. *ACM Transactions on Computer-Human Interaction* 12(1), 119–46.

Fogarty, J., Hudson, S. E., and Lai, J. (2004). Examining the robustness of sensor-based statistical models of human interruptibility. In *Proceedings of the ACM Conference on Human Factors in Computing Systems, CHI 2004, Computer-Human Interaction*, April 24–9, Vienna, Austria, pp. 207–14.

Fogarty, J., Ko, A. J., Aung, H. H., Golden, E., Tang, K. P., and Hudson, S. E. (2005). Examining task engagement in sensor-based statistical models of human interruptibility. In *Proceedings of the ACM Conference on Human Factors in Computing Systems, CHI 2005, Computer Human Interaction*, April 2–7, Portland, Oregon, USA, pp. 331–40.

Fogarty, J., Lai, J., and Christensen, J. (2004). Presence versus availability: The design and evaluation of a context-aware communication client. *International Journal of Human-Computer Studies* 61(3), 299–317.

Franke, J. L., Daniels, J. J., and McFarlane, D. C. (2002). Recovering context after interruption. In *Proceedings of the 24th Annual Meeting of the Cognitive Science Society, CogSci 2002*, August 8–10, Fairfax, Virginia, USA, pp 310–15.

Gievska, S., Lindeman, R., and Sibert, J. (2005). Examining the qualitative gains of mediating human interruptions during HCI. In *Proceedings of the 11th International Conference on Human-Computer Interaction, HCI 2005*, July 22–27, Las Vegas, Nevada, USA.

Gillie, T. and Broadbent, D. E. (1989). What makes interruptions disruptive? A study of length, similarity and complexity. *Psychological Research Policy* 50, 243–50.

Gladwell, M. (2000). *The tipping point: How little things can make a big difference*. Boston, MA: Little, Brown and Company.

Goldhaber, M. H. (1997). The attention economy and the net. *First Monday* 2(4).

Gonzalez, V. M. and Mark, G. (2004). Constant, constant, multitasking craziness: Managing multiple working spheres. In *Proceedings of the ACM Conference on Human Factors in Computing Systems, CHI 2004, Computer-Human Interaction*, April 24–9, Vienna, Austria, pp. 113–20.

Healey, C. G. (December 2005). Perception in visualization. Available at: http://www.csc.ncsu.edu/faculty/healey/PP/ (accessed June 30, 2006).

Heylighen, F. (2004). Tackling complexity and information overload: From intelligence amplification and attention economy to the global brain. Technological Forecasting and Social Change [Submitted]. Available online at: http://pcp.vub.ac.be/Papers/PapersFH2.html.

Ho, C., Nikolic, M., Waters, M., and Sarter, N. (2004). Not now! Supporting interruption management by indicating the modality and urgency of pending tasks. *Human Factors* 46(3), 399–409.

Ho, J. and Intille, S. S. (2005). Using context-aware computing to reduce the perceived burden of interruptions from mobile devices. In *Proceedings of the ACM Conference on Human Factors in Computing Systems, CHI 2005, Computer Human Interaction*, April 2–7, Portland, Oregon, USA, pp. 909–18.

Horvitz, E. and Apacible, J. (2003). Learning and reasoning about interruption. In *Proceedings of the 5th International Conference on Multimodal Interfaces, ICMI 2003*. November 5–7, Vancouver, British Columbia, Canada. New York: ACM Press, pp. 20–7.

Horvitz, E., Kadie, C., Paek, T., and Hovel, D. (2003). Models of attention in computing and communication: From principles to applications. *Communications of the ACM* 46(3), 52–9.

Horvitz, E., Koch, P., and Apacible, J. (2004). Busybody: Creating and fielding personalized models of the cost of interruption. In *Proceedings of the Conference on Computer Supported Cooperative Work, CSCW 2004*, November 6–10, Chicago, Illinois, USA. New York: ACM Press, pp. 507–10.

Horvitz, E., Koch, P., Kadie, C. M., and Jacobs, A. (2002). Coordinate: Probabilistic forecasting of presence and availability. In *Proceedings of the Eighteenth Conference on Uncertainty and Artificial Intelligence, UAI 2002*, August 1–4, Edmonton, Alberta, Canada. San Francisco: Morgan Kaufmann, pp. 224–33.

Hudson, J. M., Christensen, J., Kellogg, W. A., and Erickson, T. (2002). I'd be overwhelmed, but it's just one more thing to do: Availability and interruption in research management. In *Proceedings of the SIGCHI Conference on Human Factors in Computing Systems: Changing our world, changing ourselves, CHI '02*, Minneapolis, Minnesota, USA. New York: ACM Press, pp. 97–104.

Iqbal, S. T., Adamczyk, P. D., Zheng, X. S., and Bailey, B. P. (2005). Towards an index of opportunity: Understanding changes in mental workload during task execution. In *Proceedings of the ACM Conference on Human Factors in Computing Systems, CHI 2005, Computer Human Interaction*, April 2–7, Portland, Oregon, USA, pp. 311–20.

Jameson, A., Schafer, R., Weis, T., Berthold, A., and Weyrath, T. (1999). Making systems sensitive to the user's time and working memory constraints. In *Proceedings of the 4th International Conference on Intelligent User Interfaces*, Los Angeles: ACM Press, pp. 79–86.

Kaptelinin, V. and Czerwinski, M. (eds) (2007). *Beyond the desktop metaphor: Designing integrated digital work environments*. Boston: MIT Press.

Kvavilashvili, L., Messer, D. J., and Ebdon, P. (2001). Prospective memory in children: The effects of age and task interruption. *Developmental Psychology* 37(3), 418–30.

Lester, J., Converse, S., Kahler, S., Barlow, T., Stone, B., and Bhogal, R. (1997). The persona effect: Affective impact of animated pedagogical agents. In S. Pemberton (ed.), *Proceedings of the ACM CHI '97 Human Factors in Computing Systems Conference*, March 22–27, Atlanta, Georgia, USA, pp. 359–66.

McAfee, A. P. (2006). Enterprise 2.0: The dawn of emergent collaboration. *Sloan Management Review* 47(3), 21–8.

McCrickard, D. S., Catrambone, R., Chewar, C. M., and Stasko, J. T. (2003). Establishing tradeoffs that leverage attention for utility: Empirically evaluating information display in notification systems. *International Journal of Human-Computer Studies* 58(5), 547–82.

McCrickard, D. S. and Chewar, C. M. (2003). Attuning notification design to user goals and attention costs. *Communications of the ACM* 46(3) 67–72.

McFarlane, D. C. and Latorella, K. A. (2002). The scope and importance of human interruption in human-computer interaction design. *Human-Computer Interaction* 17(1), 1–62.
Mark, G., Gonzalez, V. M., and Harris, J. (2005). No task left behind? Examining the nature of fragmented work. In *Proceedings of the ACM Conference on Human Factors in Computing Systems, CHI 2005, Computer Human Interaction*, April 2–7, Portland, Oregon, USA, pp. 321–30.
Marlow, C., Naaman, M., Boyd, D., and Davis, M. (2006). Tagging paper, taxonomy, Flickr, academic article, ToRead. In *Proceedings of the Seventeenth Conference on Hypertext and Hypermedia, Hypertext 2006*, August 22–25, Odense, Denmark. New York: ACM Press, pp. 31–40.
Marsh, R. L., Hicks, J. L., and Bryan, E. S. (1999). The activation of un-related and cancelled intentions. *Memory & Cognition* 27(2), 320–7.
Maslach, C., Schaufeli, W. B., and Leiter, M. P. (2001). Job burnout. *Annual Review of Psychology* 52, 397–422.
Meacham, J. A. and Leiman, B. (1982). Remembering to perform future actions. In U. Neisser (ed.), *Memory observed: Remembering in natural contexts* (pp. 327–36). San Francisco: Freeman.
Miller, G. (1956). The magical number seven, plus or minus two. *Psychological Review* 63, 81–97.
Nabeth, T. and Roda, C. (2006). Les espaces sociaux virtuels: Approches, pratiques émergentes et perspectives. In A. Bounfour (ed.), *Capital immatériel, connaissance et performance*. Paris: L'Harmattan, pp. 225–65.
Nagata, S. F. (2003). Multitasking and interruptions during mobile web tasks. In *Proceedings of the 47th Annual Meeting of the Human Factors and Ergonomics Society*, October 13–17, Denver, Colorado, USA, pp. 1341–5.
Nardi, B., Whittaker, S., and Schwarz, H. (2000). It's not what you know, it's who you know: Work in the information age. *First Monday* 5(5) (May).
Nisbett, R. E. (2003). *Geography of thought: How Asians and westerners think differently... and why*. New York: Free Press.
Nonaka, I. and Takeuchi, H. (1995). *The knowledge-creating company: How Japanese companies create the dynamics of innovation*. New York: Oxford University Press.
Obermayer, R. W. and Nugent, W. A. (2000). Human-computer interaction for alert warning and attention allocation systems of the multi-modal watchstation. In P. Hamburger (ed.), *Integrated Command Environments: Proceedings of SPIE 2000*, Vol. 4126. Bellingham: The International Society for Optical Engineering (SPIE), pp. 14–22.
O'Conaill, B. and Frohlich, D. (1995). Timespace in the workplace: Dealing with interruptions. In *Companion Proceedings of Human Factors in Computing Systems, CHI 1995*. Denver: ACM Press, pp. 262–3.
O'Reilly, T. (2005). What is web 2.0? Design patterns and business models for the next generation of software. Available at: http://www.oreillynet.com/pub/a/oreilly/tim/news/2005/09/30/what-is-web-20.html (accessed September 30, 2005).
Picard, R. W. (1997). *Affective computing*. Cambridge, MA: MIT Press.
Rensink, R. A. (2000). Seeing, sensing, and scrutinizing. *Vision Research* 40(10–12), 1469–87.
Robertson, T. J., Prabhakararao, S., Burnett, M., Cook, C., Ruthruff, J. R., Beckwith, L., and Phalgune, A. (2004). Impact of interruption style on end-user debugging. In *Proceedings of the ACM Conference on Human Factors in Computing Systems, CHI 2004, Computer-Human Interaction*, April 24–9, Vienna, Austria, pp. 287–94.
Roda, C. and Nabeth, T. (2007). Supporting attention in learning environments: attention support services, and information management. In E. Duval, R. Klamma, and M. Wolpers (eds), *Creating new experiences on a global scale: Second European Conference on Technology Enhanced Learning, EC-TEL 2007, Crete, Greece, September 17–20, 2007, Proceedings*. New York: Springer-Verlag, pp. 277–91.
Roda, C., Stojanov, G., and Clauzel, D. (2006). Mind-prosthesis metaphor for design of

human-computer interfaces that support better attention management. In *Proceedings of the AAAI 2006 Fall Symposia on Interaction and Emergent Phenomena in Societies of Agents*, October 13–15, Arlington, Virginia, USA, pp. 52–9.

Roda, C. and Thomas, J. (2006). Attention aware systems: Theories, applications, and research agenda. *Computers in Human Behavior* 22(4), 557–87.

Rubinstein, J. S., Meyer, D. E., and Evans, J. (2001). Executive control of cognitive processes in task switching. *Journal of Experimental Psychology: Human Perception and Performance* 27(4) 763–97.

Rudman, P. and Zajicek, M. (2006). Autonomous agent as helper – helpful or annoying? In *Proceedings of the IEEE/WIC/ACM International Conference on Intelligent Agent Technology, IAT 2006*, December 18–22, Hong Kong, pp. 170–6.

Schroeder, R., and Axelsson, A. (eds). *Avatars at work and play: Collaboration and interaction in shared virtual environments*. New York: Springer-Verlag.

Sellen, A. J., Louie, G., Harris, J. E., and Wilkins, A. J. (1996). What brings intentions to mind? An in situ study of prospective memory. *Memory & Cognition* 5(4), 483–507.

Senge, P. (1994). *The fifth discipline: The art and practice of the learning organization*. New York: Doubleday.

Sifry, D., Marks, K., Çelik, T., and Hayes, E. (2006). Attention.Xml. Available at: http://developers.technorati.com/wiki/attentionxml (accessed June 30, 2006).

Speier, C., Vessey, I., and Valacich, J. S. (2003). The effects of interruptions, task complexity, and information presentation on computer-supported decision-making performance. *Decision Sciences* 34(4) 771–97.

Stone, L. (2006). Linda Stone's thoughts on attention and specifically, continuous partial attention. Available at: http://continuouspartialattention.jot.com/WikiHome (accessed June 2007).

Summers, L. and Dahod, S. (2003). You've got the power: Using goal-driven performance management to empower. Available at: http://www.workinfo.com/free/Downloads/141.htm (accessed November 10, 2008).

Toet, A. (2006). Gaze directed displays as an enabling technology for attention aware systems. *Computers in Human Behavior* 22(4), 615–47.

Vedantam, S. (2004). Human responses to technology scrutinized. *The Washington Post*, June 7.

Vertegaal, R., Chen, D., Shell, J., and Mamuji, A. (2006). Designing for augmented attention: Towards a framework for attentive user interfaces. *Computers in Human Behavior* 22(4), 771–89.

Wolfe, J., Klempen, N., and Dahlen, K. (2000). Postattentive vision. *Journal of Experimental Psychology: Human Perception & Performance* 26(2), 693–716.

Wolpers, M., Martin, G., Najjar, J., and Duval, E. Attention metadata in knowledge and learning management. In *Proceedings of the 6th International Conference on Knowledge Management, I-KNOW 2006*, September 6–8, Graz, Austria.

Wright, P. M. and Snell, S. A. (1998). Toward a unifying framework for exploring fit and flexibility in strategic human resource management. *Academy of Management Review* 23(4), 756–72.

Zijlstra, F. R. H., Roe, R. A., Leonova, A. B., and Krediet, I. (1999). Temporal factors in mental work: Effects of interrupted activities. *Journal of Occupational and Organizational Psychology* 72, 163–85.

12 Leveraging organizational capital for innovation

The process of marketing knowledge co-creation

Florian Kohlbacher

Introduction

This chapter deals with organizational capital and processes for innovation from a marketing and knowledge management perspective. Knowledge has frequently been identified as a crucial enabler for innovation (e.g. Bounfour, 2003; Drucker, 1985; Hanvanich *et al.*, 2003; Ichijo, 2002). At the same time, marketing affairs are one of the most knowledge-intensive functions of a corporation, and marketing processes like customer relationship management/customer knowledge management and new product development are very closely related to innovation (cf. e.g. Gibbert *et al.*, 2002; Kohlbacher, 2007; Leonard, 1998; Nonaka and Takeuchi, 1995). Speaking from the knowledge-based view of the firm (e.g. Nonaka and Toyama, 2005), which sees knowledge and competencies as decisive foundations for the performance and abilities of organizations, and building on Kohlbacher's (2007) framework of knowledge-based marketing, this chapter presents and analyzes the organizational process of marketing knowledge co-creation for generating innovation.

Theoretical background

The theoretical foundation of this chapter is Nonaka's theory of organizational knowledge creation (Nonaka, 1994; Nonaka and Takeuchi, 1995) and Kohlbacher's (2006; 2007) framework of knowledge-based marketing and knowledge co-creation in the business ecosystem. Kohlbacher identified and described four core marketing processes in which knowledge (co-)creation plays an essential role (cf. Figure 12.1). Of course, many more marketing processes can be identified and analyzed in a similar way, as well as more entities in the business ecosystem involved in the joint creation of knowledge and value. The models in Figures 12.1 and 12.2 are meant to illustrate only the core processes and actors. Note that the marketing knowledge base and the marketing processes together represent a firm's organizational capital in marketing.

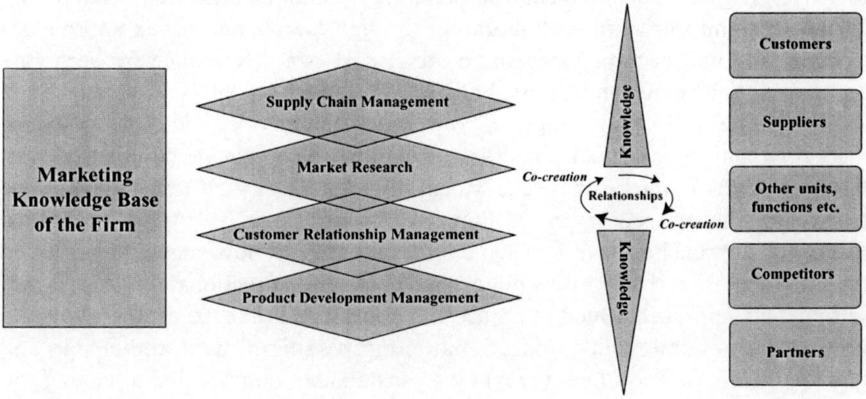

Figure 12.1 Knowledge-based marketing processes.
Source: Kohlbacher, 2007a: 117

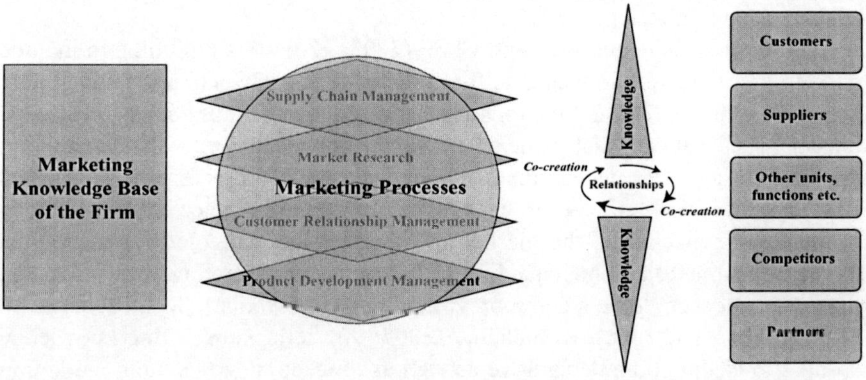

Figure 12.2 Knowledge-based marketing processes (integrated model).
Source: Kohlbacher, 2007a: 118

Marketing knowledge and knowledge-based marketing

Despite the fact that the theory of organizational knowledge creation has been applied to numerous fields (cf. e.g. Nonaka *et al.*, 2006b), this does not seem to be the case for marketing and marketing research. Indeed, even though "marketing functions lend themselves particularly well for an investigation of knowledge transfer within MNCs," "there is a dearth of research on knowledge transfer in the field of marketing" (Schlegelmilch and Chini, 2003: 220–221). Yet, in an increasingly global business environment, the creation and transfer of marketing knowledge and intra-firm collaboration through knowledge-based approaches to marketing will become more and more crucial as a determinant for corporate competitive advantage and survival of firms (Kohlbacher, 2007).

Kohlbacher (2007) developed a conceptual framework of knowledge-based marketing and the essential processes of marketing knowledge co-creation with the main actors in the business ecosystem of global firms – customers, suppliers, competitors, business partners (cf. Figure 12.1 and 12.2 above). While traditional marketing approaches have focused overly on explicit knowledge and neglected the important role of tacit knowledge, specifically in international (cross-cultural) settings, his approach aimed to adjust this imbalance in the extant literature and proposed a new knowledge-based marketing paradigm, with knowledge and knowledge co-creation being the key to sustainable competitive advantage in the global network economy. Facing the current global business environment and fierce competition, knowledge-based marketing has already become crucial as a determinant for corporate competitive advantage and as such a sine qua non for leading MNCs. Besides, as large parts of marketing knowledge are tacit and hard to codify, face-to-face communication and the integration of local staff into marketing processes and decision-making is an important factor for global marketing knowledge sharing that leads to successful marketing and sales achievements (Kohlbacher, 2007).

According to Schlegelmilch and Chini (2003: 226) "it is high time to include marketing into the research agenda for knowledge management and to overcome the paradox that marketing functions are neglected in the discussion on knowledge transfer." As a matter of fact, "[b]eing among the first to internationalize, marketing functions are key to the development of knowledge transfer processes in a dispersed MNC context" (ibid.). However, despite the obvious importance of knowledge to the marketing discipline, the marketing literature has struggled for more than 10 years to come to an understanding of the nature of marketing knowledge and there does not seem to be a common ground unifying scholars (Kohlbacher *et al.* 2007; Kohlbacher, 2006). Kohlbacher (2007: 96) defines marketing knowledge as "all knowledge, both declarative as well as procedural, concerning marketing thinking and behavior in a corporation."

Knowledge-based marketing processes

Hanvanich *et al.* (2003: 124) argue that while marketing scholars have been interested in the topic of marketing knowledge, "they have focused mainly on how firms acquire, disseminate, and store knowledge," with related research areas being market orientation and organizational learning. Taking a new approach to re-conceptualizing marketing knowledge and innovation, Hanvanich *et al.* (2003: 130) proffer that "marketing knowledge resides in three key marketing processes: product development management (PDM), customer relationship management (CRM), and supply chain management (SCM)." This notion is based on the framework of Srivastava *et al.* (1999) that redefines marketing as a phenomenon embedded in the three core marketing processes of PDM, SCM and CRM. Bjerre and Sharma (2003: 140) seem to agree when they posit that the "important thing is not one specific piece of knowledge, but an entire package that includes knowledge about clients, competitors, local institutions, suppliers etc."

I will subsequently discuss each of the three core processes of PDM, SCM and CRM from a marketing knowledge perspective. Kohlbacher's (2007) framework presented in Figures 1 and 2 includes market research as a forth process. But a discussion of market research would go beyond the scope of this chapter. In a sense, it could also be viewed as a sub-process of customer knowledge management (see below, CRM) or as an antecedent of PDM.

Supply chain management

Supply chain management might actually be the least obvious process to analyze from a marketing knowledge perspective. However, suppliers are able to generate and provide valuable insights and knowledge about competitors, customers, and customers' customers; and they can play an important role in product development processes, help to cut costs, and provide superior value propositions to customers. Indeed, suppliers must be "prepared to develop team-based mechanisms for continuously exchanging information about needs, problems, and emerging requirements, and then taking action" because in a successful collaborative relationship, joint problem solving displaces negotiations (Day, 1994: 45). Suppliers must also be prepared to participate in the customer's development processes, even before the product specifications are established. That is why the channel bonding capability has many features in common with the customer-linking capability, and hence the same skills, mechanisms, and processes might be readily transferred between those related domains (Day, 1994: 44fn).

Ahmadjian (2004: 227) contends that "[k]nowledge creation occurs not only within firms, but also through relationships between firms." In fact, customer-supplier partnerships (Konsynski and McFarlan, 1990) as well as strong supplier networks, have frequently been put forth in this context (cf. e.g. Chaston, 2004; Cusumano and Takeishi, 1991; Dyer and Hatch, 2006; Dyer and Nobeoka, 2000; Lincoln *et al.*, 1998). In the latter case it was notably those of Japanese companies, and here again especially the ones in the automotive, but also the electronics sector. These networks or strong relationships between firms in Japan have frequently been termed and analyzed as so-called *keiretsu*, described as "the webs of relations that envelop many Japanese companies" (Lincoln *et al.*, 1996: 67) or as "clusters of interlinked Japanese firms and the specific ties that bind them" and their "long-term, personal and reciprocal character" (Lincoln *et al.*, 1992: 561). Furthermore, "the openness and richness of networks are believed to foster a fertile environment for the creation of entirely new knowledge" (Lincoln *et al.*, 1998: 241). However, it must not necessarily only be big firms that successfully manage and share knowledge in the supply chain. Glisby and Holden (2005) for example, present the case of a Danish small specialist manufacturer that applied knowledge management concepts to the supply chain and thus managed to co-create the market with their

Japanese business partners through a synergistic process of knowledge sharing (cf. also Kohlbacher *et al.*, 2007).

Customer relationship management

The continuous need to learn from and about customers and competitors, and to exploit such knowledge to stay ahead, has frequently been stressed and discussed (cf. e.g. Chaston, 2004; Davenport *et al.*, 2001; Davenport and Klahr, 1998; Gulati and Oldroyd, 2005; Li and Cavusgil, 1998). Indeed, "customer focus," "customer knowledge co-creation," and "customer interaction" are crucial keywords in this context (cf. e.g. Griffin and Hauser, 1993; Gulati and Oldroyd, 2005; Prahalad and Ramaswamy, 2004b; Thomke and von Hippel, 2002; Vandermerwe, 2004).

Wikström and Norman (1994: 64) argue that because marketing is no longer "a clearly delineated function at the end of the production chain" and that since nowadays "there are many functions and people who influence the customer relationship," then it is not logical to have marketing handled solely by a specialist department. Thus, knowledge about customers needs to be shared throughout the organization (Bennet and Gabriel, 1999). Indeed, "knowledge on customers and their preferences must be located or solutions for a particular kind of customer problem need to be identified" (Schlegelmilch and Penz, 2002: 12). For the latter task, CRM and data mining tools for decision support have proven useful and effective – CRM is "critically dependent upon having accurate and up-to-date knowledge about customers" (Chaston, 2004: 225). However, even though tools and technology are important, they are not enough (cf. e.g. Davenport *et al.*, 2001; Gulati and Oldroyd, 2005). In fact, although CRM has received much scholarly and management attention, it frequently does not go beyond the surface and remains restricted to collecting and managing mere data and information, but not knowledge – especially tacit knowledge – despite its importance (cf. also Zaltman, 2003). Indeed, Gouillart and Sturdivant (1994: 117) criticize that "most managers do not understand the distinction between information and knowledge" and that even if they "include information from all points on the distribution channel, most general market data do not show a manager how each customer relates to the next or how customers view competing products and services." Besides, CRM has been traditionally popular as a means to tie customers to the company through various loyalty schemes, but it left perhaps the greatest source of value under-leveraged: the knowledge residing in customers (Gibbert *et al.*, 2002: 464).

A relatively new approach that tries to overcome the short-comings of CRM is "customer knowledge management" (CKM) (e.g. Davenport *et al.*, 2001; Desouza and Awazu, 2005; Gibbert *et al.*, 2002; Wayland and Cole, 1997). According to Gibbert *et al.* (2002: 461), CKM differs from CRM and knowledge management in general, as customer knowledge managers "require a different mindset along a number of key variables." "Customer knowledge managers, first and foremost focus on knowledge *from* the customer (i.e. knowledge residing in customers), rather than focusing on knowledge *about* the customer, as characteristic of customer relationship management" (Gibbert *et al.*, 2002: 461, original emphasis). Indeed, customer-driven companies need to harness their capabilities to manage the knowledge of those who buy their products (Davenport and Klahr, 1998; Gibbert *et al.*, 2002).

Nevertheless, CRM still plays an important role as market driven organizations "develop intimate relationships with their customers, instead of seeing them as a means to a series of transactions" and these capabilities are "built upon a shared knowledge base that is used to gather and disseminate knowledge about the market" (Day, 1999: xi). Indeed, as buyer-seller relationships "continue their transformation, a customer-linking capability – creating and managing close customer relationships – is becoming increasingly important" (Day, 1994: 44). The customer-linking capability "comprises the skills, abilities, and processes needed to achieve collaborative customer relationships so individual customer needs are quickly apparent to all functions and well-defined procedures are in place for responding to them" (Day, 1994: 49). I therefore view CKM as one – from a knowledge-based perspective essential – process within CRM.

Product development management

Obviously, market research and CKM are – or at least should be – closely related. In a similar vein, knowledge from market research and customer knowledge and its management are not only essential for understanding customers and their needs to successfully advertise and market products, but also as early as in the product development process. Indeed, as marketing organizations serve as corporate links between customers and their organization's manufacturing and R&D operations (Riesenberger, 1998), the integration of and knowledge exchange between R&D and marketing has also been treated as an important issue (e.g. Griffin and Hauser, 1996; Song and Parry, 1993).

According to Bell *et al.* (2002: 82), product development is "a particularly salient area for organizational learning inquiry for a number of reasons": it is often a team-based pursuit, it requires a high degree of interfunctional coordination, and it is frequently project based. Indeed, there is a strong body of literature that deals with product development and product introduction for an organizational learning, Knowledge Management or market orientation perspective (cf. e.g. Baker and Sinkula, 2005; Kusunoki *et al.*, 1998; Madhavan and Grover, 1998; Schulze and Hoegl, 2006, to name but a few). But, product development is often difficult because "the 'need' information (what the customer wants) resides with the customer and the 'solution' information (how to satisfy those needs) lies with the manufacturer" (Thomke, 2003: 244). Traditionally, "the onus has been on manufacturers to collect the customer need information through various means, including market research and information gathered from the field," a process that "can be costly and time-consuming because customer needs are often complex, subtle, and fast-changing" (ibid.).

Nonaka and Takeuchi (Imai *et al.*, 1985; Takeuchi and Nonaka, 1986) have already discussed the issues of learning and transferring knowledge in product development projects more than twenty years ago, and the theory of organizational knowledge creation is thoroughly grounded in and backed up by empirical research on such projects (Nonaka and Takeuchi, 1995; Nonaka *et al.*, 1996). In fact, even though many vital processes of innovation, change, and renewal in organizations can be analyzed through the lens of knowledge conversion (Nonaka *et al.*, 2006b), knowledge creation and transfer in product development projects seem to be particularly important, as the research focus by eminent Western scholars has also shown (cf. e.g. Leonard, 1998; Leonard and Sensiper, 1998; Leonard-Barton, 1992; von Hippel, 1994). Indeed, "the ability to import knowledge from the market" is a principal component of the product development process (Leonard, 1998: 179). Baba and Nobeoka (1998), in their study on the introduction of 3-D CAD systems, even speak of "knowledge-based product development." Moreover, Nonaka *et al.* (2006b) suggest that members of a product development project share ideas and viewpoints on their product design in a *ba* – a shared context – that allows common interpretation of technical data, evolving rules of thumb, an emerging sense of product quality, effective communication of hunches or concerns, and so on.

One way of capturing customer needs and translating them into a product concept has been termed "empathic design" (Leonard, 1998; Leonard and Swap, 2005). Leonard (1998: 194, emphasis removed), defines empathic design as "the creation of product or service concepts based on a deep (empathetic) understanding of unarticulated user needs." It is "a set of techniques, a process of developing deep empathy for another's point of view and using that perspective to stimulate novel design concepts" (Leonard and Swap, 2005: 82). Empathic design differs from contextual inquiry precisely because it does not rely on inquiry; in the situations in which empathic design is most useful, inquiry is useless or ineffective (Leonard, 1998: 288fn). The more deeply a researcher can get into the mindset, the perspective, of a prospective or actual user, the more valuable is the knowledge thus generated (Leonard, 2007).

Obviously, the knowledge gained and generated through market research, empathic design and product development etc. should not vanish after the project finishes. Indeed, it is essential to retain vital knowledge and share and transfer across functions, between projects as well as generations of projects and products (e.g. Aoshima, 2002; Cusumano and Nobeoka, 1998; Nobeoka and Cusumano, 1997). As Cusumano and Nobeoka (1998: 175) put it: "In addition to overlapping projects and using cross-functional teams, companies have various organizational and technological mechanisms to help them capture knowledge about designs or manufacturing processes and then transfer this knowledge across different projects or different generations of products." Indeed, successful new product development at least partially depends on the ability to understand technical and market knowledge embodied in existing products, and the adaptation of this knowledge to support new product development (Aoshima, 2002; Iansiti, 1997; Iansiti and Clark, 1994).

Knowledge-based innovation

"Knowledge is a crucial enabler for innovation, that is, corporate transformation, which requires the involvement of all organizational members" (Ichijo, 2002: 478). Viewing innovation as a continuous process of re-invention, Bounfour (2003) places knowledge creation at the heart of innovation, and Drucker (1985: 107) proffers that "amongst the history-making innovations, knowledge-based innovations rank high." Hanvanich *et al.* (2003: 126) maintain that "knowledge plays a critical role in innovation generation" (cf. also Cavusgil *et al.*, 2003) and Chaston (2004: 150) contends that innovation "involves the application of knowledge to create new products and/or services." Kogut and Zander (1992) argue that innovations are products of a firm's "combinative capabilities" to generate new applications from existing knowledge. Teece *et al.* (1997) term such capabilities "dynamic capabilities," i.e. a firm's ability to use existing firm-specific capabilities and to develop new ones. Dynamic capabilities provide a firm with the basis for its sustainable advantage over time and, according to Teece (1998: 62), a "critical dimension of knowledge management has emerged: capturing value from innovative activity."

For Leonard (1998: 4) the "starting point for managing knowledge in an organization is an understanding of core capabilities," which "constitute a competitive advantage for a firm" and "have been built up over time and cannot be easily imitated." It is exactly these core competencies that are building and sustaining the sources of innovation in organizations. Together, these capabilities and competencies form the organizational capital of a firm. Finally, "[i]n a world where other firms are seeking to expand their market share, successful firms often can only stay ahead of the competition by exploiting new knowledge to offer improved products or processes that deliver new forms of added value to their customer" (Chaston, 2004: 155). However, it is important to note that "the knowledge necessary to come up with valuable innovations is neither in-house nor nearby" (Santos *et al.*, 2004: 37), or at least this is not necessarily the case.

According to Leonard and Sensiper (1998: 116), "[t]he process of innovation is a rhythm of search and selection, exploration and synthesis, cycles of divergent thinking followed by convergence." Besides, "[i]nnovation, the source of sustained advantage for most companies, depends upon the individual and collective expertise of employees" and creative cooperation is critical (Leonard and Sensiper, 1998: 112). Indeed, knowledge building for an organization occurs by combining people's distinct individualities with a particular set of activities, and it is this combination that enables innovation (Leonard, 1998: 8). On a global scale, there is a need for a process for innovating "that transcends local clusters and national boundaries," becoming what Santos *et al.* (2004: 31) have termed "metanational innovators." This is a strategy of utilizing localized pockets of technology, market intelligence and capabilities, and which has provided a powerful new source of competitive advantage: more, higher-value innovation at lower cost (Doz *et al.*, 2001; Santos *et al.*, 2004). According to Santos *et al.* (2004: 31), it is the "logical next step beyond augmenting in-house R&D with external ideas" in what has been called the "era of open innovation" (e.g. Chesbrough, 2003). Indeed, Chesbrough

(2006: 15) argues that in "a world of widely distributed useful knowledge, one can only sustain innovation by actively licensing in external ideas and technologies alongside developing and deploying one's own ideas." As firms look to advance their technology, they can or should use both external ideas and internal ideas, and both internal and external paths to market. Companies should make much greater use of external ideas and technologies in their own business, while letting their unused ideas be used by other companies. Open innovation is a paradigm that offers the prospect of lower costs of innovation, faster times to market and the chance to share risks with others (Chesbrough, 2003, 2006). This shares commonalities with the idea of leveraging external knowledge from entities in the business ecosystem.

The process of marketing knowledge co-creation

As Kohlbacher (2007) has shown, applying knowledge management concepts and practices to the knowledge-intensive field of marketing, and to marketing functions, bears out particularly efficient and effective. Especially when introducing new products or when entering new markets, knowledge creation and transfer, and intra- as well as inter-firm collaboration, prove critical for the success of the projects. It is especially the process of knowledge co-creation – joint knowledge creation – which is of outmost importance in this context.

Knowledge co-creation

Knowledge co-creation, and especially knowledge co-creation with customers, is at the heart of knowledge-based marketing. Indeed, as Nonaka (2007: xiv) puts it, "[f]irms and managers have to take the standpoint of the customer, and collaborate with them and dwell in them to share and co-create tacit knowledge." However, Sawhney (2002: 96, original emphasis) notes that even though "[c]ollaboration has become an established way of doing business with suppliers, channel partners and complementors," with a few exceptions, "working directly with *customers* to co-create value remains a radical notion." But a "critical aspect of creating a successful market is the ability to integrate the customer into every key process" and collaborators "may play a major role in initiating knowledge creation in the marketspace" (Kotler *et al.*, 2002: 36, 38).

According to Achrol and Kotler (1999), the creation of marketing know-how is the most important function of marketing in the global knowledge-based economy. Indeed, "in marketing, a wide array of knowledge needs to be created" and "knowledge on customers and their preferences must be located or solutions for a particular kind of customer problem need to be identified" (Schlegelmilch and Penz, 2002: 12). Most of the time the knowledge creation or application is only conducted in a unilateral, one-sided way. Firms generate, collect and analyze knowledge about customers, customers' needs, competitors, suppliers etc. Customer knowledge from customers can be seen as a little exception to this, but here as well, the knowledge might be communicated unilaterally from the customers to the firm. But the real challenge and source of essential knowledge for competitive advantage is to go beyond knowledge creation and application as a unilateral concept. In fact, interactions and knowledge co-creation become more and more crucial.

Therefore, knowledge and value co-creation with customers – but also with suppliers and other business partners – has also received significant attention recently (cf. e.g. Doz *et al.*, 2001; Gummesson, 2002; Lawer, 2005; Prahalad and Ramaswamy, 2000; Prahalad and Ramaswamy, 2004b; Prahalad and Ramaswamy, 2003; Sawhney and Prandelli, 2000b; Sawhney, 2002; Thomke and von Hippel, 2002; Wikström, 1996; Zack, 2003). According to Prahalad and Ramaswamy (2000: 80), the market has become "a forum in which consumers play an active role in creating and competing for value," with the distinguishing feature of this new marketplace being "that consumers become a new source of competence for the corporation" (cf. also Prahalad and Ramaswamy, 2003; Prahalad and Ramaswamy, 2004b). Indeed, "co-creation converts the market into a *forum* where dialogue among the consumer, the firm, consumer communities, and networks of firms can take place" (Prahalad and Ramaswamy, 2004b: 122, original emphasis). According to Zack (2003: 71), anyone who can help the business – customers, trading partners, suppliers, consumers, interest groups – should be involved to create the knowledge the company needs. In fact, as discussed above, the "array of relationships in the set has been expanded from the dyad of seller and customer to include partners up and down the value chain (e.g., suppliers, the customers of customers, channel intermediaries)" (Day and Montgomery, 1999: 4).

Gibbert *et al.* (2002: 463) contend that since CKM is about innovation and growth, customer knowledge managers "seek opportunities for partnering with their customers as equal co-creators of organizational value." According to Prahalad and Ramaswamy (2003), the value of products or services is in the co-creation experience that stems from the customer's interaction with the product and/or the firm (cf. also Prahalad and Ramaswamy, 2004b). Gummesson (2002: 8) further notes that "[e]specially in services and often in B-to-B, customers are co-producers." Lovelock and Gummesson (2004: 29) use the term "coproducer" in the narrow sense of "a transfer of work from the provider to the customer" and contend that "[i]n its purest form, coproduction means that customers engage in self-service, using systems, facilities, or equipment supplied by the service provider." However, research in this area is still rather scarce, and as Lawer (2005: 11) has noted, "the organizational learning or marketing literature does not yet adequately define or empirically identify the nature or scope of the capability changes required for co-creation of knowledge with customers." Indeed, "the challenge is to view customers as co-producers of knowledge" (Desouza and Awazu, 2005: 143) and in order "to be successful at co-producing knowledge, the organization must seek customers who have open knowledge-sharing cultures, are willing to engage in learning and knowledge-creating activities, and are willing to take a certain degree of risk" (Desouza and Awazu, 2004: 15). Finally, companies must "redesign their businesses from a customer-driven starting point, so that they gather deep knowledge about customers and then have the capacity to offer customized products, services, programs, and messages" (Kotler *et al.*, 2002: 164).

Furthermore, customer interactions (Furukawa, 1999b, 1999a; Vandenbosch and Dawar, 2002), customer experiences (Berry *et al.*, 2002; Carbone and Haeckel, 1994; Pine II and Gilmore, 1999; Prahalad and Ramaswamy, 2000; Prahalad and Ramaswamy, 2004b; Prahalad and Ramaswamy, 2003), and communities of creation (Sawhney and Prandelli, 2000a) have become key terms in this context. In fact, "[h]igh-quality interactions that enable an individual customer to co-create unique experiences with the company are the key to unlocking new sources of competitive advantage" (Prahalad and Ramaswamy, 2004a: 7). Prahalad and Ramaswamy (2003: 15) propose the concept of "experience environment," which "can be thought of as a robust, networked combination of company capabilities [...] and consumer interaction channels [...] flexible enough to accommodate a wide range of individual context-and-time-specific needs and preferences." The network creates an experience environment with which each customer has a unique interaction. The consumer actively co-creates his or her personalized experience, which forms the basis of value to that consumer (Prahalad and Ramaswamy, 2003: 15). Because we must continually co-create new knowledge to co-create value continually, so-called "knowledge environments" for managers resemble experience environments for consumers (Prahalad and Ramaswamy, 2004b: 171). To be effective, "a knowledge environment must engage the total organization, including multiple levels, functions, and geographies," and the knowledge environment "is also where *the manager, as consumer, interacts with the experience network* to co-create value" (Prahalad and Ramaswamy, 2004b: 179, 185, original emphasis).

Customers' ideas – specifically those of so-called "lead users" (e.g. von Hippel, 1986; von Hippel, 1977) – and the ideas of those that interact directly with customers, or those that develop products for customers, have become important (cf. e.g. Leonard, 1998, 2007; Zaltman, 2003). "Lead users have foresight (knowledge) to help an organization better plan for product innovations" and organizations have "begun to host user conferences for the specific purpose of getting to know how their customers utilize their products and how they have customized or modified them to meet their needs" (Desouza and Awazu, 2004: 14). In the 1970s, von Hippel (1977) found that most product innovations come not from within the company that produces the product, but from end-users of the product. Note that lead users can be part of or can also form networks and share their ideas and knowledge within them (Furukawa, 1999b, 1999a). More recently, Thomke and von Hippel (2002) suggested ways in which customers can become co-innovators and co-developers of custom products (cf. also Gibbert *et al.*, 2002; Thomke, 2003). Indeed, "[c]ontrary to the mythology of marketing, the supplier is not necessarily the active party" and in B-to-B, "customers initiate innovation and force suppliers to change their products or services" (Gummesson, 2002: 15). As Prahalad and Ramaswamy (2004a: 10–11, original emphasis) put it: "In the co-creation view, all points of interaction between the company and the consumer are opportunities *for both value creation and extraction.*"

The process of marketing knowledge creation

A key issue in the literature on organizational learning and knowledge management is how successfully firms learn when they are exploiting current knowledge and skills versus exploring new knowledge and skills, and a long tradition of research suggests that these are competing strategies (Kyriakopoulos and Moorman, 2004; March, 1991; Miller *et al.*, 2006). But this view has also been challenged, with the argument that firms must engage in both strategies (e.g. He and Wong, 2004; Jansen *et al.*, 2005; Kyriakopoulos and Moorman, 2004; Levinthal and March, 1993; Lewin and Volberda, 1999). Levinthal and March (1993: 105) put it like this:

> An organization that engages exclusively in exploration will ordinarily suffer from the fact that it never gains the returns of its knowledge. An organization that engages exclusively in exploitation will ordinarily suffer from obsolescence. The basic problem confronting an organization is to engage in sufficient exploitation to ensure its current viability and, at the same time, to devote enough energy to exploration to ensure its future viability. Survival requires a balance, and the precise mix of exploitation and exploration that is optimal is hard to specify.

Kyriakopoulos and Moorman (2004) identified research in various fields that has recently shifted focus from whether to how firms can achieve a complementarity of the exploitation and exploration strategies: Brown and Eisenhardt (1997), e.g. introduce semi-structured and time-paced strategies as managerial tools to achieve this dynamic balance in product innovation. Likewise, the integration of exploration and exploitation is central to work examining dynamic or combinative capabilities (Grant, 1996; Kogut and Zander, 1992; Teece *et al.*, 1997). In the product development literature, scholars often study the degree of fit between a new product and prior activities (e.g. marketing and technological synergy, Henard and Szymanski, 2001; Montoya-Weiss and Calantone, 1994; Moorman and Miner, 1997; Song and Parry, 1997). Kyriakopoulos and Moorman (2004: 220) contribute to this literature by suggesting that a firm's market orientation can systematically promote synergies between exploratory and exploitative marketing strategy activities because "a firm's market orientation reduces the tensions between exploration and exploitation strategies and creates the opportunity for cross-fertilization and complementary learning between the two strategies."

While knowledge exploitation "means enhancing the intellectual capital of a company with existing knowledge", knowledge exploration "is a strategy for a company to increase its intellectual capital by creating its unique private knowledge within its organizational boundary" and therefore "means enrichment of the intellectual capital that a company achieves by itself" (Ichijo, 2002: 479–478). According to Ichijo (2002), both knowledge exploitation and knowledge exploration are indispensable for a company to increase its competitive advantage and Kyriakopoulos and Moorman (2004: 234) found that – despite the common assumption that these are competing strategies – "market-oriented firms can gain important bottom-line benefits from pursuing high levels of both strategies in product development." In fact, "[i]n a world where other firms are seeking to expand their market share, successful firms often can only stay ahead of the competition by exploiting new knowledge to offer improved products or processes that deliver new forms of added value to their customers" (Chaston, 2004: 155). If we interpret Chastons's expression "exploiting new knowledge" to be a mix of exploiting old knowledge and exploring new knowledge, we might well conclude that his statement is consistent with the above. Vicari and Cillo (2006: 195) follow Kyriakopoulos and Moorman (2004) and define market knowledge exploitation strategies as "those that imply a leverage on existing knowledge to refine marketing strategies, without exiting the existent path." On the other hand, they define market exploration strategies as "those that enact new approaches in the relationship with the market, by challenging existent convictions and routines of the organization" (Vicari and Cillo, 2006: 195–196).

Dynamic capabilities enable "both the exploitation of existing internal and external firm-specific capabilities and developing new ones" (Teece *et al.*, 1997: 515; cf. also Eisenhardt and Martin, 2000). Kyriakopoulos and Moorman (2004: 222) – who build their concepts of marketing exploitation and exploration on the resource-based view of the firm – conceptualize a firm's market orientation as "a dynamic capability that facilitates a firm's ability to explore and exploit knowledge and skills." Indeed, dynamic capabilities are rooted in both exploitative and exploratory activities (Benner and Tushman, 2003). Kyriakopoulos and Moorman (2004: 235, 236) finally conclude that "as a dynamic capability to sense market changes and relate to markets, a firm's market orientation helps it reconfigure and integrate knowledge generated from both strategies to serve existing and future customer needs" and that "market orientation is one important firm-level factor that allows high levels of both marketing exploitation strategies (improving current knowledge and skills) and marketing exploration strategies (developing new knowledge and skills) to be used profitably by firms." The ability to pursue both exploration and exploitation at the same time – and/or within the same organization – has also been termed ambidexterity (e.g. O'Reilly III and Tushman, 2004; Tushman and O'Reilly III, 1996).

Based on the above, Kohlbacher (2007: 103) defined knowledge-based marketing as "a knowledge management approach to marketing that focuses both on the exploitation (sharing and application) and exploration (creation) as well as the co-creation of marketing knowledge from contexts, relations and interactions in order to gain and sustain competitive advantage." Knowledge-based marketing therefore asks for ambidexterity. Figure 12.3 illustrates the interconnected processes of organizational knowledge creation and innovation, i.e. the marketing knowledge (co-)creation process. Through the SECI process – the process of organizational knowledge creation defined and explained by Nonaka (Nonaka, 1994; Nonaka and Takeuchi, 1995) – new knowledge is constantly created and refined over time, lifting the knowledge from the tacit and explicit organizational knowledge base to a higher dimension, namely in the form of holistic knowledge. In a sense, this holistic knowledge bridges explicit and tacit knowledge and can therefore be seen as a kind of synthesis of both. Indeed, bridging the gap between explicit and tacit knowledge means bridging the gap "between the formula and its enactment." Taylor (1993: 57) contends that the "person of real practical wisdom is marked out less by the ability to formulate rules than by knowing how to act in each particular situation." Note that the tacit and explicit knowledge base and the holistic knowledge created from them are crucial organizational capital, as is the process as a whole.

Dixon (2000: 13) defines knowledge "as the meaningful links people make in their minds between information and its application in action in a specific setting" and states that it "is always linked to action", as it is "derived from action and it carries the potential for others to use it to take action". In a similar vein, tacit knowledge refers to a kind of knowledge which is highly personal, hard to formalize and thus difficult to communicate to others, as it is deeply rooted in action (Nonaka and Takeuchi, 1995). In fact, in management, "knowledge about situations is of prime importance [...] not just knowledge about facts or people or technology, et cetera, but situational knowledge that combines all these factors" (Ghosn and Riès, 2005: 175).

Note that the marketing knowledge co-creation process in Figure 12.3 is exactly the knowledge co-creation process – and actually also an exploration and exploitation process – that can be found in the model of knowledge-based marketing processes (cf. Figures 12.1 and 12.2). In a sense, this model of the marketing knowledge co-creation process explains on the micro level and in

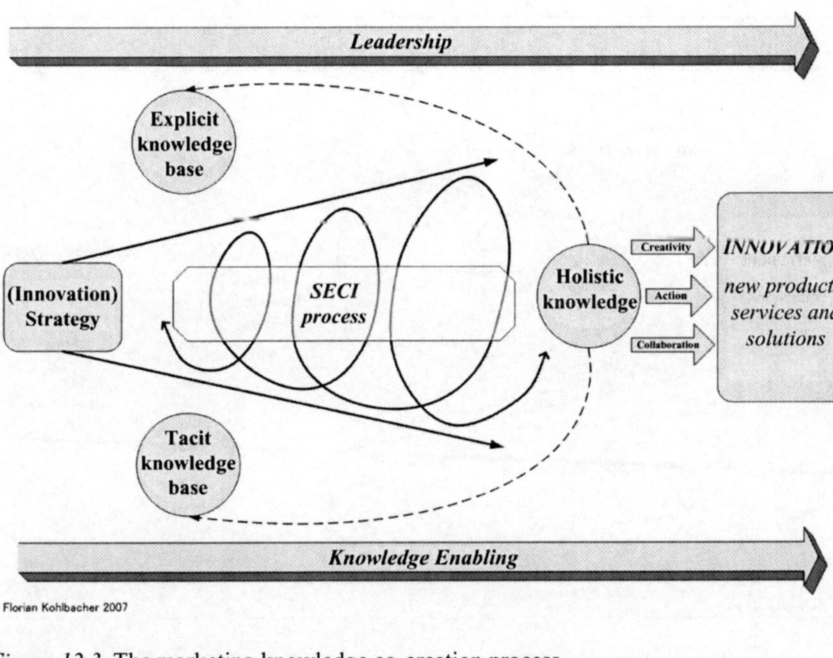

Figure 12.3 The marketing knowledge co-creation process.

Source: Author's own illustration

greater detail what is shown in the macro model of knowledge-based marketing processes in general.

The marketing knowledge creation process is an iterative process that starts with setting an innovation strategy and constantly loops back again. The final outcome is innovation in the form of new and innovative products, services and solutions. The continuous process of creating and refining concepts, ideas and knowledge through direct communication and interaction fosters the emergence of innovation and competitive advantage. Put differently, the whole process could also be described as a process of building up, refining and re-creating organizational capital. Indeed, organizational capital is both the input and the output of the process, as well as the ability to execute the process. Finally, the knowledge creation process is supported and nurtured by leadership – usually by middle managers (Nonaka and Takeuchi, 1995) and knowledge activists (von Krogh, Ichijo, and Nonaka, 2000) – as well as certain enablers or enabling conditions (von Krogh *et al.*, 2000).

Last but not least, as shown by Nonaka and associates (Nonaka, Toyama, and Konno, 2000; von Krogh *et al.*, 2000), organizational knowledge creation needs a shared context/*ba* or it is least enhanced by it. Figure 12.4 takes this fact into consideration and incorporates *ba* into the model. The knowledge creation process takes place in *ba* and is at the same time nurtured by it. For the case of the interaction and subsequent knowledge exchange and creation between firms and customers, Furukawa (1999b; 1999a) proposes the concept of 'meeting *ba*' (*deai no ba*). This meeting *ba* needs to be designed to communicate actively with customers

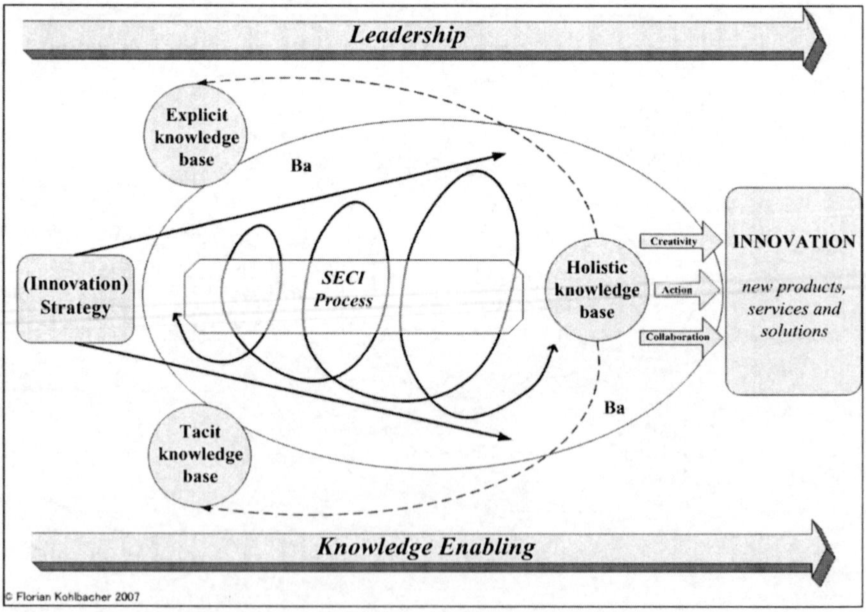

Figure 12.4 The marketing knowledge co-creation process and *ba*.

Source: Author's own illustration

and consumers within the social network. In a similar vein, Nonaka (2007: xiv) emphasizes the importance of *ba* and contends that a "theory of knowledge-based marketing must also be one of contextual marketing."

Knowledge-based marketing in practice

Despite the growing recognition of the need for knowledge-based approaches to marketing and systematic, strategic marketing knowledge (co-)creation, there are only few pioneer firms that are already taking or trying to take such an approach (Kohlbacher, 2007; Kohlbacher *et al.*, 2007). These firms face the challenge of an increasingly global business environment with fierce competition, and they take up and master the challenge with the help of knowledge-based marketing. The most outstanding example is probably Toyota. Indeed, Toyota has often been found to be very strong at organizational learning and knowledge creation and sharing (cf. e.g. Ichijo, 2007; Ichijo and Kohlbacher, 2007; Liker, 2004; Spear, 2004; Spear and Bowen, 1999). One aspect that has particularly been under the scrutiny of researchers is knowledge sharing and learning within its supplier network and the way Toyota leverages this co-created knowledge for both itself and its suppliers (e.g. Dyer and Hatch, 2004; Dyer and Nobeoka, 2000; Evans and Wolf, 2005; Liker and Choi, 2004). Additionally, Toyota also learns from its competitors and co-creates new knowledge with them. In particular, the joint venture between Toyota and GM – New United Motor Manufacturing, NUMMI – has already become legendary and has repeatedly been discussed from a knowledge-based perspective (cf. e.g. Badaracco, 1991; Easterby-Smith and Araujo, 1999; Inkpen, 2005; Liker, 2004, to name but a few). More recently, Toyota has established an international joint venture between with PSA Peugeot Citroën in Kolín, Czech Republic (Toyota Peugeot Citroën Automobile Czech, TPCA). This joint venture enables Toyota to pursue a marketing strategy perfectly suited for the emerging markets in Eastern Europe, and the collaboration with PSA also resulted in mutual learning, marketing knowledge co-creation, and other advantages for Toyota's European operation and its strategy of using external, local resources (Ichijo and Kohlbacher, 2007b; Kohlbacher, 2007; Ichijo and Kohlbacher, 2008).

Kohlbacher (2007) reports Swiss-based Schindler Elevator's knowledge-based marketing strategy for the market introduction of a new escalator product into Asian markets (cf. also Kohlbacher *et al.*, 2007). This case, for example, showed that even for a large MNC with its vast network of subsidiaries that are well connected by e-mail, intranet, databases, telephone and video conferences, the sharing of tacit knowledge on a personal level is still a very reasonable – or even indispensable – approach. In fact, a combination of both a codification and a personalization strategy for marketing knowledge management in order to leverage both tacit and explicit knowledge proved highly successful and led to the co-creation of crucial marketing knowledge. Similarly, Hewlett Packard (HP) Consulting and Integration leverages both tacit and explicit marketing, sales and application knowledge from its field people – consultants and system engineers – through communities of practice and the process of knowledge co-creation through them (Kohlbacher and Mukai, 2007).

Last but not least, German conglomerate Siemens – like HP, frequently featured as a company with a strong background in knowledge management – leverages competitive advantage and new business opportunities through a cross-selling and marketing knowledge sharing and co-creation project that spans the boundaries of its different business divisions (Kohlbacher, 2007).

As for knowledge-based new product development management, Nonaka *et al.* (2006a) give an account of how Mazda enabled empathic design in developing the third generation Roadster Miata that won the Japan Car of the Year Award 2005/2006 (cf. also Kohlbacher, 2007). The product development team was indeed able to capture customer needs and translate them into a successful product concept because of their capacity to leverage even tacit customer needs and knowledge, and to achieve a high level of experience co-creation between the customers and the product. Finally, Maekawa Manufacturing Ltd – famous for its decentralized structures and project-based management approach (e.g. Peltokorpi and Tsuyuki, 2006) – found that producing and selling industrial parts is not enough any more. Through co-creation of common contexts and knowledge with its customers it was able to combine its products with its process knowledge to offer an integrated service including consulting. However, they do not simply offer pre-defined process and manufacturing models, but actively co-create the solutions together with their customers (Kohlbacher, 2007), an achievement that helped them to escape the red oceans of cutthroat competition and create new market space (blue ocean), yet "untainted by competition" (Kim and Mauborgne, 2004: 77). Indeed, as Prahalad and Ramaswamy (2004b: 12, original emphasis) state, the future of competition "lies in an altogether new approach to value creation, based on *an individual-centered co-creation of value between consumers and companies.*"

Even though discussing the concrete process of marketing knowledge co-creation in detail for each of these best practice companies would go beyond the scope of this chapter, it should have become clear that knowledge-based marketing and marketing knowledge (co-)creation can successfully be applied in practice and indeed lead to sustainable competitive advantage.

Conclusion

Building on Kohlbacher (2007), this chapter presented and discussed a knowledge-based approach to essential marketing processes and offered a model of marketing knowledge co-creation for generating innovation. However, as is the case with Nonaka's SECI process of organizational knowledge creation, it is important to note that there is no silver bullet or single right approach. Indeed, depending on each company's individual circumstances, the process may look different, and a particular knowledge-based approach to marketing will have to be developed and strategically managed. Nevertheless, at the least, the following five general conclusions can be drawn (cf. also Kohlbacher, 2007: 193–194):

- As knowledge has become a critical source for competitive advantage, marketing – and management in general – has to become knowledge-based.

- Marketing scholars and practitioners have focused too much on explicit marketing knowledge in the past. Combining and synthesizing both tacit and explicit knowledge and, subsequently, leveraging holistic marketing knowledge, is a sine qua non for corporate success and the source of innovation.
- Marketing knowledge needs to be co-created. Not only inside the firm, or across different units of a corporation, but also together with other stakeholders – most importantly customers, but also with suppliers, partners and competitors.
- Managers have to perceive their firms as interconnected in the global network economy, and thus have to take relationship marketing and the co-creation of knowledge and value with other entities in the business ecosystem seriously.
- Building, re-creating and sustaining organizational capital in the form of knowledge and knowledge-creating processes is a crucial driver of innovation.

Aligning a knowledge-based innovation strategy with the micro processes of generating and co-creating knowledge will be a major challenge for corporations in the network economy of the twenty-first century. As a result, organizational capital in the form of knowledge and knowledge-based marketing processes will become decisive for competitive advantage and thus corporate success and survival. Further research needs to be done to identify and analyze full-fledged best practices, but the "next practices" (Prahalad and Ramaswamy, 2004b) mentioned above show that at least some truly global, leading companies are on their best way to successfully implement and leverage knowledge-based marketing and marketing knowledge (co-)creation to gain and sustain competitive edge.

References

Achrol, R. S. and P. Kotler, 'Marketing in the network economy', *Journal of Marketing* 63(4) (1999), 146–62.

Ahmadjian, C. L., 'Inter-organizational knowledge creation: knowledge and networks', in H. Takeuchi and I. Nonaka (eds), *Hitotsubashi on knowledge management*, Singapore: John Wiley & Sons (Asia), 2004, 227–45.

Aoshima, Y. 'Transfer of system knowledge across generations in new product development: empirical observations from Japanese automobile development', *Industrial Relations*, 41(4) (2002) 605–28.

Baba, Y. and K. Nobeoka, 'Towards knowledge-based product development: the 3-d CAD model of knowledge creation', *Research Policy* 26(6) (1998) 643–59.

Badaracco, J. L. *The knowledge link: how firms compete through strategic alliances.* Boston: Harvard Business School Press, 1991.

Baker, W. E. and J. M. Sinkula, 'Market orientation and the new product paradox', *The Journal of Product Innovation Management* 22(6) (2005) 483–502.

Bell, S. J., G. J. Whitwell, and B. A. Lukas, 'Schools of thought in organizational learning', *Journal of the Academy of Marketing Science* 30(1) (2002) 70–86.

Benner, M. J. and M. L. Tushman, 'Exploitation, exploration, and process management: the productivity dilemma revisited', *Academy of Management Review* 28(2) (2003) 238–56.

Bennet, R. and H. Gabriel, 'Organisational factors and knowledge management within large marketing departments: an empirical study', *Journal of Knowledge Management* 3(3) (1999) 212–25.

Berry, L. L., L. P. Carbone, and S. H. Haeckel, 'Managing the total customer experience', *MIT Sloan Management Review* 43(3) (2002) 85–9.

Bjerre, M. and D. D. Sharma, 'Is marketing knowledge international? A case of key accounts', In A. Blomstermo and D. D. Sharma (eds), *Learning in the internationalisation process of firms*. Cheltenham: Edward Elgar, 2003, 123–41.

Bounfour, A., *The management of intangibles: the organisation's most valuable assets*. London: Routledge, 2003.

Brown, S. L. and K. M. Eisenhardt, 'The art of continuous change: linking complexity theory and time-paced evolution in relentlessly shifting organizations', *Administrative Science Quarterly* 42(1) (1997) 1–34.

Carbone, L. P. and S. H. Haeckel, 'Engineering customer experiences', *Marketing Management* 3(3) (1994) 8–19.

Cavusgil, S. T., R. J. Calantone, and Y. Zhao, 'Tacit knowledge transfer and firm innovation capability', *The Journal of Business and Industrial Marketing* 18(1) (2003) 6–21.

Chaston, I., *Knowledge-based marketing: the twenty-first century competitive edge*. Thousand Oaks: Sage Publications, 2004.

Chesbrough, H. W., *Open innovation: the new imperative for creating and profiting from technology*. Boston: Harvard Business School Press, 2003.

Chesbrough, H. W., *Open business models: how to thrive in the new innovation landscape*. Boston: Harvard Business School Press, 2006.

Cusumano, M. A. and K. Nobeoka, *Thinking beyond lean: how multi-project management is transforming product development at Toyota and other companies*. New York: The Free Press, 1998.

Cusumano, M. A. and A. Takeishi, 'Supplier relations and management: a survey of Japanese, Japanese transplants, and US Auto plants', *Strategic Management Journal* 12(8) (1991) 563–88.

Davenport, T. H., J. G. Harris, and A. K. Kohli, 'How do they know their customers so well?' *MIT Sloan Management Review* 42(2) (2001) 63–73.

Davenport, T. H. and P. Klahr, 'Managing customer support knowledge', *California Management Review* 40(3) (1998) 195–208.

Day, G. S., 'The capabilities of market-driven organizations', *Journal of Marketing* 58(4) (1994) 37–52.

Day, G. S., *The market driven organization: understanding, attracting, and keeping valuable customers*. New York: The Free Press, 1999.

Day, G. S. and D. B. Montgomery, 'Charting new directions for marketing', *Journal of Marketing* 63 (Special Issue) (1999) 3–13.

Desouza, K. C. and Y. Awazu, 'Gaining a competitive edge from your customers: exploring three dimensions of customer knowledge', *KM Review* 7(3) (2004) 12–15.

Desouza, K. C. and Y. Awazu, *Engaged knowledge management: engagement with new realities*. Basingstoke: Palgrave Macmillan, 2005.

Dixon, N. M., *Common knowledge: how companies thrive by sharing what they know*. Boston, MA: Harvard Business School Press, 2000.

Doz, Y., J. Santos, and P. Williamson, *From global to metanational: how companies win in the knowledge economy*. Boston: Harvard Business School Press, 2001.

Drucker, P. F., *Innovation and entrepreneurship: practice and principles*. New York: HarperCollins, 1985.

Dyer, J. H. and N. W. Hatch, 'Using supplier networks to learn faster', *MIT Sloan Management Review* 45(3) (2004) 57–63.

Dyer, J. H. and N. W. Hatch, 'Relation-specific capabilities and barriers to knowledge transfers: creating advantage through network relationships', *Strategic Management Journal* 27(8) (2006) 701–19.

Dyer, J. H. and K. Nobeoka, 'Creating and managing a high-performance knowledge-sharing network: the Toyota case', *Strategic Management Journal* 21(3) (2000) 345–67.

Easterby-Smith, M. and L. Araujo, 'Organizational learning: current debates and opportunities', in M. Easterby-Smith, L. Araujo and J. Burgoyne (eds), *Organizational learning and the learning organization: developments in theory and practice*. London: Sage, 1999, 1–21.

Eisenhardt, K. M. and J. A. Martin, 'Dynamic capabilities: what are they?' *Strategic Management Journal* 21(10/11) (2000) 1105–21.

Evans, P. and B. Wolf, 'Collaboration rules', *Harvard Business Review* 83(7/8) (2005) 96–104.

Furukawa, I., 'Shakaiteki nettowaku to maketingu (social networks and marketing)', in I. Nonaka (ed.), *Nettowaku bijinesu no kenkyu – fureai ga tsukuru kyokan komyuniti [network business research – empathy communities created through contacts]*. Tokyo: Nikkei BP, 1999a, 87–154.

Furukawa, I., *Deai no 'ba' no kosoryoku – maketingu to shouhi no 'chi' no shinka [the imagination of the meeting 'ba' – the evolution of marketing and consumption 'knowledge']*. Tokyo: Yuhikaku, 1999b.

Ghosn, C. and P. Riès, *Shift: inside Nissan's historic revival* (J. Cullen, trans.). New York: Currency Doubleday, 2005.

Gibbert, M., M. Leibold, and G. Probst, 'Five styles of customer knowledge management, and how smart companies use them to create value', *European Management Journal* 20(5) (2002) 459–69.

Glisby, M. and N. Holden, 'Applying knowledge management concepts to the supply chain: how a Danish firm achieved a remarkable breakthrough in Japan', *Academy of Management Executive*, 19(2) (2005) 85–9.

Gouillart, F. J. and F. D. Sturdivant, 'Spend a day in the life of your customers', *Harvard Business Review* 72(1) (1994) 116–25.

Grant, R. M., 'Prospering in dynamically-competitive environments: organizational capability as knowledge integration', *Organization Science* 7(4) (1996) 375–87.

Griffin, A. and J. R. Hauser, 'The voice of the customer', *Marketing Science* 12(1) (1993) 1–27.

Griffin, A. and J. R. Hauser, 'Integrating R&D and marketing: a review and analysis of the literature', *The Journal of Product Innovation Management* 13(3) (1996) 191–215.

Gulati, R. and J. B. Oldroyd, 'The quest for customer focus', *Harvard Business Review* 83(4) (2005) 92–101.

Gummesson, E., *Total relationship marketing*. Oxford: Butterworth-Heinemann, 2002.

Hanvanich, S., C. Dröge, and R. Calantone, 'Reconceptualizing the meaning and domain of marketing knowledge', *Journal of Knowledge Management* 7(4) (2003) 124–35.

He, Z.-L. and P.-K. Wong, 'Exploration vs. exploitation: an empirical test of the ambidexterity hypothesis', *Organization Science* 15(4) (2004) 481–94.

Henard, D. H. and D. M. Szymanski, 'Why some new products are more successful than others', *Journal of Marketing* 38(3) (2001) 362–75.

Iansiti, M., *Technological integration: making critical choices in a turbulent world*. Boston: Harvard Business School Press, 1997.

Iansiti, M. and K. B. Clark, 'Integration and dynamic capability: evidence from product development in automobiles and mainframe computers', *Industrial and Corporate Change* 3(3) (1994) 557–605.

Ichijo, K., 'Knowledge exploitation and knowledge exploration: two strategies for knowledge creating companies', in C. W. Choo and N. Bontis (eds), *The strategic management of intellectual capital and organizational knowledge*. New York: Oxford University Press, 2002, 477–83.

Ichijo, K., 'The strategic management of knowledge', in K. Ichijo and I. Nonaka (eds), *Knowledge creation and management: new challenges for managers*. New York: Oxford University Press, 2007, 121–45.

Ichijo, K. and F. Kohlbacher, *Toyota's global knowledge creation strategy*. Paper presented at the 49th Annual Meeting of the Academy of International Business (AIB). Indianapolis, 2007a.

Ichijo, K. and F. Kohlbacher, 'The Toyota way of global knowledge creation: the "learn local, act global" strategy', *International Journal of Automotive Technology and Management* 7(2/3) (2007b) 116–34.
Ichijo, K. and F. Kohlbacher, 'Tapping tacit local knowledge in emerging markets – the Toyota way', *Knowledge Management Research and Practice* 6(3) (2008) 173–86.
Imai, K.-i., I. Nonaka, and H. Takeuchi, 'Managing the new product development process: how Japanese companies learn und unlearn', in K. B. Clark and R. H. Hayes and C. Lorenz (eds), *The uneasy alliance: managing the productivity-technology dilemma*. Boston: Harvard Business School Press, 1985, 337–81.
Inkpen, A. C., 'Learning through alliances: General Motors and Nummi', *California Management Review* 47(4) (2005) 114–36.
Jansen, J. J. P., F. A. J. Van den Bosch, and H. W. Volberda, 'Exploratory innovation, exploitative innovation, and ambixterity: the impact of environmental and organizational antecedents', *Schmalenbach Business Review* 57(4) (2005) 351–63.
Kim, W. C. and R. Mauborgne, 'Blue ocean strategy', *Harvard Business Review* 82(10) (2004) 76–84.
Kogut, B. and U. Zander, 'Knowledge of the firm, combinative capabilities, and the replication of technology', *Organization Science* 3(3) (1992) 383–97.
Kohlbacher, F., '*Knowledge-based approaches to international marketing – in search of excellence*'. Paper presented at the IFSAM VIIIth World Congress, Berlin, 2006.
Kohlbacher, F., *International marketing in the network economy: a knowledge-based approach*. Basingstoke: Palgrave Macmillan, 2007.
Kohlbacher, F., N. J. Holden, M. Glisby, and A. Numic, *Knowledge-based approaches to international marketing: unleashing the power of tacit local and global knowledge to create competitive advantage*. Paper presented at the 49th Annual Meeting of the Academy of International Business (AIB), Indianapolis, 2007.
Kohlbacher, F. and K. Mukai, 'Japan's learning communities in Hewlett-Packard Consulting and Integration: challenging one-size fits all solutions', *The Learning Organization* 14(1) (2007) 8–20.
Konsynski, B. R. and F. W. McFarlan, 'Information partnerships: shared data, shared scale', *Harvard Business Review* 68(5) (1990) 114–20.
Kotler, P., D. C. Jain, and S. Maesincee, *Marketing moves: a new approach to profits, growth, and renewal*. Boston: Harvard Business School Press, 2002.
Kusunoki, K., I. Nonaka, and A. Nagata, 'Organizational capabilities in product development of Japanese firms: a conceptual framework and empirical findings', *Organization Science* 9(6) (1998) 699–718.
Kyriakopoulos, K. and C. Moorman, 'Tradeoffs in marketing exploitation and exploration strategies: the overlooked role of market orientation', *International Journal of Research in Marketing* 21(3) (2004) 219–40.
Lawer, C., *On customer knowledge co-creation and dynamic capabilities*. Working Paper, Cranfield School of Management (2005).
Leonard, D., *Wellsprings of knowledge: building and sustaining the sources of innovation*. Boston: Harvard Business School Press, 1998.
Leonard, D. and S. Sensiper, 'The role of tacit knowledge in group innovation', *California Management Review* 40(3) (1998) 112–32.
Leonard, D. and W. C. Swap, *When sparks fly: harnessing the power of group creativity*. Boston: Harvard Business School Press, 2005.
Leonard, D., 'Market research in product development', in K. Ichijo and I. Nonaka (eds), *Knowledge creation and management: new challenges for managers*. New York: Oxford University Press, 2007, 146–57.
Leonard-Barton, D., 'Core capabilities and core rigidities: a paradox in managing new product development', *Strategic Management Journal* 13(Special Issue) (1992) 111–25.
Levinthal, D. A. and J. G. March, 'The myopia of learning', *Strategic Management Journal* 14 (Winter Special Issue) (1993) 95–112.

Lewin, A. Y. and H. W. Volberda, 'Prolegomena on coevolution: a framework for research on strategy and new organizational forms', *Organization Science* 10(5) (1999) 519–34.

Li, T. and S. T. Cavusgil, 'Decomposing the effects of market knowledge competence in new product export', *European Journal of Marketing* 34(1/2) (1998) 57–79.

Liker, J. K., *The Toyota way: 14 management principles from the world's greatest manufacturer*. New York: McGraw-Hill, 2004.

Liker, J. K. and T. Y. Choi, 'Building deep supplier relationships', *Harvard Business Review* 82(12) (2004) 104–13.

Lincoln, J. R., C. L. Ahmadjian, and E. Mason, 'Organizational learning and purchase-supply relations in Japan: Hitachi, Matsushita, and Toyota compared', *California Management Review* 40(3) (1998) 241–64.

Lincoln, J. R., M. L. Gerlach, and C. L. Ahmadjian, '*Keiretsu* networks and corporate performance in Japan', *American Sociological Review* 61(1) (1996) 67–88.

Lincoln, J. R., M. L. Gerlach, and P. Takahashi, '*Keiretsu* networks in the Japanese economy: a dyad analysis of intercorporate ties', *American Sociological Review* 57(5) (1992) 561–85.

Lovelock, C. and E. Gummesson, 'Whither services marketing? In search of a new paradigm and fresh perspectives', *Journal of Service Research* 7(1) (2004) 20–41.

Madhavan, R. and R. Grover, 'From embedded knowledge to embodied knowledge: new product development as knowledge management', *Journal of Marketing* 62(4) (1998) 1–12.

March, J. G., 'Exploration and exploitation in organizational learning', *Organization Science* 2(1) (1991) 71–87.

Miller, K. D., M. Zhao, and R. Calantone, 'Adding interpersonal learning and tacit knowledge to march's exploration-exploitation model', *Academy of Management Journal* 49(4) (2006) 709–22.

Montoya-Weiss, M. and R. Calantone, 'Determinants of new product performance: a review and meta-analysis', *The Journal of Product Innovation Management* 11(5) (1994) 397–418.

Moorman, C., and A. S. Miner, 'The impact of organizational memory in new product performance and creativity', *Journal of Marketing Research* 34(1) (1997) 91–106.

Nobeoka, K. and M. A. Cusumano, 'Multiproject strategy and sales growth: the benefits of rapid design transfer in new product development', *Strategic Management Journal* 18(3) (1997) 169–86.

Nonaka, I., 'A dynamic theory of organizational knowledge creation', *Organization Science* 5(1) (1994) 14–34.

Nonaka, I., 'Foreword', in F. Kohlbacher, *International marketing in the network economy*. Basingstoke: Palgrave Macmillan, 2007, xi-xv.

Nonaka, I., F. Kohlbacher, and N. Holden, *Aging and innovation: recreating and refining high-quality tacit knowledge through phronetic leadership*. Paper presented at the 66th Annual Academy of Management Meeting, Critical Management Studies Research Workshop, Managing the Aging Workforce: Leadership Towards a New Weltanschauung, August 11–16, 2006, Atlanta, USA, 2006a.

Nonaka, I. and H. Takeuchi, *The knowledge-creating company: how Japanese companies create the dynamics of innovation*. New York: Oxford University Press, 1995.

Nonaka, I., H. Takeuchi, and K. Umemoto, 'A theory of organizational knowledge creation', *International Journal of Technology Management* 11(7/8) (1996) 833–45.

Nonaka, I. and R. Toyama, 'The theory of the knowledge-creating firm: subjectivity, objectivity, and synthesis', *Industrial and Corporate Change* 14(3) (2005) 419–36.

Nonaka, I., R. Toyama, and N. Konno, 'SECI, ba and leadership: A unified model of dynamic knowledge creation', *Long Range Planning* 33(1) (2000) 1–31.

Nonaka, I., G. von Krogh, and S. C. Voelpel, 'Organizational knowledge creation theory: evolutionary paths and future advances', *Organization Studies* 27(8) (2006b) 1179–208.

O'Reilly III, C. A. and M. L. Tushman, 'The ambidextrous organization', *Harvard Business Review* 82(4) (2004) 74–81.

Peltokorpi, V. and E. Tsuyuki, 'Knowledge governance in a Japanese project-based organization', *Knowledge Management Research and Practice* 4(1) (2006) 36–45.

Pine II, B. J. and J. H. Gilmore, *The experience economy: work is theatre and every business a stage*. Boston: Harvard Business School Press, 1999.

Prahalad, C. K. and V. Ramaswamy, 'Co-opting customer competence', *Harvard Business Review* 78(1) (2000) 79–87.

Prahalad, C. K. and V. Ramaswamy, 'The new frontier of experience innovation', *MIT Sloan Management Review* 44(4) (2003) 12–18.

Prahalad, C. K. and V. Ramaswamy, 'Co-creation experiences: the next practice in value creation', *Journal of Interactive Marketing* 18(3) (2004a) 5–14.

Prahalad, C. K. and V. Ramaswamy, *The future of competition: co-creating unique value with customers*. Boston: Harvard Business School Press, 2004b.

Riesenberger, J. R., 'Executive insights: knowledge – the source of sustainable competitive advantage', *Journal of International Marketing* 6(3) (1998) 94–107.

Santos, J., Y. Doz, and P. Williamson, 'Is your innovation process global?' *MIT Sloan Management Review* 45(4) (2004) 31–7.

Sawhney, M., 'Don't just relate – collaborate', *MIT Sloan Management Review* 43(3) (2002) 96.

Sawhney, M. and E. Prandelli, 'Communities of creation: managing distributed knowledge in turbulent times', *California Management Review* 42(4) (2000a) 24–54.

Sawhney, M. and E. Prandelli, 'Beyond customer knowledge management: customers as knowledge co-creators', in Y. Malhotra (ed.), *Knowledge management and virtual organizations*. Hershey: Idea Group Publishing, 2000b, 258–82.

Schlegelmilch, B. B. and T. C. Chini, 'Knowledge transfer between marketing functions in multinational companies: a conceptual model', *International Business Review* 12(2) (2003) 215–32.

Schlegelmilch, B. B. and E. Penz, 'Knowledge management in marketing', *The Marketing Review* 3(1) (2002) 5–19.

Schulze, A. and M. Hoegl, 'Knowledge creation in new product development projects', *Journal of Management* 32(2) (2006) 210–36.

Song, X. M. and M. E. Parry, 'How the Japanese manage the R&D-marketing interface', *Research Technology Management* 36(4) (1993) 32–8.

Song, X. M. and M. E. Parry, 'The determinants of Japanese new product successes', *Journal of Marketing Research* 34(1) (1997) 64–77.

Spear, S., 'Learning to lead at Toyota', *Harvard Business Review* 82(5) (2004) 78–86.

Spear, S. and H. K. Bowen, 'Decoding the DNA of the Toyota production system', *Harvard Business Review* 77(5) (1999) 96–106.

Srivastava, R. K., T. A. Shervani, and L. Fahey, 'Marketing, business processes, and shareholder value: an organizationally embedded view of marketing activities and discipline of marketing', *Journal of Marketing* 63 (Special Issue) (1999) 168–79.

Takeuchi, H. and I. Nonaka, 'The new new product development game', *Harvard Business Review* 64(1) (1986) 137–46.

Taylor, C., 'To follow a rule', in C. Calhoun, E. LiPuma and M. Postone (eds), *Bourdieu: critical perspectives*. Cambridge: Polity Press, 1993, 45–60.

Teece, D. J., 'Capturing value from knowledge assets: the new economy, markets for know-how, and intangible assets', *California Management Review* 40(3) (1998) 55–79.

Teece, D. J., G. Pisano, and A. Shuen, 'Dynamic capabilities and strategic management', *Strategic Management Journal* 18(7) (1997) 509–33.

Thomke, S. H., *Experimentation matters: unlocking the potential of new technologies for innovation*. Boston: Harvard Business School Press, 2003.

Thomke, S. H. and E. von Hippel, 'Customers as innovators: a new way to create value', *Harvard Business Review* 80(4) (2002) 74–81.

Tushman, M. L. and C. A. O'Reilly III, 'Ambidextrous organizations: managing evolutionary and revolutionary change', *California Management Review* 38(4) (1996) 8–30.

Vandenbosch, M. and N. Dawar, 'Beyond better products: capturing value in customer interactions', *MIT Sloan Management Review* 43(4) (2002) 35–42.

Vandermerwe, S., 'Achieving deep customer focus', *MIT Sloan Management Review* 45(3) (2004) 26–34.

Vicari, S. and P. Cillo, 'Developing a brokering capacity within the firm: the enactment of market knowledge', in B. Renzl, K. Matzler and H. Hinterhuber (eds), *The future of knowledge management*. Basingstoke: Palgrave Macmillan, 2006, 184–204.

von Hippel, E., 'Lead users: a source of novel product concepts', *Management Science* 32(7) (1986) 791–806.

von Hippel, E., 'Sticky information and the locus of problem-solving: implications for innovations', *Management Science* 40(4) (1994) 429–39.

von Hippel, E. A., 'Has a customer already developed your next product?' *Sloan Management Review* 18(2) (1977) 63–74.

von Krogh, G., K. Ichijo, and I. Nonaka, *Enabling knowledge creation: how to unlock the mystery of tacit knowledge and release the power of innovation*. New York: Oxford University Press, 2000.

Wayland, R. E. and P. M. Cole, *Customer connections: new strategies for growth*. Boston: Harvard Business School Press, 1997.

Wikström, S., 'The customer as co-producer', *European Journal of Marketing* 30(4) (1996) 6–19.

Wikström, S. and R. Norman, *Knowledge and value: a new perspective on corporate transformation*. London: Routledge, 1994.

Zack, M. H., 'Rethinking the knowledge-based organization', *MIT Sloan Management Review* 44(4) (2003) 67–71.

Zaltman, G., *How customers think: essential insights into the mind of the market*. Boston: Harvard Business School Press, 2003.

13 Organisational capital and competence building

Anjali Bakhru

Introduction

The terms 'knowledge economy' or 'knowledge society' have become increasingly accepted, and form part of the management lexicon as recognition grows of the valuable role that intangible assets and knowledge perform in firm success. The challenge of managing and developing these assets is nevertheless a real and complex task. Those assets which potentially contribute the most value to firms are often difficult to measure, given that they are intangible and even difficult to identify because of their lack of visibility. While the heightened importance and role of intellectual property is emphasised within a knowledge economy, less transparent is the value of knowledge, which tends to be more tacit and bound up with individuals in the performance of their specific task roles. Given that the value of these assets is increasingly assumed in respect of their realised and potential contribution to competitive advantage, the focus of this chapter is the means through which firms manage and develop their 'organisational capital' over time.

In order to address this issue, two perspectives on organisational capital are provided. First, an intellectual capital approach illustrates that research has begun to adopt a dynamic perspective. While the traditional emphasis has been on assessing and measuring an organisation's intellectual capital, there is increasing appreciation of the need to explore the means through which organisational capital and its constituent knowledge stocks can be developed and enhanced over time. The second perspective presented here is a capabilities-based perspective, which is rooted in the resource-based view. A dynamic approach is implicit in a capabilities-based perspective with the emphasis on organisational process. Given the centrality of organisational adaptation and change to sustaining competitive advantage from a resource-based perspective, recent work on dynamic capabilities directly addresses the issue of ongoing competence development needed for organisational adaptation and renewal.

Identifying organisational capital

The term 'organisational capital' is sometimes used interchangeably with the term 'intellectual capital'. Typically, an intellectual capital approach emphasises the value of knowledge in its different forms and applications within the organisation. Bontis (2002), for example, defines a firm's intellectual capital as the stock of its human capital, its structural capital and its relational capital. Human capital is referred to as the knowledge that is embedded within individuals, and which often proves difficult to codify. The implication is that the value of human capital is the tacit knowledge of individuals, which affects how tasks are carried out and ultimately task performance itself. In contrast, structural capital is the knowledge that is embedded within an organisation's processes and procedures, and which is therefore more likely to be codified, such as in the form of operating manuals or hard-coded in software and systems. And finally, the third type of capital identified is relational capital. It refers to the knowledge that can be gleaned externally from customers, suppliers, the government or trade and industry associations and, hence, it represents the potential of 'ex-firm intangibles'.

While there is broad agreement over the value to firms of their organisational or intellectual capital, there exists some divergence in the underlying meaning of these terms. For example, organisational capital is used also to denote a specific categorisation of knowledge similar in meaning to structural capital above. Subramaniam and Youndt (2005: 451) refer to organisational capital as 'the institutionalised knowledge and codified experience residing within and utilized through databases, patents, manuals, structures, systems and processes'. Alternatively, organisational capital is used to refer to a specific group of elements. Martin-de-Castro *et al.* (2006), for example, refer to organisational capital as comprising the culture, structure, and organisational learning of a firm. While the former definition focuses on organisational knowledge, the latter encompasses all the tangible and intangible elements of an organisation through which knowledge is both developed and transferred over time. In other words, definitions of intellectual or organisational capital highlight the value of a number of intangible assets and knowledge-based assets – from the corporate culture, which affects both the actions and behaviours of employees, to the knowledge embodied in an organisation's intellectual property. The problem facing managers and researchers is a complex one. Terms such as 'organisational capital', for example, are not uniformly defined and interpreted, and different elements of intellectual capital are likely to vary in importance across firms and even over time. The further difficulty lies, therefore, in identifying the competences organisations need in order to develop their intellectual or organisational capital.

Linking organisational capital to competitive advantage

Common to both an intellectual capital perspective and a capabilities perspective is the resource-based view, which highlights the link between a firm's intangible assets and its competitive advantage. From the 1980s to the present day, the contribution of intangible assets to the value of publicly-traded companies is estimated to have doubled. In the case of American companies, for example, it is estimated to have grown from forty per cent to seventy-five per cent.[1] Consideration of competitive advantage in a dynamic context suggests, however, that the notion of sustainability is a limited one, and it is widely accepted that there is a need to 'innovate or die' for success in a knowledge economy. The innovation implicit in organisational adaptation is likely to depend, in part, on the firm's intellectual capital or knowledge assets. The implication is, therefore, that an imperative exists to both enhance and renew the firm's intellectual capital base.

Bontis' (2002) definition of intellectual capital suggests that knowledge might be considered to be a category both separate from, as well as integral to, a firm's intangible assets, given that much potentially valuable knowledge is that which is not codified and tends to be embedded in individuals rather than in systems, or protected in the form of intellectual property. While structural capital focuses on the systems and processes through which knowledge can be stored, human and relational capital are distinguished by the fact that both types of capital can be considered to be both a source of knowledge and, importantly, a source for renewal. Bontis (2002: 631) explains that the importance of human capital lies in the fact that 'it is a source of innovation and strategic renewal, whether it is from brainstorming in a research lab, daydreaming at the office, throwing out old files, reengineering new processes, improving personal skills, or developing new leads in a sales representative's little black book'. In other words, human capital is not only a stock of knowledge, but also a source of knowledge renewal, since the essence of human capital is the underlying intelligence of the individual. The challenge is, nevertheless, to identify whether there are any general or specific competences of individuals which are more valuable than others.

The value of entrepreneurial skills, given the role of entrepreneurship in idea generation and business opportunity recognition, is recognised as a force for exploration, even within established organisations (Shane, 2000; Alvarez and Busenitz, 2001). It is within research on entrepreneurship that there has been an attempt to link venture success to individual competences and to identify whether successful entrepreneurs share common personality characteristics. Typical of this approach are studies such as that of Markman and Bacon (2003), which shows that the most successful entrepreneurs are those exhibiting the characteristics of self-efficacy, opportunity recognition, personal perseverance, human and social capital, and superior social skills. The implications of such research for organisations operating in a knowledge economy are self-explanatory. Depending on the degree to which these characteristics are innate to individuals, organisations might seek to adopt certain selection criteria in employee recruitment or to favour training instead. However, the characteristics identified also serve to demonstrate the vagueness with which terms such as 'human capital' and 'social capital' are used. While the value of human capital could be considered to relate, in part, to the entrepreneurial abilities of individuals, Markman and Bacon (2003) suggest that entrepreneurial abilities are, in turn, a function of the human and social capital of individuals. In other words, human and social capital are sometimes considered a requirement as well as an outcome of competence development.

Within the literature, there have also been studies that have aimed to address directly the role of intellectual capital, and to assess the link between a firm's intellectual capital and its ability to innovate. Subramaniam and Youndt (2005) acknowledge that, while the link between knowledge and innovation is widely-accepted, there is little understanding of how knowledge links to specific capabilities. Conducting a longitudinal, US-based study across a diverse sample of 93 organisations, they assess how the human, organisational and social capital elements of intellectual capital affect innovation. The theoretical basis of this study relates to the fact that different types of knowledge affect an organisation's ability to innovate incrementally or radically. It is argued that organisational capital is conducive to incremental innovation, since it refers to knowledge which is codified and preserved via an organisation's systems and processes, and is likely to reinforce existing knowledge rather than transform it. Social capital, as represented by the role of group or team work, enables interaction and an exchange of ideas and, hence, serves to refine knowledge; while human capital is most likely to transform knowledge on the basis that individuals are themselves likely to be the dominant source of new knowledge within organisations. Their findings support the role of organisational capital in enabling incremental innovation, although social and human capital have a positive effect on radical innovation only in combination. The interactive effect between social and human capital reinforces prior research on the role of individuals as the source of new knowledge (Grant, 1996) and highlights their role in the transfer of new knowledge prior to the development of routines and capabilities (Bakhru, 2004). A primary benefit of this approach is that it specifies the role played by different types of capital in enabling organisational adaptation. Its disadvantage is that it is less conclusive in terms of identifying the specific competences that underpin and augment the different types of capital. For example, in Subramaniam and Youndt's (2005) study, constructs for the different types of capital are subjective and rely on respondent perceptions to statements such as 'our employees are highly skilled' and 'our employees are creative and bright' in respect of human capital. However, this research suggests that value is realised through the interaction and interdependency between different types of intellectual or organisational capital.

While the traditional focus of research on intellectual capital is on assessing and measuring different types of intellectual capital, research is increasingly reflecting the need to account for the complex operational reality of organisations. Marr (2006), for example, discusses not only the interdependencies and interactions of intangible assets with each other, but also with the tangible assets in which they might be embedded. While this further highlights the difficulties of identifying specific competencies, it directly acknowledges that elements of a firm's intellectual capital base are not productively valuable in isolation. As it will be shown, the advantage of a capabilities perspective is that it directly addresses the issue of resource co-ordination and combination with a focus on process.

A capabilities perspective

Similar to research on intellectual capital, research relating to the RBV continues to assess the contribution of valuable resources to competitive advantage (Ahuja and Katila, 2004; Dutta *et al.*, 2005; Ethiraj *et al.*, 2005). The origins of the

RBV lie in the VRIN approach developed by Barney (1991), which argues that competitive advantage is attributable to those resources which are valuable, rare, inimitable and non-substitutable. Value is ultimately associated with inimitability, and the most valuable resources are likely to be those intangible resources which are harder to imitate, such as an organisation's brand, its corporate culture or its intellectual property. At the same time, the existence of causal ambiguity and the role of path dependency in the development of organisational capabilities over time points to the potentially more enduring advantage provided by capabilities, where capabilities refer to the capacity at an organisational level to perform a specific task or group of tasks (Grant, 1991). Research on new market entry and research on firm diversification (Chandler, 1992; Grant, 1988, 1996; Klepper and Simons, 2000; Markides and Williamson, 1994) illustrates the value of existing capabilities in terms of the ability to leverage and replicate existing capabilities to a new business or in the application of prior learned experience to a new setting. Klepper and Simons (2000) show that successful pioneers in the US television industry were those entrants who could build on complementary capabilities and apply the experience they had acquired within the radio industry. This highlights the critical role of capabilities in enabling organisational adaptation, which is necessary for survival in the long term at least.

Organisational change is an inevitable and ongoing challenge faced by organisations. Miller and Shamsie's (1995) study of the Hollywood film studios showed how, during a period of environmental stability from 1936 to 1950, property-based resources were valuable, with the emphasis on film production on-site in studios, film distribution through owned chains of movie theatres, and film stars employed on long-term contracts. From the 1950s, the situation altered as the industry experienced significant environmental uncertainty following the disbandment of movie theatre chains in light of an anti-trust ruling. Knowledge-based resources came to be valued more highly as teams of production staff and film stars were brought together on a project basis and films were shot on location. The study showed that the firms that prospered in each period were those with the requisite endowment of either property-based or knowledge-based resources. While some environmental shifts can be considered to be significant (requiring radical innovation), such as in the case of the Hollywood film industry, many more require the level of adaptation associated with incremental innovation. For many firms, for example, entry into online markets left existing business models intact, requiring only the addition of a front-end web interface for customers to transact online. Innovation, from a capabilities perspective, is clearly focused on an organisation's ability to adapt. Over a period of time, a firm's ability to innovate requires consideration of an organisation's capabilities and its capacity to alter these as an addition to the entrepreneurial mindset emphasised from an intellectual capital approach.

Throughout the literature, there is recognition of a paradox in relation to capabilities – while capabilities are critical in enabling change, the ability to change or adapt capabilities themselves is viewed as fraught with difficulties, since capabilities are subject to the constraints of path dependency as well as structural and cognitive inertia. The challenge is therefore to consider how to make them more dynamic, and the appeal of 'dynamic capabilities' as a concept is thus as a means of overcoming the rigidities inherent in adapting capabilities. From a competence-building perspective, however, it is possible to overlook the fact that we often need only to improve our capabilities rather than change them in any significant way. Capabilities are not finite, and the degree to which they are developed is largely a matter of managerial deliberation, subject to satisficing criteria linked to firm performance (Winter, 2000). Helfat and Peteraf's (2003) discussion of a 'capability life cycle' serves to reinforce the notion that capabilities evolve over time through various stages such as birth, growth and decline. However, what we understand about the capability development process itself is a matter of degree, given that research in this area has been less systematic, particularly in relation to providing empirical verification at the micro process level (Bakhru, 2007). One exception is Montealegre's (2002) study, which demonstrates how development of a capability in e-commerce at a stock exchange itself relied upon the existence of other key resources and capabilities. Specific capabilities that formed a pre-requisite for development during different stages included a capability to strategise, a capability to be flexible and, finally, a capability to integrate and engender trust. The need for strategic integration, for example, involved a number of tasks, including combining the various business and personal skills and functional backgrounds of managers to create revenue-producing products and services, while at the same time ensuring integration with existing organisational processes. In turn, the capability to integrate was itself facilitated by the exchange's long-term view, information technology and organisational culture, as well as by specific actions directed toward gaining internal commitment and investing in complementary infrastructure. In other words, competence-building itself requires integration of a range of other key capabilities and resources to support the development process.

Dynamic capabilities

A dynamic capabilities perspective is an extension of a capabilities approach and, as stated, its appeal lies in its potential to offer a panacea to resolving the rigidities inherent in capabilities over time and therefore as an attempt to make capabilities more dynamic. While capabilities are the means through which resources are configured, dynamic capabilities can be considered to be the means through which resources and capabilities are reconfigured and, hence, are central to competence-building over time. The focus is on the processes directed towards effecting change. In line with a capabilities approach, a dynamic capabilities approach advocates that competitive advantage cannot be sustained but rather that it needs to be renewed. As such, dynamic capabilities cannot be a source of sustained competitive advantage but rather the source of renewing competitive advantage. Teece *et al.*'s (1997) original conceptualisation of dynamic capabilities stemmed from an interest in explaining how organisations can create and sustain competitive advantage in dynamic or rapidly changing environments. The ability of organisations to reconfigure themselves is not left to chance, they argue, but that it is a learned skill. The field has developed as research has attempted to refine and develop our understanding of what dynamic capabilities are.

A patterned element of activity is emphasised in the dynamic capabilities literature (Helfat *et al.*, 2007). Since Teece *et al.*'s (1997) seminal paper, two main approaches to dynamic capabilities have been outlined, where one approach is distinguished by its attempt to describe mechanisms of making capabilities more dynamic, while another focuses on a routinised approach to change (see also Schreyögg and Kliesch-Eberl, 2007). According to the former approach developed by Eisenhardt and Martin (2000), dynamic capabilities are viewed as specific and identifiable processes. In moderately stable markets, dynamic capabilities take on the appearance of other organisational capabilities, i.e. new product development, strategic decision-making and alliancing. Commonalities in practice across firms and even best practice across firms suggests that dynamic capabilities might even share key features across firms. Alternatively, it is argued that dynamic capabilities resemble a routinised approach to change, with routines created for the specific purpose of adapting existing operational routines (Zollo and Winter, 2002; Winter, 2003). As Zollo and Winter (2002: 340) state, 'dynamic capability is exemplified by an organisation that adapts its operating processes through a relatively stable activity dedicated to process improvements'.

Both approaches emphasise the deliberate and managed process of creating dynamic capabilities, at least in relatively stable environments. Under conditions of high environmental volatility, however, both approaches break down somewhat and show greater convergence. In more dynamic markets, the means required to respond to change are likely to operate on the basis of simple rules developed (Eisenhardt and Martin, 2000) or to rely on *ad hoc* rather than routinised processes (Zollo and Winter, 2002). The implication for competence building is, therefore, that firms rely to a greater extent on improvisation, experimentation and problem-solving in more volatile environments. We can infer that the challenge of responding to change, in terms of competence building, becomes more difficult when we need to change most.

An empirical study aimed at 'unbundling' the concept of dynamic capability is that of Verona and Ravasi (2003), who researched Oticon (a Danish hearing aid manufacturer). The company is renowned for its capacity to develop and launch new products and, since the introduction of new products is one of the primary drivers of change and renewal at the firm level, the study focuses on Oticon's dynamic capability in product development and the knowledge-based processes which underpin them. The findings illustrate the importance of leveraging resources such as other actors, physical resources, the structure and systems, as well as the company culture. It further highlights the importance of knowledge in engendering dynamic capabilities, and ensuring knowledge integration and the associated management of knowledge resources. While organisational structure assumes importance for creating flexibility, where this was achieved through the firm's project-based organisation, it was notably the absence of other physical and structural barriers within the firm that allowed the integration of knowledge that would otherwise be dispersed across the organisation.

The debate over the form and substance of dynamic capabilities continues. In line with prior research, Helfat *et al.* (2007:1) define dynamic capability as 'the capacity of an organisation to purposefully create, extend or modify its resource base'. In a departure from prior research, they extend the conceptualisation of dynamic capabilities. They argue that dynamic capabilities come in many forms, albeit directed at effecting change: they allow firms to enter new businesses, extend old businesses, and create new products and processes. They also further refer to the leadership and entrepreneurial capabilities of individual managers as part of an organisation's dynamic capability set, as well as the concept of relational capabilities, which enables firms to access the resources and capabilities of alliance partners. The notion of dynamic capabilities referred to by Helfat *et al.* (2007) is an increasingly abstract one. The latter are no longer defined as specific organisational processes themselves, but rather they rely on organisational processes for their fulfilment. However, this development is therefore a move closer to an intellectual capital perspective as knowledge and, in particular, access to the knowledge of individuals as well as organisations is increasingly accentuated in relation to competence development.

Discussion and conclusions

The aim of this chapter has been to approach the topic of competence-building in relation to organisational capital from two different perspectives. Both an intellectual capital and a capabilities approach share much in common, particularly in relation to the contribution of intangible assets and knowledge to an organisation's competitive advantage. The complexity of the challenge of identifying those competences which are relevant and important to renewing and developing valuable organisational capital is highlighted in both approaches and demonstrates increasing convergence in approach. While there is need for more systematic empirical research, studies to date demonstrate that any attempt to build a competence in one area itself relies on the combination and co-ordination of other resources and capabilities across the organisation. Underpinning competence or capability development is the assumption that a system of integrated skills is required to leverage the organisation's capital. From an intellectual capital perspective, the challenge is approached more directly in relation to the task of knowledge renewal. It supports the need for competence development at the individual as well as the organisational level, where the focus relates ultimately to the means through which organisations are able to create and renew their knowledge assets. Recent advances in relation to dynamic capabilities, however, also point to the importance of integrating knowledge at the level of the individual as well as the organisation, since the leadership and entrepreneurial capabilities of individual managers are increasingly considered to be part of an organisation's dynamic capability set (Helfat *et al.*, 2007). In conclusion, prior research highlights that competence building is reliant upon effective management of the complex interaction of individual and organisational level knowledge, and that it is important to focus on ensuring that firm processes are designed to provide the means through which dispersed knowledge can be integrated across the organisation.

Note

1 'A market for ideas – A survey of patents and technology', *The Economist*, October 2005.

References

Ahuja, G. and R. Katila (2004) 'Where do resources come from? The role of idiosyncratic situations', *Strategic Management Journal*, 25: 887–907.

Alvarez, S. A. and L. W. Busenitz (2001) 'The entrepreneurship of resource-based theory', *Journal of Management*, 27: 755–75.

Bakhru, A. (2004) 'Managerial knowledge to organisational capability: new e-commerce businesses', *Journal of Intellectual Capital*, 5(2): 326–36.

Bakhru, A. (2007) 'Creating and developing organisational capabilities – do we know more than we can say?', *International Journal of Learning and Intellectual Capital, Special Issue on Twenty Years after The Resource-Based Theory of the Firm: New Challenges*, 4(1/2): 174–86.

Barney, J. B. (1991) 'Firm resources and sustained competitive advantage', *Journal of Management*, 17(1): 99–120.

Bontis, N. (2002). 'Managing organizational knowledge by diagnosing intellectual capital: framing and advancing the state of the field', in C. W. Choo and N. Bontis (eds) *The Strategic Management of Intellectual Capital and Organizational Knowledge*, Oxford, Oxford University Press.

Chandler, A. (1992) 'Organizational capabilities and the economic history of the industrial enterprise', *Journal of Economic Perspectives*, 6(3): 79–100.

Dutta, S., O. M. Narasimhan and S. Rajiv (2005) 'Conceptualizing and measuring capabilities: methodology and empirical application', *Strategic Management Journal*, 26: 277–85.

Eisenhardt, K. M. and J. A. Martin (2000) 'Dynamic capabilities: what are they?', *Strategic Management Journal*, 21: 1105–21.

Ethiraj, S. K., P. Kale, M. S. Krishnan and J. V. Singh (2005) 'Where do capabilities come from and how do they matter? A study in the software services industry', *Strategic Management Journal*, 26: 25–45.

Feldman, M. S. (2000) 'Organizational routines as a source of continuous change', *Organization Science*, 11(6): 611–29.

Grant, R. M. (1988) 'On "dominant logic", relatedness and the link between diversity and performance', *Strategic Management Journal*, 9: 639–42.

Grant, R. M. (1996) 'Prospering in dynamically-competitive environments: organizational capability as knowledge integration', *Organization Science*, 7(4): 375–87.

Helfat, C. E. and M. A. Peteraf (2003) 'The dynamic resource-based view: capability lifecycles', *Strategic Management Journal*, 24: 997–1010.

Klepper, S. and K. L. Simons (2000) 'Dominance by birthright: entry of prior radio producers and competitive ramifications in the US television receiver industry', *Strategic Management Journal*, 21(10/11): 997–1016.

Markides, C. and P. J.Williamson (1994) 'Related diversification, core competencies and corporate performance', *Strategic Management Journal*, 15(5):149–65.

Markman, G. D. and R. A. Bacon (2003) 'Person-entrepreneurship fit: why some people are more successful as entrepreneurs than others', *Human Resource Management Journal*, 13(2): 281–301.

Marr, B. (2006). 'Using strategic value creation maps to visualize intangible performance drivers', in A. Bonfour (ed.) *Capital Immateriel, Connaissance et Performance*, Paris, L'Harmattan.

Martin-de-Castro, G., J. E. Navas-Lopez, P. Lopez-Saez and E. Alama-Salazar (2006) 'Organizational capital as competitive advantage of the firm', *Journal of Intellectual Capital*, 7(3): 324–37.

Miller, D. and J. Shamsie (1995). 'A contingent application of the resource-based view of the firm: the Hollywood studios', *Academy of Management Best Papers Proceedings*, pp. 57–61.

Montealegre, R. (2002) 'A process model of capability development: lessons from the electronic commerce strategy at Bolsa de Valores de Guayaquil', *Organization Science*, 13(5): 514–31.

Schreyögg, G. and M. Kliesch-Eberl (2007). 'How dynamic can organizational capabilties be? Towards a dual-process model of capability development', *Strategic Management Journal*, 28: 913–33.

Shane, S. (2000) 'Prior knowledge and the discovery of entrepreneurial opportunities', *Strategic Management Journal*, 11: 448–69.

Shane, S. (2003) *A General Theory of Entrepreneurship: the individual-opportunity nexus*, Cheltenham, Edward Elgar.

Subramaniam, M. and M. A. Youndt (2005) 'The influence of intellectual capital on the types of innovative capabilities', *Academy of Management Journal*, 48(3): 450–63.

Teece, D., G. Pisano and A. Shuen (1997) 'Dynamic capabilities and strategic management', *Strategic Management Journal*, 18: 509–33.

Verona, G. and D. Ravasi (2003) 'Unbundling dynamic capabilities: an exploratory study of continuous product innovation', *Industrial and Corporate Change*, 12(3): 577–606.

Winter, S. G. (2000) 'The satisficing principle in capability learning', *Strategic Management Journal*, 21: 981–96.

Winter, S. G. (2003) 'Understanding dynamic capabilities', *Strategic Management Journal*, 24: 991–5.

Zollo, M. and S. G. Winter (2002) 'Deliberate learning and the evolution of dynamic capabilities', *Organization Science*, 13(3): 339–51.

14 IT, organisational capital and the reporting (measurement) issue

Ahmed Bounfour

To what extent does organisational capital present a value in euros, dollars or any other currency for a company, and, more generally, at the macroeconomic level? If organisational capital creates value, then we need to better measure it and report on it. The previous chapters developed different *facettes* of organisational capital and organisational design in the knowledge economy. In this chapter I will mainly review some of the results of the literature, especially those focusing on IT and organisational processes as sources of value for companies. In the last section, I will present a framework that might be used by companies and policy makers for reporting on organisational capital. This framework has to be considered by taking into account the general *acquis* of the intangible research movement over the last fifteen years. But let's consider, as a starting point, the arguments developed by Nicolas Carr when he talks about IT as a commodity, which therefore does not create value, meaning implicitly that value creation has to be looked for somewhere in idiosyncratic processes. But, as we will see later, organisational processes and IT are inseparable twins, and therefore we have to be very cautious about any argument putting forward the general commoditisation of such a huge investment.

But let's start by considering Carr's arguments, and comparing them to those of some of his opponents, and later on to the academic production on IT, organisational processes and performance.

In his famous article in *Harvard Business Review*, 'IT Doesn't Matter', Nicolas Carr (2003) develops a hypothesis he sees as reasonable, if not as intuitive (p. 6): as information technologies gain ubiquity, their strategic importance decreases: they are becoming increasingly 'commodities'. According to Carr, the essence of what constitutes a competitive advantage is not the ubiquity of a resource, but its rarity. This echoes an argument largely put forward by the strategic literature over the last fifteen years.

Let us consider his arguments in detail.

The author first develops a historical perspective, considering the dynamics of revolutions that have shaped the industry over the past two centuries: that of the steam engine, the railroads, the telegraph and telephone, then the explosion engine. Information technology is the last of them. As these technologies popularise, they become trivialised inputs, and hence thereby lose their unique character. According to Carr, this should be the same for information technology.

The author introduces a distinction between 'proprietary technologies' and 'infrastructure technology'. The former must be the subject to control by a single enterprise, typically via a patent, and can therefore generate a rent, while the latter does not have a unique character and merit to be shared with others (for reasons of efficiency of production). During its early stages of construction, however, the infrastructure technology can be likened to a proprietary technology and thus ensures a rent to the first user(s).

Despite their complexity, information technologies are to be associated with infrastructure technologies. They deserve widespread networking. For the author, the benefits of adaptation of these technologies to enterprises are largely outweighed by the costs of insulation (p. 8). The 'commoditisation' of information technology has been greatly accelerated by the internet. Based on these arguments, what should companies do?

Carr tells us that the more technology is becoming widespread, the more it becomes less relevant to the strategy (as is the case today with electricity). As for him, the real risk that companies have to bear is an overinvestment in IT.

According to Carr, three basic rules should be observed by managers:

- spend less;
- be followers rather than leaders;
- focus attention on vulnerabilities rather than on opportunities.

These arguments of Carr's have been challenged during the debate organised by *Harvard Business Review* in the June issue of 2003, immediately following the May issue in which Carr's paper was published. The arguments put forward by Carr's opponents can be summarised as follows:

Creating value from IT can be done only by the transformation of managerial practices. The needs of processing and related transaction costs are often underestimated by companies. The incremental innovation is important, and the gap between the potential of IT and the reality of organisational innovations has increased considerably in recent years (Brown and Hagel III).

- For managers, what is important is the economy of information technology, according to Moore's law, in particular the intangible elements (services) that they can provide to its users. Innovation gives an advantage to the innovator. For the leaders, it is important to consider both cost control, but also the organisational and networking aspects allowed by the information technology (McFarlan, Nolan).
- Carr's assertions (information technologies have no strategic value, information technologies are 'commodities', etc.) have no empirical foundation, and attest to a misunderstanding of the complexity of IT functionalities. The comparison with electricity – a homogeneous product – is pejorative and inappropriate, just as there is an underestimation of the role of IT in developing the knowledge capital of companies (Strassmann).

- The historical and sectoral analogies (railways, electricity, etc.) do not have much relevance (Lewis).
- A careful reading of the article attests to an underestimation of the complexity of the topic, and considering all information technologies as primarily infrastructure technologies poses a problem. A minimum knowledge of the field should encourage extreme caution on the subject. Considering all information technologies as a 'commodity', in a sense marries with the general arguments of those who promote 'tous azimuts' outsourcing. It also underestimates the complementary assets, which are necessarily idiosyncratic, that companies can build around IT. In any case, the discussion that followed this paper invites us to consider this issue further, and not to evacuate IT and related services into the exclusive field of 'commodities'.

This is what we propose to do now, considering the achievements of academic research on the topic on the last twenty-five years.

When considering the literature on the contribution of IT to business performance, the proposed approaches are both quantitative and qualitative (Chan, 2000). Considering the bulk of the work done at international level, with respect to the contribution of IT to performance and value creation (around one hundred articles published in major international academic journals), the problem of IT /IS performance and value was approached via several perspectives:

- the contribution of IT to productivity;
- the contribution of IT to the development of corporate competitive advantage;
- the impact of IT on the consumer surplus;
- the organisational perspective (especially in terms of processes);
- the intangibles valuation perspective;
- the economic analysis of projects (and project portfolios).

Brynjolfsson and Hitt (1996) particularly developed the first three perspectives, around three issues for IT investments:

- Do they increase business productivity?
- Do they improve corporate competitive position?
- Do they create value for customers?

The contribution to productivity

The question of the contribution of IT to productivity has been popularised by the famous Solow paradox (1987) – Solow said that he could see computers everywhere, except in the productivity statistics. In simple terms, for an organisation (a business or a nation), the question posed can be expressed as follows: Does a marginal investment of a Euro in IT generate a positive net income, given the cost of investment? In other words, what is the level of marginal productivity of investment in a determined resource (in this case information technology)? This approach has been the subject of numerous applications in the evaluation of intangible investments related to R&D (Berndt, 1991). It has also been applied to information technology. Mukhopadhyay and Cooper (1993) have used it for the assessment of the impact of managerial information systems, such as the assessment of inventories control systems. As recalled by Hitt and Brynjolfsson (1996), the theory states that the firm transforms a set of resources – the inputs – into determined outputs, and that this transformation may be explained through a mathematical formulation: a production function. The theory states that companies will invest in a resource in a rational manner until the last unit of output generates a value lower than its cost. At the equilibrium, net incomes will be nil. Also, the assumption that the two authors have sought to test is as follows: IT spending has a positive gross marginal profit. The analysis verifies the assumption research: IT contributes to the productivity of firms surveyed. The same arguments have been developed by the authors in another study (Brynjolfsson and Hitt, 1996).

Based on a Cobb-Douglas function, three types of investments (computer investment, non-computer investment and labour) have been measured in constant 1990 dollars, and were reported to added value. The econometric analysis of the two authors concludes to a clear correlation between IT inputs and value-added, with a gross marginal contribution of 86.5 per cent versus 8.5 percent for the labour factor. This hypothesis is consistent with the findings of previous works (Berndt and Morrisson, 1995; Loveman, 1994; Lichtenberg, 1993; Brynjolfsson and Hitt, 1993). Simply put, companies should invest in information technologies because they produce marginally positive net worth (net of costs). The findings of Brynjolfsson and Hitt are consistent with more recent works (Dewan and Minn, 1997; Rai *et al.*, 1997; Bharadwaj *et al.*, 1999; Tam, 1999). But the existence of an indisputable positive effect on productivity was also challenged by some researchers (Osei-Bryson and Ko, 2003).

Competitive analysis

The competitive analysis (competitive strategy) considers the issue from the point of view of the observable competitive performance on the marketplace, and its global results, measurable by global indicators such as return on equity, return on turnover or relative market share. From this point of view, what is relevant is the extent to which IT enables a company to have a competitive advantage, generating rent and thus subnormal profits. This is, of course, related to a possible existence of barriers to entry, as developed by industrial economics (Bain, 1956) and popularised by Porter in the 1980s (Porter, 1980). Several studies have tried to address this issue, taking different angles (Box 1).

As we can see, there is a debate among scholars on the existence of a demonstrable link between IT investment and corporate performance. That some studies did not observe such a link can be explained by a missing link: an intermediate step of the analysis which would integrate organisational processes and the complementary assets generated by information technology. This will be further developed later.

Several recent works have confirmed the difficulty of linking IT investment and competitive position (Rai *et al.*, 1997; Shin, 2001). Rai *et al.* (1997) evaluated the impact of IT spending on productivity and financial performance (as measured by ROA and ROE ratios). They have concluded that there is an impact on the first dimension, and also underlined the lack of correlation with the second dimension. Others stressed, on the contrary, the possibility of demonstrating such a link: Bender (1986) has indicated the importance and the opportunity for companies to establish it (from his study of the insurance industry). Weill (1992) reported the existence of such a link, especially for the early adopters. The impact of IT on the latter can be spectacular during the early stages of adoption, but as soon as the technology becomes commonplace, the competitive advantage disappears. Weill (1990) has also highlighted the importance of 'conversion effectiveness' for the effective creation of value from IT. Dos Santos *et al.* (1993), based on the analysis of 97 IT investments, have analysed the impact of the announcement of such investments on the stock market value of the companies involved in these projects over the period 1981–1988. They concluded that innovative investments have an impact on this value, while non-innovative investments do not. Mahmood and Mann (1993) concluded that there was an overall impact of IT on business performance. Barua *et al.* (1995) have developed a two-step model that links IT investments to business performance at the level of business units. According to them, the intermediate level refers to activities or functions such as marketing, production and logistics. Strassmann (1997), for his part, has indicated that it is impossible to establish any relationship between economic performance and financial status of the company and its investments. Bharadwaj *et al.* (1999) have concluded that there was a correlation between investment in IT and related financial performance measured by Tobin's Q ratio. For the entire period (1988–1993), and for the sample of enterprises covered (631 companies), the inclusion of IT expenditure as a variable in the model significantly increases the variance of Q. More generally, for the authors, IT should be integrated into an overall perspective of the formation of intangible assets by companies, as well as other resources such as R&D, marketing and advertising. Lee and Menon (2000), on the contrary, have discussed the existence of an impact in the hospital sector. Im, Dow and Grover (2001) have concluded that there was a positive effect of the announcement of investment projects in IT on the financial markets. Dedrick *et al.* (2003) and Weill (2002) have also concluded that there was a positive effect, and that companies are indistinguishable in terms of this effect. The same conclusion is drawn by Lee and Bose (2002), who considered including other intangible expenses.

Bharadwaj (2000) and Santhanam and Hartono (2003) were interested in highlighting the importance of the behaviour of the leading firms in an industry as an explanatory factor for the differentiation of the observed performance. Brynjolfsson *et al.* (2000), in a more recent study, showed that investments associated with IT create value in the market.

Sircar, Turnbow and Bordoloi (2000) have concluded that there is a positive impact on sales and assets, but not on net income, from the study of a sample of 624 firms over the period 1988–1993.

Box 14.1 A review of recent researches on IT, IS and competitive strategies

The organisational perspective

The difficulty of establishing a clear correlation between investments and overall corporate financial performance has prompted several researchers to be interested in an intermediate modelling of performance, considering not only the input dimension, through the analysis of productivity, but focusing their research on the evaluation of the impact on organisation and processes. Others have sought to valorise organisational capital, considering that the real value created by information technology is at the level of such capital. Others were interested in contingency factors that affect the conditions for proper use of information technology. Some research finally insisted on the interest of considering information technology from an approach centred on intangible resources.

An approach centred on IT conversion effectiveness and key processes

From the proposal made by Soh and Markus (1995), we can deduct the interest of considering processes as key contributors to the performance of IT and information systems (IS). The authors suggest that the right question is not whether IT creates value, but how to determine the conditions under which such a value is likely to be created. It is in this context that we should consider the work of Weill (1992), cited above, when he introduced the concept of 'IT conversion effectiveness', to emphasise the failure of IT projects in meeting the economic goals of the firm. Hence, the interest remains in developing a theory of the practical conditions of realising the value, which inevitably must embrace the organisational aspects. In this study the authors review a number of models based on this perspective, before proposing an integrated model (Box 2).

The model of Lucas (1993) highlights the importance of two variables in the success of an investment in IT: good design of the technology and the tasks to be carried out; and an appropriate use of that technology. The model of Grabowski and Lee (1993) stresses the importance of adapting, not in terms of tasks, as is the case with Lucas, but more in strategic terms. The question posed is that of an adaptation between the strategic profile of the company (prospector, defender, analyser and reactor according to Miles and Snow's typology), its cost structure and technology portfolio. The prospectors, for example, who work in changing environmental conditions, have a decentralised organisation – the best suited IS profile in this context appears to be the most diversified.

Markus and Soh (1992), whose approach is in line with that of Weill (1992), suggested the importance of considering an intermediate step in the creation of value: IT assets. Simply because if the value is not there, it is only because of the failure of IT projects that were not capable of integrating organisational processes. IT assets (infrastructure, software, application portfolio) are important to control and evaluate these processes. Beath *et al.* (1994) considered that the approach of IT assets is necessary, but not sufficient, and it is appropriate to add the control of three key processes: systems development, operations (business operations), and planning. The process control is treated here as particularly critical for the recovery of IT assets.

Sambamurthy and Zmud's 1994 study highlighted the impact of IT on the organisation, rather than looking at the assessment of IT assets (new products or services, processing of business processes, increasing the intelligence of the organisation, etc.). It is through these impacts that the value is created.

Box 14.2 A review of the literature on the importance of organisational processes

From there, a link between these five visions can be made, around three (meta) key processes:

- The competitive processes are the focal point of the analysis, and are intended to ensure a good relationship between information technology and market needs.
- The usage processes are intended to ensure that the built IT assets contribute to the production of the impact sought by the company. (new or improved products and services, new organisational processes, support for new business models).
- The conversion processes of information technology are intended to ensure good rooting of information technology in IS business processes; they are

intended to turn an expense into IT/IS assets (infrastructure, software, business applications).

The issue of conversion capability has been the subject of interesting developments in the literature. The question has been addressed by Richardson *et al.* (2003), who consider at the outset that the issue for researchers and managers is not to decide whether IT is a necessity, but rather to determine the factors that will influence the differentiation of effective levels of performance. This question is rarely discussed in the literature; as noted, earlier works have sought – for the most part – to demonstrate the impact of information technology on business performance. The authors here refer to the work of Hitt *et al.* (2002), Bharadwaj (2000), and Santhanam and Hartono (2003).

In response to this question, the authors introduce the concept of 'IT conversion capability' by examining a selection of American companies that have invested in information technology over the period 1992–1997. They suggest that the link between IT investment and business performance depends strongly on the level of 'IT conversion capability', and consider this a key criterion. This helps to develop a more nuanced view of the relationship investments in information technology/performance.

The ability to convert IT has been defined as a specific attribute of a business, reflecting its ability to leverage the potential of IT (p. 11). This concept reflects a company's ability to use IT inputs, such as commonly available hardware and software, consulting services and training staff, to develop processes and specific assets that enhance organisational performance.

An approach centred on resources/complementary assets

For these approaches an organisation must consider taking into account the resources (assets) needed for the effective creation of value. In some ways, the conversion capability itself is a complementary asset, as are organisational processes. Compared to the previous approaches, the difference lies in the fact that the focus here is on the combinatory dimension of value creation, e.g. IT and IS intervene, in conjunction with other resources, to create value (R&D, technology, organisational processes, brands, and information systems).

Several studies may be mentioned here as forming part of a resources/complementary assets view. Ross *et al.*(1996) addressed the issue of defining conditions under which a company can increase its competitive advantage by using IT. On the basis of surveys in various business sectors, the authors consider three complementary assets as critical in achieving competitive advantage:

- *The human asset*, through IS teams having updated skills and abilities to understand the dynamics of their organisation's business needs;
- *The technology asset*, through databases, and shared and efficient technology platforms (providing a cost advantage to the company);
- *The relationship asset,* through a shared vision and responsibility with top

management, which in this case is really involved in corporate technological and operational choices, and establishing the necessary steering teams.

In the same vein, Powell and Dent-Micaleff (1997), on the basis of a research in the retail sector, have identified why some companies were more successful than others using the same technological base. The difference lies in the way companies combine technological resources with the necessary resources for success: human resources and complementary business resources (supplier relationships, IT training, business processes, etc.). In a more recent article, Davern and Kauffman (2000) have highlighted the importance of differentiating the realised value with the potential value of IT. They insist on two important complementary assets: business process design and human capital.

Vargas *et al.* (2004), for their part, targeted the interaction of human factors, IT investment and value creation by firms, seeking to identify the factors most likely to produce the positive combinatorial function. In referring to some earlier work (Neo, 1988; Kettinger *et al.*, 1994; Mata *et al.*, 1995), the authors have identified a number of complementary resources and made two assumptions they have sought to be tested empirically in the field of distribution of pharmaceutical products in Spain:

- Hypothesis 1: the level of use of IT, considered alone, is not correlated to the obtaining of a competitive advantage.
- Hypothesis 2: Complementary human resources, associated with information technology, lead to the obtaining of a competitive advantage.

All together, the authors analysed 18 intangible resources with positive complementarities to IT. The assumptions of the model have been validated and the importance of human resources was put forward as essential to creating value in the studied industry.

Through these four pieces of research, we can foresee the importance of the concept of complementary assets for modelling and measuring the performance of information systems, especially for benchlearning purposes. This concept of complementary resources incorporates, as part of a broader approach, the IT resources of the company and their valorisation.

A resource-based view approach

As a dominant theory in strategic management, the resource-based view stipulates, on the one hand, the idiosyncratic nature of the performance of enterprises and, on the other hand, the fact that this performance is attributable to a combination of resources, essentially of an intangible nature. In IS, several studies have focused on the identification of resources of particular relevance to the development of corporate competitive advantage.

For Mata, Fuerst and Barney (1995), four attributes of IT were considered in this perspective:

- capital requirements (with the associated risks: technological risks, market risks);
- proprietary technology (which can be subject to patent protection or secret, but generally this factor has become less important because of the 'commoditisation' of IT);
- technical competences in IT (which are subject to codification and therefore to an easy transfer to the outside);
- managerial competences in IT (they usually have a tacit and idiosyncratic character). A model has been defined for the attributes of the considered resources. While this model has not been the subject of an empirical test, the authors believe that only those managerial skills are likely to ensure a sustainable competitive advantage to the company.

Anandhi Bharadwaj (2000), for her part, has sought to empirically demonstrate the relevance of the framework of the resource-based view, focusing her analysis on the concept of corporate IT capability, defined as the organisation's 'ability to mobilise and deploy IT resources in combination or in presence of other resources and capabilities' (p. 171). Adopting the typology of Grant, the author distinguishes between three types of resources:

- IT physical resources (technology infrastructure);
- IT Human Resources;
- IT intangible resources (knowledge assets, market orientation, and synergy).

Two types of hypothesis were tested:

- Hypothesis 1: Superior IT capabilities will be associated with significantly higher ratios profits.
- Hypothesis 2: Superior IT capabilities will be associated with significantly lower cost ratios.

The research leads to the validation of these two hypotheses, in other words, companies with higher IT capability perform better, both from a financial standpoint as well as in terms of cost control.

A more recent study by Ravichandran and Lertwongsatien (2004) confirms the importance of IT resources in the formation of the competitive advantage of enterprises, from a sample of 129 companies in the United States. The model is deployed around four modules:

- IS resources (human capital, IT infrastructure, quality of IS partnership);
- IS capabilities (planning, development, exploitation);
- Support in IT to key competences (market-oriented competences, functional competences);
- performance (operating performance, market performance).

The research results indicate that the differentiation of performance between companies can be explained mainly by the attention given to support for key corporate competences.

Melville *et al.* (2004) proposed a model linking IT resources, human resources and complementary organisational resources, around processes intended to provide the expected organisational performance. Therefore, we can see that the resource-based aproach, by an extension of the assets perspective, proposes an integrated model for value creation by organisations, based on their investments in IT.

Organisational capital and processes

We have already referred to the process dimension in the performance of IT/IS. Some studies have put forward a number of critical processes, such as procurement and supply of a wide range of IT services, the design of a strong and flexible IT architecture, good connectivity between internal and external networks, and so on. This is the approach adopted by Devaraj and Kohli (2000) in the hospital sector. These developments can also be linked to the proposals made earlier by experts and consultants in the field of process reengineering (Hammer and Champy, 1993). But the concept of process may also be approached in a strategic perspective: via what type of process does an organisation develop a vision of its information system? Tallon *et al.*(2000) have highlighted the importance of integrating processes in the evaluation of the impact of IS, having noted the inability of traditional accounting aggregates to include this dimension. A model was developed to measure the impact of IT on corporate business processes. The evaluation focused on the perception by the leaders of IS performance, based on a survey of 304 executives around the world. Based on their survey, the researchers proposed a typology of companies in four categories:

- non-focused companies;
- companies focused on operational aspects;
- companies focused on marketing aspects;
- companies with a dual focus.

Focused companies are those that appear to have a better perception of IT/ IS performance. On the other hand, the existence of a strategic alignment and the deployment of assessment procedures for IT/IS greatly increase the perception of the created value. More recently, Kéfi *et al.* (2006) put forward the process dimension of the performance by linking it to the issue of strategic alignment. The results of their research indicate that the perceived strategic alignment has an impact on the strategic and operational performance, while organisational processes based on IS resources have an impact only on the operating performance of the firm.

Processes can also be considered from a financial perspective, by considering the total value of organisational capital. In other words, organisational processes, coupled with efficient IT infrastructure, might lead to a higher value, perceived by the financial markets (at least for listed companies). That is the perspective developed by Brynjolfsson *et al.* (2002), who considered the complementarity between organisational assets and IT assets, and addressed the issue of measuring the level of contribution of each of these assets to the creation of value.

Based on data collected for 1216 companies during the period 1987–1997, the analysis leads to the confirmation of the essential assumptions made by the research design, in particular:

- Every dollar invested in computers is associated with an increase in the market value of $10, this compared to an increase of just over $1 for investments in other tangible assets.
- Companies that use IT intensively are also likely to be those that adopt work practices that involve a combination of specific organisational characteristics, in particular those relating to the organisation of work in project mode, and greater decentralisation of tasks.
- This combination of specific organisational characteristics increases the value of the enterprise as a higher calling than physical asset.
- A greater valuation in the market is associated with companies that have adopted these organisational characteristics, combined with a strong investment in equipment.
- More recently, Lev and Radhakrishnan (2004) developed a model aimed at evaluating the importance of organisational capital for cross-sectional differences in the market value of firms. The model shows that organisational capital is an important contributor to value creation, and includes *ad hoc* case studies of companies such as IBM.

From all these theoretical and empirical developments, we can derive an important message: organisational capital is an important intangible resource, of particular relevance for value creation within and around organisations. Such a resource needs to be further documented, including consideration of how it intervenes as a complement to other intangibles. Another perspective that should be further considered is related to the measurement issue: how to measure investments made by companies in their organisational processes, and what kind of framework should used. This was notably the subject of B2B Metrics, an EU project aimed at modelling and measuring B2B processes.

Organisational capital into context: B2B reporting[1]

Even before we measure the contribution of IT and related assets to corporate performance, there is still the question of how to model and report on organisational processes in the knowledge economy, especially in a context increasingly dominated by automated processes and information flows. This question has been posed within the European framework and several research projects have tried to address this important issue. This was the core subject for B2B Metrics. B2B e-business necessarily includes an important intangible dimension. Indeed B2B is an intangible subject and, at least with regards to the proposed framework, three dimensions are to be considered for qualification and quantification: resources (investment in), processes (the hub of the analysis) and outputs (alias impacts). In fact, looking into the details of how the analysis is conducted, it is clear that the organisational dimension is the main focus of the project, and therefore that any development at this level will substantially increase the awareness and understanding of intangibles, in Europe, but also on a more global scale. By focusing on processes – including their standardisation – B2B is expected to provide valuable inputs into the ongoing debate on intangibles in the international arena. The debate is just starting; it is both analytical and practical. This option is certainly the most coherent one.

The project's main focus: the organisational dimension

As has been underlined earlier, at the analytical level, over the last ten years, several theories and works have emphasised the importance of the organisational dimension as a key component for building corporate – and, more generally, organisations' – competitive advantage. Resource-based views, as well as capabilities approaches, have strongly contributed to such an emphasis. Several scholars have tried to circumscribe the concept of organisational capital by considering it from the general perspective of intangible assets. For B2B, organisational capital is defined as a set of processes designed to improve performance within the value-added chains of companies and industries. These processes are mainly organised in modules and might be used for defining *ad hoc* metrics and statistical reporting.

Categories of intangibles

By considering the hub of B2B Metrics – the four modules – it is clear that the categories used are closely related to, and included within, the intangibles categories (Figure 14.1).

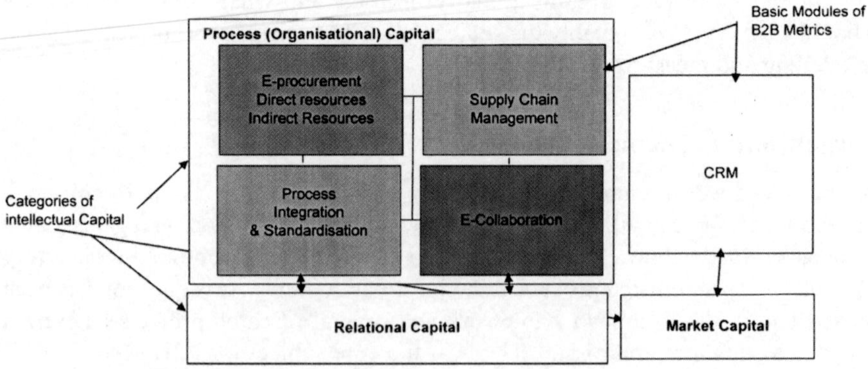

Figure 14.1 B2B and intangibles categories.

Table 14.1 Elements of relational capital

Relational capital (upstream)/ e-procurement	*Relational capital (vertical)/ e-collaboration*
Process time reduction	Process time reduction
Integration of systems	Increase in product quality
Standardisation of systems	Market (formative) power
Reliability of supply	
Market (formative) power	

Table 14.2 Elements of market capital

Process time reduction
Increased transparency/availability of information
Turnover
Market share
Share of new products in % of total turnover
Turnover with existing customers/customer retention
Customer satisfaction, service

Outside companies, and therefore within the value-added chain, it is clear that e-procurement, SCM and e-collaboration are designed to reinforce corporate relational capital. This relational capital includes a specific component dedicated to innovation resulting from e-collaboration. The main elements of relational capital – for which *ad hoc* metrics can be defined – are indicated hereafter (see Table 14.1 and Figure 14.2).

CRM processes are naturally defined and implemented with the aim of reinforcing companies' market capital. Specific components of market capital are indicated in Table 14.2.

B2B Metrics and statistical reporting

The problematic of managerial and statistical reporting in the knowledge economy is one of those justifying the conduct of B2B Metrics and other similar projects within the IST programme. By conducting surveys and generating monographs on a relatively large scale, including the international perspective, the project is contributing to a better understanding of the knowledge (and virtual) economy as a concept. For instance, in the automotive sector, the pilot phase tends to suggest that B2B as an organisational design is still limited in terms of diffusion, even though it is also largely recognised that such a path will be adopted by many of the value-added chain players. There are still important barriers upstream and downstream the value-added chain. Most of these are related to the complementary assets (training of managers) as well as to the weak absorptive capacity of these organisations.

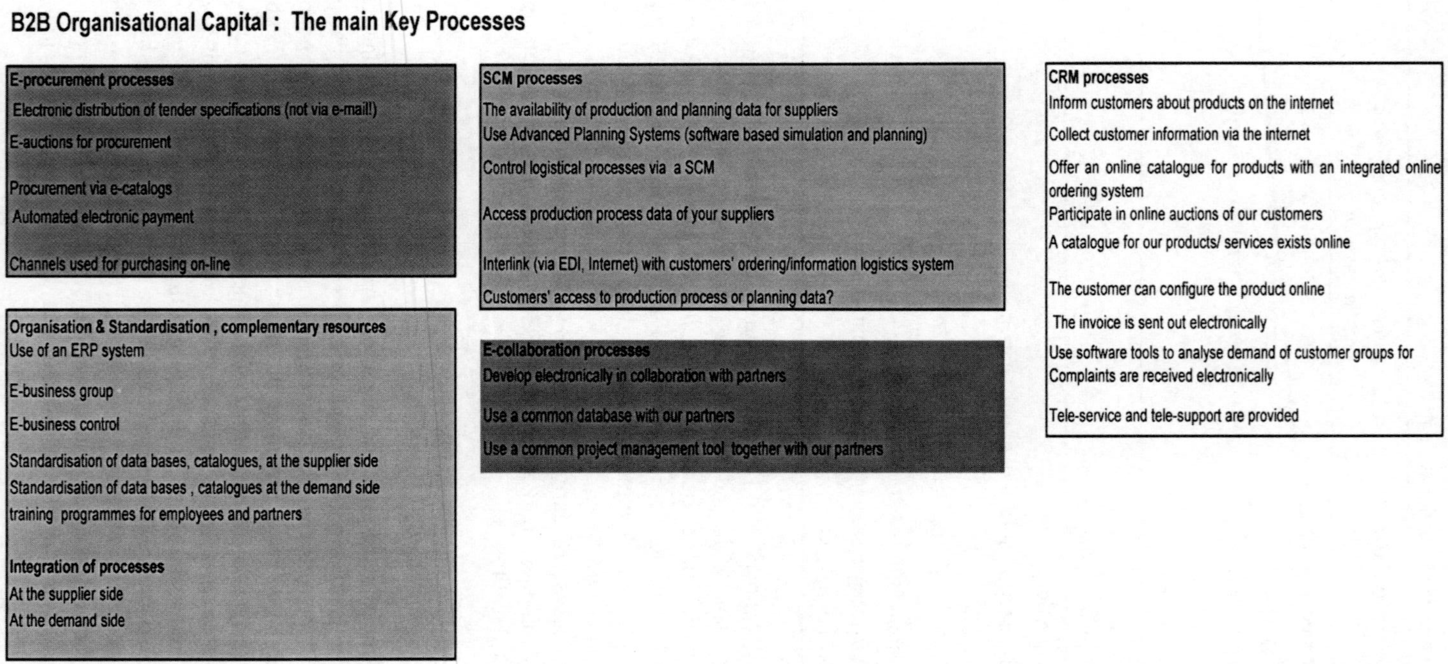

Figure 14.2 Organisational capital: key processes.

Table 14.3 A possible structure for intangibles (organisational) B2B reporting: the horizontal dimension

Investment in (Organisational capital)	*Impact of investment (other components of intellectual capital)*
E-procurement processes for direct resources	Relational capital – upstream
E-procurement processes for indirect resources	Relational capital – upstream
Supply chain management processes	Relational capital – upstream
CRM processes	Market capital
E-collaboration processes	Relational capital
Standardisation of all processes	Relational capital
Complementary innovation	Human capital

Table 14.4 A proposed structure for an ad hoc annex on B2B (intangibles) cross-sectoral reporting

Dimension of B2B Reporting	*Examples of the main items*	*Accounting rule*	*Present accounting channel for disclosure*
Process Indexes – Organisational capital	Expenditures on: *Generic processes* such e-procurement, SCM, e-collaboration, CRM, standardisation of processes, complementary innovation	Registration at their internal costs According to a harmonised definition	Profit and loss statement Ad hoc annex
	Expenditures on ad hoc *business processes* These processes have to be agreed at the sectoral level. They have to be very limited in number (10 processes maximum) and agreed among *ad hoc* professional associations.	Registration at their internal costs According to a harmonised definition	Profit and loss statement Ad hoc annex
Impact Indexes – Relational capital, market capital, human capital	Calculated Indexes such as: Market capital Overall market shares Market share maintenance (development) Share of turnover due to new products Process time reduction Increase in transparency Relational capital – upstream, lateral and downstream process time reduction standardisation of systems reliability of supply formative power Human capital Investment in training Investment in new organisational forms	Assessment of outputs performance based on voluntary *ad hoc* basis (Benchmarking groups, eventually supported within the IST programme)	Balance sheet- Ad hoc annex

From the managerial/statistical reporting, B2B Metrics has contributed to the clarification – and recommendation – of different types of statistical reporting schemes. For instance, some items – those relating to objectives, barriers and infrastructures – are already easily subject to traditional reporting initiatives. Those of more sophisticated forms and contents (impacts, organisational forms) might need the building – and initiating – of voluntary communities of practice. These might consist of professional associations and companies who are ready to share relatively sensitive information that they control, in terms of production and access.

From the analytical elements available today, it is clear that intangibles can be better reported on a more 'community of practice' level.

The horizontal versus vertical dimension for reporting on intangibles

According to the IC-dVAL® approach (Bounfour, 2003), two dimensions for reporting are suggested:

- The **horizontal dimension**, which refers to the definition and implementation of cross-sectional information. It requires better harmonisation, in order to reinforce the meaning of the information by reinforcing its reliability and comparability.
- The **vertical dimension**, which refers to the necessary contingent nature of an organisation, sectional business strategies, process strategy and performance.

Horizontal (cross-sectoral) reporting

Horizontal reporting is based on very few indicators, comparable from one sector to another. A potential structure for reporting on organisational intangibles might be as shown in Table 14.3.

How to report

At the accounting level, this reporting can be the subject of an *ad hoc* annex within the general accounting system of companies. Accounting rules to be implemented can be based on those suggested in Table 14.4.

This reporting can be carried out with national statistics, using an amended version of the B2B questionnaire.

Vertical (sector specific) reporting

The vertical dimension is specifically necessary for reporting at the level of sectors, communities of practice or individual companies. It is recommended here because we assume that, in the knowledge economy, idiosyncrasy of performance is an important dimension, often neglected by statistical reporting. The approach here might be organised from two perspectives (see Table 14.5):

Table 14.5 A possible structure for intangibles (organisational) B2B reporting: the vertical dimension

Pure narrative approach	*Mix of narrative and metrics*
Vision	Vision
Effective organisational models/structure/ processes	Effective organisational models/structure/ processes
Emerging organisational models/structure/ processes	Related metrics
Registered/expected performance	Emerging organisational models/structure/ processes
Lessons learned: failures versus successes	Related metrics
	Lessons learned: failures versus success

- A *pure narrative perspective*: here what is important is the description of visions, and already effective or prospective organisational modes;
- A mix of narrative and quantitative data.

How to report

Vertical reporting is recommended at the level of professional or trade associations, clubs of volunteers or benchmarking groups.

Note

1 This section refers to the final report of B2B Metrics, Statistical Indicators for the Information Society, Measuring Forms, Content, Strategy and Impacts of B2B E Commerce IST-2001-32193, a project and conducted under the European IST programme, and coordinated by IFO Institute (Munich), with contributions from NRI, VATT, University of Manchester and RCS. The final report is available from: http://www.b2b-metrics.de/

References

Bain, J. (1956). *Barriers to New Competition*. Cambridge, MA: Harvard University Press.

Barua, A., Kriebel, H. C. and Mukhopadhyay, T. (1995), 'Information technologies and business value: an analytic and empirical investigation', *Information System Research*, Vol. 6, No. 1: pp. 3–23.

Beath, C. M., Goodhue, D. L. and Ross, J. R. (1994). 'Partnering for business value: the shared management of the IS infrastructure'. *Proceedings of the 15th International Conference on Information Systems*. Vancouver, British Columbia: pp. 459–60.

Bender, D. H. (1986). 'Financial impact of information processing', *Journal of Management Information Systems*, Vol. 3, No. 2 (Summer): pp. 232–8.

Berndt, E. (1991). *The Practice of Econometrics: classic and contemporary*. Reading, MA: Addison-Wesley.

Berndt, E. R. and Morrison, C. J. (1995), 'High-tech capital formation and economic performance in US manufacturing industries: an exploratory analysis', *Journal of Econometrics* Vol. 65, No. 1: pp. 9–43.

Bharadwaj, A. S. (2000). 'A resource-based perspective on information technology capability and firm performance: an empirical investigation', *MIS Quarterly*, Vol. 24, No. 1 (March): pp. 169–96.
Bharadwaj, A. S., Bharadwaj, S. G. and Konsynski, B. R. (1999). 'Information technology effects on firm performance as measured by Tobin's q', *Management Science*, Vol. 45, No. 7 (July): pp. 1008–24.
Brynjolfsson, E. and Hitt. L (1993). 'Is information systems spending productive? New evidence and new results', *Proceedings of the 14th International Conference of Information Systems*, Orlando, FL: pp. 47–64.
Brynjolfsson, E. and Hitt, L. (1995). 'Information technology as a factor of production: the role of differences among firms', *Economics of Innovation and New Technology*, Vol. 3, No. 3–4: pp. 183–200.
Brynjolfsson, E. and Hitt, L. (1998). 'Beyond the productivity paradox', *Communications of the ACM*, Vol. 41, No. 8 (August): pp. 49–55.
Brynjolfsson, E., Hitt, L. and Yang, S. (2002) *Intangible Assets: Computer and Organisational Capital*, eBusiness@MIT, paper No. 138. Available at http://ebusiness.mit.edu/research/papers/138_Erik_Intangible_Assets.pdf
Brynjolfsson, E. and Yang, S. (1996). 'Information technology and productivity: a review of the literature', *Advances in Computers*, Vol. 43, pp. 179–214.
B2B Metrics. *Statistical Indicators for the Information Society: measuring forms, content, strategy and impacts of B2B e-commerce*, Final Report, IST-2001-32193. Available at: http://www.b2b-metrics.de/Final%20Report170505.pdf.
Carr, Nicolas (2003). 'IT doesn't matter', *Harvard Business Review*, Vol. 81, No. 5: pp. 41–50.
Chan, Y.E. (2000). 'IT value: the great divide between qualitative and quantitative and individual and organizational measures', *Journal of Management Information Systems*, Vol. 16, No. 4: pp. 225–61.
Davern, M. J. and Kauffman, R. J. (2000). 'Discovering potential and realizing value from IT investments', *Journal of Management Information Systems*, Vol. 16, No. 4: pp. 121–43.
Dedrick, J., Gurbaxani, V. and Kraemer, K. L. (2003). 'Information technology and economic performance: a critical review of the empirical evidence', *ACM Computing Surveys*, Vol. 35, No. 1: pp. 1–28.
Devaraj, S. and Kohli, R. (2000). 'Information technology payoff in the health-care industry: a longitudinal study', *Journal of Management Information Systems*, Vol. 16, No. 4: pp. 41–67.
Devaraj, S. and Kohli, R. (2003). 'Performance impacts on information technology: is actual usage the missing link?', *Management Science*, Vol. 49, No. 3: pp. 273–89.
Dewan, S. and Min, C. (1997). 'Substitution of information technology for other factors of production: a firm-level analysis', *Management Science*, Vol. 43: pp. 1660–75.
Dos Santos, B. L., Peffers, K. and Mauer, D. (1993). 'The impact of information technology investment announcements on the market value of the firm', *Information Systems Research*, Vol. 4 (March): pp. 1–23.
Grabowski, M. and Lee, S. (1993). 'Linking information systems application portfolio and organizational strategy', in R. Banker, R. Kauffman and M. A. Mahmood (eds) *Strategic Information Technology Management: perspectives on organizational growth and competitive advantage.* Harrisburg, PA: Idea Group Publishing, pp. 33–54.
Hammer, M. and Champy, J. (1992). *Business Process Reegineering: a manifesto to business revolution*. New York: Harper Business.
Hitt, L. and Brynjolfsson, E. (1996). 'Productivity, business profitability, and consumer surplus: three different measures of information technology value', *Management Information Systems Quarterly*, Vol. 20, No. 2 (June): pp. 121–42.
Hitt, L., Wu, D. J. and Zhou, X. (2002). 'ERP Investment: business impact and productivity measures', *Journal of Management Information Systems*, Vol. 19, No. 1: pp 71–98.
Im, K. S., Dow, K. E. and Grover, V. (2001). 'A reexamination of IT investment and the

market value information systems spending', *Management Science*, Vol. 42, No. 4 (April): pp. 541–58.
Kéfi, H., Shwarz, A. and Kalika, M. (2006). 'Modèle basé sur les processus versus alignement stratégique: quels facteurs explicatifs de la performance', paper presented at the XIème congrès de l'AIM (Association Information et Management), June 8–9, Luxembourg.
Kettinger, W. J., Grover, V., Segars, A. H. and Guha, S. (1994). 'Strategic information systems revisited: a study in sustainability and performance', *Management Information Systems Quarterly*, Vol. 18, No. 1 (March): pp. 31–58.
Kohli R. and Devaraj, S. (2003), 'Measuring information technology payoff: a meta-analysis of structural variables in firm-level empirical research', *Information Systems Research*, Vol. 14, No. 2: pp. 127–45.
Lee, B. and Menon, N. M. (2000). 'Information technology value through different normative lenses', *Journal of Management Information Systems*, Vol. 16, No. 4 (Spring): pp. 99–119.
Lee, J., Bose, U. (2002). 'Operational linkage between diverse dimensions of IT investments and multifaceted aspects of a firm's economic performance', *Journal of Information Technology*, Vol. 17: pp. 119–31.
Lev, B. and Radhakrishnan, S. (2004). 'The valuation of organization capital'. Available at: http://pages.stern.nyu.edu/~blev/docs/TheValuationOfOrganizationCapital.pdf.
Lichtenberg, F. (1993). 'The output contribution of computer equipment and personnel: a firm level analysis', Columbia Business School Working Paper.
Loveman, G. W. (1994). 'Assessing the productivity impact of information technologies', in T. J. Allen and M. Scott Morton (eds) *Information Technology and the Corporation of the 1990s: research studies*. Cambridge, MA: MIT Press.
Lucas, H. C. (1993). 'The business value of information technology: a historical perspective and thoughts for future research', in R. D. Banker, R. J. Kaufman and M. A. Mahmood (eds) *Strategic Information Technology Management: perspectives on organizational growth and competitive advantage*. Harrisburg, Pennsylvania: Idea Group Publishing, pp. 127–39.
Luftman, J. L. (2000). 'Assessing Business-IT alignment maturity', *Communications of the Association for Information Systems*, Vol. 4, Article 14 (December), pp. 11–50.
Mahadevan, B. (2000). 'Business models for Internet based e-commerce: an anatomy', *California Management Review*, Vol. 42, No. 4: pp. 55–69.
Mahmood, M. A. and Mann, G. J. (1993).'Measuring the organisational impact of information technology investment: an exploratory study', *Journal of Management Information Systems*, Vol. 10, No. 1: pp. 97–122.
Markus, M. L. and Soh, C. (1993) 'Banking on information technology: converting IT spending into firm performance', in R. D. Banker, R. J. Kaufman and M. A. Mahmood (eds) *Strategic Information Technology Management: perspectives on organizational growth and competitive advantage*. Harrisburg, Pennsylvania: Idea Group Publishing, pp. 375–403.
Mata, F. J., Fuerst, W. L. and Barney, J. B. (1995). 'Information technology and sustained competitive advantage: a resource based analysis', *MIS Quarterly*, Vol. 19, No. 4 (December): pp. 487–504.
Melville, N., Kraemer, K. and Gurbaxani, V. (2004). 'Review: information technology and organizational performance: an integrative model of IT business value', *MIS Quarterly*, Vol. 28, No. 2: pp. 283–322.
Mukhopadhyay, T. and Cooper, R., (1993). 'A microeconomic production assessment of the business value of management information systems: the case of inventory control', *Journal of Management Information Systems*, Vol. 10, No. 1: pp. 33–5.
Neo, B. S. (1988). 'Factors facilitating the use of information technology for competitive advantage: an exploratory study', *Information and Management*, Vol. 15: pp. 191–201.
Porter, M. E. (1980). *Competitive Strategy*. New York: The Free Press.

Powell T. C. and Dent-Micaleff, A. (1997). 'Information technology and competitive advantage: the role of human, business and technology resources', *Strategic Management Journal*, Vol. 18, No. 5, pp. 375–405.

Rai, A., Patnayakuni, R. and Patnayakuni, N. (1997). 'Technology investment and business performance', *Communications of the ACM*, Vol. 40, No. 7 (July): pp. 89–97.

Richardson, V. J., Subramani, M. and Zmud, R. W. (2003). 'Benefiting from information technology investments: the role of IT conversion capability', Paper under the Second Round Review at *MIS Quarterly*.

Richardson, V. J. and Zmud, R. W. (2001). 'The value relevance of information technology investment announcements: Incorporating industry strategic IT role'. Working paper.

Ross, J. W., Beath, C. M. and Goodhue, D. L. (1996). 'Develop long-term competitiveness through IT assets', *MIT Sloan Management Review*, Vol. 38, No. 1: pp. 31–42.

Sambamurthy, V. and Zmud, R. W. (1994). 'IT management competency assessment: a tool for creating business value through IT'. Working paper, Financial Executives Research Foundation.

Santhanam, R. and Hartono, E. (2003). 'Issues in linking information technology capability to firm performance', *MIS Quarterly*, Vol. 27, No. 1: pp. 1–29.

Shin, N. (2001). 'The impact of information technology on financial performance: the importance of strategic choice', *European Journal of Information Systems*, Vol. 10, No. 4: pp. 227–36.

Sircar, S., Turnbow, J. L. and Bordoloi, B. (2000). 'A framework for assessing the relationship between information technology investments and firm performance.' *Journal of Management Information Systems*, Vol. 16, No. 4: pp. 69–97.

Osei-Bryson, K. M. and Ko, M. (2004). 'Exploring the relationship between Information Technology Investment and firm performance using regression splines analysis', *Information & Management*, Vol. 42, No. 1; pp. 1–13.

Soh, C. and Markus, L. (1995), 'How IT creates business value: a process theory synthesis', in De Gross, J. *et al.* (eds) *Proceedings of the Sixteenth International Conference on Information Systems*, Amsterdam, pp. 29–41.

Solow, R. M. (1957) 'Technical progress and aggregate production function', *Review of Economic and Statistics*, Vol. 39: pp. 312–20.

Strassmann, P. A. (1997). 'Will big spending on computers guarantee profitability?', *Datamation*, Vol. 43, No. 2 (February): pp. 75–82.

Tallon, P. P., Kraemer, K. L. and Gurbaxani, V. (2000): 'Executives' perceptions of the business value of information technology: a process-oriented approach', *Journal of Management Information Systems*, Vol. 16, No. 4: pp. 145–73.

Tam, K. Y. (1998). 'The impact of information technology investments on firm performance and evaluation: evidence from newly industrialized economies', *Information Systems Research*, Vol. 9, No. 1 (March): pp. 85–98.

Vargas, A., Hernandez, M. J. and Bruque, S. (2004). 'Human factors and IT competitive value', *Human IT*, Vol. 7, No. 1: pp. 47–73.

Weill, P. (1992). 'The relationship between investment in information technology and firm performance: a study of the valve manufacturing sector', *Information Systems Research*, Vol. 3, No. 4 (December): pp. 307–33.

Weill, P., Subramani, M. and Broadbent, M. (2002). 'Building IT infrastructure for strategic agility', *Sloan Management Review*, Vol. 44, No. 1: pp. 57–65.

Index